East Africa and the Orient

Cultural Syntheses in
Pre-Colonial Times

D1242903

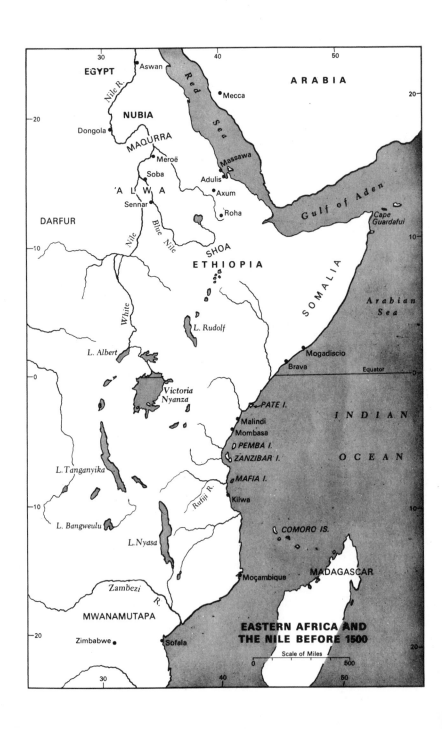

30   40   50

EGYPT

Aswan

ARABIA

Nile R.

Mecca

Red Sea

20

NUBIA

Dongola

MAQURRA

Meroë

Massawa

Soba

Adulis

'A L W A

Axum

Sennar

Roha

Gulf of Aden

Cape Guardafui

DARFUR

Nile

Blue Nile

SHOA

ETHIOPIA

10

White

SOMALIA

Arabian Sea

L. Rudolf

L. Albert

Mogadiscio

Brava

Equator

0

Victoria Nyanza

PATE I.

Malindi

Mombasa

I N D I A N

PEMBA I.

ZANZIBAR I.

O C E A N

L. Tanganyika

MAFIA I.

Rufiji R.

Kilwa

10

L. Bangweulu

L. Nyasa

COMORO IS.

MADAGASCAR

Moçambique

Zambezi R.

MWANAMUTAPA

EASTERN AFRICA AND THE NILE BEFORE 1500

20

Zimbabwe

Sofala

Scale of Miles

0   500

30   40   50

EAST AFRICA
AND THE ORIENT

Cultural Syntheses in
Pre-Colonial Times

EDITED BY

H. Neville Chittick

AND

Robert I. Rotberg

AFRICANA PUBLISHING COMPANY, New York and London

A Division of Holmes & Meier Publishers, Inc.

Edited under the auspices of the
Center for International Affairs, Harvard University

Published in the United States of America 1975 by
Africana Publishing Company
a division of Holmes & Meier Publishers, Inc.
101 Fifth Avenue
New York, New York 10003

Published in Great Britain 1975 by
Holmes & Meier Publishers, Ltd.
Hillview House
1, Hallswelle Parade, Finchley Road
London, NW11 0DL

LIBRARY OF CONGRESS CATALOGING IN PUBLICATION DATA

Main entry under title:

East Africa and the Orient.

Papers presented at a conference on pre-colonial history in East Africa
held in Kenya in 1967, and sponsored by the Harvard University Center for
International Affairs, the British Institute in Eastern Africa, and the University of Nairobi.
    Bibliography: p.
    Includes index.
    1. Africa, East—History—Congresses. 2. Africa, East—Relations (general) with the Indian Ocean region—Congresses. 3. Indian Ocean region—Relations (general) with East Africa—Congresses. 4. Africa, East—Relations (general) with Asia—Congresses. 5. Asia—Relations (general) with East Africa—Congresses. I. Chittick, H. Neville, ed.   II. Rotberg, Robert I., ed. III. Harvard University. Center for International Affairs. IV. British Institute in Eastern Africa. V. Nairobi. University.
DT432.E18   301.29'67'05   73-89568
ISBN 0-8419-0142-2

PREFACE

The present collection of essays consists of papers originally delivered at a conference devoted to aspects of the precolonial history of the East Africa, and especially the relations of that region with the Orient. Although the existence of these relations had long been known in outline, their diversity and significance had been too little examined. The region had been subject to the influence of outsiders from the first centuries of the Christian era, if not before. Not only Arabs, but Indonesians, Persians, and Indians had contributed to the development of the polities of the coast and Madagascar. Commercial links extended as far as China.

For too long the civilizations of the lands bordering the Indian Ocean, and East Africa's involvements with the wider world, had been studied from a series of parochial perspectives, and within the traditional categories of particular disciplines. There had been few attempts to relate the concerns of the different disciplines to each other, or to place those concerns in a cross-cultural context.

The conference, held in 1967 in Kenya, sought to remedy these deficiencies and to bring new perspectives to bear on the problems of interpreting East Africa's interaction with the Orient by gathering together Africanists and others with experience in, and know-ledge of, the regions of the Indian Ocean basin, Southeast Asia, and China. The participants in the conference represented a variety of disciplines and, collectively, exemplified a commitment to the use of new techniques of historiography. Textual historians and archaeologists welcomed and made full use of the insights of collaborating ethnobotanists, musicologists, anthropologists, geog-raphers, and other specialists.

Discussing prepared papers presenting these various viewpoints and working together for a week, the participants sought to define our knowledge of East Africa in relation to the Indian Ocean region as a whole, and to provide a foundation for future research. In order to limit this book to a reasonable size, however, only the papers most pertinent to the main theme of the conference are included here. Some of the other contributions have already been published in learned journals. (In addition, the lengthy discussions of each paper were recorded on tape, the resulting 350-page transcript contributing to the process of editing and revising the contributions.)

Although the authors of the following chapters revised them for publication (in some cases more than once) they have generally been unable to take account of studies published since about 1970. (The editors have endeavored, nevertheless, to keep the overall bibliography up-to-date.) One of the following chapters, that by Grottanelli, has indeed been published, in the Italian journal *Africa* (XXVII [1972], 363–394), under the same title, and appears here in a slightly revised form.

The editors, who convened the conference, are grateful for the financial support of The Ford Foundation and the sponsorship of the meetings by the Harvard University Center for International Affairs, the British Institute in Eastern Africa, and the University of Nairobi. They have fortunately enjoyed the patience and cooperation of the contributors to this book and the other participants. For uncommonly devoted and skillful assistance in organizing the conference and preparing the proceedings for publication, the editors owe major debts of gratitude to Mrs. Jane French Tatlock, Mrs. Jill Geser, Mrs. Helen Morrison, the late K.O. Mathan, Mrs. Shirley C. Quinn, the late Mrs. Marina Finkelstein, and Stephanie D. Jones. The index was prepared by Evalyn Seidman. Mrs. Anne Greer and the *Voice of Kenya* kindly recorded the meetings. Norman Bennett and the late Al Castagno were unfailingly helpful in facilitating this book's appearance in print. The Hon. J.J. Nyagah, then Minister of Education of Kenya, declared the conference open, and Dr. Arthur Porter, then Principal of University College, Nairobi, generously permitted the conference to use the facilities of his institution.

H.N.C. and R.I.R.

April 1973

CONTENTS

LIST OF MAPS

A NOTE ON NOMENCLATURE

Place names are given in the transliterated or Romanized form generally accepted in the modern country concerned (except where the English equivalents are too widely used to be ignored) or in the original text quoted or cited.

Transliterations from Arabic follow the usual English system, while transliterations from Chinese are predominantly in the Wade-Giles romanization.

The word "medieval" has been eschewed, largely because it, and associated terminology derived from the study of Europe. bears no relation—except possibly and very roughly by the accident of chronology—to the very different African experience. The use of "medieval" implies much that cannot be shared or appropriated by Africa. To employ it as a term of convenience would mislead without adding anything of great significance; the editors accordingly have made it anathema.

INTRODUCTION

The Indian Ocean basin has an intrinsic cultural and economic unity which has always been shared by the peoples of the East African coast. They, like others living on the eastern and northern shores of the basin, have long enjoyed the similar climatic and ecological conditions which facilitated unity and comparable perspectives. The moist lands around the Ocean's rim share a warm, usually humid, climate with a heavy rainfall. The soils, often derived from the old coral reefs which grow almost everywhere in these latitudes, are sandy, well-drained, and suited to the cultivation of similar staple crops. There is an exception, the generally arid northern seaboard, and it was the presence of this desiccated region, with its uncultivable hinterland of desert and mountain, which stimulated the development of trade in the basin. Commerce was facilitated by the monsoons, which blow from the northeast from November or December until April and from the southwest from May or June onward, with a period of calm or rain in between. The monsoons are wholly reliable as far south as Zanzibar and almost as far as Kilwa (7° S.). Vessels can therefore sail from southern Arabia, the Persian Gulf, and the southern Iranian coast to East Africa during the northeastern monsoon (the warm season in East Africa) with an assurance that the winds will always be abaft the beam. After a period of trading in East Africa, the southwestern monsoon carries traders homeward. On the northern coast of Africa, and, indeed, as far south as Zanzibar or Mafia, there is sufficient time not only to sell cargoes from the north which have been brought in dhows, and to purchase cargoes for the return voyage (in modern times mangrove poles), but also to trade in local goods between the ports of East Africa. Beyond, south of

1

Kilwa to Moçambique and Sofala, the monsoon regime is unreliable and could, with other factors, have affected the settlement of Indonesians in Madagascar. A dhow from the Persian Gulf cannot count upon a roundtrip in a year, particularly since the current flowing in the channel between Madagascar and the mainland in a north-south direction makes it difficult for sailing vessels reaching the southern end of that channel to return. Moreover, the winds of the southern Indian Ocean are from east to west, and in an opposite direction even further south. There also is an east-west current in the same latitudes.

The similarity of habitat throughout the basin was reflected in a roughly similar way of life. The staple food was predominantly rice, and, in East Africa, knowledge of its cultivation was derived largely from Southeast Asia. Fish added protein, and the desire to improve catches probably stimulated the development of shipbuilding. The coconut palm, again disseminated from the east, furnished a food eaten with rice and fish, and, from its inner husk, cords and ropes for both rigging and, in the earliest period, the stitching of sewn boats. Fronds from the coconut were used for the thatch-like covering of the high-pitched roofs (to throw off the heavy rains) of the usual rectangular houses, an innovation whose form is ultimately derived from Indonesia.

Islam provided a further cross-cultural bond in the basin. It reached southern Arabia and the Persian Gulf by the end of the seventh century. Soon it was in western India, and then spread to Southeast Asia and Indonesia. There were Muslim trading settlements in East Africa not later than the tenth century. And it was during these early years of the spread of Islam that the lands of Iraq sheltered the world's most civilized and prosperous region. There, and in the nearby Fars province of Persia, important trade routes converged as a result of the commercial interests of the Umayyad and Abbasid caliphates. Their ships and traders were also dispatched to search for ivory and gold, visiting East Africa as had other Arabs and Persians for at least a millennium. Most of these merchants visited East Africa and returned on the following monsoon, and we know that from the time of the *Periplus of the Erythraean Sea* (c. 120 A.D.), a crucial document examined below

with great care by Gervase Mathew, some of these men of commerce settled on African shores, learned the languages of the
people, and intermarried with the indigenous inhabitants. It is
likely that these first settlers came from southwestern Arabia; few,
as far as can be ascertained, came from Mesopotamia or inland
Persia. But fierce quarrels between the sects of young Islam in the
Persian Gulf region and elsewhere, the aridity of the shores of
Arabia, and the growth of population in a zone of inadequate
resources, favored a more broadly based immigration which coincided with or overlapped movements on a smaller scale of people
from farther east—from western India, Southeast Asia, and
Indochina.

These immigrants found two strikingly different zones in eastern
Africa. From Cape Guardafui to Kisimayu the coast is barren
and inhospitable, totally lacking good harbors. Along the narrow
coastal plain are fishing settlements. Behind are ranges of sand
dunes which give way to a flat, acacia-covered plain which carries
less tree cover in the northernmost part of the region. This is now
the home of nomad Somali and their camels and cattle. Most of
this coast is unbroken; it is nowhere cut by navigable waterways
leading into the interior. There are a few coral islands close to the
coasts and connected by isthmuses of sand, but they afford inadequate shelter to sailors.

South of Kisimayu the shores are more hospitable. The line of
the coast is broken by numerous inlets, the lower reaches of rivers
now drowned by the encroaching ocean. Bur Gao (Port Durnford)
in Somalia and Dar es Salaam and Kilwa in Tanzania are all
towns on or in such estuaries. There are substantial rivers, too:
the Juba near Kisimayu, the Tana and the Sabaki in Kenya, and
the Ruvu, Rufiji, and Ruvuma in Tanzania. The largest is the
Rufiji, which has a very extensive delta and is thought to have
provided access to the interior for early immigrants. The Rufiji,
the Tana, and the Juba are all navigable by small boats for 30
or more miles inland. The Rufiji delta, additionally, boasts very
large areas of mangrove forest.

The islands off this coast, of which there are a substantial
number, have played an important role in the history of East

Africa. Some, close inshore, are comparatively low-lying; the most important are those of the Lamu archipelago, particularly Manda, Pate, and Lamu itself. Pemba, Zanzibar, and Mafia, the bigger islands along this long stretch of coast, lie well off-shore and are largely coraline in structure. All of these islands afforded valuable shelter both for ships plying along the coast and for vessels in port, the water in their lee being protected.

This is the region to which immigrants eventually came, and it is with what they brought, what they found, what they contributed, and the eventual cultural synthesis, that the following essays are primarily concerned. Of the immigrations, the least well understood and most confusing for analysis, is that of the Indonesians. Yet there are abundant cultural indications of their arrival. As Michael Gwynne demonstrates below, several of the staple food crops of eastern Africa—of the interior as well as the coast—indisputably originated in Southeast Asia. The banana is preeminent, but certain species of yams and cocoyams, as well as coconuts, are additional examples. Like pigs, which were probably derived from the same source, these cultigens were capable of surviving over long distances and of being diffused easily, whether or not their actual conveyance by Southeast Asians was intentional. However this may have been, these crops now provide subsistence for large numbers of Africans, and the variety of their mutants, particularly of the banana, testifies to considerable longevity (perhaps about two millennia) in eastern Africa. Unfortunately, this clear botanical indication of fairly early Southeast Asian influence is compromised by cultural and linguistic evidence which argues for a much more recent and direct participation in the affairs of Africa and its offshore islands by Southeast Asians or, more narrowly, Indonesians. The peoples of the Malagasy Republic today speak varieties of the predominant languages of Indonesia. Merina, the language of the aristocratic Malagasy, is akin to the variant of Bahasa Indonesian which is spoken in southwestern Borneo. Indonesians and Malagasy can converse as easily as can French and Italians or speakers of Swahili and Nyanja. Congruence of language in Madagascar could hardly have occurred without common languages, prolonged intermingling, and settlement, a plausibility to which the physiognomy of the present inhabitants of Madagascar—seeming Indonesians in all respects—bears witness. There may well be important indigenous components in the cultural baggage of the Malagasy—the arguments for which both Aidan Southall and Pierre Vérin discuss in their chapters below—but thus far none have been isolated which are indisputable or widely accepted. Instead, we are left with a problem which perplexed the contributors to this symposium: How could Indonesians have populated Madagascar without, at the very minimum, seriously affecting the development of the mainland—a mere 250 miles distant—or the peoples of the mainland, in some notable and definable way?

The evidence for direct Indonesian or Southeast Asian penetration of the mainland is fragmentary and limited. No Africans speak languages with Indonesian connections, although there are indications that the Bantu tongues of the Makonde and Makua (of Moçambique) may, once they are examined carefully, reveal ancient associations with Indonesia. There are no significant physical resemblances (admittedly, a full serological analysis is lacking), and, indicative as the botanical evidence may be, it implies ultimate origin (as Gwynne makes clear) rather than direct transmission by human agency. Yet this implication, and the lack of any positive evidence, should not exclude the possibility that Southeast Asians may have directly introduced food crop cultivation and iron working to mainland eastern Africa by means of some form of mercantile settlement or colonial occupation over a relatively long period. If we ignore or explain away the apparently separate earlier introduction of Asian food staples, this intervention could have occurred as late as the beginning of the Christian era since it is generally agreed that the earliest Indonesian emigration to Madagascar must have taken place before the introduction of the Sanskrit language and culture to Indonesia in about 200 A.D. If Indonesians, with their portable, durable, and rapidly maturing cultigens (bananas or yams), and a superior ability to forge spears, in fact settled in Africa (at the mouth of the Zambezi or Rufiji rivers?) two or three hundred years after the beginning of the Christian era, their influence (and tutelage?) could conceivably account for the enlargement of scale of the Bantu-speaking peoples and their ability to populate large areas of eastern and southern Africa in the face of competition from Kushitic- and Khoisan-speaking pastoralists. The confirmation of such direct influence by Indonesians would lend credence to the controversial similarity (argued persuasively by A.M. Jones' "The Influence of Indonesia," a paper delivered to the original conference [published in *Azania*, IV (1969), 131–145] and in his *Africa and Indonesia* [Leiden, 1964]) of African and Indonesian musical modes and instruments—preeminently the xylophone.

But, why and how did Indonesians migrate? What routes did they follow? We know that Indonesians were among the world's first builders of large ocean-going vessels; their sailors could have followed Sharp's current directly across the southern Indian Ocean (6,000 miles from Sumatra), returning on the equatorial countercurrent. Or they could have sailed in stages from Sumatra to Ceylon, to the Maldive Islands, and thence to Madagascar. Or, using the monsoons, they could have followed the coastal route around India and Arabia and so down the East African coast, a course which would have complemented the trading interests of Indonesians. The last is the most logical route, but there is a noticeable lack of linguistic, social, and cultural evidence to support the supposition that Indonesians were ever in India or Arabia. (Vinigi L. Grottanelli, in discussing the settlement of the Horn of Africa, however, noted several items which seem to be Indonesian in origin.) Without knowledge of the culture of the Maldive and Seychelle Islands, the second route remains no more than a logical alternative. If the Indonesians sailed directly, they must initially have done so inadvertently. There can have been no knowledge of what was to be found, and the establishment of colonies would have required (and may have occasioned) return journeys home (the Indonesians navigated by the stars) and a subsequent series of purposeful voyages. But why would Indonesians in number have emigrated from their fertile homelands? Hubert Deschamps, in a paper presented to the conference but not published here, argued in favor of a settlement by pirates or buccaneers, and several contributors recalled the Waqwaq—conceivably Indonesians—who attacked eastern Africa and the islands in a thousand ships in 945 A.D. (J. Spencer Trimingham discusses this and the other Arabic accounts in his chapter.) But women usually are responsible for the consolidation of language. What little we know of the origins of Malagasy culture also argues in favor of the gradual diffusion of the Indonesian languages and cultures to Madagascar and, separately if not simultaneously, the diffusion of technology and particular material items to the mainland.

Confirmation of these possibilities, and strong support for Indonesian intervention in Africa, awaits further research in Africa, in Madagascar, and in Southeast Asia. Both Southall and Vérin delineate the kinds of questions to which answers must be sought, suggest and explore the methodological problems and difficulties, and advance hypotheses about the components of Malagasy culture on the basis of their own archaeological and anthropological research. They consider, for example, the arguments in favor of Indonesians settling on the mainland prior to their arrival in Madagascar, and reject as inconclusive Deschamps's suggestion that African names for Malagasy animals and some plants must imply movements of population rather than random borrowing. They also note the existence in Madagascar of two groups of dialects of Indonesian origin, which have in common only about 60 per cent of their vocabularies. Because of these differences, Vérin postulates two successive waves of immigration, the earlier in the west, the later in the east. But Southall considers the range of dialectical variation to be a result of the development of linguistic groups in the relatively isolated milieux of Madagascar. Both contributors also discuss the origin of the fortified villages of the central plateau and a range of issues which bear upon the nature of the contribution of Southeast Asians to Malagasy and, by possible extension, African life.

Research on and about the mainland during the last decade, although revealing little about the impact of Indonesia, has profoundly transformed our knowledge of the history of the peoples of the coast. Much of this new work has been archaeological in origin, as will be evident from the papers by Neville Chittick and James Kirkman. But linguistic investigations and a reassessment of the available textual and numismatic evidence have contributed equally to the synthesis which is contained in many of the following chapters. The *Periplus of the Erythraean Sea* is the earliest written record of the region. From it we learn that the inhabitants of southwestern Arabia settled in East Africa as long ago as the first century B.C., and had conceivably lived there or paid visits for a considerable time before. They intermarried with East Africans —probably pre-Bantu—learned their languages, and exported the exotic products of the coast—notably ivory and, from what is now Somalia, slaves. The *Periplus* has long been known, but only as a result of Mathew's new analyses (as presented below) is it now possible fully to appreciate its significance and assign to it a probable authorship and date. Even so, because of the refractory nature of the data contained in the *Periplus* and its fragmentary descriptions of peoples and ports—the identifications of which are still in dispute—along the coast south of Somalia, its explication cannot alone resolve the Indonesian conundrum.

After the *Periplus* and the meager information provided by Ptolemy, almost all the written accounts are in Arabic. But the first of these travel reports dates from the tenth century, and, as Trimingham emphasizes, their authors were not interested primarily in history. Similarly, as is demonstrated by Paul Wheatley in his rich essay on China's relations with Africa, China's knowledge of Africa before the fifteenth century was remarkable, but second-hand. There are a few early, local, brief inscriptions which are noted by Chittick and Kirkman, but the fullest and most significant non-archaeological sources for pre-colonial eastern Africa are redactions of the local chronicles. However, until recently these have been taken far too readily at their face value. Although every small port or island town boasts a chronicle, only the Kilwa chronicle is of any antiquity. The others, particularly those concerning Pate and the island towns of the Lamu archipelago, are in their present form less than 100 years old. For the most part they are simply written versions of oral traditions as remembered and recorded during the nineteenth century. They exhibit the chronological telescoping and tendency to ruling-family apotheosis common to this kind of documentation, and the information they contain must be subjected to the checks afforded by archaeology. Thus far, fresh examination of the two most important chronicles, of Kilwa and Pate, have led to a reinterpretation of the former and a drastic reassessment and devaluing of the latter.

As a result of the investigations reported in the following chapters, and data unearthed since those chapters were initially presented, it is possible to conclude that from the ninth century until the latter part of the thirteenth, eastern Africans traded primarily with the peoples of the Persian Gulf. Dhows brought immigrants from this region, notably people who, perhaps because they came from or had originated in the Persian province of Fars of which Shiraz is the capital, were called Shirazi. Chittick suggests, below, that they settled first along the coast of Somalia south of Cape Guardafui, and then along the northern Kenya coast, between the ninth and twelfth centuries. There they lived, trading imported goods for ivory with people (conceivably the ancestors of the Nyika and others) who probably spoke Bantu tongues, and who may have claimed the city of Shungwaya as their pre-diasporan home. The conferees, among them several of the contributors to this volume, discussed the probable location of this place of origin at some length, and Chittick has subsequently searched for it unsuccessfully in the vicinity of Bur Gao. Since many of the peoples of northern Kenya and southern Somalia still claim it as their home, and since the dispersal from Shungwaya may have been stimulated by external influence, its discovery remains one of the prime targets of archaeological research in eastern Africa.

Wherever and whatever Shungwaya may have been, the migration of people who are called Shirazi in the chronicles, and who may have influenced the development and/or the demise of Shungwaya, is now interpreted as a movement of people whose ancestors came from the Persian Gulf. In the case of Pemba there was also an immigration of other peoples, perhaps Iraqis, before the tenth century. By then there was an important Islamic settlement on the island, whose inhabitants traded with the Gulf. At about this same time there was a similar Islamic outpost on the small, now unimportant, island of Manda in the Lamu archipelago. It is the earliest excavated site in this historically important region, but the later history of Manda, like that of Pemba, is known only in a fragmentary way.

The early towns of the coast were essentially entrepôts. They obtained products for export from the peoples of the interior and welcomed the annual visits of seafaring merchants from the Arabian and Gulf ports. Yet the peoples of the interior, no matter how assiduously they traded, seem to have been influenced little by the culture of the coastal towns. As late as the nineteenth century, the coastal village polities and the peoples of the interior enjoyed an essentially diarchical relationship. The goods required by the Muslim merchants, especially the ivory, may have been carried considerable distances, but without the organization or interference of the traders of the coast. Only in the far south, in what is now Moçambique, did Muslims penetrate the interior. As Merrick Posnansky's chapter indicates, not until the nineteenth century did Arabs reach the great states in and around the interior lakes, and the long-distance carriage of goods to the coast by the interior-dwelling Bisa, Yao, and Nyamwezi probably began only in the eighteenth century. Posnansky also emphasizes the paucity of imported objects discovered in the lacustrine region. Hardly any antedate the nineteenth century.

Lacking more than the most speculative of evidence, it is still impossible meaningfully to discuss either the relations of the peoples of the East African coast with their Bantu-speaking neighbors or the impact of these small Islamic trading communities upon the historical development of inner Africa. They were, however, an integral part of the Indian Ocean commercial network and, certainly from the tenth century (if not before) to the nineteenth century, constituted eastern Africa's window on the world. Notions of modernization were mediated by and transmitted through the entrepôts and, during the heyday of the major city-states, from the eleventh through the fifteenth centuries, their influence both in terms of Africa and in terms of the basin may have been far greater than we can now suppose.

For pre-Islamic times we have only the *Periplus* and the findings of archaeologists—which have been few and scattered—as guides. During the first centuries of the Christian era, brass, copper, tin, and iron were imported into Somalia north of Cape Guardafui. Glass, iron tools, and weapons were the main items of trade to the south. Lances, for example, were made in the Yemen especially for the African trade. But none of the imported objects have been excavated. Similarly, where there have been finds of Roman and Ptolemaic coins, the circumstances of their discovery have been dubious. No Roman pottery has ever been found.

From about the seventh century, East Africa traded primarily with the peoples of the northern rim of the Indian Ocean. The earliest imported Islamic pottery dates from the ninth and tenth centuries and closely resembles wares recently excavated at Sirâf, a Persian port on the northern side of the Gulf. The unglazed jars which have been found on Manda, the only excavated site of the period, were probably fashioned near Sirâf. Of the glazed ware which has been found, blue "Sassanian-Islamic" jars predominate and are known to have been widely used in Mesopotamia and along the coast of Fars. The glass of this early period seems to be of Persian origin, although some may have been derived from Egypt via the Gulf. The Arabian principality of Oman doubtless also participated in this trade; al-Mas'udi, who is discussed by Trimingham, embarked from Oman on his famous voyage to Qanbalu—probably the modern Pemba. From the eleventh century, merchants appear to have preferred to import Islamic sgraffiato wares (Geza Fehérvári discussed this category of pottery in a paper delivered to the conference but not included here) from Persia. The polychrome and blue-and-white bowls which were used for decoration in the fifteenth century, and were inserted, for example, in the vaults of buildings at Kilwa, also appear to be Persian.

The undoubted early connections between the Arabian peninsula and eastern Africa are supported only in the most cursory fashion by material finds. There are written reports (discussed by Trimingham) of a regular thirteenth-century trading route from Aden to Mogadishu, Kilwa, and Madagascar, and of the importation of ambergris from Zanj (East Africa) to Aden in the fourteenth century, but southern Arabia, as Egypt, would probably have been able to offer comparatively little to East Africa before about 1300, when political links were forged. The Abu'l-Mawahib dynasty, which came to power about then in Kilwa, was derived from southwestern Arabia. Ibn Battuta, the well-known Tangerian traveler, met learned men from the Hijaz at Kilwa in the mid-fourteenth century, and in the fifteenth a deposed sultan of Aden took refuge in Kilwa. During the fourteenth century, too, a new type of decorated yellow-glazed pottery was made near Aden and exported to Kilwa and to Gedi and other towns along the Kenyan coast.

The quality of East Africa's relations with communities farther east—beyond the Gulf—is more difficult to judge from artifacts alone. When the Portuguese arrived in East Africa at the very end of the fifteenth century they found Gujarati merchants from the vicinity of Bombay trading cotton cloth and copper in the main ports. This commerce had probably flourished for some time, but its importance is difficult to gauge and there is no mention of peoples from India in the written sources for the period. During the era of the *Periplus*, the products of Cambay (northwestern India) do not appear to have been transported south of Guardafui. Later, however, perhaps from about the eighth century, traders from Daybul, a port of prominence near the mouth of the Indus River, seem—according to oral tradition—to have been present on the coast of what is now Tanzania. From the Indian sub-continent Africans were presumably importing iron objects and breads, pottery from India being almost lacking before the seventeenth century. The first beads were carnelian from Cambay; from about the twelfth century glass beads, some of which later came from Negapatam on the Coromandel coast (southern India), began to be imported. But common as these glass beads are in the excavations of East Africa and the pre-colonial trade of the entire Indian Ocean basin, they remain a particularly unstable indicator of the age or pattern of commerce. Beads have been classified, notably by the late W.G.N. van der Sleen, who presented a paper to the conference, but thus far not in ways which command universal acceptance or are applicable to the problems of modern archaeology. Work is now being undertaken on the chemical analysis and classification of Indian Ocean beads.

India may have provided Africa with new methods for the

mining of gold. Indeed, the techniques of gold mining in Rhodesia (Zimbabwe) were probably derived from India, conceivably directly. Indian brass cups have occasionally been found in fourteenth- or fifteenth-century contexts, but the most notable objects of Indian origin in East Africa are two large fragments of decorative inscriptions with Qur'anic texts cut from marble-like calcite. The carved work on the back of one is clearly from a Hindu hand of the tenth century. The stones seem to have been taken by Muslims from a Hindu temple and were reworked in the late fifteenth or early sixteenth centuries. But when they were removed to East Africa, and found their way to Kilwa, is not yet known.

Wheatley's assessment of China's involvement with Africa is based largely upon Chinese sources. It is clear from the receiving end, from East Africa, that the porcelain of China was prized from early times. Remarkable amounts have been found by archaeologists, and there are references to Chinese porcelain in the later Swahili literature. The excavation at Manda disclosed some ninth- and tenth-century Yueh and white wares, but only in the fourteenth century do similar imports, predominantly celadon plates, become common. During and after the fifteenth century, the quantities of celadon (later blue-and-white) exceed those of Islamic wares. A few specimens of porcelain from Annam (Vietnam) and many of the Sawankhalok type from western Thailand have also been found. There is a surprising absence of jade. (Lacquer goods, which must have been traded, would not have survived.) The goods of the Orient were probably not imported directly into East Africa. Before the fifteenth century, the Chinese never sailed to East Africa, and then only to Malindi. Sirâf was, in the tenth century, a major transshipment port.

Chinese and other foreign coins have also been found in East Africa, but they appear to have been desired primarily for ornamentation. Coins of foreign provenance are particularly plentiful at Kisimani Mafia, which was important during the thirteenth century. Of the many copper coins, two are Mongol, one was struck by the Ayyubid rulers of Egypt, and another is from the Chola kingdom of southern India. But the amount of the foreign coinage of the coast is insignificant compared to the very many good quality copper coins which were minted by the sultans of Kilwa, probably for currency, and in Mogadishu and Zanzibar.

Complementary excavations in India and Southeast Asia may someday establish the configuration of East Africa's export trade; in this process the indigenous coinage may prove useful. Until then, it is possible to say only that East Africans offered primarily their natural products. Rhinoceros horn, tortoise or turtle shell, and similar goods are mentioned in the *Periplus*. African ivory, which was softer than the Asian variety and more easily worked, was always important and highly prized, especially in India. Gold was a significant export, particularly when Kilwa controlled Sofala in the fourteenth and fifteenth centuries. Iron, according to Idrisi and others, was smelted on the coast (this is attested to by excavations), exported to India, and made into the famous steel goods which were re-exported to Africa. Ambergris is frequently mentioned, especially by the Chinese, but, being rare, its total value may never have been high. Gum copal was not an important product until Portuguese times. Mangrove poles, now the main cargo of dhows, are rarely mentioned but were probably also important for export to the northern rim of the Indian Ocean, where timber is scarce.

The extent of the slave trade is in dispute. As Trimingham indicates, large numbers of black, perhaps "Zanji," slaves were present in Iraq and elsewhere in western Asia and China during the first centuries of Islam, but it is not at all certain if any of these slaves were of East African origin. They may have been shipped through the ports of northern Somalia, slaves being notably lacking in the exports of the southern coast. Indeed, the only account which exists of slave trading in the region of Sofala implies that such activity was unusual.

In this, as in so many other spheres of knowledge concerning the interaction of East Africa and the Orient, definitive statements are more often negative than positive. The following chapters must therefore be viewed as cautious attempts not to rewrite, but for the first time to provide a basis for writing the history of this cultural synthesis. The lacunae and conundrums remain, if more specifically delineated than before. The research opportunities and requirements are equally defined: as Gwynne explains, a further understanding of the genetics and diffusion of food crops and domesticated animals is essential. It is clear that archaeological surveys and excavations in southern Somalia—the putative general area of Shungwaya—should have high priority. Similarly, too little is known about the Moçambique coast, southern Arabia (an area crucial to a further appreciation of the *Periplus*), and southwestern Ethiopia; archaeological investigations in those regions are in their infancy. Because of the unanswered questions which surround the movement of Indonesians westward, biogeographical histories of the Maldive and Seychelle island groups are critical; Socotra, another little known island, may have been another diffusionary center of importance. Archaeological explorations on those islands, in Madagascar, in the Persian Gulf, and throughout Southeast Asia and the Indonesian archipelago will likewise prove crucial. The renewed energies of musicologists and linguists must be directed to a range of problems; numismatists, mariners, art historians, Sinologists, and many other specialists can all assist. Few reliable texts exist of the Arabic and Chinese accounts. New, carefully prepared redactions are therefore urgently needed. It is clear, moreover, that new discoveries will and should amplify and revise the report that is contained in the following chapters. Perhaps first-hand documentation will be discovered in Shiraz or Fars, or new sites be excavated on the northern or eastern rims of the Indian Ocean and in Madagascar. The present collection is intended to provide a foundation for such research.

THE EDITORS

THE PEOPLING OF THE EAST AFRICAN COAST

Neville Chittick

Neville Chittick

THE ORIGINAL INHABITANTS

Anthropological and Archaeological Evidence

Skeletal evidence of the physical nature of the past inhabitants of the East African coast is almost entirely lacking. This is perhaps not so great a loss as might at first appear, since the validity of the interpretation of physical characteristics of skulls, unless based on a large related series, is often open to dispute. Apart from the historical sources, which are of overriding importance, we therefore have to rely mainly on what we can learn from the archaeological evidence and from the cultural characteristics, languages, and present distribution of peoples.

The problem is further complicated by the fact that recent work has suggested that the different physical characteristics of peoples in Africa who are phenotypically different (e.g. the San [Bushmen] and the Bantu) and genotypically the same are due to environmental factors such as habitat and diet.[1] If this view is correct its implications are far-reaching. Given our present knowledge, however, we must base our inferences on the phenotypes as they now exist.

1. Ronald Singer and J.S. Weiner, "Biological Aspects of some Indigenous African Populations," *Southwestern Journal of Anthropology*, XIX (1963), 168–176.

Before the Iron Age the greater part of Africa was occupied by peoples who lived by hunting and by collecting wild vegetable foods. It is generally accepted that at least in the southern part of the continent these people were of the Bushman-Hottentot (Khoisan-speaking) type. It is believed that these hunting peoples made most or all of the artifacts classified as Late Stone Age in Africa. Such artifacts have been found on or near the coast at a number of sites ranging from Kilwa in the south[2] to Kilifi in the north.

The only surviving hunting peoples near the coast are the Sanye-Boni group in northern Kenya and southern Somalia, but there is good evidence that the Boni formerly lived as far north as the Webi Shabeli[3] The present inhabitants of Pate still consider the Sanye to be the earliest inhabitants of that island, in the usual way that settled people regard their hunting neighbors as aboriginals.[4] There has been, however, some doubt about how the Sanye and Boni should be classified racially and linguistically; it seems that their language should be considered South Kushitic (proto-Hamitic) as opposed to a "Bushman" tongue.[5]

There is also evidence that the Rift Valley, as far south as northern Tanzania, and regions to the west were in the first millennium B.C. occupied by pastoral peoples, possibly of Caucasoid character. No relics of these people, who used stone bowls and pottery as well as flaked stone tools, have, however, been found on the coast or in its hinterland.

The view generally held is that the hunting peoples of East Africa were displaced by Bantu-speaking people. Oliver, largely on the basis of the linguistic work of Guthrie, maintained that the Bantu spread from a nuclear area south of Lake Tanganyika eastwards and westwards to the coasts, following the "southern

2. Joan R. Harding, "Late Stone Age Sites on the Tanganyika Coast," *Man*, LXI (1961), 221.
3. Enrico Cerulli, *Somalia*, (Roma, 1957), I, 53.
4. See references quoted by G.W.B. Huntingford in "The Peopling of the Interior of East Africa by its Modern Inhabitants," in Roland Oliver and Gervase Mathew (eds.) *History of East Africa* (Oxford, 1963), I, 63.
5. Harold C. Fleming, "Asa and Aramanik: Cushitic Hunters in Masai-Land," *Ethnology*, VIII (1969), 1. On this subject see also A.H.J. Prins, "The Didemic Diarchic Boni," *Journal of the Royal Anthropological Institute*

woodland belt."[6] To the east the Bantu-speakers reached the sea near and to the south of the Ruvuma River. From this region they are thought to have spread north and south along the coast during the second half of the first millennium A.D. This theory assumes that the Bantu peoples of the southern woodland belt have stayed put for something like 1500 years, or at least that their languages have remained little affected by population movements. This assumption may be true, but it presents a picture different from the great movements of population which we know to have taken place over the last half millennium.

The difficulty in attempting to correlate archaeological finds with this theory lies in the impossibility of deducing what type of language the makers of particular artifacts spoke, and, if we equate "Bantu" with Negroid in this connection, the lack of skeletal material associated with the finds. There are, however, some grounds for supposing that the Bantu-speaking peoples brought the knowledge of iron to most of equatorial Africa.[7] The earliest Iron Age pottery wares known over a wide area of eastern Africa from the Limpopo River to Lake Victoria display certain common characteristics.[8] It is tempting to equate these apparently related types of pottery (that with a more northerly distribution is known as dimple-based, or Urewe, ware) with the spread of the Bantu-speaking peoples in East Africa. On this assumption (and it is no more) Robert Soper's recent finds of pottery, termed Kwale ware and related to the Urewe (dimple-based) ware of the Lake Victoria region, would support Oliver's theory of the comparatively early spread of the Bantu peoples up the coast. The sites of these finds are no great distance from the coast (southwest of Mombasa and in the South Pare hills respectively) and have yielded radiocarbon dates of around the third century A.D. These dates agree with

XCIII (1963), 174, where further references are given. Cerulli, *Somalia*, I, 52, considers them of mixed origin.

6. Roland Oliver, "The Problem of the Bantu Expansion," *Journal of African History*, VII (1966), 361.
7. Robert Soper, "A General Review of the Early Iron Age of the Southern Half of Africa" *Azania*, VI (1972), 5–36; Merrick Posnansky, "Bantu Genesis," *Uganda Journal*, XXV (1961), 86–93.
8. Brian M. Fagan, "Early Iron Age Pottery in Eastern and Southern Africa," *Azania*, I (1966), 101.

those calculated for related wares in the interior and are rather earlier than that suggested by Oliver for the Bantu migration northwards along the coast. So far as historical evidence is concerned, however, there is no reason to reject such a date.

Historical Evidence

(a) Graeco-Roman sources

Our earliest historical source is the *Periplus of the Erythraean Sea*, the date of which is still disputed but is about 120 A.D. This document tells us nothing about the physical characteristics of the native inhabitants of the East African coast save that they were very tall.[9] The fact that nothing is said about their color has been taken as indicating that they were not Negroid.[10] But we are not really justified in drawing such a conclusion. The writer of the *Periplus* made few comments on the physical nature of the inhabitants of the countries which he described, except in his description of people on the borders of This (China); therefore nothing can be based on the mere omission of any mention of skin color.

It is further said by some historians that in the *Periplus* the people of this coast are clearly contrasted with those further north, the supposed Berbers of the seaboard fronting on the Red Sea and the Gulf of Aden.[11] I can see little evidence for such contrast; there are certainly insufficient grounds for saying that these more southern people are different racially or linguistically from the "Berbers" to the north. As to the remaining evidence, the fact that they were seafarers using sewn boats might be said to be rather opposed to the view that they were Kushitic; that each place had its own chief is evidence neither way, nor is the fact that the people are said to have been piratical. Their interest in the sea and the cultivation of the coconut are consonant with an Indonesian origin; but this interest suggests an immigration earlier

9. § 16, 28. See also Gervase Mathew, "The Dating and Significance of the *Periplus of the Erythraean Sea*," below, 158.
10. Oliver, "Bantu Expansion," 308; Gervase Mathew, "The East African Coast Until the Coming of the Portuguese," in Oliver and Mathew, *History of East Africa*, 95
11. Mathew in *History of East Africa*, 95.

than most authorities would accept, and it has been surmised that the Indonesians who came to Madagascar (and perhaps first to the mainland) were of short stature.[12] In brief, all that we can gather from the *Periplus* is that the hunting peoples who were the aboriginal inhabitants had already, at least in some places, been replaced by other people whose identification is disputable. The fact that iron objects figure so prominently among imports suggests that these people either had no knowledge of smelting that metal, or smelted it only on a small scale.

Our next source is Ptolemy, whose work—in the form in which it has come down to us—is maintained to be effectively of the fifth century so far as it concerns East Africa.[13] From the *Geography* all that we learn of the inhabitants of the coast of what is now southern Tanzania is that some were "man-eating Ethiopians." Oliver has suggested that these may have been Bantu.[14] The name "Ethiopian" is evidence neither one way nor the other, for it was used by the Greeks to describe almost any African of black or dark color. However, cannibalism may perhaps be said to be more characteristic of the Negroid than the Kushitic peoples. Ptolemy says that the "Ethiopians" who made sewn boats lived "above," or north, of the cannibals; these are evidently the same seafarers referred to in the *Periplus*. We should note, too, that Ptolemy refers to the promontory Zingis (Ζιγγις), probably at the northern end of Azania; the root occurs again in Cosmas Indicopleustes (mid-sixth century) as Zingion (το ζίγγιον). This is certainly the equivalent of the Arabic Zanj, or Zinj, the name applied to both the country and the inhabitants beyond the Berber region. When applied to people, "Zanj" is, as we shall see, usually held to denote Negroid, and probably Bantu-speaking, persons.

The name "Zand Afrik Shah" occurs in Herzfeld's publication of the inscription of the Sassanian King Narsah at Paikuli in Kurdistan.[15] Henning has, however, shown that Herzfeld's reading

---

12. George Peter Murdock, *Africa, its Peoples and their Culture History* (New York, 1959), 9. See also Aidan Southall, "The Problem of Malagasy Origins," below, 192; Pierre Vérin, "Austronesian Contributions to the Culture of Madagascar: some Archaeological Problems," below 164.
13. Mathew, *History of East Africa*, 96, and below, 156.
14. Oliver, "Bantu Expansion," 368.

is wrong,[16] and this supposed reference should be expunged from the literature into which it has found its way.

(b) *Chinese sources*

Before turning to the earlier Arabic sources, it is well to mention what we can learn from the Chinese, most of which, however, appears to have been derived from the Arabs. Paul Wheatley has written of the evidence from China elsewhere in this volume, and the material is summarized by Duyvendak.[17]

The hearsay knowledge which the Chinese had of the Berbera coast as early as the ninth century indicates that the inhabitants were pastoralists, living on meat, milk, and blood which they drew from living cattle, as the Maasai do today. The people of Ma-lin (*Muâ-liĕn) were described as black and fierce, but were evidently Muslims. It is maintained that Ma-lin in this passage must be Malindi, as the same name occurred in a Ming history where the identification is certain.[18] If this is correct, the information we are given is of little value, for what we are told about the place cannot be true of the comparatively verdant region of modern Malindi, the land of Ma-lin being described as having no trees or herbs, and the people as eating dates and feeding their horses on fish. The date-palm will not bear in modern Malindi; horses are lacking, and would succumb to sickness.

In the work of Chao Ju-Kua, finished in 1226, we find the Zanj mentioned as Ts'eng Chi, and are told of an island whose inhabitants are as black as lacquer, have frizzy hair, and are captured and sold as slaves to the Arab countries.[19] In another passage

15. Ernst Herzfeld, *Paikuli: Monument and Inscription of the Early History of the Sassanian Empire* (Berlin, 1924).
16. W.B. Henning, "A Farewell to the Khagan of Aq-Aqatärän," *Bulletin of the School of Oriental and African Studies*, XIV (1952), 514–516.
17. J.J.L. Duyvendak, *China's Discovery of Africa* (London, 1949).
18. *Ibid.*, 15.
19. *Ibid.*, 22. Duyvendak considers the island to be Madagascar because of the reference to giant birds. But taking into account the Negroid nature of the inhabitants and the Zanj association, this seems doubtful; the story of the *Rukh* bird has no doubt come through the Arabs and could be attached to any part of this region (cf. Buzurg ibn Shahriyar [ed. P.A. van der Lith, trans. L. Marcel Devic] *Livre des Merveilles de l'Inde*, XXXIV/XXXVI [Leiden, 1883–1886], 61–64); they are said to swallow wild camels, which are nonexistent in Madagascar.

thought to refer to Zanzibar (Ts'ong Pa), though the description accords rather ill with that island, we are told of Arab Muslim inhabitants.[20]

These Chinese accounts, however, because they are not first hand, are of much less importance to us than the Arabic sources, some of which are at least based on eyewitness accounts.

(c) *Arabic sources*

The Arab historians tell us little of Zanj save in connection with the revolts of slaves in Iraq, notably in the latter part of the ninth century. Though the Zanj are distinguished from slaves from other parts of Africa, their racial character is not wholly clear.

The earlier Arab geographers and travelers describing eastern Africa were primarily concerned with the native inhabitants; all of the southern part of the coast appeared to have been pagan, and little was said of immigrants, who, we can assume, were few. Our understanding of what the geographers wrote is made more difficult by the fact that "Zanj" was used in two senses: as a general term for the whole region,[21] and for a restricted stretch of this coast, extending from the Webi Shabeli River to the beginning of the land of Sofala.[22] The latter, it should be emphasized, did not include the settlement which the Portuguese occupied on their arrival; the northern limit of the land of Sofala was probably where the Usambara mountains, which I would equate with Jebel 'Ajrad, come down to the sea opposite the island of Pemba.[23] There is a similar confusion in the use of "Zanj" as applied to people. In some contexts, the term seems to indicate little more than that they were black.[24] Al-Mas'udi, in his *Muruj adh-*

---

20. Greville S.P. Freeman-Grenville, *The East African Coast: Select Documents from the First to the Earlier Nineteenth Century* (Oxford, 1962), 21.
21. cf. L. Marcel Devic, *Le Pays des Zendjs* (Paris, 1883), 34.
22. See J. Spencer Trimingham, below, 120. V.V. Matveyev, *The Northern Boundaries of the Eastern Bantu* (*Zinj*) *in Tenth Century According to Arabic Sources* (Moscow, 1960), prefers the Juba, as a boundary, on the grounds that the Webi Shabeli does not flow into the sea; but it may have done so a thousand years ago.
23. Al-Idrisi (1st Climate, 7th Section) and see Trimingham, below 138.
24. Devic, *Pays des Zendjs*, 122.

Dhahab, (III, 1–2) distinguishes the Zanj from the Nubians and Beja but includes among them the people of Berbera. It is clear, however, from a general passage (I, 163–164) that he considers what we would call Negroid characteristics to be typical of the Zanj. He includes among them the people of Sofala (III, 6).[25]

An outstanding characteristic of the social organization of the peoples on or near the coast is that they were ruled by a king, or kings, who were apparently elected. This characteristic is indicated in all of the early sources, starting with al-Jahiz (died c. 869), and again by al-Mas'udi (tenth century) and, slightly later, by Buzurg ibn Shahriyar.[26] These kings had troops under their command and made war on each other. It was a society with a religious bent; accounts of preaching by holy men are given by al-Jahiz and subsequent authors, including al-Mas'udi (III, 30), who tell us that their sermons were delivered in their own language, and that they had no religious law (thus contrasting them with the Muslims). Al-Jahiz further informs us that the sermons were preached in the presence of the king. This information suggests a fairly highly developed society, one we should not expect at this time and place.

Al-Mas'udi is our best source on this region. He himself sailed more than once at least as far as the island of Qanbalu (probably Pemba)—for the last time in 916–917 A.D. Much the most important conclusion which has been drawn from his writings is that Bantu speakers were present in the Zanj country, and in particular in the Sofala country and Waqwaq, their seat of government. This conclusion is based on al-Mas'udi's statement that they chose a king for themselves whom they called *waqlīmī* or *waflīmī*, which we are told means "son of the great lord."[27] Elsewhere we are told that this title was applied to all of the kings of Zanj, though

25. I have used the version of al-Mas'udi, translated by Barbier de Maynard and Pavet de Courteille and edited by Charles Pellat, *Les Prairies d'or* (Paris, 1962), consulting on occasion V.V. Matveyev and L.E. Kubbel, *Arabic Sources of the VII–X Centuries on the Ethnography and History of African Regions South of Sahara* (Moscow, 1960) [Russian translation].

26. V.V. Matveyev, "Records of Early Arab Authors on Bantu Peoples," VII International Congress of Anthropological and Ethnological Sciences (Moscow, 1965), summarizes the evidence.

27. Al-Mas'udi, III, 6–7 and 29–30.

a more likely title for the ruler would be one derived from the "enye" root, such as *mwenye*.[28] The case for equating this word, *waqlimi* or *waflimi*, with the Bantu *mfalme* (pl. *wa-*), "king," is strengthened by the similarity of the Zanj word for God, *mklnjlū* (mkulunjulu?) which is said by Mas'udi to mean "Great Lord," to a southern Bantu word for God, u-nkulu-nkulu.[29] It may equally be related to the Bantu *mkuu* (great person), or *juu* (above). However, even if these words are Bantu, we cannot go on to deduce that Swahili was being spoken.[30] With regard to *waqlimi*, we should also note that *waqa'* in Kushitic languages is a word for "God", while the Limis are a people of the interior, as recorded by Ibn Battuta.

Al-Mas'udi also tells us the staple food of the Zanj was sorghum-millet (*dhura*)[31] and a food dug out of the ground like the *qulqās* (taro, or coco-yam). The people also cultivated coconut palms extensively on the islands and ate bananas as well as honey and meat.[32]

One passage of al-Mas'udi (III, 6) is of particular interest in connection with the character of the people: "The Zanj alone among all the tribes of the Aḥābīsh [Abyssinians] crossed the canal [Khalīj] which leaving the upper course of the Nile discharges into the Zanj sea. They established themselves in this country, extending their settlements up to the country of Sofala."

It has been suggested that this passage may refer to a movement of Kushites southwards. Further references to the use by the Zanj of Sofala and Waqwaq cattle as beasts of burden, and even for war,[33] lend color to the view that there was a migration of cattle-keeping peoples who became dominant over the Bantu but adopted the Bantu language. This is a possible interpretation. However,

28. *Ibid.*, II, 292.
29. G.A. Wainwright, "The Diffusion of -Uma as a Name for Iron," *Uganda Journal*, XVIII (1954), 115.
30. As does G.S.P. Freeman-Grenville, "Medieval Evidences for Swahili," *Swahili*, 29/1 (1959), 11. The validity of the identification of these words has recently been cautiously examined by W.H. Whiteley, *Swahili, The Rise of a National Language* (London, 1969).
31. Not maize, as translated by Pellat.
32. Al-Mas'udi, III, 30.
33. *Ibid.*, 7, 26.

the reference to the southern Zanj as one of the Abyssinian peoples need not necessarily mean that they were Kushitic; it may arise from an imprecise use of racial terms. "Habash" may perhaps here be used in the same sense that "Ethiopian" was used by Graeco-Roman writers—an expression that may be compared to the general use of Zanj for all black people.

The reference to cattle being used as beasts of burden is puzzling, and reminds one of the cattle armies of the Tutsi in Rwanda,[34] though it does not seem that the latter rode their cattle. The Tutsi are generally believed to be of Kushitic stock, but they speak a Bantu language and research is throwing some doubt on the validity—so far as their ancestral stock goes—of their being distinguished from the nonpastoral peoples over whom they now rule. (Different ways of life, and particularly different diets, may produce very different outward physical characteristics.) Al-Mas'udi's account, on the other hand, may be partly mythical, arising from the fact that the Zanj did not, as he says, have any horses, mules, or camels. In the next sentence (III, 7) he says that some of the Zanji tribes sharpened their teeth and were cannibals; both of these characteristics pertained to the "Bantu" rather than to Kushites. Today many of the Makua-Makonde peoples, the Yao, and the Luvale file their teeth.

The statement of al-Mas'udi that the Zanj moved south (apparently across the Juba or Webi Shabeli) is, if the Zanj were Bantu-speakers, difficult to reconcile with the theory of the spread of the Bantu up the coast northwards from the Ruvuma River area. It may be that al-Mas'udi was misinformed and, in terms of travel from the known to the unknown, simply presumed that the Zanj spread from north to south. This is conjecture only, and al-Mas'udi's statement must be given much weight.

There is no doubt that by the time of Ibn Battuta's visit in 1331-32 the indigenous population of the southern coast was

34. Marcel d'Hertefelt, A. Trouwborst, and J. Scherer, *Les Anciens Royaumes de la zone interlacustre meridionale* (London, 1962), 65. The "preachers" of whom the early Arabic sources speak may be compared also to the high religious dignitaries known as *iiru* at the Rwanda court: *ibid.*, 71; Alexis Kagame, *L'Histoire des armées-bovines dans l'ancien Rwanda* (Bruxelles, 1961).

Negroid; it is virtually certain that they were Bantu-speaking. Of particular interest is his statement that the inhabitants of Kilwa, of very black complexion, tattooed their faces in the same way as did the Limis who lived in the country whence the gold was brought (presumably what is now Rhodesia).[35] Tattooing is a present-day characteristic of the Makua-Makonde tribes, and it is remarkable that a skull found in an early well at Kilwa—probably dating before this period—displays filed teeth.[36] The conclusion that one is tempted to draw—that people of Makonde type were living on Kilwa Island in the fourteenth century—is contrary to the fact that the present homeland of these people extends only a short distance into Tanzania from Moçambique and that they have been moving northwards in recent times.

(d)   *African sources*

The local sources, which are mostly of very doubtful value, have little to say about the aboriginal inhabitants. The Kilwa Chronicle, originally set down in the 1520's, recorded Swahili-sounding names for the chief of Kilwa and for certain of the early sultans.[37] The authenticity of these names is doubtful, as the Chronicle is referring to a period which I would ascribe to the late twelfth/early thirteenth century.[38]

More important is the evidence that there was a Negroid

35. Hamilton A.R. Gibb (trans.), *The Travels of Ibn Battuta* (Cambridge, 1959), II, 380.
36. Discovered in the course of the British Institute excavations at Kilwa. After finding the human bones, the men digging this well refused to continue.
37. Freeman-Grenville, "Medieval Evidences," 4–8. The Kilwa Chronicle is an account of the history and rulers of Kilwa which was originally written at the command of a sultan of that city who ruled in the first half of the sixteenth century. It has survived in two versions, both of which evidently omit some of the material set down in the original chronicle. One version (the one referred to here) is in Arabic, and was copied in Zanzibar in 1877; the other is an account based largely on the same or a similar original source incorporated in the *Deçadas da Asia* by João de Barros. Critical translations of these works are given in G.S.P. Freeman-Grenville, *Medieval History of the Coast of Tanganyika* (London, 1962); the chronology is further examined in Neville Chittick, "The 'Shirazi' Colonization of East Africa," *Journal of African History*, VI (1965), 275–294.
38. *Ibid.*, 275. See also 38 of this chapter.

population at an early date in southern Somalia which was subsequently submerged by the Galla and Somali.[39] This conclusion is indicated not only by written and oral traditions, but also by the survival of Negroid groups, and, at Barawa, of a form of Swahili. On the evidence that ad-Dimishqi in the fourteenth century referred to Mogadishu as "Maqdishū of the Zanj," and as belonging to the Zanzibar coast, Cerulli has also suggested that the population of that town was then at least partly Negroid;[40] but this suggestion must be regarded as doubtful in view of the vague use of the "Zanj" referred to above. These Negroid people ("Kashur" in Arabic, "Nyika" in Swahili) were undoubtedly Bantu-speaking. The date of their arrival is doubtful. The Book of the Zanj (Kitab al-Zunuj)[41] maintains that Himyaritic Arabs found them already settled a century before the birth of Christ. Little confidence can be placed in this statement, however, for the Book of the Zanj is a late nineteenth-century redaction, and its information about the pre-Islamic period is uncorroborated by earlier sources. It is, however, perhaps legitimate to suppose that the Negroid Kashur were present before there was any substantial Arab immigration to the coast. This I would place in the ninth century, partly on the archaeological evidence from Unguja Ukuu and Manda.[42] Their country (and capital) was known as Shungwaya. The main settlement of this name may have been at different places at different times; the Book of the Zanj indicates that it was close to the Juba River. The site has been identified with Port Durnford (Bur Gao)[43] just north of the Kenya border. However, on a recent visit to this place I found no sign of occupation earlier than the fifteenth or sixteenth centuries, and there is no convincing historical evidence that a town (as opposed to a region) named Shungwaya existed before that time. Together with Grottanelli I am suspicious of the reported find of coins, some Ptolemys, at this site; if buried

39. Cerulli, *Somalia* I, 54–57; II, 115–121.
40. *Ibid.*, I, 44–46.
41. *Ibid.*, I, 231 ff.
42. Neville Chittick, "Discoveries in the Lamu Archipelago," *Azania*, II (1967), 37–67.
43. Vinigi L. Grottanelli, "A Lost African Metropolis," *Afrikanistische Studien* (Berlin, 1955), 231.

together they cannot in any case have been placed there at a date before that of the latest of them, which are of Ottoman Egypt, or after 1500.[44] The graves at Bur Gao can, on grounds of style, hardly be earlier than the sixteenth century, and the defensive wall is certainly later than some of the graves.[45] If there was an earlier Shungwaya town, one must look for it elsewhere.

Yet there is no doubt that this Negroid population center was the nucleus of the northeastern group of Bantu tribes, who have spread over the eastern part of Kenya and into northern Tanganyika during the last few centuries.[46]

It seems to me there are three solutions to the question of the spread of the Negroid "Bantu" in the region described by al-Mas'udi, which I take to be primarily eastern Tanzania and northeastern Moçambique.

The first is that the early Bantu peoples moved southwards from Somalia, a migration similar to, but much earlier than, that of the Segeju and associated tribes. This conclusion is supported by the evidence of the Book of Zanj as to the antiquity of Negroid peoples in Somalia and can be said to accord tolerably well with what al-Mas'udi tells us of the southward movement of the Zanj. It is, however, opposed to the linguistic (glottochronological) evidence and leaves unsolved the question of how, if we adopt the generally accepted view that the Bantu peoples originated far to the west or southwest, they reached their home in Somalia. A route through, or north of, the ,region of the great lakes might have been possible.

The second solution is that, in accord with the linguistic evidence, the Bantu peoples moved up from the south but were

44. Vinigi L. Grottanelli, *Pescatori dell'Oceano Indiano* (Roma, 1955), 385.
45. Neville Chittick, "An Archaeological Reconnaissance of the Southern Somali Coast," *Azania*, IV, (1969), 115–130.
46. Prins, "Die Urheimat der Nordost-Bantu," *Anthropos*, L (1955), 273; Grottanelli, below, 64; Herbert J. Lewis, "The Origins of the Galla and Somali," *Journal of African History*, VII (1966), 27–46. R.F. Morton, "The Shungwaya Myth of Miji Kenda Origins," *International Journal of African Historical Studies*, V (1972), 397–423, dismisses the authenticity of the tradition that these Miji Kenda (Nyika) tribes originated in the Shungwaya region. I find his arguments wholly unconvincing, involving as they do an unsubstantiated and incomplete evaluation of the *Kitab al-Zanuj*.

overcome by a cattle-keeping people, perhaps Kushitic, who came from the north and who established themselves as a ruling class over the Bantu, while adopting the Bantu language. The account of al-Mas'udi seems to agree best with this explanation. The miscegenation of these two stocks might account for the comparatively low proportion of Negroid traits found in Bantu-speaking peoples in eastern Africa as observed by some authorities.[47] The comparatively highly organized social structure, with "kings," armies, and preachers might have been brought by the cattle-keeping conquerors or adopted from the Bantu themselves. Against this second solution is the fact that the coast and its immediate hinterland are ill-suited to a pastoral society, and that we have to accept the total submersion of the ruling pastoral people within, it seems, a short period.

The last solution is that the Bantu spread northwards from the Moçambique region, displacing pre-existing hunting peoples, but not becoming involved with any other race. The evidence for this is linguistic only. For there to have been Negroid peoples, apparently Bantu-speaking, north of Kenya well before the end of the first millennium, this migration would have had to have taken place at an early date; but, as we have seen, a date as early as the *Periplus* is not impossible. This theory is contradicted by the statement of al-Mas'udi that the Zanj came from the north, and it is difficult to reconcile it with what he said about using cattle as beasts of burden, a practice which is unknown among the northern or central Bantu.

Which of these theories is most likely to be correct is a matter for argument. If we accept the validity of the deductions based on linguistic evidence, the second—that there were present both Negroid peasants who derived from the south and west and a cattle-keeping upper caste from the north—seems most convincing. But the validity of some of these deductions is open to doubt and coming under increasing criticism by linguists. If we ignore the linguistic evidence of how the Bantu might have spread along the coast, the theory that they dispersed southwards from the Somali region is the most acceptable. It may be that their descendants

47. Sonia Cole, *Races of Man* (London, 1963), 116.

are among those peoples, notably the Nguni, with well-developed political institutions, who finally settled toward the extreme south of Africa. It is remarkable that the Nguni and other peoples in that region until only recently used the cattle, to which they attach great importance, as beasts of burden and for riding. So far as I have been able to verify, this practice is quite unknown in any other region of Bantu Africa, though it was reportedly found among the Hottentots.

THE IMMIGRANTS

Historical Evidence

Up to this point we have neglected the immigrant peoples. I do not propose to deal here with the question of the Indonesian immigration; I would only point out that the single Arab reference to ships coming from the east, by Buzurg ibn Shahriyar, concerns a raid which is stated to have taken place in 334 A.H. (A.D. 945–946).[48] The "thousand ships" are said to have come from "Waqwaq," which, though in one view equated with Japan,[49] may have been any of the islands in the Far East. The raid might have come from the kingdom of Sri Vijaya (a kingdom centered on Sumatra), which, Mathew points out, controlled the sea routes to China at the time. But the suggestion that people from that kingdom settled on the coast is wholly speculative.[50] This "Waqwaq" must be distinguished from that near the Sofala country, though here, as in other contexts, confusion has arisen from the erroneous idea that Africa turned to the east to join the Far Eastern lands.

In sum, on the East African coast there have been settlers from the lands bordering the northern shores of the Indian Ocean from at least as early as the beginning of the Christian era. We know from the *Periplus* that Arab merchants from southwestern Arabia intermarried with the natives of Azania (the interior of East Africa southwest of Cape Guardafui) and that they knew their language.[51]

48.   Lith and Devic, *Livre des merveilles*, 175. See also below, 133, 273.
49.   Lith and Devic, *Livre des merveilles*, Excursion F, 295 ff.
50.   Mathew, in *History of East Africa*, 108. For Sri Vijaya see O.W. Wolters, *Early Indonesian Commerce* (Ithaca, 1967), 63–70.
51.   See § 16.

This immigration of Arabs from various lands has continued down to recent times, but the details of these movements are difficult to establish with certainty for they depend on sources of doubtful reliability.

(a) *Arabic sources*

Very little is to be learned from the early Arabic sources about the settlement of overseas peoples. It is clear that most of the coast was pagan down to the fourteenth century, the few Muslim settlements, other than those on islands, being isolated enclaves. Al-Idrisi, as late as the mid-twelfth century, mentions Merca as the southernmost Muslim town. Al-Mas'udi (I, 232) states that Qanbalu had a mixed population of Muslims and pagan Zanj at the beginning of the tenth century.

Qanbalu has been argued to be Zanzibar rather than Madagascar.[52] The latter is certainly impossible, but the arguments for its being Zanzibar could equally well apply to Pemba, which I think is in fact Qanbalu. The main evidence for this identification is in Yaqut (a geographer of the early thirteenth century) who refers to one of the two towns in Pemba (Jazirat al-Khadra) as Mknblū (Mkanbalu?) which seems likely to be the same name as Qanbalū and probably also identical with Mkumbuu, a place on the eastern coast of the island.[53] Moreover "Qanbalā" is marked on Ibn Hawqal's map as being opposite the "desert" between Balad al-Habash (Ethiopia) and Balad al-Zanj.[54] It is also pertinent that Pemba is the first large island one reaches coming from Oman, as al-Mas'udi did. He further said (I, 205) that the Muslims spoke the Zanj language and that they conquered the island and made the Zanj inhabitants captive "in the same way that the Muslims conquered the island of Crete in the Mediterranean at the time of the beginning of the Abbasid and end of the Umayyad dynasty." This statement may imply that the Muslims had been there for a considerable time, as also does their adoption of the Zanj language, and would almost certainly be of mixed blood by

52.   Lith and Devic, *Livre des merveilles*, 283.
53.   See Trimingham, below 126 of this volume.
54.   J.H. Kramer and Gaston Wiet (eds.), *Configuration de la terre* (Paris, 1964) I, 135.

the tenth century. We are told nothing of the origin of these Muslims; the reference to Crete may imply however that they were Arabs from overseas, not Muslims from farther north up the coast.

Al-Idrisi (mid-twelfth century) stated that the population of what is probably Zanzibar island was mixed but mostly Muslim. Yaqut stated that the king of Zanj lived on that island. There were two sultans in Pemba, one an Arab from Kufa[55]—the only reference to origins which I have observed.

Yaqut presented Maqdishu as the most important Muslim town on the mainland; its inhabitants were dark Berbers and were governed by elders.[56] A century later, Ibn Battuta stated that the town was ruled by a single shaykh, a Berber, who, though he knew Arabic, spoke in the Maqdishi language.[57] This is usually taken to refer to Somali, but could equally well be a Bantu language. The inhabitants of Zanzibar were also described as Berber, "a people of the Zanj." The people of this place, and of Mombasa and Kilwa, were all described as being of the Shafi'i persuasion, one of the orthodox, Sunni, rites of Islam.

(b) *African sources—the chronicles*

Let us now turn to the later sources of information about immigration to the coast. All but one of these sources were recorded on the East African coast itself; with the sole exception of the Kilwa Chronicle, which was set down in the first half of the sixteenth century, none can be traced back to before the eighteenth century, and most are more recent.

The first thing to be said about these records, and said with emphasis, is that they have hitherto been treated by the historians of East Africa as far more reliable than is justified. Though some scholars have shown some suspicion about the earliest periods dealt with in these records, the greater part of their information has been accepted as true unless proved false by some other written account.

In many or most cases these sources record the historical facts

55. John Gray, *History of Zanzibar* (London, 1962), 18.
56. J. Spencer Trimingham, *Islam in East Africa* (Oxford, 1964), 6n.
57. Gibb, *Ibn Battuta*, II, 375.

remembered at the time when the record was set down. Unless, therefore, we have good grounds for believing that the author was relying on an earlier written source, we should treat these chronicles with the same circumspection as we should an orally recorded tradition, taking into account the date at which the documents were committed to writing. A simple chronicle set down at a given date represents the remembered history at that time; it will be most accurate in dealing with events nearest to the time in which the historian is writing. If no earlier written source were available to the chronicler, it becomes less accurate the further back in time it goes (with the proviso set out below).

We should therefore view these chronicles in the same light as we would "traditional history." The chronicles of the coast are mostly an account of the rulers of a particular town-state. We should bear in mind certain factors of a primarily genealogical or "reign-list" nature applicable to such accounts. Some of these factors are:

1. Many or most such chronicles are concerned with establishing the right of a people to its land, or of a ruling family to its position.

2. In general, the earliest events and names are remembered comparatively reliably; the "middle" period is often much muddled; recent events are well remembered.

3. In the muddled middle period there is frequently a duplication of names (thus 'Ali b. Muhammad b. 'Ali b. Muhammad b. 'Ali...).

4. Average figures for the span of generations and reigns must be used to control the chronology where it is nonexistent or defective.

5. The importance and exploits of the state, town, or people concerned are often much exaggerated, while other places are somewhat ignored.

6. In the case of Muslim societies, there is a tendency to exaggerate the Arab element in the forebears and often to claim fictitious descent from the Prophet's, or Sherifian, families.

When considering the written chronicles, we should also take account of the evidence from purely oral sources and, where appropriate, from archaeological work.

Of the written sources only the Book of the Zanj gives an account of pre-Islamic immigration.[58] These immigrants are said to have been Arabs from Himyar and to have founded most of the more important towns of the coast, from Maqdishu to Mombasa, and also Kilwa. Arabs from almost every other region are supposed to have followed. It is possible—one can say no more—that this statement preserves the memory of traders and settlers from southwestern Arabia first mentioned in the *Periplus*, but the story of the founding of the towns is almost certainly mythical. Archaeology as yet offers no confirmation on this point: No remains dating from before the eighth century have been found at any of the excavated coastal sites. Until the end of the twelfth century Kilwa was a place of no great wealth, and the first contemporary writer to mention it was Yaqut in the early thirteenth century.

The Chronicle of Pate and the Chronicle of Lamu claim that Syrians were sent to the East African coast by the Umayyad caliph 'Abd al-Malik (A.D. 685–705); the former source states that he founded thirty-five towns on the coast. These accounts, too, are probably mythical. The Pate Chronicle is, as we shall see, very unreliable for a much later period, and any immigrants there may have been at this period were very unlikely to have come from Syria (such an origin was probably suggested by the fact that Damascus was the seat of the Umayyad dynasty). Mythical too, we can assume, is the story of the expedition sent by the Abbasid caliph al-Mansur (754–775) against the disloyal towns of the coast, the account in the Book of the Zanj of the dispatch of governors to various towns by Harun al-Rashid, and the statement in the Pate Chronicle that Harun sent Persians to colonize the coast. No confirmation whatever, not even a hint, of these supposed events is to be had from records remaining in the Arab homelands.

We must note here, however, the story of the emigration of two joint rulers of the Julanda family, the brothers Sa'id and Sulaiman ibn 'Abbad, together with their families and followers, from Oman to the land of Zanj. This occurred, we are told, after their defeat by the Umayyad forces in the reign of 'Abd al-Malik.

58. Cerulli, *Somalia*, I, 231 ff; translation 253 ff.

But, having been set down in the early eighteenth century, the story is of doubtful authenticity.[59] It might appear to be confirmed by a passage in the Book of the Zanj which states that the Kilindini of Mombasa were originally of the Julanda tribe.[60] But this tradition is otherwise uncorroborated, and other derivations given in the same passage are very doubtful. The most we can say is that these traditions may enshrine the memory of an early migration from Oman, which is not in itself unlikely as many settlers are known to have come from this region in later times.

The next reference to the arrival of settlers brings us to the only sources of any antiquity, the Kilwa Chronicle and work of the Portuguese historian João de Barros, Deçadas da Asia. The latter was published in 1552 and incorporates much of the substance of the Arabic Sunna al-Kilawiyya (the Kilwa Chronicle), probably written in the 1520's, as well as other matters concerning the earlier history of the coast.[61]

In his work, Barros (Dec. I, Bk. VIII, Cap. IV) tells us of the emigration of the followers of the Shi'a Zaid to East Africa, probably after the latter's death in 122 A.H. (A.D. 740).[62] Although we have no other authority for this emigration, the circumstantial account given by Barros rings true, in spite of the fact he understood no Arabic and probably little of the matter with which he was dealing. The Zaidites would probably have sailed from the Persian Gulf, as apparently they were prominent in adjacent

59. See Samuel Barrett Miles, The Country and Tribes of the Persian Gulf (London, 1966; 2nd. ed.), 16. The account is published in Salil ibn Razik (ed. George Percy Badger), History of the Imams and Sayyids of Oman (London, 1871), 18. Joseph Schacht expressed scornful doubt of the reliability of the story in his review of Freeman-Grenville, "Medieval History of the Coast of Tanganyika," Bibliotheca Orientalis, XXI (1964), 111.

60. Cerulli, Somalia, I, 238, 265.

61. Freeman-Grenville, The Medieval History, 45 ff. See also Chittick, "Shirazi Colonization," passim.

62. Trimingham, Islam in East Africa, 3, states that they settled at Shungwaya, but I have not been able to trace the source for this statement. Although Schacht in his review of Freeman-Grenville's work is clearly right in pointing out that it cannot have taken place in the first century of the Hijra, I do not follow the rest of his criticism on the supposed Zaidite immigration.

regions; at the present time they are found only in Iraq and the Yemen.

Barros goes on to say that, after spreading along the coast, the heretical Zaidites retreated in a subsequent period to the interior as a result of the arrival of a new group of Arabs. The new arrivals were of a different sect of Islam, probably orthodox Sunni, and the Zaidites were unwilling to submit to them. In the course of time, the Zaidites intermarried with the pagans and became known as Baduis [Bajun?].

As for the new arrivals, they were said to have come from near al-Ahsa, not far from Bahrain. Although the account of their emigration is similar to that of the later Shirazi,[63] it may well record the memory of a historical movement from the region. Al-Ahsa was the capital of the fearsome Qarmatians, and the story may refer to refugees from that region. They are said to have founded Mogadishu and Barawa. The date of this story is very doubtful, though it would certainly be before the founding of the "Shirazi" dynasty at Kilwa.[64] Barawa is referred to as a pagan town by al-Idrisi early in the twelfth century; although not mentioned by him, Mogadishu certainly existed at that time.

Further discussion of immigration is to be found in Cerulli, who recorded a tradition of immigration of Qahtanis (from southern Arabia) to Mogadishu in the tenth century.[65] In suggesting this date, however, he relied largely on a date of around 1000 for the beginning of the Shirazi dynasty at Kilwa. One wonders whether there is not here some confusion with the immigration of Banu Majid in the middle of the twelfth century, at the time when the town seems to have acquired its present name, as Trimingham points out elsewhere in this volume.[66] Cerulli also cited two genealogies of persons who are said to have settled at Mogadishu in the mid-eighth century.[67] The dates are of doubtful reliability, but one of the persons was called al-Sirafi. Further evidence of

63. Chittick, "Shirazi Colonization," 278.
64. Rather more than seventy years, according to Barros.
65. Cerulli, Somalia, I, 20.
66. See below, 124.
67. Cerulli, Somalia, I, 25–26. The dates are 149 and 150 A.H.

settlers from Sirâf, the great port on the eastern side of the Persian Gulf, is the present existence at Merca of a group of seagoing people who call themselves Sirafi. According to their traditions they constituted a wealthy community on the coast before the arrival of the Somali around the twelfth century. Sirâf declined after the tenth century, and it may be reasonable to assign the arrival of the immigrants to the period of its prosperity.[68] At the same time it should be remembered that excavations at Sirâf have shown the town to have continued to exist until a much later date.

The trade of Sirâf with the Zanj country is better attested than that of any other region. Al-Mas'udi (*Muruj*, I, 233) traveled with two Sirâfis, and Ibn Hawqal stated that timber for building in Sirâf came from the Zanj country.[69] Because Sirâf was the port of Shiraz, our attention is drawn to the traditions of early Shirazi settlement in the region of Mogadishu and to the thirteenth-century inscriptions of Persians, one a Shirazi (the only epigraphic mention of the name) in that town.[70] The Shirazi are also associated with Shungwaya.[71]

At this point let us turn for a moment to the evidence which archaeology has to offer. The earliest sites on the East African coast yet identified are ascribed to the ninth century; of these the only ones which appear to be of major importance are at Unguja Ukuu and at Manda.[72] Only the second of these has been the subject of excavations, but at both of the sites a type of blue-glazed Islamic ware, mostly with underglaze decoration in relief, is by far the commonest import. This ware has been found at Ctesiphon and Susa; though usually assigned to the turn of the Islamic era (seventh century),[73] its production evidently continued through the ninth century and probably well into the tenth. The very large proportion of imported material, construction in stone,

68. *Ibid.*, 98.
69. Kramer and Wiet, *Configuration de la terre*, II, 277.
70. Cerulli, *Somalia*, I, 3 and 98.
71. Prins, "Die Urheimat der Nordost-Bantu," 280.
72. Neville Chittick, "Unguja Ukuu: The earliest imported pottery, and an Abbasid Dinar," *Azania*, I (1966), 161; Chittick, "Discoveries in the Lamu Archipelago," *ibid*, II (1967), 37–67.
73. Arthur Lane, *Early Islamic Pottery* (London, 1957), 9, and Plate 3.

and the use of lime mortar at Manda indicate the presence of substantial numbers of settlers, presumably Muslims. The imported pottery, both glazed and unglazed, is for the most part very similar to finds from the recent excavations at the site of Sirâf; in the view of Whitehouse, the excavator, some of the unglazed pottery from Manda could have been made near that port.[74] This underlines the close connection of the East African coast with the Persian Gulf during this period.

The Kilwa Chronicle gives an account of the emigration and settling at various places on the coast of the sultan of Shiraz and his family, one of the sons establishing a dynasty at Kilwa. I have maintained that this dynasty was established at the end of the twelfth century, not in the latter part of the tenth century as hitherto held, and have also suggested, and am now persuaded, that the immigrants came not from the Persian Gulf but from the Benadir coast, from Mogadishu to Shungwaya, where some of those more remote ancestors from Shiraz or the eastern side of the Gulf had settled earlier.[75] Further evidence for this conclusion is a garbled tradition that was recorded by Burton a century ago: He said that a certain Shaykh Yusuf of Shangaya (Shungwaya) bought land from the heathen chief of Kilwa island, for the cloth that he could spread over it, and established a dynasty of Shirazi kings.[76] This Yusuf may be compared with the ʿAli of Shangaya who is associated with the flags of the *mitepe* (sewn boats) and who is thought to be identical with the founder of the Kilwa dynasty,[77] and with the Shirazi Yusuf bin Hasan who, according

74. David Whitehouse, "Excavations at Shiraf, First Interim Report," *Iran*, VI (1968); "Second Interim Report," *Iran*, VII (1969).
75. Chittick, "Shirazi Colonization."
76. Richard Francis Burton, *Zanzibar, City, Island and Coast* (London, 1872), II, 360–361.
77. Francis Barrow Pearce, *Zanzibar, the Island Metropolis of East Africa* (London, 1920), 29. "All *mitepe* fly three flags on the masthead. The white pennant is the flag of a certain ancient Persian Sultan named Ali, who lived at Shangaya on the east African coast. It is possible that this potentate may be identical with one of the earliest settlers from Shiraz in the tenth century. Below the white pennant is flown an enormously long streamer, known as *utakataka*. Under the streamer is flown the red flag of the Sultans of Shangaya, in ancient times the capital of the Persian settlements on the Azanian coast. The small white pennants on

to a tradition recorded at Kilwa Kivinje at the turn of the present century, established the dynasty there. The statement in Baros's version of the Kilwa Chronicle that the mother of ʿAli, the founder of the dynasty, was an Abyssinian slave, may well be an etiological explanation of the fact that, as a result of intermarriage on the Benadir coast, the sultans were dark in color.

There are persistent traditions on the coast south of Tanga and in the Zanzibar islands, of a people from overseas, referred to as the Debuli, who were present on the coast before the Shirazi. The Debuli probably took their name from the great port of ad-Daybul near the mouth of the Indus, which flourished up to the thirteenth century.[78] They were certainly Muslims, and I suspect that probably more Arabs settled at that town, which fell to the Muslims in 711–712 A.D., than did converted Hindus. This immigration of Debuli is the only one recorded from that region. One informant told the writer that the Debuli did not remain long. This remark is of little evidential value, but the Debuli were presumably all or mostly merchants, and, in view of the rarity of Muslim remains before the Shirazi dynasty in the region concerned, it seems that few of them settled permanently on the coast.

At the end of the thirteenth century there was a change of dynasty at Kilwa. The new rulers had the surname Mahdali, or Ahdali, which indicates that they had their origin in the western Yemen, although the family may have already been resident at Kilwa. Under the new dynasty the main connection of Kilwa seems to have shifted from the Persian Gulf to southern Arabia. There is a marked change in architectural style, which may be associated with this shift in focus, although no parallels to the style of the new buildings at Kilwa are yet known in the Yemen or Hadramaut, or indeed, in the period concerned, anywhere else.[79]

It remains to consider the traditions of the Pate region. Here, attention has centered on the Pate Chronicle, which exists in numerous versions, most of which were set down about half a century ago. They give an account of the arrival of three brothers

the prow represent, it is said, the sons of the Sultan Ali of Shangaya."
78. Chittick, "Shirazi Colonization," 290.
79. Neville Chittick, *Kilwa: An Islamic Trading City on the East African Coast* (Nairobi, 1974), I, 239.

of the Nabhani family of Oman and of their founding of a dynasty
which ruled in Pate from 600 A.H. (A.D. 1203/4 onwards).
According to the Chronicle, in the fourteenth century the Nabhanis
are supposed to have conquered all of the coast from Mogadishu
to the Kerimba islands. I have maintained[80] that the Nabhanis
did not attain power until the seventeenth century and that they
were preceded by a dynasty of Batawi who are supposed to have
come from the Hadramaut.[81] Some Nabhanis may have settled in
Pate at a rather earlier date; they were apparently present in
Pemba at the beginning of the seventeenth century and seem to
have dominated the northern part of the island until the middle
of the eighteenth century.[82] Immigration from Oman and from
the Hadramaut has continued up to recent times.

We have said nothing so far of Indian immigration to the coast.
This is a matter on which we have little evidence; neither the local
nor the foreign sources tell us anything of value, and it is probable
that the number of Indians settled before 1500 was very small.
At the same time there is little doubt that their ships traded with
East Africa, especially those from Cambay. Such trade was
evidently on a substantial scale when the Portuguese arrived, and
at that time there were some settlers from the subcontinent, both
Hindu, probably of the Battia caste, and Muslims.[83]

Conclusions

What can we deduce about the immigrants to East Africa? It is
probably a mistake to picture a large number of people sailing
in a group at one time. Rather, we should presume that at all
periods a few individuals were coming from diverse regions and
settling on the coast, but that at certain times there were more
massive waves of immigration from particular areas, probably
spread over years.

80. Neville Chittick, "A New Look at the History of Pate," *Journal of African History*, X (1969), 55–66. See also Chittick, "Discoveries in the Lamu Archipelago," *Azania*, II (1967), 37–67.
81. Stigand, *The Land of Zinj*, 163.
82. John Gray, "Zanzibar Local Histories II," *Swahili*, 31 (1960), 130.
83. Justus Strandes (trans. Jean F. Wallwork, ed. James S. Kirkman), *The Portuguese Period in East Africa* (Nairobi, 1961), 93.

The salient fact is that almost all of the newcomers settled originally on the Benadir coast and on the islands of Zanzibar and Pemba. It was from the Benadir coast that descendants of these immigrants, particularly the Shirazi, remigrated southwards. Similar migrations took place as late as the seventeenth century; witness the settlement of the Khatimi-Barawi clan at Kunduchi and other places on the Mrima coast (that portion of the coast opposite the islands of Zanzibar and Pemba), where they became the dominant family.

The exceptions—those who came directly from overseas to the southern part of the coast—seem to have been only the dimly remembered Debuli, and, later, immigrants from southwestern Arabia. The last of their descendants are associated with the establishment of the dynasty of Abu'l-Mawahib and are thought to have come from the Hadramaut.

The main region of origin of the early immigrants seems to have been the Persian Gulf. The Zaidites, if they existed, probably sailed from these shores; they were followed by Arabs from the Bahrain region (al-Ahsa). After them came settlers from Fars, Shiraz, and Sirâf, its port. The extent to which they were Persian is disputable. A few certainly were, as witness the two inscriptions from Mogadishu, but certainly the cultural impact of the Persians on the East African coast was very slight. It has often been maintained that the existence in Swahili of words of Persian origin is evidence of the presence of large numbers of Persians, but in fact most of these words could have stemmed from the Arabic dialects of the Gulf. This is also true of the "Persian" calendar, and it is significant that the oft-cited Swahili *Nairuzi* (the New Year) is nearer to the Arabic form of the word, *Nairuz*, than it is to the Persian, *Nauruz*. Though I am not competent to assess the proportion of Arabs among the inhabitants of the coast of Fars in the period with which we are concerned, there seem to have been many of them. Shiraz, moreover, is the capital of Fars, and the name of the capital, or a prominent town, is often applied to a whole region. (At the present day, for example, all immigrants to the coast from the Hadramaut are referred to as Shihiris.)

Basra and the head of the Gulf are not mentioned in the better sources, but we can presume, remembering the ruler in Qanbalu who came from Kufa, that some immigrants derived from those shores.

As to the immigration from other regions in the early period, there is the story of doubtful authenticity of the followers of Sulaiman and Sa'id from Oman, and it is evident from traditions and inscriptions at Mogadishu that prominent families, and possibly small groups, from the Hadramaut and other parts of the Arabian peninsula, settled there. But the main period of immigration from the Arabian peninsula would seem to have been from the later thirteenth century on. This immigration has continued up to recent times—notably of course that of Muscati Arabs from Oman.

What of the relationship between the immigrants and the indigenous peoples? Probably in most cases there was some association with the local tribes, as there was in recent times between the Muslim ruling families of mixed Arab descent in the village states of the Mrima coast and their tribal counterparts. Such a relationship is described in the Book of the Zanj: "So each tribe of the Zanji associated itself with a tribe of the Arabs" in Mombasa.[84] We are told that in the earliest period each Arab had a Zanji patron, and if an Arab came to the town of the Zanj and happened to have a dispute with another Zanji, he would be under the protection of his patron and of his patron's tribe. On the other hand, the Arabs protected the Zanji in war against common enemies.[85]

The immigrants would have arrived with few, if any, women, so that it is evident that the population would rapidly have become mixed. No doubt the leading families tended to intermarry and thus to retain a greater proportion of Arab blood. Throughout history, as seen through the eyes of the people, the general ethnic categories of these communities have probably been similar to those discernible down to recent times:

First, pure-blooded Arabs, the "Manga" (from Oman) and the

84. Cerulli, *Somalia*, I, 238, 265.
85. *Ibid.*, 236, 261.

"Shihiri" (from the Hadramaut) in Swahili; and recent arrivals or transient residents, in early times including a few Persians. These Arabs would have formed the ruling class for only a restricted period after their arrival, and then only where, in exceptional circumstances, they had established an ascendancy.

Second, Afro-Arabs, the "Arabu" of Swahili. Of mixed blood, these have in the past usually constituted the ruling section of the population.

Third, Islamized Africans with some Arab blood, known as "Swahili" to the Europeans; these are the contemporary "Shirazi" of Zanzibar.

Fourth, the African tribesmen, outside the settlement or recently arrived in them, and little affected by Islamic culture.

The same name does not however necessarily designate the same group in all periods. After they first established themselves on the Benadir coast, the Shirazi would fall in the first category; the sultans of the Shirazi dynasty at Kilwa, by then of mixed blood, would fall in the second; whereas those who now call themselves Shirazi fall in the third group.

This essay is full of uncertainties; therefore, I would like finally to suggest how we may amplify our knowledge. First, I would wholeheartedly support the plea for fresh, critical redactions and translations of the early Arabic and Chinese sources which deal with eastern Africa. Second, an urgent task is to carry out archaeological survey excavations in southern Somalia, while continuing the work which is already underway in the coastal hinterland further south. Third, we need to examine afresh the local historical evidence, casting on it the light to be derived from other sources, notably epigraphy and archaeology, anthropology, and present-day traditions.

THE PEOPLING OF THE HORN OF AFRICA

Vinigi L. Grottanelli

The Horn of Africa is a roughly triangular area, the vertices of which can be placed in Tajura Gulf in the north, Ras Kiamboni (Ras Chiambone) in the south, and Cape Guardafui in the east. Though immense, the Horn has a remarkable geographical homogeneity. It is a monotonous plateau, a dry savannah in places sparsely covered by thorn bush, which gradually slopes down from the highlands in the west and northwest toward the coastal plains. For anyone approaching it by land, the area offers no natural obstacles except two main rivers and a few minor streams which wind their way through the bush, in places being fringed by a thin strip of forest. To strangers coming from the sea, the country presents a barren rocky coast, or a uniform line of low reddish dunes, almost entirely lacking in bays or harbors;[1] behind the coast, the endless expanse of steppe remains arid for most of the year, bursting into green foliage and blossoms for only the few weeks that follow the spring and autumn rains.[2]

1. As late as 1887, F.L. James could rightly title a report of his pioneer reconnaissance of these lands *The Unknown Horn of Africa* (London, 1888).
2. Ibid., 7. Cf. also Ernst Georg Ravenstein, "Somal and Galla Land, embodying information collected by the Rev. Thomas Wakefield," *Proceedings of the Royal Geographical Society*, VI (1884), 255–273.

Land and People

However unattractive, this landscape has in fact appealed to immigrants of various races and origins. Although they can be classified racially and linguistically, I find that geo-ecological criteria provide the most convenient order for a basic grouping. I will therefore consider four main groups: a) the hunters who first roamed through the arid mainland stalking game; b) the herdsmen who thousands of years later followed in the wake of the hunters and found that the thorn bush and steppe provided grazing for their cattle, sheep, and camels; c) the farmers who settled along the river banks to cultivate the narrow strips of rich black soil; and d) the sailors and merchants from faraway lands who, having found landing places to establish their trading posts, eventually became the founders of towns along the coast. As might be expected, mixed societies emerged from the contacts between these different waves or strata of population. But to this day characteristics of the four main groups can be observed within the area. We shall examine each in turn.

The Hunters

There can be no doubt that the earliest inhabitants were hunters. Their presence is documented from prehistoric times, starting with Seton-Kerr's doubtful Upper Acheulean surface findings in former British Somaliland and with better established Acheulo-Levalloisian and Stillbay deposits (Hargeisa and other sites), and continuing with a number of Mesolithic cultures (Magosian, Eibian or Doian, Wilton industries, and a variety of a blade-and-burin culture reminiscent of Capsian and named Hargeisan by J. Desmond Clark) widely scattered throughout the Horn. Apart from some findings by Graziosi, Neolithic levels proper appear to be lacking, industries of the Wilton type lingering on "until they were gradually superseded by iron; before this, there is no real indication of domestication of stock, or of cultivation, and no ground or polished celts have been found."[3]

3. Sonia Cole, *The Prehistory of East Africa* (Harmondsworth, 1954), 159–163, 224. Paolo Graziosi, *L'età della pietra in Somalia* (Firenze, 1940), 14–15, 84, and *passim*.

I am not competent to discuss the details of prehistoric industries as such, but apart from the obvious interest of their dating there are connected tasks which belong to anthropologists, i.e., to ascertain the racial types to which the early inhabitants belonged and to establish possible relationships between them and the groups which still hunt in the area.

Unfortunately, no skeletal remains have so far been found in the Horn which can with certainty be associated with the use of the successive types of stone implements; the racial attribution of the ancient hunters must therefore be conjectural as it can only be inferred from the broader frame of African prehistory. An exception is the finding by Clark near Bur Hakaba of a number of human and animal bones associated with the Mesolithic Doian industry. Cole has said that these remains were "almost certainly Hamitic," an assertion somewhat weakened by her admission that "the bones were too fragmentary to determine their racial type."[4]

It is a well-known fact that the Somali, the present inhabitants of most of the Horn, are not hunters and, indeed, despise this activity. The only major groups among them who hunt at all are the Sab, or "non-noble" tribes, such as the Rahanwen and the Digil.[5] The professional hunters, whose whole (or main) subsistence is based on this occupation, are to be found among the so-called "low castes" aggregated to the noble tribes—the Midgan in northern Somalia, the Eile in the Bur Hakaba region, the Ribe in the middle Juba Valley, and the Boni in Trans-Juba.[6] Their inferior position in the general structure of modern Somali society, their enforced endogamy, their archaic mode of life, and the ritual duties which they are called upon to perform for the herdsmen, leave no doubt as to the fact that the Midgan and similar groups are remnants of an earlier stratum of population. Are they then the direct

4. Cole, *Prehistory*, 103–104.
5. N. Puccioni and V.L. Grottanelli, "Gli Etiopici meridionali," in R. Biasutti (ed.), *Razze e Popoli della Terra* (Torino, 1959), III, 252.
6. For literature on these "serf tribes," cf. V.L. Grottanelli, "Note sui Bon, cacciatori di bassa casta dell'Oltregiuba," *Annali Lateranensi*, XXI (1957), 191–212; A.H.J. Prins, "The Somaliland Bantu," *Bulletin of the International Committee for Urgent Research*, 3 (1960), 25–27; A.H.J. Prins, "The Didemic Diarchic Boni," *Journal of the Royal Anthropological Institute*, XCIII (1963), 174–185.

descendants of the Mesolithic inhabitants of the Horn? Or, on the other hand, has an aboriginal race of hunters and food-collectors been submerged, or partially absorbed, by further waves of steppe nomads, which were in turn met and to some extent incorporated by the Kushitic (Hamitic) cattle-breeders in the course of their gradual occupation of the country?

The question is connected with, and complicated by, the hypothesis of a Khoisanoid (Bushmanoid) peopling of the whole of East Africa in the distant past, suggested by some of the older anthropologists and never fully rejected. One argument in favor of this thesis is the presence in East Africa of peoples like the Hadza-Tindiga and the Sandawe, who, in addition to having a *Steppenjäger* culture, speak indisputably click languages; it was also supposed that cultural links connect the Hadza with the more northerly hunting groups such as the Dorobo, Sanye, Ariangulu, and Boni, and even the Wata (Watta, Watwa) of the Galla countries.

The unity of these widely scattered peoples is questionable. Dorobo, for instance, is a collective name embracing Teuso- as well as Nandi-speaking groups of "primitive forest-dwelling hunters"[7] (savannah-dwelling would be more appropriate) spread from eastern Uganda to Kenya and parts of Tanzania. According to Tucker, corroborating Ernst Dammann, Sanye also contains click sounds; its speakers "are perhaps identical with the Ariangulu (Langulo) and Boni, in the same area, and may also be known as Watta."[8] But the lexical materials I collected among the Boni are, however scanty, sufficient to show that Boni cannot (now) be equated with Sanye;[9] Dammann has shown that Sanye fails to link up with Sandawe and Hadza;[10] and Köhler in turn has pointed out how questionable are the attempts to classify Hadza with "Khoisan" languages, which again are far from being uniform themselves.[11] Therefore, although the possibility of finding a uniting link among these dispersed little groups is no doubt tempting, linguistic

7. A.N. Tucker and M.A. Bryan, "The non-Bantu Languages of Northeastern Africa," *Handbook of African Languages*, III (London, 1956), 93, 115.
8. *Ibid.*, 138, 157.
9. Grottanelli, "Note sui Bon," 208–212.
10. Ernst Dammann, "Einige Notizen über die Sprache der Sanye (Kenya)," *Zeitschrift für Eingeborenen-sprachen*, XXXV (1950), 227–234.
11. Verbal communication, Munich, November, 1966.

evidence, when pieced together, turns out to be inconclusive. Anthropological links are equally frail. Among the Boni, for instance, slight indications of a Khoisanoid racial component were noted by various authors.[12] More generally, Baumann wrote: "Die khoisanische Beimischung ist teilweise im ganzen Ostafrika zu verspüren, meist in Gebieten, die sich gerade durch viel Fundstätten miolitischer Jägerkultur auszeichnen und auch Resten rezenten Wildbeutertums Heimat geben,"[13] and he quotes Seligman,[14] Menghin, Biasutti, and other authorities, who believe that Bushmen occupied a much larger territory in the past—from Nubia to Malawi and beyond. Another argument supporting the idea that Bushmen occupied a large territory is provided by the wide distribution of rock paintings and petroglyphs in eastern and northeastern Africa, some of which (but by no means all) recall South African parallels and are locally attributed to ancient and now vanished inhabitants of the respective areas.[15]

No matter how fascinating, the search for traces of survivals and shreds of evidence of distant connections cannot blind us to the fact that far more obvious cultural, linguistic, and racial similarities connect the modern hunters of the Horn with their present neighbors and overlords, the Kushites. Cultural and linguistic affinities are easely explained by centuries of contacts; but racial similarity is not as easily accounted for when one bears in mind the lasting endogamy imposed on these pariahs. The only satisfactory explanation is that both the submerged castes and the noble herdsmen must be traced back to a common racial stock, of which they represent two successive offshoots.

12. R. Parenti, "Gli Uaboni," *Rivista di Biologia Coloniale*, IX (1949); N. Puccioni, "Osservazioni sugli Uaboni," *L'Universo*, XVII (1936), 1–8; R. Battaglia, "I Bon di Hola Wager nell'Oltregiuba," *Annali Lateranensi*, XXI (1957), 322–346.
13. H. Baumann, R. Thurnwald, and D. Westermann, *Völkerkunde von Afrika* (Essen, 1940), 15.
14. C.G. Seligman, *Races of Africa* (London, 1930), 24. He describes the ancestors of the Bushmen as "having perhaps occupied the greater part of tropical East and east-central Africa."
15. For the most recent survey of this problem, see H. Baumann, H. Rhotert, and A.R. Willcox, "Paleoafricane Culture," *Enciclopedia Universale dell'Arte*, X (Roma, 1963), 416–438.

In the course of their long wanderings through eastern Africa, the early representatives of what Biasutti calls "an archaic form of the Ethiopian race"[16] may well have incorporated the remnants of a still earlier Bushmanoid type; at a later date, in the southern parts of the Horn and beyond, these hunters certainly interbred with Negro elements. These contacts account for the indisputably mixed characteristics of the East African low-caste groups shown by anthropological measurements: The common traits of all of these groups, as Cerulli has rightly pointed out, are due not so much to an original racial unity as to similarities in the processes of their (pre)historical formation.[17]

Some modern authors have suggested a probable connection between these archaic hunters and representatives of the East African Capsian culture. The racial type attributed to the latter "made its appearance in northern and eastern Africa by the end of the Upper Palaeolothic period, about ten thousand years ago. This was a race akin to the Caucasian—it is called by Leakey 'proto-Hamite'—and almost certainly it had evolved its special characteristics in south-west Asia, from where some of its members moved into Africa."[18] Owing to the great scarcity of skeletal data so far available for comparison, the above is no more than a working hypothesis. The same can be said of the supposed derivation of both the East African and Tunisian Capsian from the "comparable" Natufian culture of Palestine.[19]

In a sense, apart from the time factor, hypotheses such as these represent a parallel to the old theory of broad Hamito-Semitic unity. In more general terms, it is not unreasonable to assume that "Caucasoid" peoples, originating or assembling in the area between the middle Euphrates, the Mediterranean coast, and Sinai, initiated

16. Puccioni and Grottanelli, "Gli Etiopici," 267. Unless otherwise indicated, all translations into English are by the author.

17. Enrico Cerulli, "The Folk-literature of the Galla of Southern Abyssinia," Harvard African Studies, III (1922), 9–228; Enrico Cerulli, Somalia (Roma, 1957), I, 52.

18. Roland Oliver and John D. Fage, A Short History of Africa (Harmondsworth, 1962), 19.

19. Ibid. The respective dating of Natufian and early Kenya Capsian creates some difficulties: See Cole, Prehistory, 194.

a southward migration in pre-Neolithic times, taking two separate but parallel routes: one along the eastern fringes of the Egyptian desert and coastal Eritrea into what is now Somalia, the other east of Sinai along the Tihama, through Hijaz to the Yemen and beyond. (In predynastic times, the Nile Valley itself could offer a devious but attractive alternative to the former route.) Anthropological affinities—partial but undeniable—between the peoples on either side of the Red Sea may well date back to preagricultural and prepastoral epochs. And one should of course not forget that pariah classes and tribes, some of which (e.g., the Sleb) still hunt wild animals, also exist to this day in Arabia.[20]

One must beware, however, of oversimplifying what has surely been a highly complex series of obscure ethnic processes. Both in the prehistorical and in the anthropological field, our knowledge of these primitive hunting-and-collecting cultures is so fragmentary that generalization and comparison remain dangerously conjectural and scientific conclusions altogether premature.

The Herdsmen

The second, and far more considerable, wave of population was that of the Kushitic-speaking people, of whose early culture and tribal structure we know little. In all probability they too came from the north, possibly following the same routes as the hunters who preceded them. Whichever may have been their "original homeland" (if the expression itself makes any sense), the Kushites acquired their character as a group of nations, and, indeed, most of the cultural traits that distinguish them to this day, when they came into possession of livestock and emerged as typical cattle-breeders.

It was largely the expanding needs of a pastoral economy that caused the Kushites' migrations and, eventually, their conquest of the Horn. And it was their pride as cattle-owners that caused them

20. For full literature on these groups, see Joseph Henninger, "Pariastämme in Arabien," *Festschrift des Missionshauses St. Gabriel* (Wien-Mödling, 1939), 501–539; Henninger, "Tribus et classes de parias en Arabie et en Egypte," *Atti del XIV Congresso Internazionale di Sociologia*, IV (Roma, 1950–1952), 266ff.; Henninger, "Die Familie bei den heutigen Beduinen Arabiens...," *Internationales Archiv für Ethnographie*, XLII (1943), 157–162.

to look disdainfully upon and refuse to mix with their distant kin, those hunters lacking cattle who had preceded them.[21]

For centuries, although we have no means of establishing how many, considerable groups of Kushitic herdsmen occupied only that part of the Horn that faces the Gulf of Aden. This barren territory, far less hospitable than the northern Ethiopian highlands where another branch of Kushites was already settled at the time, must have become inadequate when its inhabitants and their herds began to multiply; from here they started—perhaps a thousand years ago—that slow series of southward migrations that were to lead to the occupation of the whole territory we are here considering as far as Jubaland and beyond. The first to engage in this long trek were the Oromo or Galla, who came, stayed a few centuries, and went; in their footsteps followed their kindred, the Somali, who are still masters of this whole territory.

Somali traditions are unanimous in affirming that the region immediately south of the Gulf of Aden belonged to the Galla before the Somali themselves moved into it. The first European who recorded this tradition is, to my knowledge, Avanchers, a Capuchin missionary and a subject of the king of Sardinia, who in the 1850's was told by Somali informants that the Galla had formerly held the Berbera area.[22] Thirty years later, Paulitschke wrote: "Among the Somali of the Aden Gulf one comes across no tradition that does not mention the Galla as the earlier inhabitants of the African Horn."[23] The same traditions are also

21. East Africans do not always draw a clear-cut distinction between the hunters and the herdsmen. The Kamba call both the Galla and the Somali *atwa* (WaTwa, Wata), a general name for "serf classes": Cf. Gerhard Lindblom, *The Akamba* (Uppsala, 1920), 21. To this day, physical differences between Galla and Wata are practically nonexistent: Haberland admits that in the early stages of his stay among the Borana he lived for several weeks with a Wata group without suspecting that they were not real Borana. Cf. Eike Haberland, *Galla Süd-Äthiopiens* (Stuttgart, 1963), 4–5.
22. Léon des Avanchers, "Esquisse géographique des pays Oromo ou Galla, des pays Somalis, et de la côte orientale de l'Afrique," *Bulletin de la Société de Géographie*, XVII (1859), 160.
23. Philipp Paulitschke, "Die Wanderungen der Oromo oder Galla Ost-Afrikas," *Mitteilungen der Anthropologischen Gesellschaft*, IX (1889), 174. The same author has elsewhere quoted from G. Bianchi (*Alla terra dei*

found among the southeastern Danakil,[24] and ancient graves and cairns in the neighborhood of Zayla' (Zeila) are also attributed to the Galla.[25]

The Greek inscription from a stone throne in Adulis, now lost but fortunately copied by Cosmas Indicopleustes about A.D. 520,[26] gives a precise list of regions and peoples conquered by an unknown Axumite king in the early centuries of the Christian era. It mentions, among others, a people called Rhausi, inhabiting the interior of the "land of Barbaroi" where incense grows in vast plains without water. The country is no doubt the hinterland of Berbera, or more generally what used to be British Somaliland; and Saint-Martin has convincingly identified Rhausi with Arusi.[27] If this identification is accepted, it suggests the presence of a well-known Galla tribe in the area south of the Gulf of Aden some time between the second and third centuries A.D.[28] On the basis of other evidence, Lewis has recently concluded that the Galla

Galla [Milano, 1884], 318) "die lebhafte Tradition der Arussi und Borana, dass ihre Vorfahren in alten Zeiten zwischen Harar und dem Cap Âsir die Wohnsitze gehabt hätten. Die Sango von Aussa sollen angeblich die Galla aus dem heutigen Afar- und Somâl-Lande vertrieben haben...." Cf. Paulitschke, _Ethnographie Nordostafrikas_ (Berlin, 1893), I, 21.

24. Carlo Conti Rossini, _Etiopia e genti d'Etiopia_ (Firenze, 1937), 325.

25. G. Révoil, _La Vallée du Darror, voyage aux pays Çomalis_ (Paris, 1882), 275; for further references, see J.P. Michels, _De Godsdienst der Galla_ (Nijmegen, 1941), I, 11. This argument has been somewhat weakened by the recent observations of I.M. Lewis (see below, n. 29). See also G.W.B. Huntingford, "Field Archaeology in Kenya and Somaliland," _Atti del VI Congresso Internazionale delle Scienze Preistoriche e Protostoriche_, III (Roma, 1966), 242.

26. [Adulis inscription] _Corpus inscriptionum graecarum_, t. III, n. 5127 _b._; Cosmas, "Topographia Christiana," in Jacques Paul Migne (ed.), _Patrologiae Cursus Completus. Series Graeca_ (Paris, 1860), LXXXVIII, 140. On Adulis in general, see Roberto Paribeni, "Ricerche sul luogo dell'antica Adulis (Colonia Eritrea)," in _Monumenti Antichi publicati per cura della Reale Accademia dei Lincei_, XVIII (Milano, 1908), 439–572.

27. Vivien de Saint-Martin, _Le Nord de l'Afrique dans l'antiquité grecque et romaine_ (Paris, 1863), 235, and cf. the second of the two maps marked n. 1.

28. Saint-Martin favored the earlier date (_ibid._, 229–231); Conti Rossini (_Storia d'Etiopia_ [Bergamo, 1928], 122) suggests the central years of the third century. The attribution of the throne to Zoskales, which would date the inscription to the times of Vespasian (D.H. Müller, "Epigraphische Denkmäler des Axumitischen Reiches," _Abhandlungen der K. K. Akademie_, XLIII [Wien, 1894], 4, 10) can no longer be followed.

were still in northern Somalia during the eleventh century.[29]

The traditions indicating that the northern section of the Horn was the ancient homeland of the Galla are too widespread to be overlooked, but it is equally certain that at an early date this people must have begun to migrate in a southwesterly direction, which led them to the occupation of the country now known as Ogaden, to the upper courses of the Webi Shabeli River and of its affluents, to those of the Juba River as far as Liban, and ultimately to the present Boran region close to Kenya's northern frontier.

All of these territories lie south of the Ethiopian highlands proper. The first historical document we possess about this people is very precise: "The Galla came from the west and crossed the river of their country, which is called Galana, to the frontier of Bali, in the reign of Wanag Sagad."[30] Bali (Bale), the mountainous region east of Lakes Margherita and Awasa, was thus the first part of the high plateau invaded by the Galla, and the assailants must have come from the valley of the Dawa or some neighboring area in the upper reaches of the Juba system.

Bahrey's passage which I have just quoted, and which is confirmed by Almeida,[31] disposes in my opinion of Haberland's recent

29. I.M. Lewis, "The Galla in Northern Somaliland," *Rassegna di Studi Etiopici*, XV (1959–1960), 21–38. This does not mean, of course, that *some* of the numerous Oromo tribes had not begun to move southward by that time. "The Galla migrations from Somaliland must have begun at least by the twelfth century, for the Arab historian Yaqut claims the complete Islamization of the 'Somali of the Zayla coast' by that time": G.W.B. Huntingford, *The Galla of Ethiopia* (London, 1955), 19.

30. I. Guidi (tr.), *Historia Gentis Galla*, in *Scriptores Aethiopici*, III (Paris, 1907), 195. Cf. C.F. Beckingham and G.W.B. Huntingford (trs. and eds.), *Some Records of Ethiopia*, 1593–1646 (London, 1954), 111. Amharic literature has not added much to our understanding of these matters; cf., however, the traditions translated by A. Caquot, "Histoire amharique de Gran et des Gallas," *Annales d'Ethiopie*, II (1957), 123 ff.

31. Beckingham and Huntingford, *Some Records*, 134. Manoel de Almeida, who composed his History of Ethiopia between 1628 and 1646 when the memory of Galla invasions was still fresh, and who had direct access to Ethiopian sources, states that the Galla invaded Bale at the same time as Adal. The latter is the well-known Muslim state of the Harar highlands, whose old capital Dakar, according to Conti Rossini, probably corresponds to modern Fiambiro.

hypothesis that Bale should be considered the Galla *Urheimat*.[32] Doubtless, however, the occupation of the fertile, well-watered mountainous country left a lasting impression on the Oromo, many of whom still claim that they came from a mountain called Walabu (or Ulabo, Ulammo, etc.), a delightful abode where they were all united under a single *bokku* (scepter), and lived in leisure on the milk and meat of a miraculous white breed of cattle, with no need to till the soil.[33] Mount Walabu belongs to the watershed range between the basin of the Juba and Lake Margherita,[34] and the mode of life in this land of Eden clearly reflects the ideal of a pastoral people, and its dislike and contempt of agriculture.

There is no contradiction between the latter tradition, which points to a southern Ethiopian origin, and the tradition of a Somali origin, because they obviously refer to different phases in Oromo history. Indeed, in the version collected in 1878 by Cecchi, the two traditions are blended into one: "From the African coast facing southern Arabia, the Galla had settled in the country of Ulamo or Ulabo, near the territory now occupied by the Arusi."[35] In his reconstruction of Galla origins, Cecchi suggested an even earlier phase, one in which the ancestors of these people were settled in southwestern Arabia.[36] Claims to Asiatic ancestry are, however, a common attempt in northeastern Africa to ennoble a nation and are often based on legends, though they may of course contain grains of truth.

We have no means of ascertaining whether the movements of the Oromo prior to the sixteenth century took the form of a sudden rush of conquerors or of a slower penetration. The latter appears more likely, but we remain in the field of conjecture. One can also only guess at the causes that prompted this migration, the most likely being pressure from the neighboring Somali and the search for more and better grazing grounds made necessary by demographic expansion. Indeed, even in normal situations pastoral

32. Haberland, *Galla Süd-Äthiopiens*, 4–5. But see below, 102.
33. Enrico Cerulli, *Etiopia Occidentale* (Roma, 1932–1933), II, 169–170; Cerulli, *Somalia* (Roma, 1957–1964), II, 127; Conti Rossini, *Etiopia e genti*, 326.
34. *Ibid.*
35. Antonio Cecchi, *Da Zeila alle frontiere del Caffa* (Roma, 1885), I, 510.
36. *Ibid.* (1887), II, 472–473.

tribes need little encouragement to embark on the exploration, and possibly the permanent conquest, of new territories. The lack of major natural obstacles must have been an encouraging factor, and the roaming bands of hunters which until then formed the sparse population of most of the plateau cannot have put up any real resistance. The Galla did meet strong resistance, however, when they approached the organized states—of which Bale was only the first, chronologically—in the highlands of southern Ethiopia, where an earlier Kushitic strain (the so-called Sidama) had preceded them, and when they reached the banks of the Webi and Juba which, as we shall see, had been partly colonized by Negro farmers.

To sum up: Judging by the slender shreds of evidence at our disposal, it would appear that by the early centuries of the present millennium the Galla had abandoned the northern territories of the Horn to the Somali and had occupied most of its central and southern parts. They had probably reached the Indian Ocean at some points, but to these nomadic, almost exclusively pastoral, tribes, the sea was of no practical interest; they had no boats, abstained from eating fish or other sea food, and seem always to have avoided the coast. According to the picture of their early cultural conditions drawn by Conti Rossini[37]— not on the basis of conjectural ethnological reconstructions but from factual information in Ethiopian and other sources—the Galla before their invasion of Ethiopia had practically no knowledge of metals, of weaving, of pottery, nor indeed of agriculture as the Amhara understood it; they neither bred nor used horses or mules and, strangely enough, kept no sheep. A contrasting thesis, recently propounded by Haberland, is that the Galla possessed an "archaic" farming culture.[38] In general, one must concede that the traditional and prevalent opinion which regards the Galla as totally ignorant of cultivation, voiced among others by Bruce ("although the principal food of this people at first was milk and butter, yet...they learned of the Abyssinians to plough and sow the fields, and to make bread"),[39] should be taken *cum grano salis*. One cannot

37. *Etiopia e genti*, 64–65.   38.   *Galla Süd-Äthiopiens*, 363–370, 773–774.
39.   James Bruce, *Travels to Discover the Source of the Nile* (Edinburgh, 1790), II, 217.

accept as a fact that any Kushitic people, no matter how passion-
ately specialized in animal husbandry, had to wait till the sixteenth
century A.D. to become acquainted with some form of agriculture.
It *may* be, as Haberland asserts on purely ethnological grounds,
that an extensive cultivation of barley was practiced by the Oromo
prior to their contacts with the "Sidama" in southern Ethiopia
(and the Bantu of Somalia). But because in these latitudes barley
is a highland cereal, it is difficult to accept it as the basis of Galla
"original" agriculture (*ursprünglicher Feldbau*) unless one assumes
that these people's ancestral homeland (*ursprüngliche Heimat*) was
a highland such as Bale, an assumption contradicted by historical
evidence. The unscientific usage of the word *ursprünglich* only adds
to the confusion.

Historical records concerning the Galla begin with the sixteenth
century but are of little use for the purpose of this paper because,
by that time, most of the Oromo tribes had already left the Horn
and had begun their invasion of Ethiopia. According to Cerulli,
they evacuated the Webi Shabeli area around the fifteenth century
and the Bur Hakaba region in the seventeenth, whereas they stayed
on in the Juba Valley until the eighteenth and even the first half
of the nineteenth century.[40]

The gradual withdrawal of the Galla coincides with the advance
of the Somali, which again is to be explained partly in terms of
demographic growth and the economic and political expansion of
powerful new tribes, and partly as a consequence of outside
pressure, mainly on the part of the Ethiopian kingdom. The wars
between Christian Ethiopia and its southern neighbors, the Muslim
states of Ifat, Dawaro, and Adal, continued over a considerable
period; but they reached their peak from the reign of Amda Syon
(1314–1344) to that of Zari'a Ya'qob (1434–1468). During this
period the Ethiopians held the initiative. Just as these wars caused
intense tribal movements among the Sidama in the southwest of
Ethiopia (which incidentally must have had repercussions on the
"Hamitization" of the lacustrine Bantu), they exerted strong
pressures on the Somali in the southeast, causing great numbers

40. Cerulli, *Somalia*, I, 58.

of the latter to leave the Harari highlands with their herds and to move southwards. There, in turn, they encroached on the Galla who were then living in the upper basin of the Webi Shabeli. These Galla were known as the Warday (Warra Daya: The name is used to this day to indicate the Galla in Jubaland, the region to which the Warday were forced to retire). This first major victory of the Somali is attributed to the Ajuran tribes, later ousted by the Hawiyya, and seems to have taken place during the fifteenth century.[41]

But Somali migrations to the Benadir coast, which were obviously not all undertaken in the course of one century, may well date from earlier epochs. If we are to place any reliance on Arab medieval cartography, al-Idrisi's map of 1154 shows that the Somali (named "Berbera") had already extended along the coast as far south as Merca,[42] outflanking, as it were, the Galla who at that time occupied the territories farther inland. Conti Rossini suggests that these early migrations may have been the outcome of Ethiopian raids to Ifat and beyond in the ninth and tenth centuries, following which, if we believe Ibn Hawqal, Zeila came under Ethiopian rule. Apart from this isolated document, local traditions collected by Cerulli confirm the general fact that Somali conquests started from the region facing the Gulf of Aden (where, as we have seen, the Somali had at an earlier date replaced the Galla), and followed two different routes: either descending the river valleys toward the coast (i.e., in a roughly northwest-southeast direction), or following the line of the coastal wells not far from the ocean shore, from northeast to southwest.[43]

It is of course impossible to attempt here even a summary of the migrations in which different Somali tribes were engaged over the centuries. The final result was the chasing from the Horn of all of the Galla groups as such, though no doubt here and there a considerable amount of Galla blood was absorbed by the conquerors, as in the case of the Gurra of the lower Webi who

41. *Ibid.*, I, 62–64.
42. Carlo Conti Rossini, "Geographica," *Rassegna di Studi Etiopici*, III (1943), 167–171, and J. Spencer Trimingham, "The Arab Geographers and the East African Coast," below, 115, 139.
43. Cerulli, *Somalia*, I, 60–61.

were formed by dissident Ogaden mixed with the surrounding Oromo,[44] and in the case of the Warday of Jubaland who were incorporated as serfs and herdsmen by the Somali after their occupation of the river's right bank around 1848.[45]

There is hardly any need to add that the two nations, the Galla and the Somali, not only were for centuries in close territorial contact, but are related in every respect, racially, linguistically, and culturally. "As regards the antecedents of the Somali," James wrote, "I think Sir Richard Burton's opinion may be taken as quite correct, namely, that by their own traditions, as well as by their distinct physical peculiarities, customs, and geographical distribution, they must be accepted as a half-caste offshoot of the great Galla race, allied to the Caucasian type by a steady influx of pure Asiatic blood."[46] This theory was partly accepted and partly rejected by Sergi who found no differences in type between Galla and Somali and, further, no character suggesting an Arab origin of the Somali. He thought that the origin of the Somali must be sought among the Galla because, according to him, the Somali, taken as a whole, are anthropologically Galla: "A slight Semitic element has penetrated them in historical times, especially in the maritime areas, but it has been absorbed and can therefore be said to have disappeared from the physical characters forming the Somali types of today, which are fundamentally Galla."[47]

I have cited these two authorities not only to show that the anthropological unity of Galla and Somali, an undisputed fact today, was already recognized in the nineteenth century, but also because their views bring up a point fundamentally relevant to our present considerations, i.e., the degree and nature of the possible Asiatic affinities of both peoples. Burton and James, who stressed the "Caucasian" streak in the formation of the Somali (as opposed to the Galla), explained it by emphasizing the extent of interbreeding with Arab elements. To a limited degree, this

44. Cerulli, *Somalia*, II, 128.
45. F. Elliot, "Jubaland and Its Inhabitants," *Geographical Journal*, XLI (1913), 558.
46. James, *Unknown Horn*, 7.
47. Giuseppe Sergi, *Africa: Antropologia della Stirpe Camitica* (Torino, 1897), 194, 198.

phenomenon is real, but most genealogies which aimed to prove the Arabian ancestry of the various Somali tribes are obviously legendary. Sergi, a professional anthropologist, was not taken in and correctly distinguished between the agelong processes which led to the formation of his "Hamitic" race (represented, among others, by the Somali and Galla) and the recent admixtures with "Semitic" elements, which he did not deny but dismissed as statistically irrelevant.

This conclusion does not mean that the basic idea of assigning an Asiatic ancestry to the peoples of the Horn should be rejected, but that it must be reconsidered in a different perspective. Anthropologically speaking, Biasutti's conception of "metamorphic" or derived races seems to me the preferable hypothesis. To these he assigns the "Ethiopic" race (a better name for Sergi's "Hamitic," which has confusing linguistic implications), showing that its intermediate characters cannot be accounted for by the mere assumption of Europoid-Negroid hybridisms on a large scale. This race is geographically widespread (from the Ababdeh of southeast Egypt to the Tutsi of Burundi) and morphologically stable; it has a documented antiquity on African soil if, as Biasutti believed, the Upper Palaeolithic or at least Mesolithic skeletal remains from Kenya and Tanganyika correspond to its types; osteological affinities connect it prevalently with Europoid races, of which it may represent an archaic (pre-Europoid) variety.[48] Infusions of Negro blood have no doubt taken place over the millennia, but significantly the infusions are less noticeable among the pastoral tribes than among the agricultural ones.

It is pointless to try to locate the "ancestral homeland" of nomadic tribes such as the ones which we have discussed; it is more reasonable to consider their probable migration routes. Poverty of prehistorical and archaeological data does not permit precise conclusions, but a combination of other elements suggests certain inferences. All traditions, as well as the pattern of historically ascertained movements in recent centuries, point to a general north-to-south direction for the Kushitic migrations. The indisputably Asiatic origin of the domestic animals on which the economy

48. Biasutti, *Razze e Popoli*, I, 445–447, III, 88–91.

of these peoples is founded (all the Kushitic domestic breeds except the donkey ultimately derived from southwestern Asia[49]), and the evidence we possess about the diffusion of the same domestic species in Africa as a whole, suggest that groups of Kushitic stock (whose racial affinity to the main human type of ancient Egypt is well established) very probably introduced those species into Africa, or, at least, that they contributed to their introduction. This means that the migration routes of some of their early nuclei originated in southwestern Asia—probably, because of their physical similarity, in the area already suggested for the hunters. Judging from what is known about the chronology of early domestication in the Fayyum, Merimde, Badari, and other Neolithic sites of the lower Nile Valley, one could cautiously suppose that the forefathers of the present Kushites entered Africa from Sinai with their first small flocks of goats, sheep, and cattle towards the end of the fifth or in the course of the fourth millennium B.C.

These incipient pastoralists supplemented their diet with game; indeed, for all we know, there may have been no clear distinction between their migrations and those of pure hunters of the same racial stock who preceded them in time along the same routes and possibly continued to roam along with them in later centuries. At any rate, what we can safely argue—because it is shown by the wide territorial dispersion of their nations in historical times and by their linguistic differentiation—is that those migrations extended over many centuries. But it is of course only in dynastic times that we have evidence of Kushitic (or "Ethiopic" in Biasutti's sense) tribes of cattle-breeders occupying the arid areas between the Nile Valley and the Red Sea. Because their respective habitats were the same, these tribes have usually been identified with the Blemyes of Hellenistic and Roman times[50] and these, in turn, with the Beja;

49. Cf. M. Hilzheimer, "Die ältesten Beziehungen zwischen Afrika und Asien, nachgewiesen an Haustieren," *Africa*, III (1930), 472–483.
50. For the Blemyes, see Ugo Monneret de Villard, *Storia della Nubia Cristiana* (Roma, 1938), 24–35; Andrew Paul, *A History of the Beja Tribes of the Sudan* (Cambridge, 1954), 20–37. On the problem of the identification of the present-day Beja with the Blemyes and their forerunners, see R. Herzog, "Zur Frage der Kulturhöhe und der Wirtschaftsform der frühen Bedja," *Paideuma: Mitteilungen zur Kulturkunde*, XIII (1967), 54–59.

but it is not impossible that the ancestors of the Galla and Somali may also have been early offshoots of this ancient ethnic stock.[51]

The Farmers

The Kushites' southward migrations have affected the ethnic situation of a larger part of Africa than the one considered here. Apart from the "Hamitization" of the lacustrine area, with which we are not concerned (and for which, incidentally, neither the Galla nor the Somali are responsible), Galla groups have extended as far south as the Sabaki River and, at one point, beyond. But they have left territorial gaps, and a look at an ethnic map shows that these gaps or pockets correspond to the valleys of the Horn's main rivers, which are occupied by Negroes. This applies to the basins of the Juba and Webi Rivers in southern Somalia as well as to that of the Tana in southern Kenya.

There is no doubt that the Negro (Bantu-speaking) groups were already settled in these valleys by the end of the first millennium A.D., and possibly earlier,[52] and that the incoming Galla attacked them, chased them from part of their lands or subjugated them, and kept them under control as serfs or subordinate allies. However, while the Bantu preferred the humid, often wooded areas where water was available for irrigation and the soil more fertile for their crops, the Kushites kept to the drier territories away from the rivers, where malaria was rare and the tsetse fly did not threaten their cattle. Moreover, so long as they allowed their Negro neighbors to retain their *shamba* (farms), the Kushites could exploit

51. "Gli Abissini considerano i Galla come originari della costa orientale d'Africa, cioè del Mar Rosso." Giulio Ferrario, *Il costume antico e moderno o storia...di tutti i popoli antichi e moderni*, XVI: *Il costume degli antichi Etiopi, de'Nubi, degli Abissini* (Milano, 1819), 100. Unfortunately no bibliographical reference is quoted.
52. A *terminus a quo* could roughly be established if we accept Murdock's hypothesis of "the first century as an estimated date for the beginning of the Bantu expansion" and of "the period from A.D. 575 to 879" for their arrival on the East African coast. George Peter Murdock, *Africa: Its Peoples and Their Culture History* (New York, 1959), 274, 307. As Murdock declares, these are only conjectures; but the first date may well not be far from the mark. See also, H.N. Chittick, "The Peopling of the East African Coast," above, 16.

them and, by way of tribute, by looting, or by exchange, obtain from them a steady supply of vegetable foods.

But conditions vary as one proceeds from southwest to northeast. The Pokomo on the Tana River retained their racial and cultural integrity and, up to a point, their political autonomy;[53] the Juba Bantu were forced to flee from their lands in large numbers when the Galla attacked them, even if some returned at a later date; the Shabeli Negroes, farther away from their kin and entirely surrounded by the Galla first and the Somali later, were largely acculturated, if not altogether absorbed by the conquerors.

No thorough study has ever been made of the Bantu-speaking peoples in the Webi area. Their main groups are: the Shidla, formerly clients of the Mobilen Somali on the middle Webi north of Maqdishu; the Shabeli further up the Webi, in the territory of the Ajuran; the Dube still farther upstream, at the foot of the Arusi plateau, now confederates of the Karanle Somali but still speaking a Rahanwen dialect; and the Elay or Helay of the Baydowa plateau, a federation of Negro villages bearing the name of the pastoral Elay (a tribe of the Rahanwen Somali, now in the Bur Hakaba region).[54] According to Cerulli, each of these major groups was organized as a federation of villages, which in turn acknowledged the sovereignty of the local Somali subtribe. But on their own lands the Bantu appeared to have full rights; encroachments by the Somali were strenuously resisted as unlawful, and when cattle of the latter were shifted to the riverside for watering during the dry seasons the Somali are said to have paid for this traditional privilege with a few head of cattle. Other aspects of this symbiosis that cannot be quoted here show that the position of the Webi Bantu was in many respects higher than that of serfs.

Partly because of a national superiority complex, and partly no doubt because the social structure of the Bantu speakers was so different from their own patriclanic, segmented structure, the

53. A.H.J. Prins, *The Coastal Tribes of the Northeastern Bantu* (London, 1952), 4–5.
54. Cerulli, *Somalia*, II, 115–121; Cerulli, "Tribu di pastori e genti di agricoltori lungo i grandi fiumi della Somalia," *Rivista di Antropologia*, XLVI (1959), 11–19.

Somali never troubled to learn and use the proper ethnic names of their Negro neighbors. A further practical cause of this lack may have been the fact that Bantu villages not only were not formed on strict lineage bases but may often have included members of more than one tribe, as well as runaway slaves of mixed or uncertain origin. This would account for the general name applied by the Darod to the Webi Bantu—*Addon* (slaves)—which would otherwise contrast with the nature of the inter-ethnic (Bantu-Somali) relationship to which we have just referred. The Hawiyya, on the other hand, have borrowed the general term *Habesho* from the coastal Arabs.[55] This may point to the interesting inference that the Hawiyya had no word in their own language to indicate "Negro" before they reached southern Somalia and the coast and hence had previously known no Negroes.

The collective local name for the Juba Bantu, *Gosha*, is again not altogether a Somali word, but a Bantuized form of a Somali term, meaning "people of the forest," the river banks being more thickly wooded than the steppes forming the herdsmen's customary habitat. While we lack historical documents on the Webi tillers, we do have information about those on the Juba River in an Arab chronicle, known as the Book of the Zanj, that has recently been edited, translated, and commented on by Cerulli.[56] It says that in bygone days the coast of the Indian Ocean south of the equator, and the Juba Valley, belonged to a people called Kashur by the Arabs (now known as Nyika in Swahili).[57] These people kept cattle, sheep, and fowl, they cultivated maize,[58] beans, and millet, and their capital was called Shungwaya. The chronicle states that these were the only people in this area; after twelve (or fifteen) days' march one reached Ethiopia. They had a king with royal court in Shungwaya, and well established laws; their state lasted

55. Cerulli, *Somalia*, II, 119.
56. *Ibid.*, I, 229–357. A brief abstract of the same *Kitab* had been given by J.A.G. Elliot, "A Visit to the Bajun Islands," *Journal of the African Society*, XXV (1925–1926), 150 ff. See also Chittick, above, 34.
57. *Nyika*, again, means "people of the bush." On the name *Kashur*, see V. L. Grottanelli, "A Lost African Metropolis," in J. Lukas (ed.), *Afrikanistische Studien Diedrich Westermann*, (Berlin, 1955), 232.
58. In the manuscript known to Elliot, there is no mention of this plant. Elliot, *A Visit*, 151, n. 3.

until the great Galla invasion, which ousted the Kashur from the Juba area and forced them to migrate southward. The Kashur were divided into twelve tribes, which "lived all together on the banks of the Juba River and around it and upstream, since the day on which God the Highest created them."[59] The list of the twelve tribes published by Cerulli (A), compared with the corresponding list in Elliot's abstract (B), is as follows:[60]

(A)	Digu	Shamba	Lungu	Sifi	Giryama	Shuni
(B)	Ndigo	Chembe	Lungu	Segeju	Giriama	Chonye
(A)	Kamba	Ribi	Jibana	Taita	Kadiyaru	Dara
(B)	Kamba	Riba	Jamban	Taita	Kathiyara	Ndara

The list has been commented upon by Alice Werner, in a footnote to the Elliot paper, and by Cerulli. With slight modifications in the spelling, all of the names but one correspond to those of northeastern Bantu tribes or subtribes existing to this day, mostly in southern Kenya,[61] and, with the exception of the Segeju and the Taita, customarily grouped under the Swahili name of Nyika. No tribe called Kathiyara is now known, but it is remembered as the former name of a mountain north of Usambara.[62] Dara or Ndara is again explained by Cerulli as the name of a mountain (in Taita), but it could also be compared with Ndera and Ndura, subtribal names among the Pokomo.

The Book of the Zanj goes on to narrate how the Yemeni Arabs came to the coast "in the days of paganism" and built the coastal towns of Maqdishu (Mogadiscio), Mombasa, Kilwa, etc. When they arrived at the Juba River the Zanj fled from them. Hence they were given the name Kashur, which supposedly means "the runaways." However, contact was later established, and the Zanj, once they had accepted gifts from the Arabs, gave up their fears and made lasting friendship with the immigrants. Then came the Bajuni, and more Arabs from Oman, Syria, Hijaz, Iraq, and

59. Cerulli, *Somalia*, I, 256.
60. *Ibid.;* Elliot, *A Visit*, 151. I have dropped all prefixes, which are in the normal plural form *wa-* in list (B) and in the singular *m-* in list (A). I think Werner was right in explaining "Sifi" as a copyist's error: See V. L. Grottanelli, *Pescatori dell'Oceano Indiano* (Roma, 1955), 41, n. 1.
61. Prins, *Coastal Tribes*, 35 ff.
62. Cerulli, *Somalia*, I, 257, n. 5.

the Yemen, mostly by sea, but some also by land, *via* Suakin and Berbera. And after the conversion of all of these to Islam in the year 41 A.H. (sic!), the Galla came from Ethiopia to the Juba, and started "killing the Kashur day and night," because between the two peoples "there was nothing but enmity and hatred." So this time the Kashur left for good, "and only those remained behind who were at Wama and Shungwaya."[63]

The chronicle thus confirms two related historical facts, the occupation of the Juba basin by the Galla, and the consequent migration of the Nyika to the Tana Valley and beyond, where we still find them today. No dates are given for these events, but we have elements to establish them with fair approximation. If we were to take literally the assertion of the Book of Zanj that the invaders came "from Abyssinia," the period could not be earlier than the second half of the sixteenth century, because we know from Ethiopian sources that Galla invasions of that country did not begin before the reign of Galawdewos (1540–1559), and, strictly speaking, their occupation of parts of the kingdom took place only after the death of that king. On the other hand, a Portuguese document proves that the Galla were already on the Juba River by 1550,[64] while the Nyika are known not to have made their appearance in the coastal area of Kenya until *after* the arrival of the Portuguese.[65] This would point to the first half of the sixteenth century as the likeliest period of the Galla-Nyika wars. Huntingford's tentative dating of the same events to about 1200–1300[66] seems, on the whole, much too early, though one must admit that a long period of raids and skirmishes may have preceded the actual chasing of the Bantu tribes from the Juba banks, and that the large-scale series of migrations that ensued cannot obviously have taken place all at once but may have involved several generations.[67]

63. *Ibid.*, 259–263.
64. Conti Rossini, "Appunti e comenti," *Rassegna di Studi Etiopici* II (1942), 99–101.
65. Prins, *Coastal Tribes*, 48.
66. G.W.B. Huntingford, "The Peopling of the Interior of East Africa by its Modern Inhabitants," in Roland Oliver and Gervase Mathew (eds.), *History of East Africa* (London, 1963), I, 89.
67. V.L. Grottanelli, "I Bantu del Giuba nelle tradizioni dei WaZegua,"

The identification of Shungwaya has met with difficulties in the past, because this place, usually understood to be a coastal city, is inaccurately marked on old maps and, after 1700, absent from modern ones. Several Bantu tribes still retain the memory of its name, but not its exact location. Indeed, the name appears to be used in two different ways, either as a town or as a whole area ("the wide and vague region known as Shungwaya," as Kirkman puts it).[68] I have elsewhere given the reasons in favor of the identification of this lost capital of the Zanj as the modern site of Bur Kavo (or Bur Gao, Bur Gab, renamed Port Durnford by the British), which I visited in 1952.[69]

The next question is: To what extent are the so-called Gosha the descendants of the Nyika who "remained behind"? Unfortunately, no serious study of the Juba Bantu has ever been attempted. It is a great pity, because on the one occasion in which I had the opportunity of devoting some time to them (during an interval of fieldwork in an adjoining area) I found that they had preserved a remarkable wealth of tradition. From my materials, which are scanty and naturally require checking, it appears that the situation at the beginning of the nineteenth century could roughly be summed up as follows: Most if not all of the Bantu (Nyika) farmers had been chased away from the lower course of the Juba; of the older inhabitants probably only the Boni remained. Some pockets of Warday Galla, on the left bank near the coast, still held out against the Somali, while the bulk of the southern Galla had already occupied their present territories in Kenya. The Somali (Rahanwen, Kablallah, Marrehan, etc.) controlled practically all of the area east of the Juba, while the costal strip was left to the Bajun.[70]

Geographica Helvetica, VIII (1953), 259. James Kirkman, who confirmed this tradition for the Giryama, Pokomo, Digo, Durama, and Taita, suggested the first quarter of the seventeenth century as the earliest possible date for this migration. James Kirkman, *The Arab City of Gedi* (Oxford, 1954), 74–75.

68. James Kirkman, "Some Conclusions from Archaeological Excavations on the Coast of Kenya, 1948–1966," below, 226, 236. Kirkman, *The Arab City of Gedi;* cf. Prins, *Coastal Tribes*, 43.
69. Grottanelli, "Lost African Metropolis," 231 ff.
70. Grottanelli, "I Bantu del Giuba," 249–260.

In the meantime, the slave trade was introducing more and more human material into the coastal towns. Arab slave dealers in Maqdishu, Barawa, etc., were no doubt links in a long-established chain that ran to Arabian and Persian ports; but part of the human merchandise remained in Somalia, to be used mainly on the agricultural tasks that the Somali and Arabo-Persians were unable or unwilling to carry out themselves. Recruits were gathered mostly from the coastal Bantu of present-day Tanzania and Moçambique, in addition to those of Kenya. (Information collected by Italian and British authors, as well as my own data, show that the present Bantu of lower Jubaland include groups of Yao, Makua, Nyamwezi, "Nyasa," Shambala, Makale, Ngindo, Zaramo, Zigua, and "Nyika.")

Most of these people were probably employed as laborers in Juba *shamba* when the slave trade was officially abolished in 1873 by Sayyid Barghash in all of the territories under his control from Kilwa to Maqdishu. But there was no radical change in the existing situation until after the 1886 treaty between Great Britain and Germany, and especially after the cession of the Benadir coast to Italy in 1892, when the freed slaves strove to reassemble according to their tribal origins and the agricultural areas in the river valleys became magnets for runaways from all over the country.

Yet, in some cases, the liberation movement and the resettlement on tribal lines were the result of mass revolts and preceded the abolition of slavery and colonial regulations. This was the case with the Zigua, who now form a considerable group on the Juba River downstream from Gelib, just north of the equator, and in 1952 occupied some thirty-five villages, mostly on the right bank. Their traditions show that their forefathers were taken by the Arabs from their homeland near the coast of Tanganyika to Somalia at some time between the end of the eighteenth and the beginning of the nineteenth century;[71] that the Arabs, pretending to be their friends, had promised to transport them to a fertile land where they could freely attend to their farming but had then treacherously given them over to the Somali, at whose hands they suffered cruelly; that after a short time they broke away from their

71. *Ibid.*, 254 ff.

masters, reached the Juba, and settled there, finding that the river banks were uninhabited except for a few Boni hunters. This did not happen, of course, without a reaction from the Somali, who returned "ten times" to attack their former slaves and plunder their farms; but the Somali were not able to dislodge them.

These traditions are confirmed by reports of early European travelers in the area, Guillain in the 1850's[72] and Von der Decken in 1865,[73] who found the Zigua in control of roughly the same region which they occupy today.

It would be interesting to record the traditions of the remaining Bantu groups further upstream, mainly in the plains of Gelib and Alexandra. There seem to be no Bantu settlements worth mentioning north of these areas, but a study of toponyms might possibly provide indications of their presence in the past.

As is well known, Bantu languages akin to Swahili are also spoken along the southern section of the Somali coast: Cimbalazi (Chimiini) by the Hamarani of Barawa, and Kitikuu or Kibajuni by the Bajun between Kisimayu and Kiunga. But neither group is anthropologically Negroid, and the historical processes that led to the formation of both of these linguistic minorities can be understood only in terms of the long series of events connected with Asiatic colonization of the coast.

The Seamen and Traders

Lack of space, and the comforting knowledge that the subject will be dealt with more extensively in other parts of this book, induce me to limit this fourth section to an outline.

As we are dealing with the peopling—not the discovery—of the Horn, we are not concerned here with the countless visits paid to the country through the centuries by mariners, African or Asiatic, who did not establish permanent settlements on the coast. This applies first of all to the expeditions sent to Punt by the Pharaohs, mostly by sea, starting about the middle of the third

72. Charles Guillain, *Documents sur l'histoire, la géographie et le commerce de l'Afrique orientale* (Paris, 1856–1857), III, 180.
73. Carl Claus von der Decken (ed. Otto Kersten), *Reisen in Ostafrika in den Jahren 1862 bis 1865* (Leipzig, 1871), II, 303–304.

millennium. Punt, which can safely be identified with the coastal lands extending from southern Eritrea to the region of Berbera and possibly to Cape Guardafui, was known to the Egyptians as early as the reign of Sahure (Fifth dynasty), and revisited at intervals at the time of the Sixth, Eleventh, and especially the Twelfth dynasty, 1800 B.C. But these commercial expeditions, apparently little more than organized raids, as well as those which followed under the New Kingdom, are not likely to have exerted any appreciable influence on the indigenous population. Only one detail deserves attention for our purposes. In the Dair al-Bahri bas-reliefs, depicting the arrival in Punt of the expedition sent by Queen Hatshepsut (Eighteenth dynasty, c. 1480 B.C.), it is unmistakable that a few Negroes are portrayed with the Puntite types that are racially "red," i.e., like the Egyptians. The most plausible explanation, as already suggested by Conti Rossini, is that they were imported slaves—possibly from the lowlands of Eritrea or from western Ethiopia.[74]

It is just possible that the first Asiatic ships which touched the northern reaches of the Horn were those of the Sumerians, who, especially during the Lagash period, had developed what by third millennium standards could be called a considerable fleet and who controlled the shores of Oman and perhaps southwestern Arabia (the identification of Magan and Meluhha, as far as I know, is still an open question); but here again, as in the cases of the Egyptians and of the Phoenicians who followed them, we have no reason to imagine that any form of settlement took place. Indeed, the initial phases of the exploration and colonization of the coast by Asiatic peoples are shrouded in darkness. It is probable that occasional or even frequent voyages by South Arabian, south Persian, and possibly Indian seamen took place during the second millennium, or certainly from the very beginning of the first, and that regular contacts were by then established with the inhabitants of those parts of the coast that were later called Ἀυαλίτης, Βαρβαρία, and Ἀζανία. But there are no historical or archaeological documents to prove that this was in fact the case, and we have almost no technical information on the ancient seamanship

74. Conti Rossini, *Storia d'Etiopia*.

of the Indian Ocean peoples before the days of Alexander the Great.[75]

Glaser's opinion that South Arabian penetration of the East African coast should date back to the eighth century B.C. is no more than a working hypothesis. The same can be said of his theory that the coast was colonized before the Himyarites by seamen from the small state of Ausan, a thesis that was supported by Wainwright although Grohmann had already shown the frailty of the foundation on which it rested.[76]

By the time of the *Periplus*, at any rate, Himyaritic colonization of the coast had spread from the Gulf of Aden to the neighborhood of Kilwa or the mouth of the Ruvuma River. And we may assume that it had been established there for some time because its main features were by then clearly marked and did not undergo noticeable changes for many centuries—though the same activities were transmitted in due course from one coastal people to another: sailing seasons which alternated between the southwest and the northeast according to the monsoon; the establishment of coastal trading posts at more or less regular intervals, corresponding to twelve to fourteen hours of navigation; exploitation of a list of African merchandise that has remained unchanged to modern times (precious timber such as *saj* [mangrove], ebony, sandalwood, and aloe, frankincense, myrrh and other aromatic gums, gold, ivory, rhinoceros horn, leopard and other skins, tortoise shell, ostrich feathers, and slaves). Trade was centered on the coastal ports, to which goods were brought by caravans from the interior under the surveillance of local African chiefs. The Arab traders took

75. See R. Mookerji, *A History of Indian Shipping and Maritime Activity* (London, 1912); P.I. Srinivas Iyengar, "The Trade of India from the earliest period up to the second century A.D.," *Indian Historical Quarterly*, I (1925), 693–696, and II (1926), 38–47, 290–298, 456–463; James Hornell, "Sea Trade in Early Times," *Antiquity*, XV (1941), 234 ff.; George Fadlo Hourani, *Arab Seafaring in the Indian Ocean in Ancient and Early Medieval Times* (Princeton, 1951), ch. 3.

76. E. Glaser, "Punt und die südarabischen Reiche," *Mitteilungen der Vorderasiatisch-Aegyptischen Gesellschaft* (Berlin, 1899), 16 ff.; G.A. Wainwright, "Early Foreign Trade in East Africa," *Man*, XLVII (1947), 161; A. Grohmann, "Mapharitis Landschaft," in A. Pauly and G. Wissowa (eds.), *Real-Enzyklopädie der klassischen Altertumswissenchaft* (Stuttgart, 1894), XIV, 2, 1403–1413.

pains to ingratiate themselves with the Africans, learned their languages, and intermarried with them. Thus the process from which the mixed culture, mixed race, and mixed language of the coast was to emerge, was already under way in the first century A.D.

But how far does this maritime and trading activity apply specifically to the Horn? At the opening of our era, as we have seen, it is doubtful that the pastoral Kushites had expanded even as far as Cape Guardafui, not to mention the territories further south. It is equally uncertain whether the Bantu-speaking tillers (expanding presumably from the lake regions, or at any rate from the heart of the continent) had reached the rivers of Somalia, to this day their extreme limits in the northeast. So that it is conceivable that 2000 years ago the Asiatic merchants operating in the area of the Horn may have had to deal exclusively with hordes of hunters. One should also remember that the oceanic coast of the Horn has no natural ports, with the partial exception of Hafun and Bur Gao (Port Durnford), and that none of the existing towns of Benadir seem to antedate the tenth century A.D. In the early stages, this absence of ports must have hindered the establishing of permanent contacts with the peoples of the hinterland.

The fact that South Arabians—the Himyarites and probably the Sabaeans before them—were the organizers of the coastal trade, and for a long time the overlords of the maritime ports, does not necessarily mean that they held an absolute monopoly of power. The Persians, who had for some time been interested in the exploitation of the African littoral, almost surely seized the opportunity offered by the decline of the Himyaritic state in the sixth century, which culminated in the occupation of the Yemen by the Axumites from northern Ethiopia in 525. When the Sassanians chased the Axumites from Arabia about 572, in turn establishing their sovereignty in the Yemen, they presumably extended their political and commercial influence to the Yemenite colonies in eastern Africa.

The revolts of Zanj slaves in Mesopotamia, first in 694 and again from 868 to 883, were events of such magnitude that they can be explained only by assuming that Negroes who had been imported to work both in agriculture and in the armies of the caliphs were very large in number.[77] The organization of the slave trade, on such a scale, must have been a formidable affair, and it was surely not entirely entrusted to the Arabs. Where were the slaves recruited? The majority probably came from the coastal Bantu tribes: The fact that many of them, or at least the families of their chiefs, call themselves to this day Shirazi, thus quite fantastically claiming Persian descent, can be explained by a long-standing relationship of those chiefs with Persian merchants or surveyors living in the ports and trading posts. The list includes the Doe, Nyika, Hadimu, Mvita, and Kilindini of the Mombasa area, the Tumbatu near Zanzibar, Mbwera of Mafia, and even the Swahili and Bajun.[78] But I think that it is perfectly possible that some of those slaves may have been recruited from the pre-Nilotic tribes of western Ethiopia, through the Axumite kingdom and its ports on the Red Sea and later through the Arabs who carried on the trade when the Axumites lost their control over the coast in the late sixth century.

The presence of Persians on the African side of the Red Sea and along the northern littoral of the Horn at the time is not historically proved. (Firdusi's reference to Persian domination of Berbera is probably no more than a legend.[79]) According to persistent traditions spread along the African littoral of the Red Sea and of the Gulf of Aden, and known also to such hinterland tribes as the Dahimela, all of the important sections of these coasts were long ago occupied by the "Furs."[80] It must not be supposed that these traditions reflect a military or political occupation, but it may well be that from the sixth century onward, and possibly earlier, Persians, or "persianized" Arabs, from the Bahr al-Fars, competed with Yemenites in the commercial exploitation of these and other stretches of the African coast.

77. Ugo Monneret de Villard, "Note sulle influenze asiatiche nell'Africa Orientale," *Rivista degli Studi Orientali*, XVII (1938), 335–336; J. Spencer Trimingham, "The Arab Geographers and the East African Coast," below, 116–117.
78. References in Monneret, "Note." For the Bajun, see Grottanelli, *Pescatori*, 208–209, 214.
79. Conti Rossini, *Storia*, 200.
80. *Ibid.*, 295–296; Monneret, "Note," 326–327.

The Persians' advantageous political position after their conquest of the Yemen was short-lived; the rapid rise of Islam, the Arab invasion of Persia, the military catastrophe of Nehawend (642), and the collapse of the Sassanian armies determined the end of Persian power even before the death of the last Sassanian king, Yezdergerd III (651). But the desperate internal conditions need not have caused Persian overseas mercantile activities to lose their appeal, and internal strife occasionally encouraged emigration. The Omani Chronicle by Salil ibn Razik reports that in order to escape persecution by the caliphs of Baghdad the Azdite princes Sulaiman and Sa'id fled to the Zanj coast around A.D. 680.[81] According to the *Tarikh al-Mustabsir* by Ibn al-Mujawir (thirteenth century), Persians from Sirâf even occupied Aden.[82] By 933 Siraf, formerly the main port of the Persian Gulf, was in serious decline, following its occupation by the Buyids of Dailem, and in 366–367 A.H. (A.D. 976–978) it was destroyed by an earthquake so that the occupation of Aden by Sirafi must have been earlier than either of these dates. It is a curious parallel that the pre-Somali inhabitants of Merca, the Rer Manyo or "gens of the sea," who still form a distinct group among the Somali, should claim descent from the people of Sirâf.[83]

If we accept this tradition, the founding of Merca should be set in the first third of the tenth century at the latest and might antedate the birth of the other two main towns of the Benadir Coast, Barawa and Maqdishu. According to the Kilwa Chronicle known to Barros, these towns were founded around A.D. 924 by some Arabs from al-Ahsa in the Persian Gulf.[84] The dates mentioned in chronicles of this type are subject to caution, and Cerulli has pointed out that this version has been contradicted by local traditions, which maintain that Maqdishu was founded by a

81. George Percy Badger (ed. and trans.), *History of the Imâms and Seyyids of 'Omân, by Salil-ibn-Razik* (London, 1871), xxii, 5; Monneret, "Note," 335.
82. Gabriel Ferrand, "Le K'ouen-louen et les anciennes navigations inter-océaniques dans les mers du Sud," *Journal Asiatique*, XIII, (1919), 473–479.
83. Cerulli, *Somalia*, I, 97–98.
84. al-Ahsa (Laçah in Barros, also found in the form al-Hasa) is near the site of ancient Gerrha, in the Bahrain-Yamama region. Cf. Monneret, "Note," 338–339; Cerulli, *Somalia*, I, 18–20.

federation of various Arab tribes under the supremacy of a Qahtanid group.[85] Even so, the presence of Persians in the coastal towns of the Horn is proved by less doubtful evidence—funerary inscriptions. The oldest of those published to date belongs to a Persian from Naysabur in Khurasan who died in Maqdishu in 1215; another one, belonging to a man from Shiraz, was dated 1268–1269.[86]

What is of interest to us is the established fact that the main coastal centers of Somalia were founded sometime during the tenth century, by natives of southern Arabia or of Bahr al-Fars and its hinterland. These immigrants came to live and work side by side as representatives of a relatively uniform Arabo-Persian culture, whether they were political refugees, fugitives from religious persecutions, seamen and tradesmen settling abroad for commercial reasons, or all of these things together. Their new towns may in some cases have coincided geographically with the terminal places of the δρόμοι nine centuries before—we shall never know for sure. The *lingua franca* of these towns was Arabic, but at least in the case of Barawa (and probably in others) a Bantu dialect was also spoken: It was the language of the agricultural hinterland, which townsmen spoke with their Negro servants and their clients on the farms—the exact parallel of Swahili further south. The Somali (the Jiddu, the Ajuran, and then the Hawiyya) appeared on the Benadir coast at a later date, possibly during the twelfth century; they were certainly there in the thirteenth, because Yaqut describes Merca in 1228 as a town of the Zanj coast, but belonging to the "black Berbers" (Somali),[87] thus confirming al-Idrisi's earlier mention (c. 1150). According to Cerulli, Maqdishu became an Arabo-Somali sultanate around 1250, but the first known document in which the town tribes are listed with their Somali (and not Arab) names is as late as 1573.[88]

The presence of Indians in these cosmopolitan towns is also likely and may find precedents in the δρόμοι of Himyaritic times.

85. Cerulli, *Somalia*, I, 18, 134, 169.
86. *Ibid.*, I, 2–3, 9.
87. F. Wüstenfeld (ed.), *Jacuts Geographisches Wörterbuch* (Leipzig, 1869), IV, 502, quoted in Cerulli, *Somalia*, I, 92.
88. Cerulli, *Somalia*, I, 166.

It cannot be doubted that Indians, as well as their colleagues and rivals, visited from time to time, and occasionally resided in, the countries on which their trade was based. As the *Periplus* (§ 30) informs us, the inhabitants of Soqotra, "a mixture of Arabs and Indians and Greeks," were immigrant traders. Portuguese travelers of the early sixteenth century, such as Pero Dias and Duarte Barbosa, found an active trade going on between Maqdishu and Cambay; Indian fabrics and spices were imported in exchange for African ivory, wax, cereals, and gold.[89] Unfortunately, Indian sources on nautical, archaeological, and historical aspects of this trade have not been studied.

There are traces of Indonesian influence in Somali culture, to which I called attention many years ago.[90] A study of these traces would help to clarify some obscure aspects of the debated question of Indonesian maritime routes to the western shores of the Indian Ocean. Indonesian seamen may well have sailed at one time along the coast of northeastern Africa, but, like those other occasional visitors, the Chinese, they did not contribute in any appreciable degree to its peopling. Indeed, in spite of a more ancient and better documented presence in the coastal centers, even the other Asians, the Arabs, Persians, and Indians, exerted a cultural, not a racial, influence on the peoples of the hinterland.

89. *Ibid.*, I, 115–121; Monneret, "Note," 218–320, 344–345.
90. V.L. Grottanelli, "Asiatic Influences in Somali Culture," *Ethnos*, XII (1947); Grottanelli, *Pescatori*, 48–62, 321–344.

ANALECTA SINO-AFRICANA RECENSA

Paul Wheatley

The growth of Chinese knowledge of East Africa

Most students of Africa are now aware that materials relating to
that continent exist in Chinese historical records.[1] The search for
a connection between the Chinese and African culture realms
already has a respectable history, since it dates back to at least the
early years of the seventeenth century;[2] but it is only during the

[1] This paper is essentially a revision, incorporating some of the ideas and
interpretations advanced in both formal and informal discussions at Nairobi,
of an earlier article of mine, "The Land of Zanj: Exegetical Notes on Chinese
Knowledge of East Africa Prior to A.D. 1500," in Robert W. Steel and R.
Mansell Prothero (eds.), *Geographers and the Tropics: Liverpool Essays* (Liverpool,
1964), 139–187. That article provides additional documentation omitted from
the present paper.

[2] As early as 1614 a plate in an atlas of maps by Peter Kaerius referred to
some white natives of Madagascar "supposed to have been transplanted out
of China" (Reproduced in *Tanganyika Notes and Records*, 3 [1937], opposite 1).
In 1654, in a work entitled *Œdipus Ægyptiacus* (Romae, 1652–4. Colophon
of vol. III, dated 1655), Athanasius Kircher propounded the view that Chinese
civilization had derived from that of ancient Egypt (cf. also the same author's
China Monumentis qua Sacris qua Profanis Illustrata [Amsterdam, 1667]), and
in 1660 John Webb adumbrated a similar thesis (*Historical Essay endeavouring
a Probability that the language of the Empire of China is the Primitive Language*
[London]). This theory received more detailed expression in two works of the

last fifty years or so that the study has been placed on a firm scholarly basis. The first attempt actually to integrate the available materials into an inclusive and coherent account of Sino-African relations was made by Chang Hsing-lang in 1930 in the course of a comprehensive discussion of Chinese relations with the West.[3] Then in 1947, in two lectures given before the University of London, the late J.J.L. Duyvendak provided a compendious summary of the evidence to hand.[4] He was followed in 1961 and 1962 by Teobaldo Filesi, who subjected all of the Chinese sources available in translation to analysis from the point of view of a lifelong specialist in African affairs.[5] Even more recently V. Velgus of the Institute of

---

eighteenth century: Joseph de Guignes's *Mémoire dans lequel on prouve, que les Chinois sont une colonie égyptienne* (Paris, 1760) and John Turberville Needham's *De Inscriptione quadam Ægyptiaca Taurini inventa et Characteribus Ægyptiis olim et Sinis communibus exarata idolo cuidam antiquo in regia universitate servato . . .* (Rome, 1761). A century later Charles de Paravey ("Archéologie primitive. Traditions primitives conservées dans les hiéroglyphes des anciens peuples...," *Annales de Philosophie Chrétienne* [1853]) identified the Hsi-wang Mu 西王母 of the *Chu-shu Chi-nien* 竹書紀年 and other ancient Chinese records with the Biblical Queen of Sheba (*Saba*'), and fifty years after that, Alfred Forke equated the K'un-lun mountains, home of the legendary Hsi-wang Mu, with the *qolla* of Abyssinia ("Mu Wang und die Königin von Saba," *Mitteilungen des Seminars für Orientalische Sprachen*, VII [1904], 117–172). Finally, only thirty years ago E. H. L. Schwarz ("The Chinese Connection with Africa," *Journal of the Royal Asiatic Society of Bengal*, Letters, IV [1938], 175–193) sought to explain Hottentot physical characteristics as deriving from an infusion of Mongoloid blood when "millions of Chinese" swarmed over Africa between A.D. 900 and 1200. Of course, even in the heyday of theories ascribing an African provenance to the Chinese, there were those who doubted, as witness the scathing attack of C. de Pauw, *Recherches philosophiques sur les Egyptiens et les Chinois*, vols. IV and V of *Œuvres Philosophiques* (Paris, 1774, 1795).

[3] Chang Hsing-lang 張星烺 *Chung-Hsi chiao-t'ung shih-liao hui-p'ien* 中西交通史料匯篇 (Pei-p'ing, 1930).

[4] J.J.L. Duyvendak, *China's Discovery of Africa* (London, 1949). Cf. also L.C. Goodrich, "A Note on Professor Duyvendak's Lectures on China's Discovery of Africa," *Bulletin of the School of Oriental and African Studies*, XIV (1952), 384–387.

[5] Teobaldo Filesi, *I viaggi dei Cinesi in Africa nel Medio-evo* (Roma, 1961) and *Le relazioni della Cina con l'Africa nel Medio-evo* (Milano, 1962). This is an appropriate point at which to mention a few other authors who have touched on Sino-African relations: Albert Herrmann, "Ein alter Seeverkehr zwischen Abessinien und Süd-China bis zum Beginn unserer Zeitrechnung," *Zeitschrift*

Ethnography in the University of Leningrad has both uncovered new textual sources of information and reexamined previously known materials relating to the earlier phases of the problem.[6] The two papers in which Velgus has presented his conclusions mark a major advance in our understanding of Sino-African relations, but in China it is the works of Chang Hsing-lang and Duyvendak which are best known and which have on several occasions been pressed into service as tools of Chinese political journalism.[7] It is not my purpose to restate these materials in their entirety, but—in contrast to the majority of previous writers, Velgus excepted, who have investigated these matters from a literary and humanistic point of view—to emphasize their cultural and ecological aspects.

Apart from a few probable, but as yet not fully substantiated, references to Alexandria,[8] the earliest accounts of Africa in Chinese literature appear to date from the T'ang dynasty (A.D. 618–906),

---

der Berliner Gesellschaft für Erdkunde (1913), 553–561; G. Caniglia, "Note Storiche sulla Città di Mogadiscio," *Revista Coloniale*, XII (1917), 172–188; C.E. Fripp, "A Note on Mediaeval Chinese-African Trade," *Native Affairs Department Annual*, XVII (1940), 88–96; Fripp, "Chinese Mediaeval Trade with Africa," *ibid.*, XVIII (1941), 12–22; A. Girace, "Le Coste della Somalia e i Cinesi," *Corriere della Somalia*, CCVII (1954); M. Pirone, *Appunti di Storia dell'Africa: II, Somalia* (Roma, 1961).

[6] V. Velgus, "Strany Mo-lin' i Bo-sa-lo (Lao-bo-sa) v srednevekovykh kitayskikh izvestiyakh ob Afrike," *Africana*, XC (1966), 104–121; Velgus, "O srednevekovykh kitayskikh izvestiyakh ob Afrike i nekotorykh voprosakh ikh izucheniya," *ibid.*, 84–103; "Maris (Meroe) and Beshariya in Medieval Chinese Sources," *Second International Congress of Africanists: Papers Presented by the USSR Delegation* (Moscow, 1967), 1–16.

I wish here to place on record my indebtedness to James Bator, who provided me with clear and accurate English translations of Velgus's closely reasoned papers.

[7] Cf for example, Hsia Nai, "China and Africa—Historical Friendship," *China Reconstructs*, XI, xi (November, 1962), 27–29, and *Jen-min Jih-pao* 人 民 日 報 (1962); Yang Jen-pien, "China and Africa—2,000 Years of Friendship," *China Reconstructs*, XII (February, 1964), 14–17.

[8] *Vide* Paul Pelliot ["Li-kien, autre nom du Ta-ts'in," *T'oung Pao*, XVI (1915), 690–691], and "Les anciens rapports entre l'Egypte et l'Extrême-Orient," *Comptes Rendus du Congrès International de Géographie*, V [1926], 21–22), who claimed to recognize the name Alexandria in both *Liei-Xiɐn 黎 軒 (Shih Chi* 史 記, chüan 123, and *Wei Lüeh* 魏 略, quoted in commentary in *San-Kuo Chih* 三 國 志, chüan 30, but variously as *Liei-Xiɐn* 黎 軒 *Ch'ien-Han Shu* 前 漢 書, chüan 96, f.27 verso] and *Liei-kiɐn* 黎 鞬 [*Hou-Han Shu* 後 漢 書 chüan 88, and *Chin Shu* 晉 書, chüan 97]) and *ɣien-tuok* 賢 督 (*Wei Lüeh*). Cf. also

but even they are exiguous and somewhat obscure. The revised T'ang history of Ou-yang Hsiu and Sung Ch'i incorporates brief notices of two East African territories under the rubrics *Puât-b'uât-liək* 撥 拔 力 (Modern Standard Chinese = Po-pa-li)[9] and *Muâ-liĕn* 磨 鄰 (MSC = Mo-lin).[10] The former is a phonetically adequate transcription of *Barbarig*, a Middle Persian form of *Barbarā*, the Berbera of the English-speaking world, but *Muâ-liĕn* has proved difficult to identify.

Notices of *Muâ-ilĕn* occur in no less than five different Chinese sources, always in the form of supplementary information to a description of the country of *P'iuət-liəm* 拂 菻 (= *Frūm, for Rūm*[11] [or possibly *Rūmiya*] = the Roman Orient). In addition to the account in the T'ang history mentioned above, there are passages relating to *Muâ-liĕn* in (1) the *T'ung Tien* 通 典, an encyclopedia compiled by Tu Yu 杜 佑 in c. A.D. 812; (2) in the *T'ai-p'ing Huan Yü Chi* 太 平 寰 宇 記, a general statistical and descriptive topography assembled by Yüeh Shih 樂 史 between 976 and 983; (3) in the

---

Pelliot, "Sur les anciens itinéraires chinois," *Journal Asiatique*, CLXXII (1921), 145. Friedrich Hirth, in *China and the Roman Orient* (Shanghai, Hong-Kong, Leipzig, and Munich, 1885; [reproduced photographically in China with no imprint, 1939], 182) has also equated the *(·Uo)-d'i-sân* (烏) 遲 散 of the *Wei Lüeh* with Alexandria. For a summary of some Japanese views on this topic see Velgus, *Africana*, XC, 93.

[9] *Hsin T'ang-Shu* 新 唐 書 (completed in A.D. 1061), chüan 221B, f. 13 verso (Chin-ling edition) It is regretted that in this paper the typesetter has been unable to provide both the phonetic symbols employed in the Karlgren recon-structions of Ancient Chinese and some diacritical signs used in standard transcriptions from Arabic. Consequently, an asterisk preceding a Chinese name or term often denotes only an approximation to, rather than an accurate rendering of, an Ancient vocalization.

[10] *Hsin T'ang-Shu*, f. 13 recto.

[11] It has always been difficult for the Chinese to transcribe the phonemes *rum* and *rom*, for none of the Chinese words incorporating a final -*m* include *u* or *o* as the preceding vowel, or, from the complementary point of view, none of the words incorporating the vowels *u* or *o* in a central position include -*m* as a final consonant. Consequently, in their transcriptions of phonemes of this type the Chinese have been forced to sacrifice either the vowel or the final consonant. In the case of *P'iuət-liəm* they have retained the final -*m* at the expense of the vowel. See Friedrich Hirth, "The Mystery of Fu-lin," *Journal of the American Oriental Society*, XXX (1909–1910), 17–18; Paul Pelliot, com-munication to the *Journal Asiatique*, III (1914), 498 *et seq*; Otto Franke, *Geschichte des Chinesischen Reiches* (Berlin, 1937), III, 208–212.

T'ung Chih 通 志, an historical compendium completed by Cheng Ch'iao 鄭 樵 in about 1150; and (4) in Ma Tuan-lin's 馬 端 臨 comprehensive encyclopedia *Wen-hsien T'ung-k'ao* 文 獻 通 考 which, although finished in about 1280, was not published until 1319. All five of these notices derive ultimately from an account of *Muâ-liĕn* by Tu Huan 杜 環, a Chinese officer who, after having been taken prisoner by the Arabs at the battle of the Talas River in A.D. 751, returned to China in 762, and then wrote a memoir on his experiences entitled *Ching-hsing Chi* 經 行 記.

Tu Huan's work has long been lost, but fortune favored the pre-servation of certain parts of it in an encyclopedia generally con-sidered to be unusually trustworthy. Tu Huan was a brother of the celebrated T'ang scholar Tu Yu, the author of the *T'ung Tien*, and it is in that encyclopedia that we find the earliest account of *Muâ-liĕn*.[12] In the *T'ai-p'ing Huan Yü Chi*, the *T'ung Chih*, and *Wen-hsien T'ung-k'ao*, this passage is repeated with only insignificant alterations in the wording, but in *Hsin T'ang-Shu* the relevant section is abbreviated and the sense changed in some important respects. All five notices relate the location of *Muâ-liĕn* to that of a country reported variously as *Ts'iəu-sât-lâ* 秋 薩 羅 (*T'ung Tien* and *Wen-hsien T'ung-k'ao*), *B'uâ-sât-lâ* 婆 薩 羅 (*T'ai-p'ing Huan Yü Chi*), *Lâu-b'uət-sât* 老 勃 薩 (*Hsing T'ang-Shu*) and *B'uət-sât-lâ* 郣 薩 羅 (*T'ung Chih*). In addition Hirth recorded a variant orthography *·Iang-sât-lâ* 秩 薩 羅, allegedly from an edition of *Wen-hsien T'ung-k'ao*,[13] but such a reading has not been reported by anyone else and I have not found it myself. *Muâ-liĕn* is customarily located to the southwest of this second country, though the *Hsin T'ang-Shu* appears either to regard *Lâu-b'uət-sât* as an alternative name for *Muâ-liĕn* or to be referring to two countries, both situated to the southwest of *P'iuət-liəm*.

The identification of *Muâ-liĕn* and of the protean toponym

---

[12] The editors of the *Ch'in-ting Ssŭ-k'u Ch'üan-shu Tsung-mu* 欽 定 四 庫 全 書 總 目, the great catalog of the Ch'ing imperial library which was completed in 1790, accord the *T'ung Tien* high praise, saying it "is made up entirely of solid material, that it contains all information essential to a knowledge of the period it covers, and that it clearly and systematically traces the evolution of each of the subjects it deals with."

[13] Hirth, *China and the Roman Orient*, 122.

associated with it has been the subject of lengthy debate ever since Bretschneider, studying the T'ang history in 1871, equated *Lâu-b'uət-sât*, and therefore—as he thought—*Muâ-liĕn*, with Mauritania.[14] Subsequently, Hirth located *Muâ-liĕn* on the Egyptian coast of the Red Sea,[15] and in 1919 Laufer proposed the equation of this name with that of Malindi on the Kenya coast.[16] This last has been the preferred identification of most subsequent authors; in fact it has been almost an article of faith among writers on Sino-African topics.[17] Among the few who dissented from this interpretation were Chang Hsing-lang who, basing himself on the text of the *T'ung Tien*, identified *Muâ-liĕn* and *Ts'iəu-sât-lâ* with Morocco and Castile respectively,[18] and Kirkman who proposed a location in Somalia, "probably somewhere in the region of the Gulf of Aden."[19]

Recently, Velgus has submitted the relevant texts to renewed and more rigorous scrutiny than has been accorded them hitherto and has, moreover, elicited the filiation outlined above.[20] His researches have established that the correct form of the textually unstable toponym was *B'uət/B'uâ-sât-lâ* as preserved in the *T'ung Chih* and *T'ai-p'ing Huan Yü Chi*, the other extant orthographies being merely scribal mislections. Velgus has been able to relate this form to the geographical cognizances of Tu Huan and thereby show that it was a transcription of the ethnonym Beshariya

[14] E. Bretschneider, *On the Knowledge of the Arabs Possessed by the Chinese* (London, 1871), 25.

[15] Hirth, *China and the Roman Orient*, 204–207.

[16] Berthold Laufer, *Sino-Iranica: Chinese Contributions to the History of Civilization in Ancient Iran* (Chicago, 1919), 389–390. This identification had been made, although apparently unknown to Laufer, in the middle of the nineteenth century by Hsü Chi-yü 徐繼畬 in *Ying-huan Chih-lüeh* 瀛環志略 (1848): see, Velgus, *Africana*, XC, 85.

[17] E.g., Duyvendak, *China's discovery of Africa* 15; Duyvendak in Youssouf Kamal (ed.), *Monumenta cartographica Africae et Ægypti* (Cairo, 1935), IV, fasc. 4, folio 1415; Hsia Nai, *Jen-min Jih-pao*, (1962) and *China Reconstructs*, XI, xi (1962), 27–29; Wheatley, "Exegetical Notes," 145; Filesi, *Le relazioni della Cina con l'Africa nel Medio-evo*, 39.

[18] Chang Hsing-lang, *Chung-Hsi chiao-t'ung shih-liao hui-p'ien*, I, 165–166, 177–178, and III, 43–45.

[19] James Kirkman, review of Filesi's *Le relazioni della Cina con l'Africa* in *Journal of African History*, IV (1963), 297.

[20] Cf. Note 6 above.

(Bisharin), one of the Beja tribes which figured prominently in medieval Arabic accounts of southern Egypt and the Sudan, notably in the writings of Ya'qūbī (A.D. 897), Ibn al-Faqīh (c. 903), al-Maqdisī (985–986), and Ibn Hawqal (fl. 943–977). In fact, between A.D. 268 and 451 the Beja exercised political control over part of Upper Egypt and were powerful in Nubia. Having established this identification, Velgus was then able to demonstrate that *Muâ-liĕn* was a transcription of *Meroe*, an equation supported by Tu Huan's description of the countryside and of the customs of its people. Velgus's paper is an extremely intricate piece of argumentation which, in providing an answer to one of the most persistent of Sino-African conundrums, has demonstrated once again the essential reliability of medieval Chinese descriptions of western Asia and eastern Africa. When texts and reality appear to be at variance, the fault lies only too often with the twentieth-century investigator.

The source of the meager information about *Muâ-liĕn* preserved in the T'ang history has now been shown to have derived not from the records of the Hung Lu 鴻臚, a bureau where in T'ang times and later foreign envoys and tribute bearers were interrogated concerning the geography and customs of their homelands, but from a stratum of unofficial literature which circulated in T'ang China. The notice of *Puât-b'uât-liɔk* (Barbarā) originated in similar circumstances, for it was an abridgment of a longer passage in the *Yu-yang Tsa-tsu* 酉 陽 雜 俎 ("Assorted dishes from Yu-yang"), a miscellany of varied topical writings compiled by Tuan Ch'eng-shih 段 成 式 soon after the middle of the ninth century A.D. Tuan was in many ways a singular man, certainly an unusual Chinese bureaucrat. Never conspicuously successful in his official career, he yet manifested what one of his modern admirers has called a "voracious appetite for literary curiosities and rare nuggets of knowledge."[21] His catholicity of interests led him to seek information

[21] Edward H. Schafer, "Notes on Tuan Ch'eng-shih and his Writing," *Etudes Asiatiques*, XVI (1963), 19. The name *Yu-yang* preserved an obscure literary reference to a mountain on the south or *yang* bank of the Yu river in Ho-nan. Tuan Ch'eng-shih, whose family had identified itself with the region of the middle Yang-tzŭ, had doubtless heard of the local tradition which asserted that caves in the Yu-yang mountain had afforded shelter to scholars fleeing from the wrath of Ch'in Shih Huang (see Alexander C. Soper, "A Vacation

about topics generally deemed unworthy of an educated Chinese and, moreover, to use all sorts and conditions of men and women as informants.[22] From somewhere or other, but most probably from Arab or Persian traders, he had picked up tales of a desiccated land on the western selvedge of the world, tales which in due course he incorporated in the *Yu-yang Tsa-tsu.*

For the sober scholars who compiled the T'ang history, by contrast, such information exercised no fascination. Moreover, no embassy had come from the *Bilād al-Barbarā* during the three centuries of T'ang dominion, so presumably the Hung Lu archives afforded no information about that country. Only Tuan Ch'eng-shih, with his insatiable curiosity, empirical turn of mind, and interest in the unusual, had ferreted out a few facets of its ethnology and ecology for inclusion in his "rare documents and secret schedules," 奇 篇 秘 籍,[23] and it was these, suitably edited, which eventually found their way into the T'ang history. There is, indeed, reason to believe that much of the information about foreign countries which was current in T'ang China circulated only in unofficial literature, being considered unsuitable for the attention of true scholars.[24]

Of course, the identification of an ancient Chinese transcription with an African toponym by no means invariably specifies its precise location. Although regional nomenclature appears to have remained

---

Glimpse of the T'ang Temples of Ch'ang-an," *Artibus Asiae*, XXIII [1960], 19—though it is not strictly true, as Soper states, that the allusion is to Tuan's homeland).

[22] Including foreign envoys, priests, and merchants who visited China, and peasant farmers, slaves, secretaries, and nurses. It is not improbable, moreover, that Tuan had some acquaintance with one or more foreign languages (cf. Schafer, "Notes", 28).

[23] The phrase used in Tuan Ch'eng-shih's biography in *Hsin T'ang-Shu*, chüan 89, f. 16 recto.

[24] Just how alien this topic was to a cultivated Sung Confucian is betrayed by the fact that the compilers of the *Hsin T'ang-Shu* misunderstood Tuan Ch'eng-shih's remarks and, in transposing his exuberant language into the sober phrases of the *Annals*, completely changed the import of a sentence relating to Persian trade practices in *Bilād al-Barbarā*: cf. page 104 below. They also obscured, through excessive abridgment, the nature of the marriage customs in *Muâ-liĕn* and introduced unwarranted errors into their account of the religions of the country (page 95 below).

Figure 1. A modern reconstruction of East Africa as possibly envisaged by a Chinese official of the Sung or Yüan dynasty. Note the body of water in the interior, whence a river flowed northward, the cone of Kilimanjaro, the predominantly Muslim ports, the frankincense of the Haud and the dragon's-blood tree of Soqotrā. The *p'eng* bird (here modelled on a Persian drawing from E. W. Lane's edition of the *Arabian Nights*) and the whale both featured in Chinese accounts of the coast. The representation of the junk follows contemporary drawings and the direction indicator approximates a bronze floating-compass of the Ming period, as illustrated by Wang Chen-to, *Chung-kuo k'ao-ku hsüeh pao*, V (1951). Reproduced from Robert W. Steel and R. Mansell Prothero (eds.), *Geographers and the tropics: Liverpool Essays* (London, 1964), 158.

fairly stable during historical time, it was not unknown for boundaries to fluctuate widely and for individual settlements to migrate over considerable distances within a region of the same name. It follows, therefore, that a high proportion of the toponyms resurrected in the succeeding pages, particularly in the earlier period, relate to localities rather than to specific sites. *Barbarā* provides a good example of this uncertainty. Classical authors of the West and Arab authors differ both from each other and among themselves as to the territorial implications of this name. According to the *Periplus of the Erythraean Sea*, the Emporium and Cape of Perfumes, Ἀρώματα ἄκρον καὶ ἐμπόριον, were located "at the very end of the *Barbarā* coast toward the east"[§8]. Ptolemy's Barbaric Gulf, Βαρβαρικός κόλπος, by contrast, apparently lay beyond the Cape of Perfumes (Bk. IV, ch. 8). Mas'ūdī regarded the inhabitants of *Barbarā* as basically a tribe of *Zanj* with a strong admixture of Abyssinian blood,[25] a point of view subsequently adopted by Yāqūt[26] and Abu'l-Fidā',[27] but, generally speaking, Arab authors seem to have regarded the indigenes of the *Bilād al-Barbarā* as synonymous with the Hamitic tribes of the Horn.[28] Precisely what the name implied to the Chinese at different times it is difficult to say, but the mention of myrrh among the natural products of the country in Sung times may favor the northern rather than the eastern coast of the Horn.[29] To accommodate this uncertainty I shall in this essay use the form *Barbarā* rather than the anglicized "Berbera." Curiously enough the name seems to have dropped out of use in Chinese records after Sung times.

The extension of overseas trade during the Sung dynasties—and particularly during the Southern Sung (A.D. 1127–1279) when the

[25] *Kitāb murūj al-dhahab*, III, xxxiii, 2.

[26] Wüstenfeld's edition, IV, 602.

[27] *Taqwīn al-buldān*, 159.

[28] Cf. Ibn Khaldūn: "To the south of Zeila on the western coast of the Indian Ocean are the villages of Berbera, which extend one after the other all along the southern coast [of the Indian Ocean] to the end of the sixth section. There, to the east, the country of the Zanj adjoins them." (Franz Rosenthal, *The Muqaddimah*, I [New York, 1958], 123.)

[29] According to R.E. Drake-Brockman (*British Somaliland* [London, 1912], 241–245), the best quality myrrh in recent times has come from the central and west-central districts of the former British Somaliland Protectorate.

income from maritime commerce amounted on one occasion to as much as a fifth of the total cash revenue of the state—brought the Chinese a great deal of new information about the shores of the Indian Ocean. A proportion of this new knowledge was incorporated into the official Sung history, but the more detailed accounts are once again to be found in unofficial works, notably the *Ling-wai Tai-ta* 嶺外代答 ("Information from beyond the Mountains"), written by Chou Ch'ü-fei 周去非 in 1178, and the *Chu-fan-chih* 諸蕃志 ("Gazetteer of Foreigners"), compiled by Chao Ju-kua 趙汝适 in 1225. Both authors had personal experience of the South China coast and of the foreign merchants who frequented it, Chou Ch'ü-fei having been an assistant subprefect at Kuei-lin and Chao Ju-kua the Superintendent of Maritime Trade 市舶使 in Fu-chien. For present purposes Chao's book is by far the more valuable, although a proportion of its information is drawn from the *Ling-wai Tai-ta* or even earlier works.[30] Chao relied as much on second-hand materials as Tuan Ch'eng-shih had, but he did possess more detailed information relating to a wider area of Africa. In addition to his descriptions of North Africa and the Mediterranean (with which this paper is not concerned), he was able to present fairly detailed accounts both of the Horn of Africa[31] and of the northernmost of the Bantu territories to the south. In fact he recorded this latter realm twice under different rubrics. In the first instance he adopted a passage from Chou Ch'ü-fei's work which was headed *Kuən-luən Tsəng-kji* 崑崙層期 or the *Qumr Zangi*.

Zang زنج, or something like it, was a designation for African Negroes employed by their neighbors since at least the beginning

---

[30] There is an English translation of *Chu-fan-chih* by Friedrich Hirth and W.W. Rockhill, *Chau Ju-kua: His Work on the Chinese and Arab Trade in the Twelfth and Thirteenth Centuries, Entitled Chu-fan-chï* (St. Petersburg, 1911). A convenient annotated edition of the text was published by Feng Ch'eng-chün 馮承鈞 at Shanghai in 1938, and an analysis of some aspects of Sung overseas trade by myself, "Geographical Notes on some Commodities involved in Sung Maritime Trade," *Journal of the Malayan Branch of the Royal Asiatic Society*, XXXII (1959), 1–140.

[31] Under the rubric *Pi-pa-lo* 弼琶囉. Velgus has recently drawn attention to a somewhat different account of this country in the great Sung encyclopedia *Shih-lin Kuang-chi* which, although compiled in the twelfth or early thirteenth century, was not printed until 1325.

of the Christian era,[32] and *Qumr* was an African ethnonym of undetermined linguistic affiliation[33] which happened to be closely similar to a Southeast Asian ethnikon that the Chinese had for long transcribed as **Kuən-luən*.[34] Not unnaturally the Chinese extended this term to subsume African Negroes as well as some of the peoples of tropical Asia, a process which was helped by the circumstance that **Kuən-luən* already carried implications of swarthiness. Thus the complete name comprised a Chinese term which had come to denote Negroes, coupled with an Arabo-Persian synonym.

It has been pointed out, above, that Chao Ju-kua adopted the compound form *Qumr Zangi* from Chou Ch'ü-fei, who had been writing half a century previously. It was, as far as he was concerned, book learning. But in the meanwhile he had himself acquired additional information about East African Negroes, most probably from Arab or Persian traders, under the name *Zangibār* (**Tsəng-b'uat*), a term signifying "the Coast of the Blacks,"[35] without realizing

---

[32] Cf. the Cape *Zinggis* of Ptolemy Ζιγγὶς ἄκρα, I, xvii, 9; Ζήγγισα ἄκρα, IV, vii, 11), the *Zinggion* Ζιγγιον of Cosmas Indicopleustes (6th century A.D.), the *Bilād al-Zanj* بلاد الزنج (with the ز vocalized as *g*) of the Arab geographers, the *Zäng* زنك of Persian authors, the *zängi* of the *Qutaδyu bilig* (A.D. 1069–1070), and the *çanghibar/zaghybar/zanghibar/zanghybar* of Polo (*Z* and French MSS.).

[33] Sometimes this toponym was vocalized as *qamar* = moon, but this I think may have originated as a rationalization of an unfamiliar word, which was then adopted by Ptolemy in his toponym "Mountains of the Moon" ὄρη σεληναῖα . I suppose that it might be possible to argue that *qumr* was a corrupted vocalization of a legitimate *qamar*. I am not competent to decide the issue, but I note that Ibn Khaldūn rejected *Qamar* in favour of *Qumr* (Rosenthal, *Muqaddimah*, I, 101).

[34] On the etymology and significance of **Kuən-luən* see, *inter alia*, L. de Saussure, "L'étymologie du nom des monts K'ouen-louen," *T'oung Pao*, XX (1921), 370–371; Gabriel Ferrand, "Le K'ouen-louen et les anciennes navigations interocéaniques dans les mers du sud," *T'oung Pao*, XIII (1919), 233–239, 431–492; XIV, 6–68, 201–241; R.A. Stein, "Le Lin-yi," *Han-Hiue*, II, i–iii (1947), 209–311; Wolfram Eberhard, "Lokalkulturen im alten China," *T'oung Pao*, supplement to XXXVII (1942), 245–248; Anthony Christie, "An Obscure Passage from the Periplus," *Bulletin of the School of Oriental and African Studies*, XIX (1957), 345–353.

[35] For *Zang*, see page 86; *-bar* < Tamil *-param* (*-baram* in combination) = "the opposite shore." *Zangibār* denoted, at its maximum, a considerable stretch of the East African coast—at least from Sofala to Malindi, and perhaps even farther north. In order to distinguish this territory from the present-day island of Zanzibar, in what follows I shall use exclusively the form *Zangibār*.

that it denoted the same territory as that which he had already described under the heading of *Qumr Zangi*. It would appear that the
form *Zangibār* had only recently come into use as a designation
for the east coast of Negro Africa: The earliest extant instance of its
use occurs in Yāqūt's *Muʻjam al-Buldān*, the first draft of which
was drawn up in 1224. Chao Ju-kua's work was published in the
following year. Moreover, these two forms do not exhaust the roster
of names by which the Chinese referred to this territory, for in the
official Sung history it appeared under the rubric *Zängistān* (**Tsəng-
d'ân* 層 檀), a version betraying Persian influence.[36]

In addition to mentioning a few other unnamed localities in East
Africa,[37] Chao Ju-kua also inserted a notice of a territory under the
orthography **Tiung-lji* 中 理 which, as far as I have been able to
ascertain, is *hapax legomenon* in Chinese topographical writing.
Hirth and Rockhill were inclined to treat the element **tiung* in this
name as a transcription of *zang* (see above),[38] but the phonetic
correspondence is far from perfect, and, in any case, Chao Ju-kua
elsewhere transcribed this sound as **tsəng* [*kji*] 層 [期], which is
phonologically more acceptable. Rather than a transcription of
zang, **tiung* would seem more likely to have been an attempt, and a
reasonably successful one at that, to render some Bantu word beginning with a vocable such as *Shung-*. Moreover, the reality behind
the name was presumably a place of some importance in the eyes of
Chao's informants for he was led to accord it more space in his
schedule than he allotted to any other East African territory, as much
in fact as he devoted to Egypt. It is clear, too, that he regarded the
chief settlement of the country as substantially different in form from
that of the walled Muslim cities characteristic of the coast (page 98
below), yet such general information as Chao provides points
unequivocally towards a location near the Horn, as indeed does his
reference to mountains forming the boundary with *Barbarā*. In

---

[36] *Sung Shih*, chüan 490, ff. 20 verso-21 recto. The form *Zängistan* زنكستان
was used as early as 982 by the Persian author of *Hudūd al-ʻAlam*. It may be noted
in passing that there are also notices of African countries in the *Sung Hui-yao*
宋 會 要 ("Collected Statutes of the Sung Dynasty").

[37] One of these was a high mountain on the western border of *Zangibār*, which
inevitably suggests itself as Kilimanjaro.

[38] Hirth and Rockhill, *Chau Ju-kua*, 131–132.

these circumstances it would appear not unreasonable to suggest, with a measure of diffidence appropriate to the inchoate state of early East African history, that *Tiung-lji* may represent an attempt to transcribe the toponym which has come down to us as *Shungwaya* or *Shungaya*, the half-legendary home of the coastal tribes of the Northeastern Bantu.

The consensus of local tradition,[39] Portuguese documents,[40] and early European cartography points to a location for this toponym on the southern Somali coast in the vicinity of Port Durnford Bay (indigenous name = Bur Gao),[41] but the limits of its territorial control at any time are unknown. In one version of the Swahili *Akhbar Pate, Shungwaya* is clearly associated with the ports of the Banādir coast (*Alikanda kupija zita tangu Kiwayu na Tula na Shungwaya na bandari zote—Barawa, Marika, Mukdishu*—"He began to wage war from Kiwayu and Tula and Shungwaya and all the harbors—Brava, Merca, Maqdishū"), but I am by no means certain how much reliance should be placed on this chronicle and, in particular, on this recension.[42] On early European maps the prevalent orthography of the name was *Jungaia*[43] or something similar, but

[39] Summarized in A. H. J. Prins, *The Coastal Tribes of the North-Eastern Bantu* (London, 1952), 8–11, 43–51; and in his "Shungwaya, die Urheimat der Nord-ost Bantu. Eine stammesgeschichtliche Untersuchung," *Anthropos*, L (1955), 273–281.

[40] Justus Strandes, *Die Portugiesenzeit von Deutsch- und Englisch-Ostafrica* (Berlin, 1899). English translation by Jean F. Wallwork, under the title *The Portuguese Period in East Africa*, with notes by J.S. Kirkman, (Nairobi, 1961).

[41] Vinigi L. Grottanelli, "A Lost African Metropolis," in J. Lukas (ed.), *Afrikanistische Studien Diedrich Westermann* (Berlin, 1955), 231 *et seq*; Prins, "Shungwaya."

[42] The several extant recensions of the *Akhbar Pate*, which has been described as "incomparably the richest and most detailed of the Swahili traditional histories" (G.S.P. Freeman-Grenville, *The East African Coast. Select Documents from the First to the Earlier Nineteenth Century* [Oxford, 1962], 241), differ in detail but all appear to derive from a version transmitted by one Bwana Kitini, a member of the Nabhan royal family (see A. H. J. Prins, "On Swahili Historiography," *Journal of the East African Swahili Committee*, 28/2 [1958], 26–40). In the recension published by C.H. Stigand (*The Land of Zinj* [London, 1913]), *Shungwaya* is omitted from the passage in question but other names, such as Kiunga and Kismayu, are included.

[43] E.g., Battista Agnese's *Charta navigatoria seculi XVI* (plate 24), .. *gu.wa*; Bartolomeu Lasso's *L'atlas Portugais* (1590), *Jungaya* and *Jungaia*; Portolan portugais anonyme, probably the work of Pedro de Lemos (c. 1590), *Jungaia*;

Portuguese chroniclers favored *Mosungalo[s]*, a version derived from an original incorporating a pronominal concord. It is worth noting that, if the above identification is correct, both the Chinese and the Portuguese rendered the velar semi-vowel by a dark *l*.

Despite unprecedented advances in cartography, the quantity of new substantive information relating to Africa which found its way into Chinese literature during the Mongol hegemony over China was disappointingly small. Even Wang Ta-yüan 汪 大 淵 whose *Tao-i Chih-lüeh* 島 夷 誌 略, compiled in 1349, contains notices of no less than ninety-nine countries, ports, and noteworthy localities, added little to Chao Ju-kua's descriptions and omitted much that had been known to the earlier author. *Zangibār* appeared under a new transcription **Tsəng-b'uât-lâ* 層 拔 羅[44] and there is mention of a **Kâm-măi-lji* 甘 埋 里, which some have identified, almost certainly erroneously, with Madagascar or the Comoro Islands. Its true location is unknown.

With the Ming dynasty we come to the first authenticated voyages of Chinese missions to the African coast. The desire of the imperial court for exotica, coupled with the need to reestablish the prestige of the empire abroad, induced the Yung-lo Emperor, third of the Ming dynasty, to dispatch a series of naval expeditions to the Indian Ocean. Two of these, in 1417–1419 and 1421–1422 respectively, reached as far as the East African coast. The official reports of these expeditions were subsequently destroyed, and even the *Veritable Records of the Ming Dynasty* 明 實 錄 distorted,[45] but descriptions of four African territories, Maqdishū, Brava, Juba, and Malindi

---

Peter Kaerius's *Africae nova descriptio* (1614), *Iungaya*; several Blaeu maps from the middle of the seventeenth century, *Tungaya* (an obvious mislection).

[44] The surviving text reads **Tseng-iäu-lâ*, but there is every reason to accept the emendation of **iäu* to **b'uât* 拔 first proposed by Fujita Toyohachi 藤 田 豐 八 (*Tao-i chih-lüeh chiao-chu* 島 夷 誌 畧 校 注), and subsequently followed by W.W. Rockhill ("Notes on the Relations and Trade of China with the Eastern Archipelago and the Coast of the Indian Ocean during the Fourteenth Century," *T'oung Pao*, XVI [1915], 622) and several other commentators.

[45] The story is told by Duyvendak, "The True Dates of the Chinese Maritime Expeditions in the Early Fifteenth Century," *T'oung Pao*, XXXIV (1938), 341–412, and in *China's Discovery of Africa*, 27–28. See also Paul Pelliot, "Les grands voyages maritimes chinois au début du XVe siècle," *T'oung Pao*, XXX (1933), 237–452.

have been preserved in the *Ming Shih*, the official history of the Ming dynasty,[46] and, particularly important for our present purpose, in *Hsing-ch'a Sheng-lan* 星 槎 勝 覽, a record of the lands visited by Fei Hsin 費 信, who sailed as a junior officer on some of the voyages. Fei Hsin himself did not venture much beyond the Persian Gulf, certainly not to the African coast, but, unlike his predecessors, he did acquire his information from *Chinese* who had been that far, so that his reports constitute the most detailed accounts of East Africa ever to appear in early Chinese literature. However, the spatial coverage is less than that provided in Sung times, and neither Fei Hsin nor the *Ming Shih* mentions any locality on the African coast south of Malindi or north of Maqdishū.

Environment and Ecology

To judge from extant references, the part of Africa known to the Chinese was limited to the eastern tip of the zone of desert and low-grass savannah which stretches across the continent generally between 15° and 30° North, but which in East Africa extends southward across the Horn and, reaching almost to the equator, gives rise to the most impressive climatic anomaly in the whole of Africa.[47] Several of the Chinese authors mentioned above were impressed by what they knew of these climatic conditions in East Africa. Mostly the information amounted to little more than a vague reference to drought, though Fei Hsin was able to state correctly that rain might not fall at Maqdishū for a period of several years. Beyond the coastal towns, so far as the Chinese were concerned, there stretched an inhospitable, and largely uncultivated, expanse of country characterized by yellowish-red soils. In fact, the barrenness of the

---

[46] *Ming Shih*, chüan 326. See below, page 290.

[47] The causes of this aridity in a latitudinal and continental situation normally subject to tropical humid conditions have not been wholly explained but appear to include the divergence of both monsoons over the continental land mass, the shallow nature of the southwesterly airstream, the predominantly meridional flow of air (except in the transition seasons between monsoons), and a stable stratification of air aloft. The so-called "monsoons" (actually a normal seasonal migration of pressure and wind systems owing little or nothing to differential heating of land and sea) are local terminology for the southward flow of air from April to October and the northward flow from October to March.

soil and sparseness of vegetation in the countries of the Horn was another theme pursued by most Chinese authors. Of Brava, Fei Hsin wrote, it "lacks vegetation and the land is [nothing but] an extensive waste of salt."[48] About the hinterland of Maqdishū he was more specific: "Towards the foot of the mountain [the granite upland stretching from the Shibeli basin to Bur Meldak in the Juba valley] the country is a desert of brown soil and stones."[49] Only in the case of Zangibār was there mention of forested hills rising tier on tier towards the interior, but even here Wang Ta-yüan remarked that "most of the soil [along the coast] was saline, so that arable land was unproductive."[50] Not unnaturally, Tu Huan placed considerable emphasis on the severe aridity that characterized the environs of Meroe and was much impressed with the especially noxious miasmas encountered there. Velgus has related these phenomena to the unhealthy southern wind which medieval Arab authors referred to as the marisiyah wind, that is, the wind from Meroe. "When the marisiyah wind blows for thirty consecutive days," said al-Hamdānī, "the inhabitants of Egypt buy face-cloths and balsam, and are frequently persuaded that they will suffer from plague and a quick death."[51]

In each individual notice the environmental and ecological material is presented piecemeal and unsystematically, often in the form of casual interjections, but, when it is all assembled and collated, it becomes evident that by Ming times the Chinese had some knowledge of four of the five physiographic zones which are distinguished by the Somali in the practical business of getting a living from the soil—and which are, indeed, no less real to academic

---

[48] Hsin-ch'a Sheng-lan (edition of c. 1450), folio 4 verso.

[49] Ibid., folio 5 recto.

[50] Wang Ta-yüan, Tao-i Chih-lüeh (1349), section on *Tseng-iäu-lâ (MSC = Ts'eng-yao-lo, for *Tseng-b'uât-lâ, MSC = Ts'eng-pa-lo). For annotated editions of this work see Appendix, page 288.

[51] Al-Hasan ibn-Ahmad al-Hamdānī died in A.D. 945. Throughout the northern half of the Nile Valley the prevailing winds are northerly throughout the year, but from Meroe southward the northern fringe of the so-called monsoonal circulation of the Sudan manifests itself in a short spell of southerly winds during July and August. These are the marisiyah. Farther to the south, say in the neighborhood of Khartoum, southwesterly winds predominate from June to September.

physiographers: (i) the *ba'ad* or migratory dunes along the coast, (ii) the *arra'ad* or consolidated dunes on their landward side, (iii) the *arra gudad* or red flinty steppe of the interior, and, perhaps, (iv) the *doi*, or relatively fertile pastures between the Juba and the Shibeli Rivers, though this last point might be disputed. The physiographic unit which seems to have been overlooked in the Chinese accounts was the *arra mado*, or alluvial valley floors.

Cultivated crops usually received some mention, however brief, in Chinese descriptions of East Africa. Tuan Ch'eng-shih, for example, noted that the "five grains"[52] were not eaten in *Barbarā*, Wang Ta-yüan remarked that yams replaced grain in *Zangibār*, and Fei Hsin seems to have thought it strange that the inhabitants of Brava should have grown onions and garlic instead of gourds. Domestic animals were noted with a high degree of regularity, and, particularly in relation to those territories on the Horn of Africa, the pastoral elements in the economy were emphasized. However, in the cosmo-magical scheme of universal relationships which underpinned the Chinese theory of government, it was the teratological aspects of zoology which were of supreme importance. Strange or monstrous animals were conceived as beneficent cosmic creations born of the superabundant goodness generated by an harmonious reign, so it is not surprising that the larger game animals of East Africa, some of which were unfamiliar to the Chinese, should have figured fairly prominently in these accounts: elephants, rhinoceroses, the camel-crane (ostrich), *ma-ka* beasts 馬 哈 獸 "which resemble musk-deer,"[53] "a mule with red, black and white stripes wound girdle-like round its body" (zebra), lions, leopards and, above all, the giraffe. This last creature was of particular interest, for its Somali name *gerrin* and its singular appearance both invited its identification with the *ch'i-lin* 麒 麟 (Southern Mandarin *k'i-lin*), an animal of supremely propitious portent which had

---

[52] I.e., all kinds of cereals. The list varied at different times in Chinese history.

[53] A species of antelope: perhaps the oryx (*Oryx beisa*, Rüpp), the commonest of the larger Somali antelopes, or Kirk's dik-dik (*Madoqua Kirkii*, Günth.), commonest in the vicinity of Brava, the territory to which the notice mentioning this animal relates.

unfortunately not manifested itself since early in the Chou dynasty.[54] Duyvendak has reconstructed with grace and skill the manner in which a giraffe, the Ming avatar of the *k'i-lin*, was solicited from Malindi, how it was met at the Feng-t'ien gate of the capital by the Emperor, and how this animal, which set the seal of beneficence and felicity on the reign of the Yung-Lo Emperor, indeed on the Ming dynasty itself, was immortalized in paint and verse as "an endless bliss to the state for a myriad myriad years."[55]

According to Chou Ch'ü-fei and Chao Ju-kua, a territory adjacent to *Qumr Zangi* was the home of another creature from Chinese mythology, the *p'eng* bird 鵬. So large was it that "when it took to the air it momentarily obscured the sun." It was quite capable of swooping down on a camel and swallowing it up, and its quills could be fashioned into water jars.[56] Clearly the *p'eng* has here been identified with the *rukh* of medieval romance which Marco Polo, in writing of *Mogedaxo* (= Maqdishū), declared was capable of lifting an elephant. Tales of gigantic birds such as this were current all around the shores of the Indian Ocean in medieval times and probably represented the last lingering vestiges of an ancient theriomorphic cult.[57] The *p'eng* quills may well have been a fanciful interpretation of water vessels fashioned from large bamboos.[58]

[54] The Ch'i-lin was conceived of as a harmless herbivore with the body of a deer and the tail of an ox. To Ts'ai Yung 蔡 邕 (A.D. 133–192) it was "the noblest form of animal creation, the emblem of the highest good, the incarnate essence of the five elements."

[55] Duyvendak, "The True Dates," and *China's Discovery of Africa*, 32–35.

[56] Cf. the *Chuang Tzŭ* 莊 子: "When this bird rouses itself and flies, its wings are like clouds all round the sky . . . On a whirlwind it mounts upwards as on the whorls of a goat's horn for 90,000 *li*, till, far removed from the vaporous clouds, it bears on its back the blue sky, and then it shapes its course for the south, and proceeds to the ocean there." (Transl. J. Legge, mod., *The Texts of Taoism* [1959], 212–213).

[57] The corruption of Polo's *mogedaxo* (rendered correctly in *Z* MS) into *madaschor, madegastar, magastar et al.*, coupled with the temptation to identify the *rukh* or the *p'eng* with the now extinct *Æpyornis*, which was endemic to Madagascar, has induced some scholars to equate the territory under discussion with that island. However, Polo was certainly not referring to Madagascar (on which matter see Paul Pelliot, *Notes on Marco Polo* [Paris, 1963], II *sub Mogedaxo*, 779–781).

[58] I owe this general idea to Gabriel Ferrand, who, adhering to the Madagascar theory mentioned in Note 57, suggested that the bamboo in question was that

Culture and Society

Generally speaking, the ethnological information preserved in these Chinese accounts of Africa is reasonably accurate, sometimes unexpectedly so. Several notices incorporate a few details about the appearance and general character of the people which, not suprisingly, show neither more nor less psychological insight than those of most colonial administrators of more recent times.

The inhabitants of *Muâ-liĕn*, for example, were "black and fierce," those of Maqdishū "excitable and obstinate."[59] Only for *Zangibār* in the fourteenth century was it claimed that the people exemplified "the probity of ancient times," a phrase which shows Wang Ta-yüan harking back to the era of supposedly uncomplicated collectivism under the Sage Emperors.[60] More usually these tribal peoples of Africa failed to observe the five relationships which were the mortar of Chinese society and thus placed themselves beyond the pale of civilization. In this connection Tu Huan recorded an interesting observation concerning the Mazdeans (*Ziəm-ziəm* 尋 尋) who lived in *Muâ-liĕn* and neighboring regions: 其 尋 尋 蒸 報 於 諸 夷 狄 中 最 甚. In understanding this passage the phrase *cheng-pao* 蒸 報 presents some difficulty as it is to be found neither in *P 'ei-wen Yün-fu* 佩 文 韻 府 nor in modern dictionaries from either East or West. However, Duyvendak has drawn attention to passages in the *Tso Chuan* 左 傳 in which each of the characters is used singly to imply the commission of incest with some person of an older

---

known in Malagasy as *langana*, a variety much used for water vessels by the coastal peoples of Madagascar. Although the identification of the territory with Madagascar cannot be accepted, the idea of bamboo stems suggesting giant feathers is sound. Earlier Sir Henry Yule had proposed that it was the raffia palm which had given rise to the fantasy: *The Book of Ser Marco Polo the Venetian Concerning the Kingdoms and Marvels of the East* (London, 1903, 3rd ed.), II, 415–421, 596–598.

[59] For the blacks of *Muâ-liĕn* see *Hsin T'ang-Shu* (Chin-ling edition), 221B, folio 13 recto; for the people of Maqdishū see Fei Hsin, *Hsin-ch'a Sheng-lan*, folio 5 verso.

[60] See, Wang Ta-yüan, *Tao-i chih-lüeh*, section on *Tseng-iäu-lâ*; cf. the *Chuang Tzŭ*, X, 3, where conditions such as these are attributed to the reign of Shen-nung 神 農. A closely similar passage in *Tao Te Ching* 道 德 經 is ascribed vaguely to a golden age of unspecified date.

generation.[61] Moreover, in the *Pei Shih* 北 史 ("History of the Northern Dynasties," A.D. 386–581)[62] there is a notice relating to a tribe of the Tibetan borderlands, the *D'âng-ts'iang* 宕 昌, who are recorded as marrying their aunts, sisters-in-law, and other female relations, but who, in a parallel passage in the *T'ai-p'ing Huan Yü Chi*,[63] are described simply as "having incestuous customs" 俗 有 蒸 報. Clearly Tu Huan's sentence can only be understood as, "The Mazdeans are more given to incest than are any other foreigners," a remark which echoes the notoriety accorded the Magi throughout antiquity because they held incestuous marriages to be exceptionally meritorious.[64] In the revised T'ang history the passage in question is abbreviated to such an extent that it is rendered even more ambiguous and is, moreover, made to apply to all the inhabitants of *Muâ-liĕn* instead of to the Mazdeans alone: 不 恥 蒸 報 於 夷 狄 最 甚. The extended version of Tu Huan to which Velgus has drawn our attention also indicates the manner in which the ensuing phrases in the T'ang history should be punctuated (there is, of course, no punctuation at all in a medieval Chinese text) and renders nugatory a great deal of previous speculation about the implications of the term *cheng-pao*.[65] It may be remarked parenthetically that the whole passage is cast in a consciously archaized idiom, even to the use of the stylized phrase 於 夷 狄 最 甚, "They are [in this respect] the worst of the barbarians."[66]

[61] Duyvendak, *China's Discovery of Africa*, 15, note 4. Cf. *Tso Chuan*, Duke Huan, xvi: 衞 宣 公 烝 於 夷 姜 "Duke Hsüan of Wei had committed incest with [his father's concubine] I-Chiang;" and Duke Hsüan, iii: 文 公 報 鄭 子 之 妃 "Duke Wen committed incest with the concubine of [his uncle] Tzǔ."

[62] *Pei Shih*, chüan 96, folio 9 recto. This history was compiled by Li Yen-shou 李 延 壽 in about A.D. 670.

[63] *T'ai-p'ing Huan Yü Chi*, chüan 188, folio 11 recto.

[64] Cf., *inter alia*, E.W. West, *Pahlavi Texts*, II, in F. Max Müller (ed.), *Sacred Books of the East* (Oxford, 1882), XVIII, 428; W. Geiger, *Grundriss der iranischen Philologie II*, (Strasburg, 1904), 682; R.C. Zaehner, *The Dawn and Twilight of Zoroastrianism* (1961), 162 and 165.

[65] Cf., for example, Duyvendak's rendering of 號 曰 尋 其 君 臣 ...as "They call this: to seek out the proper master and subject," which, it can now be seen, should read, "It [their religion] is called *Ziəm*. Ruler and subject . . ."

[66] Cf., for example, the *Chiu T'ang-Shu*, chüan 198, folio 1 verso: 諸 夷 中 最 爲 甚. Earlier in the same notice *cheng-hsieh* 烝 褻 is used in the same manner and with the same implications as the *cheng-pao* we have been discussing.

Velgus has also directed attention to an account of the marriage customs of *Barbarā* which is incorporated in the Sung encyclopedia *Shih-lin Kuang-chi* 事 林 廣 記, compiled by Ch'en Yüan-ching 陳 元 靚 late in the twelfth or early in the thirteenth century.[67] This passage is of particular interest as some of the details were not noticed in either European or Arabo-Persian sources of the time:

> When a marriage is to be arranged the bride's family announces the agreement by cutting off the tail of a cow in calf as [a gesture of] good faith. The period of the betrothal starts from the day when the tail is cut, and the marriage can be consummated only after the cow has calved. The groom's family must respond to the cutting of the cow's tail as a pledge of the date [of betrothal] by bringing a severed "human tail" to the house of the bride. The "human tail" which serves as a betrothal gift is the male organ. When it arrives the bride's family, rejoicing, welcomes it with music and parades through the streets for seven days, after which the groom enters the bride's house, is married to her and they become one family. Each marriage [consequently] deprives a man of his life. Such is the custom of mutual rivalry among families wishing to display the fortitude and courage of their sons-in-law, without which no girl's family would ever consent to her marriage.

I have not come across any custom comparable to this among the Somali, although the Afar formerly required a young man to demonstrate his eligibility for marriage by slaying an enemy in combat.

The dress of the people of East Africa was described reasonably accurately by Chinese authors, whether it was the Arab *thawb*, the Somali *maro*, or even, as in the case of *Barbarā*, the virtual absence of clothing other than a loincloth. Naturally the veils of Muslim women were a subject of comment, as were the "gold" (? brass) earrings of the housewives of Brava and Maqdishū. A distinction was often made between the dress of the common people and that of the élite. In the capital of **Tiung-lji*, for example, the former "wrapped cloths around themselves" (presumably something similar to the *maro*), but courtiers and ministers "wore jackets and turbans on their heads as marks of distinction."[68] In *Zangibār* the poor wrapped themselves in drab-colored cottons, whereas the wealthier wore both brocades and white cottons, set off with colored

---

[67] Velgus, *Africana*, XC (1966), 99. A somewhat abridged version of this account is also included in the *I-wu Chih* 異 物 志 of the fourteenth century.

[68] Chao Ju-kua, *Chu-fan-chih*, (Edition of Feng Ch'eng-chün 馮 承 鈞, Shanghai, 1938), I, 59.

turbans. Chinese authors also tended to pay considerable attention to African hair styles, particularly those of the females, which contrasted strongly with the dressed hair of Chinese women, but it is difficult to correlate their descriptions with particular ethnic groups of the present day. For example, in Brava and Juba both sexes allegedly wore their hair in rolls, but a little farther along the coast, in Maqdishū, this style was restricted to men; women adopted a sort of chignon, at the same time smearing a glistening yellow varnish on the crowns of their heads.

The information about East African settlement patterns preserved by Chinese authors is deficient in both quantity and quality. They distinguished clearly enough between the port cities and the villages or nomadic encampments of the interior and added a few scraps of information about the towns, but descriptions specifically of rural settlements were entirely lacking. In *Barbarā*, for example, there were four important towns (Chao Ju-kua and Ch'en Yüan-ching compare them to Chinese departmental [*chou* 州] cities), and the rest of the population was grouped in feuding villages scattered through the countryside. It is uncertain to which towns Chao was referring. If *Barbarā* included all the coast from Zeila to the neighborhood of Maqdishū the four towns may have been Zeila, *Barbarā* itself (described by Ibn Battūta as the regional capital), Maqdishū, and possibly Brava, though this last name is not mentioned in strictly contemporary Arab records. On the other hand, if *Barbarā* denoted only the southern coast of the Gulf of 'Āden, the four towns presumably included Zeila and *Barbarā*, and perhaps *Mait*, *Juwa*, or some of the other small ports mentioned by early Arab authors. In this connection it may be significant that Leardo's map of 1448 depicted four towns on this stretch of coast, but it is unfortunate that their names are indecipherable. Juba, Brava, and Maqdishū, with their walls of piled rock and their multistoried houses of cut stone, were, in Ming times at any rate, settlements that accorded well with the Chinese conception of urbanism. *Tiung-lji*, by contrast, seems to have been of a rather different character, with a palace of bricks and ashlars serving as a focus for a settlement of palm fronds and thatch.

Chinese authors usually made a few remarks about the economic

basis of East African societies, but they were presented, not unexpectedly perhaps, in an unsystematic fashion and comprised little
more than a series of comments on those aspects which differed most
strongly from the labor-intensive, arable economy of China. However,
the contrast between the cosmopolitan societies in the ports of the
Horn and the seminomadic life of the interior comes through
strongly, supplemented by incidental references to the seasonal
hunting of game animals with medicated arrows and nets in *Barbarā*
and *Zangibār* respectively, the production of salt in coastal pans,
and fishing—an activity of great importance along the whole length
of the coast. In Brava and Juba it would appear to have been the
staple activity, but it was of almost equal importance in Maqdishū,
where the dried catch was fed to stock, specified particularly as
camels, horses, cattle, and sheep. In the inland kingdom of *Muâ-
liĕn*, according to Tu Huan, horses were also fed fish.

Occasionally a fragment of information can be confirmed by
reference to present-day conditions. In *Tiung-lji*, for example, we
read:

> Every year migrating birds alight in the open country in countless
> numbers. At sunrise they suddenly disappear, leaving no trace. The
> local folk trap them in nets and eat them, for they are of excellent
> taste. They are available until the end of spring but depart with the
> onset of summer, only to reappear in the following year.[69]

The bird referred to can hardly have been other than the harlequin
quail, *Coturnix delegorguei Delagorgue*, Vog.,[70] whose true home is
in equatorial Africa but which migrates northward to Somalia when
the *gu* rains of May bring an abundance of insect life to the plains.
Today these birds are still trapped in thousands in many parts of
Africa by means of decoys which call them up through snared runs.

[69] *Chu-fan-chih*, Li Tiao-yüan's edition, part I, 26b.
[70] See C.W.M. Praed and C.H.B. Grant, *African Handbook of Birds: Eastern
and North-Eastern Africa* (London, 1952) I, Plate 20, for a picture of this bird,
and 266 for a map of its distribution. Cf. Geoffrey Archer and E.M. Godman,
The Birds of British Somaliland and the Gulf of Aden, (London, 1937) II, lxxii:
"Both inland and along the shore of the Gulf of Aden the middle of April
constitutes the peak period of the northerly migration, and the passage is much
more marked and noticeable then than on the southerly migration in September
and October."

A marine animal of considerable importance in the economy of the East African littoral was the whale. Chao Ju-kua had heard it reported that huge "fish," up to 200 *ch'ih*[71] in length, were stranded each year on the coast of *Tiung-lji*, and that the local folk cut out the marrow, brains, and eyes to get oil, a single animal sometimes yielding more than 300 jars[72]. There is some confusion in this passage which, in any case, Chao obtained at secondhand. It is doubtful, for example, if the eyes were extracted for the sake of their oil, though there are records of whale eyes being offered as tribute to the Chinese court on several occasions.[73] The "marrow" of the text was, I suspect, a mistaken notion of the nature of spermaceti, a waxy white substance found in a cavity in the head of the cachalot (*Physeter macrocephalus*). According to Chao, oil (*yu* 油) from the whales—presumably that occurring in association with the spermaceti—was used in lamps and, mixed with lime, as a caulk for boats. It has been suggested that, in the light of contemporary practice, it was likely that the oil used in caulking was shark rather than whale oil. This is a matter for the experts to decide, but the text clearly states that the oil came from huge stranded "fish" which can only have been whales, and the use of whale oil for caulking was described as a common practice around the western shores of the Indian Ocean by Idrīsī in the twelfth century, and was also mentioned by Qazwīnī in the thirteenth century—this time in connection with the people of Basrah.[74] In any case there is no reason to doubt Chao's further statement that the poorer folk employed whale ribs as rafters,

[71] The *ch'ih* 尺 or Chinese foot varied in length at different places and times but was finally standardized at 14.1 inches or 0.3581 meters. Although the precise value of the *ch'ih* in Sung times is difficult to determine, no great error can be involved if the standardized figure of the present day is used in calculating the size of the whales. Clearly Chao Ju-kua intended to convey the impression of a creature of huge size and it is of no great significance if he preserved the exaggerations of his informants.

[72] For a justification of the translation of *teng* 㽘 as "jar," see Pelliot, *Notes*, II, *sub* Capdoille, 160.

[73] Cf. Berthold Laufer, "Arabic and Chinese Trade in Walrus and Narwhal Ivory," *T'oung Pao*, XIV (1913), 342.

[74] Al-Qazwīnī, '*Ajā'ib al-Makhlūqāt wa-Gharā'ib al-Mawjūdāt*. French translation by J. T. Reinaud, *Relations des voyages faits par les Arabes et les Persans dans l'Inde et à la Chine dans le IXe siècle de l'ère chrétienne* (Paris, 1845), I, 145–146.

backbones as door-leaves, and the vertebrae as mortars. He was also explicit that no part of the creature was eaten, which is rather surprising since in more recent times whale flesh has been a much prized supplement to the local diet. Incidentally, the whale was accounted a fish so that it was not necessary to slaughter it ritually.

Among other scraps of information relating to diet one item is of especial significance. Tuan Ch'eng-shih, with his enquiring, unprejudiced mind and passion for the unusual, preserved a snippet of information about *Barbarā* which was, unfortunately, abridged to the point of incomprehensibility in the *T'ang Shu*.[75] He had learnt from his informants that agriculture was unimportant on the *Barbarā* coast and that "the five grains were not eaten," but he then went on to describe how the inhabitants depended on a diet of meat and milk, supplemented with, significantly, blood freshly drawn by inserting a needle into the veins of cattle. The Ishaak tribal-family and the Mijertein sub-confederacy, who today inhabit the coastal tracts of the Horn from the vicinity of Dagarita to the neighborhood of Iagakalaka, that is, including the territory of the ancient *Bilād al-Barbarā*, do not drink fresh blood, and there is no reason to suppose that they were partial to it in the past. In fact, among the Somali, only the Sab and a few among the trans-Juban Darod and Dir tribes adhere to this practice.[76] Both the Darod and Dir at one time occupied habitats in the northern tracts of the Horn, and the Darod family of tribes, in particular, trace their descent from an Arabian culture hero whose tomb in the Hadaftimo range is still a place of pilgrimage.[77] It might be thought, therefore, that the blood-drinking tribes of the *Bilād al-Barbarā* referred to by Tuan Ch'eng-shih were members of the Darod or Dir tribes who at that time were inhabiting more northerly territories. However, none of the representatives of these tribal families who still live in the north now drink blood, and there is no evidence that they did so in the past. In fact it is usually believed that the trans-Juban Darod tribes acquired this practice, together with certain other culture traits,

---

[75] *Hsin T'ang-Shu*, chüan 221B, f. 13 verso.
[76] Ioan Myrddin Lewis, *Peoples of the Horn of Africa* (London, 1955), 20, 67.
[77] *Ibid.*, 18–19.

from the Galla during their migrations southward in the eighteenth and nineteenth centuries.

In a search for likely exemplars of Tuan's blood-drinkers, it might be more profitable to discard the Somali in favor of some other ethnic group who are more closely identified with this rather distinctive practice. Among the Galla the drinking of fresh blood, although by no means universal, is not uncommon[78], and it is possible that this circumstance may have some bearing on the ethnological history of this part of the world. According to I. M. Lewis's reconstruction of events,[79] which has become in effect the orthodox interpretation, the Galla migrated to the Horn from southeastern Ethiopia in the ninth or tenth century A.D. and were subsequently displaced by the Somali. Recently Herbert S. Lewis has reinterpreted the available evidence in an attempt to show that both the Somali and the Galla entered the Horn from the southwest, that the Somali expansion preceded that of the Galla, and that the Galla have never occupied more of Somaliland than they do at present.[80] If it is to be inferred from Tuan Ch'eng-shih's remarks that the drawers of blood were more likely to have been Galla than Somali, it would seem that the Chinese evidence tends to support I.M. Lewis's interpretation, as it allows Galla occupation of at least part of the *Barbarā* coast during T'ang times. As Tuan Ch'eng-shih was writing just after the middle of the ninth century, it may be prudent to antedate the Galla migration by a few years—to, say, the seventh or eighth century A.D.

Religious beliefs and customs are almost invariably inadequately recorded by casual travelers, who, of necessity, discern only the surficial forms and none of the inner dynamism. The reports of foreign religions incorporated in Chinese literature are no exception. However, the predominance of Islām on the East African coast is

[78] Cf. George Peter Murdock, *Africa, its Peoples and their Culture History* (New York, 1959), chap. 42. The practice is described in detail by Eike Haberland, *Die Galla Süd-Äthiopiens* (Stuttgart, 1963), 87, 429 and Tafel 16.

[79] Lewis, *Peoples of the Horn*, 45–48.

[80] Herbert S. Lewis, "Historical Problems in Ethiopia and the Horn of Africa," *Annals of the New York Academy of Sciences*, XCVI (1962), 504–511; Lewis, *A Galla Monarchy: Jimma Abba Jifar, Ethiopia 1830–1932* (Madison, 1965), 23–26.

clearly apparent, perhaps because a high proportion of the intermediaries in the commerce of ideas between Africa and China were
themselves Muslims. Chao Ju-kua had undoubtedly obtained his
information from such people, so that he was able to state unequivocally that the inhabitants of *Zangibār* "followed the *Tāzi* (i.e.
Arab[81]) religion." In his notice of *Barbarā* he varied the formula
to read, "They worship *T'ien* [presumably here = Allāh], not the
Buddha." The amount of information on this topic relating to
Muâ-liĕn is more detailed than is customary for such a distant
region. Tu Huan was able to distinguish devotees of Islām (the
Tāzī religion 大食法), of Eastern Christianity (the *T'âi-dz'iĕn* 大秦法
[= Byzantine, specifically Monophysite] religion), and of Mazdaism
(the *Ziəm-ziəm* 尋 尋 religion), and to add a few remarks about
their customs. The prevalence of *cheng-pao* among the Mazdeans
has already been touched upon, and Tu Huan makes it clear that the
commands and prohibitions of Islām were observed only laxly. It is
true that the *Muâ-liĕn* Muslims refrained from eating pork or the
flesh of dog, donkey, or horse, but they did drink wine, particularly
on the day of solemnized community prayer.[82] Velgus has pointed
out that this is less surprising than it might at first appear, for,
apart from the ascetic 'Umar II (717–720), the Umayyad caliphs
were not inclined to doctrinal rigor, and enforcement of the
Qur'ānic prohibition against the drinking of wine came into effect
only with the accession of the 'Abbāsid dynasty in the middle of the
eighth century. Even then the prohibition was observed more
stringently in the eastern provinces of the empire than in the western.
In these circumstances it is not altogether surprising that the
Muslims of *Muâ-liĕn* were reported to be winebibbers, even if only
on one day each week. The Christians were, according to Tu Huan,
best known for their medical skills, notably the treatment of eye
and bowel ailments and brain surgery.

In view of the persistent legends of a Shīrāzī colonization of the

---

[81] *T'âi-dz'iək* < Persian *Tâzi* < Pahl. *Tāčīk* < Arabian tribal name *Tayyi'*.
See, Pelliot, *Notes*, I, 44–45.

[82] Tu Huan speaks of a weekly day of leisure 其 俗 每 七 日 一 假 and the
Hsin T'ang-Shu of a weekly day of rest 七 日 一 休 but the relevant Qur'ānic
injunction stipulates only that business be suspended during the noon service
itself (*Qur'ān* LXII, 9–10).

East African coast, it may be worthwhile to mention two indications of Persian influence which have been preserved in Chinese literature.[83] We owe the most important, and indeed the most explicit, reference to Tuan Ch'eng-shih, who recorded the manner in which Persian (*Puâ-sie 波 斯) merchants conducted their trade in Barbarā:

> When Persian merchants wish to go into this country [Barbarā], they gather about them several thousand men, to whom they present strips of cloth. All, whether old or young, draw blood and swear an oath, and only then does trading begin.[84]

The second reference, from the Sung Shih, chüan 490, f. 20 verso, states that the ruler of *Tsəng-d'ân (= Zängistān) had adopted the title of A-mei-lo A-mei-lan 亞 美 羅 亞 眉 蘭, which Hirth and Rockhill have recognized as a transcription of the Persian style Amir-i amiran.[85] For what it is worth the Sung history also provided the dynasty to which this ruler of Zängistān belonged with a genealogy extending over five hundred years.

Trade

In view of the fact that several of the Chinese authors on whom we depend were themselves concerned to a greater or lesser extent with trade, and as a preponderance of their informants were probably engaged in that activity, it is not surprising that commercial matters should figure prominently in Chinese notices of East Africa. By T'ang times (A.D. 618–906) Chinese maritime trade with the countries of the Indian Ocean was considerable, and, although there is no evidence of direct commerce between the two culture realms at this time, a few African products were already in demand in China. Notable among them was ambergris. After Pelliot's excursus on this topic[86] and Yamada's thorough analysis of early texts relating to

---

[83] See, inter alia, Arthur E. Robinson, "The Shirazi Colonisations of East Africa," Tanganyika Notes and Records, 3 (1937); 7 (1939), 40–81; E.C. Baker, "Some Notes on the Shirazi," ibid., II (1941), 1–10; G.S.P. Freeman-Grenville, The Medieval History of the Coast of Tanganyika (London, 1962), passim; Neville Chittick, "The 'Shirazi' Colonization of East Africa," Journal of African History, VI (1965), 275–294.

[84] Transl. Duyvendak, mod., China's Discovery of Africa, 13–14.

[85] Chau Ju-kua, 127.

[86] Pelliot, Notes, I, 32–38.

it,[87] there is no need for me to do more than point out that the East African coast was known to the Chinese as a prolific source of ambergris. Tuan Ch'eng-shih mentioned it under its Arabic name of 'anbar عنبر which may possibly have had a Somali etymology.[88] This substance was introduced into China by Arab or Persian traders toward the end of the T'ang dynasty, and Tuan's reference to it must be one of the earliest in Chinese literature. By Sung times Chao Ju-kua had acquired some reasonably accurate notions of its source regions but still did not connect it with the whale, about which he was comparatively well informed (see page 100 above). Lumps of from three to ten *chin* 斤[89] in weight, he said, were either driven on shore by the wind or run across at sea. As to the origin of these lumps Chao was ambivalent. After announcing unequivocally in his notice of *Tiung-lji* that "it is not known whence ambergris comes," in the systematic section of his handbook he reverted to the popular belief in China, expounded by Chou Ch'ü-fei among others, that it was solidified dragon spittle. Dragon spittle (*lung hsien* 龍涎[90]) was, in fact, the name by which it was known from at least the tenth century onwards. Moreover, whereas Chou Ch'ü-fei had known only of the trade from Murbāt, which was merely the South Arabian staple for this substance, Chao Ju-kua had been able to trace its origins one stage farther back to the bazaars of *Zangibār* and the *Barbarā* coast. In the Muslim world ambergris was used, in addition to its role in the preparation of incense, in cosmetics and as a culinary spice, but in China it appears to have been employed only as an excipient for other perfumes. Lines from a poem by

[87] Yamada Kentaro, "A Short History of Ambergris by the Arabs and Chinese in the Indian Ocean," *Report of the Institute of World Economics, the Kinki University*, VIII (1955), 1–26; XI (1956) 1–32. See also Edward H. Schafer, *The Golden Peaches of Samarkand* (Berkeley, 1963), 174–175; Wheatley, "*Geographical Notes*," 125–130.

[88] Cf. Leo Reinisch, *Südarabische Expedition, II, Die Somali-Sprache* (Wien, 1902), II, 59. Tuan Ch'eng-shih transcribed the word as *·â-muât* 阿末.

[89] Like most Chinese measures the *chin* varied from time to time and place to place but is usually taken to have represented a mean weight of about 1⅓ lb. It was standardized for customs purposes at 21⅓ oz. avoirdupois by the Sino-British Treaty of 1858.

[90] *Lung-hsien* is the customary pronunciation but *lung-yen* is also possible and is, in fact, the vocalization on which is based the Sino-Japanese *ryūyen*.

Chu Tzŭ-tsʻai 朱 子 才, however, suggest that during the Sung period the Chinese adopted the Arab custom of scenting lamp oil with ambergris: "At night the gilded lamps, fed with ambergris, shine like pearls. . ." At all times this commodity commanded high prices in China, being of approximately the same value as gold.[91]

The other product of *Barbarā* mentioned by Tuan Chʻeng-shih was ivory, but he offered no further comment, and we have to wait until Sung times for details of the African trade. The primary sources of ivory available to the Chinese in Sung times were South and Southeast Asia, both lying within the natural range of the Indian elephant, but there were also supplementary supplies to be obtained through Arab intermediaries from the coasts of *Zangibār* and *Barbarā*, where the African elephant was laid under tribute. It is symbolic of the Arabo-Persian monopoly of trade in the Arabian and Azanian Seas that the ivory staple seems not to have been on the African continent at all, but at Murbāt on the Hadramaut coast. According to Chao Ju-kua, African ivory, with its delicate streaking on a white ground, was considered superior to that from any part of Asia. Schafer has summarized the uses to which ivory was put in China.[92]

Another commodity which was fed into the trade of the Indian Ocean from the *Barbarā* coast was rhinoceros horn, possibly the single most valuable item in the Chinese pharmacopoeia, a veritable apotropaion of apotropaia, which could also afford raw material for the jeweler.[93] The Chinese could, of course, obtain horns from their own southern provinces and from South and Southeast Asia, but the market was so elastic that from time to time Arab merchants found it worth their while to bring to China the horn of the African rhinoceros.

---

[91] Cf. Wheatley, "Geographical Notes," 127. The value of ambergris in Coastal society is sufficiently attested by the well-known tale of Bakiumbe and the conquest of Manda which is told in the *Akhbar Pate*: It was a fit gift for a sultan.

[92] Schafer, *The Golden Peaches*, 239–241.

[93] See R. Soame Jenyns, "The Chinese Rhinoceros and Chinese Carvings in Rhinoceros Horn," *Transactions of the Oriental Ceramic Society, 1954–1955* (1957), 31–62.

Among the drugs and aromatics which the Chinese knew to come from the Horn of Africa, the most important were frankincense and myrrh. Chao Ju-kua realized that the former, the so-called "nipple incense" 乳 香, was a gum-resin produced by several members of the genus *Boswellia*, all of which are endemic to South Arabia and Somaliland. It is interesting to observe that although Chao had a fair idea of the method of extraction of the gum, knew that it was transported from the Somali coast to the staples at Murbāt, Shihr, and Zafār on the Hadramaut coast, whence it was shipped to the Malay kingdom of *Sri Vijaya*, and was able to describe no less than thirteen commercial grades of frankincense,[94] he was in error in supposing that it was carried to the coast on elephants. Slips such as this serve to remind us that his knowledge of Arabia and Africa was at best secondhand.

Other products of East Africa recorded during Sung and later times include sweet oil of storax[95] and tortoise-shell from *Barbarā*, dragon's blood (in this instance the resins of *Dracaena schizantha* and *D. cinnabari*[96]) and aloes[97] from the borders of **Tiung-lji*. A type of plant yielding aloes which was exported from Zafār was described by Chao Ju-kua as resembling the tail of a king crab in appearance. This is, in fact, a reasonable description of *Aloe Perryi*, a plant endemic to Soqotrā, whence the merchants of Zafār must have acquired it.

The subtle scents and flavors of the *hsiang yao* 香 藥 were easily susceptible to confusion, and errors of identification and provenance abound in the Chinese accounts. The so-called sandalwood *t'an hsiang* 檀 香 attributed by Chao Ju-kua and Wang Ta-yüan to *Zangibār*, for example, could not have been a product of the true sandalwood tree, *Santalum album*, Linn., which is confined to South Asia and parts of Australia. Most probably it was derived from *Pterocarpus santalinus*, Linn. or from some allied species. Neither

[94] Cf. Wheatley, "Geographical Notes," 47–49.

[95] *Su-ho hsiang-yu* 蘇 合 香 油.

[96] *Hsüeh chieh* 血 碣. Not to be confused with the red kinos from species of tropical Asian *Daemonorhops* which also found their way to China under the label of dragon's blood. Cf. Edward H. Schafer, "Rosewood, Dragon's Blood, and Lac," *Journal of the American Oriental Society*, LXXVII (1957), 129–136.

[97] *Lu-hui* 蘆 薈, the expressed juice of a genus of plants of the family *Liliaceae*.

could true puchuk have been obtained in *Barbarā* as Chao Ju-kua might lead us to believe, for it is the root of the Himālayan herb *Saussurea lappa*, C.B. Clarke. In fact Chao's term *mu-hsiang* 木 香 (wood aromatic) had no botanical value, being merely a commercial label covering widely differing commodities.[98] All we can say is that Chao was attempting to describe short, sun-dried pieces of root from Arabia and Somaliland, of which those shaped like chicken bones were the most highly prized.

The commodities exported from East Africa, at least as far as the Chinese sources reflect the true course of events, seem to have remained more or less constant during precolonial times, but commercial information seems to have been recorded in more systematic fashion in the later centuries. In the fourteenth and fifteenth centuries, for example, Wang Ta-yüan and Fei Hsin itemized the Chinese trade goods that were acceptable in the several realms of East Africa. Rice was likely to be a profitable cargo all along the Somali and *Zangibār* coasts, but especially along the latter. As Wang Ta-yüan remarked, "If any ship trading there carry a cargo of rice, it makes a very large profit."[99] Textiles, particularly colored satins and taffetas, were also easily disposed of both along the coast of the Horn and farther south, silks were taken to Juba, sandalwood to Maqdishū, pepper to Juba, and ivory boxes to *Zangibār*. But the incompleteness of the Chinese accounts, even when brought together and correlated, is well demonstrated by the fact that Chinese porcelain, which is attested in quantity on numerous archaeological sites in East Africa, is recorded as a trade commodity only for *Zangibār*.[100] Nevertheless, in that one reference Chao Ju-kua does state explicitly what would otherwise have to be inferred,

[98] Cf. Berthold Laufer, *Sino-Iranica: Chinese Contributions to the History of Civilization in Ancient Iran* (Chicago, 1919), 462–463; Wheatley, "Geographical Notes," 62.

[99] Wang Ta-yüan, *Tao-i Chih-lüeh*, section on **Tseng-iäu-lâ*.

[100] The porcelain exported from China was seldom of high quality, its chief characteristic being the ability to withstand transport in the hold of a junk where "the smaller pieces were packed in the larger until there was hardly a crevice left" (quotation from Chu Yu's 朱 彧 *P'ing-chou K'o-t'an* 萍 洲 可 談, written c. A.D. 1119). Nevertheless, much of it was of a quality at least comparable to that known as "people's ware" and some of it occasionally not greatly inferior to Mandarin ware.

namely that, "Every year Gujerat and *Tāzi* [Arab] coastal localities dispatch vessels to *Zangibār* carrying white cotton cloth, porcelain, copper, and red cotton for purposes of trade."

The trade in slaves deserves special mention. As early as the ninth century Tuan Ch'eng-shih recorded that the inhabitants of the *Bilād al-Barbarā* were in the habit of selling their own womenfolk to foreign traders. Possibly this human merchandise consisted of members of either outcast groups or relict societies of pre-Hamitic Bushmanoid hunters. Just over three centuries later Chou Ch'ü-fei (followed in due course by Chao Ju-kua)[101] told how "savages with lacquer-black bodies" from *Qumr Zangi* "were enticed by [offers of] food and then captured," which would seem to be a version of incidents mentioned in Idrīsī's description of the *Zangibār* coast, where Arabs of 'Umān were reputed to abduct children into slavery, first enticing them by the offer of dates.[102] A possible interpretation of a legend on a Chinese map of Africa of c. A.D. 1315 (page 110 below) as "Island slaves" may carry this tradition into the fourteenth century. Finally, there is the question—which cannot be debated here—as to whether the "devil-slaves" (*kuei nu* 鬼 奴) in the possession of wealthy families in Sung China included among their number African Negroes or were Negroid folk from Papua or Melanesia.[103] In my opinion, some among them may well have been African Negroes who had survived the barracoons of the Hadramaut, only to be shipped along the great Arab trade routes to the Far East. In any case, it is certain that the Chinese of the Sung period were aware that East Africa functioned as a reservoir of human merchandise.

[101] Chou Ch'ü-fei, *Ling-wai Tai-ta*, III, folio 6 recto; Chao Ju-kua, *Chu-fan-chih*, I, 57.

[102] Al-Idrīsī, *Kitāb nuzhat al-mushtāq* (1154), I, 58. Substantially the same story is also related in the Persian author Marvazī's *Tabā'i 'al-hayawān* of c. 1120 (accessible in English translation in V. Minorsky, *Sharaf al-Zamān Tāhir Marvazī on China, the Turks and India* [London, 1942]).

[103] See, *inter alia*, Chang Hsing-lang, "T'ang-shih Fei-chou hei-nu shu Chung-kuo k'ao," *Fu-jen Hsüeh-chih*, I (1929), 93–112; *Chung-hsi chiao-t'ung shih-liao hui-p'ien*, III (Pei-p'ing, 1930), 48–81; "The Importation of Negro Slaves to China under the T'ang Dynasty," *Bulletin of the Catholic University of Peking*, VII (1930), 37–59; Duyvendak, *China's Discovery of Africa*, 23–24; Schafer, *The Golden Peaches*, 46, 290, note 48.

Africa in Early Chinese Cartography

It is astonishing that the earliest extant Chinese map to depict Africa, the *Yü T'u* 輿 圖 prepared by Chu Ssŭ-pen 朱 思 本 early in the fourteenth century, already showed in unambiguous outline the southward orientation and triangular shape of Africa.[104] This was in strong contrast to contemporary European cartography, which was still influenced by the Ptolemaic notion of a southern continent linking Africa to eastern Asia, but, working beyond the constraints of the Ptolemaic tradition, the Chinese cartographer was under no compulsion to distend southern Africa in an easterly direction. A large river flowing northward through the length of the continent was presumably meant to represent the Nile, and an extensive body of water in the interior was probably inspired by reports of the African lakes (Fig. 1). In the matter of place-names, Chu Ssŭ-pen was not well informed. *Zangibār* (under the orthography *Sang-ku-pa* 桑 骨 八), the only toponym which can be identified with certainty, was relegated to a position on the west coast. Off the east coast was an island labelled *Ti-pa nu* 娣 八 奴. It is possible that the first two characters transcribe the Arabic *dib* دِيب (< Pāli *dipa* < Skt. *dvipa*), in which case the legend could be read as "Island slaves." The handful of other names on the African sector of the map have not been deciphered.

The *Yü T'u* existed only in manuscript for over two centuries, but was revised and enlarged by Lo Hung = hsien 羅 洪 先 in 1541, and printed in 1555 under the title *Kuang Yü T'u* 廣 輿 圖. Meanwhile, in 1402 two maps incorporating much the same information (though

[104] This map is the subject of a monograph by Walter Fuchs, *The Mongol Atlas of China by Chu Ssŭ-pen and the "Kuang-Yü-T'u"* (Pei-p'ing, 1946). Africa is depicted on plate 44, and the commentary is on 14. Fuchs has both corrected Wang Yung's 王 庸 assertion (*Chung-kuo ti-li-hsüeh shih* 中 國 地 理 學 史 [1938], 91) that the African section of the map was introduced only in Ch'ien Tai's 錢 岱 edition of 1579, and established that the outline of the continent was pointed towards the south even in Chu Ssŭ-pen's original edition, prepared between 1311 and 1320 (personal communication to Joseph Needham, reported in his *Science and Civilisation in China* (Cambridge, 1959), III, 552. The biography of Chu Ssŭ-pen has been written by Naito Torajiro, *Geibun*, XI (1920). Cf. W. Fuchs, "Was South Africa Already Known in the 13th Century?" *Imago Mundi*, X (1953), 50–51.

belonging to a different technical tradition) which had been compiled previously by Li Tse-min 李澤民 (fl. 1330) and Ch'ing Chün 清濬 (1328–1392) respectively, were combined into a single map by Li Hui 李薈 and Ch'üan Chin 權近, both working in Korea. A copy of this map, entitled *Map of the territories of the one world and the capitals of the countries in successive ages*[105] and dating from c. 1500, has been described by Ogawa Takuji and Aoyama Sadao.[106] I have seen neither this map itself nor a reproduction of it, but Needham reports that there are about thirty-five largely unidentified place-names on the south-pointing triangular continent of Africa.[107]

The second cartographic tradition that concerns us here is connected with the Ming maritime expeditions mentioned on page 90 above. The official and private reports of those voyages are supplemented by a set of combined marine charts and sailing directions which are believed to show the tracks of the Ming fleets between 1405 and 1433. Subsequently these charts were incorporated into a work entitled *Wu-pei-chih* 武備志 ("Notes on Military Preparedness"), written by Mao Yüan-i 茅元儀 at some time prior to 1621.[108] The chart, which extends from South China to the East African coast, takes the form of a cartogram in which the coast is run as a continuous line horizontally across the page, thus making it possible to compress several divergent sailing tracks within a frame of manageable dimensions. The scale varies to suit the convenience of the cartographer but, in the neighborhood of the East African coast, it averages about 120 miles to the inch. As would be expected, the toponyms inscribed on the chart are mainly those which occur in the written reports of the Ming voyagers. Those so far identified on

[105] *Hun-i chiang-li li-tai kuo-tu-chih t'u* 混一疆理歷代國都之圖.

[106] Ogawa Takuji, "Kinsei Seiyō Kōtsū Izen no Shina Chizu ni tsuite" ("An Historical Sketch of Cartography in China prior to Modern Intercourse with the West"), *Chigaku Zasshi*, XXII (1920). Reprinted in Ogawa, *Shina Rekishi Chiri Kenkyū* (Kyōtō, 1928); Aoyama Sadao, "Ri-chō ni okeru nisan no Chōsen Zenzu ni tsuite" ("On a Few General Maps from Korea of the Yi [Li] Dynasty"), *Tōhō Gakuho*, IX (1939).

[107] Needham, *Science and Civilisation*, III, 555.

[108] The complicated question of the authorship of these charts has been elucidated by J. J. L. Duyvendak, "Ma Huan Re-examined," *Verhandelingen der Koninklijke Akademie van Wetenschappen te Amsterdam*, XXXII (1933), 1–74; "Sailing Directions of Chinese Voyages," *T'oung Pao*, XXXIV (1938), 230–237.

the African section include Soqotrā,[109] [Ras] Hāfūn,[110] Maqdishū,[111] Brava,[112] Mombasa,[113] *Monfiyeh*[114] [Mafia], Malindi,[115] and "the Blacks,"[116] this last presumably being a translation of *al-Zanj.* In addition there are directions for both cabotage and ocean sailing, the latter including instructions for a voyage of 150 watches direct from Ceylon to Maqdishū. The chart as a whole has received considerable attention from scholars[117] but, apart from some introductory remarks by Duyvendak in *Monumenta cartographica Africae et Ægypti,*[118] the African sector has been little studied. A cursory inspection would seem to indicate that it was compiled hastily by someone unfamiliar with the terrain and, not improbably, from corrupt sources. The name *Pu-la-wa* (Brava), for example, has been

---

[109] *Hsü-to-ta* 須多大 (perhaps < some Prākrit form of Sanskrit *Sukhādhāra*, attested by Agatharchides of Cnidus in the second century B.C.) "called by foreigners *Su-ku-ta-la* 速古荅刺."

[110] *Ha-pu-ni* 哈甫泥: cf. *Opone* Ὀπώνη of the *Periplus Maris Erythraei*, § 13; Hāfūnā حافوني of Ibn Sa'īd (f. 3 recto); *Khāfūnā* خافوني and *Jāfūnā* جافوني (both erroneous) in Abū'l-Fidā' (*Taqwīn al-buldān*, II, 206) and Mas'ūdī (*Kitāb murūj al-dhahab*, I, 232) respectively.

[111] *Mu-ku-tu-shu* 木骨都束.

[112] *Shih-la-wa* 十剌哇, a mislection for *Pu-la-wa* 卜剌哇.

[113] *Man-pa-sa* 慢八撒.

[114] *Men-fei-ch'ih* 門肥赤, a mislection for *Men-fei-i* 門肥亦.

[115] *Ma-lin-ti* 麻林地.

[116] *Hei-erh* 黑兒.

[117] E.g., in addition to Duyvendak's papers mentioned in Note 108, W.Z. Mulder, "The 'Wu Pei Chih' Charts," *T'oung Pao*, XXXVII (1944), 1–14; J.V. Mills, "Malaya in the Wu-pei-chih Charts," *Journal of the Malayan Branch of the Royal Asiatic Society*, XV (1937), 1–48. Corrigenda in *ibid.*, XVI (1938), 153; "Notes on Early Chinese Voyages," *Journal of the Royal Asiatic Society* (1951), 3–27; "Chinese Coastal Maps," *Imago Mundi*, XI (1954), 151–168; Wheatley, *The Golden Khersonese* (Kuala Lumpur, 1961), ch. VIII; Fan Wen-t'ao 范文濤 *Cheng-Ho hang-hai-t'u k'ao* 鄭和航海圖考 (Ch'ung-ch'ing, 1943); Feng Ch'eng-chün 馮承鈞, *Chung-kuo Nan-yang chiao-t'ung shih* 中國南洋交通史 (Shanghai, 1937), 91–107; Cheng Hao-sheng 鄭鶴聲, *Cheng Ho* 鄭和 (Ch'ung-ch'ing, 1945); Anon, *Cheng-Ho hang-hai t'u* 鄭和航海圖 (Pei-ching, 1961); Ya. M. Svyet, *In the Tracks of Travellers and Sea Voyagers of the Orient* (Moscow, 1955 [in Russian]), 100–148; A.A. Bokshchanin, "The Visit to the Countries of Africa by the Maritime Expeditions of Cheng Ho at the Beginning of the Fifteenth Century," *The History of World Culture*, (Moscow, 1959), VI, and "A Contribution to the History of the Voyages of Cheng Ho," *Brief Communications of the Institute of the Peoples of Asia*, LIII (1962). Both in Russian.

[118] Edited by Youssouf Kamal IV, iv (1926–1939), folio 1415.

misread and Malindi is misplaced with respect to Mombasa. Pelliot once suggested that the chart was based on an Arab prototype.[119] Whether this were so or not, there are strong indications that the information on the African sectors at least had an Arab provenance. Several toponyms, for example, appear to be transcriptions of Arabic forms, and important place-names are accompanied by a statement of their latitude in terms of the altitude of the Pole Star measured in *chih* 指, a direct translation of the Arabic *iṣba'* اصبع . This practice was absent on the more easterly sectors of the chart. I suspect that in East African waters the Chinese mariners followed the same practice as they had previously adopted in Southeast Asia, namely to rely on expert local opinion: in the East on Malay seamanship, in the West on Arab nautical lore. In any case the *Wu-pei-chih* chart and sailing directory together constitute the earliest detailed cartographic representation of the East African coast presently in existence.

Despite formidable difficulties of textual interpretation, particularly as far as the earlier centuries are concerned, it is apparent that, during Sung and Ming times at least, there was available in China a considerable body of information relating to the East African coast. In fact, Chinese knowledge of East Africa prior to the dawn of the sixteenth century far exceeded that possessed by contemporary Europeans. In part this reflected the intensity of intercourse between Europe or China on the one hand and the Muslim world of the Middle East on the other. Whereas the latter was separated from Western Europe by an ideo-religious barrier, Arabs, Persians, and other Muslims not only travelled freely back and forth across the eastern half of Eurasia, but also on occasion achieved high office in the Chinese bureaucracy. In fact, it is scarcely an exaggeration to say that the Chinese viewed the far southwestern fringe of their oecumene through Arabo-Persian spectacles. Much of the knowledge obtained in this manner never found its way into the official literature but circulated, as it were, in a substratum of Chinese geographical consciousness, barely respectable and unworthy of serious study. During the fourteenth and fifteenth

[119] Pelliot, "Les grands voyages," 268.

centuries some of this information was formalized, probably under the influence of Persian astronomers, one of whom, Jamāl al-Dīn, had brought to Peking in 1267 a terrestrial globe that may well have depicted the western shores of the Indian Ocean.[120] The most precise information which the Chinese obtained about the East African coast, however, was to be found not in this highly academic cartographical milieu but in quite another tradition, that of practical marine navigation as represented by the *Wu-pei-chih* charts.[121] It is one of the ironies of history that, just when the Chinese had achieved direct communication with the "barbarian regions far away hidden in a blue transparency of light vapors," when "the countries beyond the horizon and from the ends of the earth had all become subjects, and when distances and routes could be calculated to the uttermost parts of the west and the farthest bounds of the north,"[122] there should have come from even farther westward a new race of aggressive foreigners who showed no inclination to offer tribute at the Dragon Throne.

[120] *Yüan Shih* 元 史, chüan 48, f. 2 verso. Cf. Needham, *Science and Civilisation*, III, 555–556.

[121] And also in the sailing directory now known as *MS. Laud Or. 145* (Bodleian Library), which appears to represent an intermediate stage in the compilation of the *Wu-pei-chih* charts, something between simple compass directories (*chen-wei[-pien]* 鍼 位 [編]) and the chart as we now have it (see, Hsiang Ta and E.R. Hughes, in Duyvendak, "Sailing Directions").

[122] From a dedicatory inscription erected by Cheng Ho in the Temple of the Celestial Spouse 天 妃 at Ch'ang-lo "on a propitious day in the second winter moon of the cyclical year *hsin-hai*, the sixth year of Hsüan-te (5 December 1431–2 January 1432)." First published by Chin Yün-ming 金 雲 銘, "Cheng-Ho ch'i-tz'ŭ hsia Hsi-yang nien-yüeh k'ao-cheng" 鄭 和 七 次 下 西 洋 年 月 考 證 in *Fu-chien Wen-hua* 福 建 文 化, XXVI (1937), 1–48. Reproduced by Duyvendak, "True dates" and *China's Discovery of Africa*, and by Filesi, *Le relazioni*, Fig. 17.

THE ARAB GEOGRAPHERS AND THE EAST AFRICAN COAST

J. Spencer Trimingham

In recent years archaeologists have devoted much time and effort to acquiring information about the early inhabitants of the East African coast. However, to date, the Arabic written sources of information have been neglected. As yet the archaeological and written spheres of evidence coincide only moderately, but it is more than likely that in the future they will overlap and consequently illuminate many current obscurities.

The purpose of this essay is to call attention to the need for a more comprehensive reading of Arabic sources and to show that Arabic sources have much to contribute.[1] This purpose will be

1. Everyone who uses Arabic evidence seems to depend on early French translations, which in some instances only add confusion to confusion. (The translations in this essay, wherever I have had access to an Arabic text and where not otherwise indicated, are my own.) The principal materials were first collected and utilized by Charles Guillain in the first volume of his *Voyage à la côte orientale d'Afrique* (Paris, 1856). L. Devic's *Le pays des Zendjs* (Paris, 1883) superseded Guillain in regard to the Arabic writers. After that the most important work was the collection of texts translated by Gabriel Ferrand, *Relations de voyages et textes géographiques arabes, persans, et turks relatifs à l'Extrême Orient du VIIIᵉ au XVIIIᵉ siècles* (Paris, 1913–1914), 2v., which has material, e.g. translations from Ibn Saʿid, not included in Devic's book. I have not seen Friedrich Storbeck, "Die Berichte der arabischen Geographen des Mittelalters über Ostafrika," *Mitteilungen des Seminars für Orientalische Sprachen*, XVII (1914), 96–169.

　　None of these books was available to me in Beirut. This lack has had the advantage of making me rely mainly on what original texts I could find.

accomplished by discussing three related subjects: the Zanj and the formation of a coastal culture; the site of the island of Qanbalu; and the coastal itineraries provided by Idrīsī and Ibn Saʿīd.[2]

THE ZANJ

The Arabs acquired the word "Zanj" from the terminology used by the Persian Gulf people for a group of inhabitants of East Africa—those, as in Ptolemy's Ζηγγισα ἄκρα, encountered at some distance beyond the Cape of the Aromatics (Guardafui) but north of the equator. Their name first comes into prominence in connection with the insurrection of ʿAlī ibn Muḥammad, known as the Zanji Revolt (A.H. 255–270 [A.D. 868–883]).[3] Zanji formed the principal element in the slave population employed in draining the marshlands (baṭāʾiḥ) of southern Iraq.[4] The Arabs took over this

2. In preparing this essay the only edition available to me of Idrisi's *Nuzhat al-mushtāq* was the Rome Medici Press edition of 1592. It is a reproduction of a late and abridged redaction made at Nablus in Palestine in A.H. 944 (A.D. 1538) and is preserved in Paris. An edition of this work is being undertaken but I do not know how far it has progressed. In addition to the relevant sections of the *Nuzha*, we need those from Idrisi's "Uns al-muhaj wa rawd al-furaj" (Istanbul, dated A.H. 588 [1192]), which contains an atlas of seventy-three maps and is generally referred to as "the Little Idrisi"; see K. Miller, *Mappae Arabicae* (Stuttgart, 1926–1927).

3. The first rebellion involving slaves, which took place in the year A.H. 75 (694) in the time of the Caliph ʿAbd al-Malik, has been erroneously regarded as the first Zanji revolt. Al-Ḥajjāj had settled Zuṭṭ, cattle-keeping immigrants from Sindh, in Kaskar. They dominated the Baṭīḥa and when they became rebellious were joined by fugitive slaves. Trouble continued for some time; see al-Balādhurī (trans. F.C. Murgotten), *The Origins of the Islamic State*, pt. II (New York, 1924), 106–110; al-Yaʿqūbī, *Taʾrīkh* (Beirut, 1960), II, 472.

The principal source for the Zanji revolt is Ṭabari (ed. M.J. de Goeje), *Taʾrīkh* (Leiden, 1879–1901), III, 1742–1787, 1834–2103. In East African references ʿAlī ibn Muḥammad is frequently called an ʿAlid pretender, but he dropped any pretensions he may have claimed to descent from ʿAlī, and the evidence shows that he was, on the contrary, a Khārijī. Masʿūdī claims that ʿAlī ibn Muḥammad leaned toward the extreme Azrakite wing of the Khawārij (*Murūj adh-dhahab* [Cairo, A.H. 1346], II, 446, cf. 439) and other evidence supports him. The leveling Khārijī doctrine held that the best man should be chosen as Caliph, "even though he be a black slave."

4. An analysis of the followers of ʿAlī ibn Muḥammad (255–270 [868–883]) shows the following groups:

system of slave colonies, which is almost unique in Islamic history,[5] from the Sassanian administration of which they were

(a) The *Zanj*. These were Negroes imported from East Africa who constituted the bulk of the armies. They did not know Arabic, and in communicating with them ʿAlī ibn Muḥammad had to use an interpreter (Ṭabarī, III, 1756–1757). My opinion is that they were newly imported, but Theodor Nöldeke suggested (*Sketches from Eastern History* [London, 1892], 153) that as their settlements were isolated from the general population, they had no occasion to learn the language.

(b) The *Nūba* were Nilotic slaves but not Nubians, since it is unlikely that the Hamitic riverain Nubians would export their own people under the regular system of exchange known as the *baqṭ*. The term Nūba was used indiscriminately for any Negro slaves from the Nilotic region. The term *Sūdān* (lit. "blacks"), applied to Negroes from Western Sudan, is not used in connection with these slaves in Iraq.

(c) The *Furātiyya* were slaves who lived on both banks of the lower Euphrates (*Furāt*) south of Wāsiṭ. They are clearly distinguished from Zanj. Both the Nūba and Furātiyya spoke Arabic (Ṭabarī, III, 1757), having lived in ʿIrāq long enough to learn the language.

(d) The *Qarmāṭiyya* were an ill-defined group of Negro slaves, probably from Nilotic Sudan, who spoke Arabic. Their name does not imply any connection with the Qarāmiṭa movement (Ḥamdān Qarmaṭ raised his rebellion near Wāsiṭ in 277 [890]). Rāshid al-Qarmāṭī, one of ʿAlī ibn Muḥammad's outstanding lieutenants, belonged to this group (Ṭabarī, III, 1749).

The majority of ʿAlī ibn Muḥammad's followers were employed as unskilled laborers (*kassāḥīn*), whose work was to dig away the nitrous soil in the marshy flats around Basra so as to lay bare the earth beneath and to obtain the saltpeter contained in the upper stratum. Among these laborers Ṭabarī referred to yet another specific group, *ash-Shūrijiyya*, whom he also called *ghulmān ash-shūrijiyya*—the term comes from Persian *shōra*, nitrous earth, ʿIrāqī-Arabic *shōraj*. Al-ʿAṭṭār, one of ʿAlī's lieutenants, belonged to this group, which also contained some free men and freedmen, though the bulk was probably slaves. Ṭabarī also referred to the hired hands who worked for the *tammārīn wa 'd-dabbāsīn* (date-growers and molasses-makers). Finally, there were the bedouins, particularly those belonging to tribes having associations with the marshy districts to the south of Wāsiṭ and to the Banū Tamīm, who often joined the Zanj. The bedouins joined the uprising for the sole purpose of plunder; and when the revolt failed they turned against the Negroes, hunted them down, and handed them back to their masters.

In the extensive marshy flats of Shaṭṭ al-ʿArab the Zanj worked in groups at the task of reclaiming the land. Their labor was supervised by agents and overseers. The "labor units" normally ranged from 500 to 5000 laborers but might have been much larger—15,000 slaves worked in the rivulet Dujail of Ahwāz (Ṭabarī, III, 1750). Life in the marshlands and the conditions under which the slaves worked and lived must have been dreadful, for conditions of life there are hard even today. Ṭabarī showed

the successors. We presume that they also inherited the organization for obtaining slaves from East Africa.[6]

The Arabs adopted the Ptolemaic conception of the Indian Ocean: The east coast of Africa, after going south for a space, is prolonged eastwards as far as the Pacific Ocean, thus covering the whole of the southern part of the earth with land. Al-Mas'ūdī, a historian of the tenth century, after giving the traditional views, cast doubt upon this idea of entire encirclement since he had been told by sailors on the Indian Ocean (al-Baḥr al-Ḥabashī)[7] that in some places the sea had no limits to the south.[8] The peninsular nature of the African continent is clear in Ibn Ḥawqal's maps (c. 943) as contrasted with the maps of the followers of Ptolemy. Al-Bīrūnī, early eleventh century, also said that communication

that the slaves were underfed and gave details of the malarial epidemics and diseases from which the Zanj suffered (and to which one must presume many succumbed). The overseers treated the slaves harshly, causing a smoldering resentment which frequently stirred them to revolt. These revolts were subdued before the slaves found a leader in 'Alī ibn Muḥammad.

5. There is a record of Zanj slaves being bought especially for labor in the stone quarries of Aden. See Ibn al-Mujāwir (ed. O. Löfgren), Ta'rīkh al-Mustabṣir (Leiden, 1951), I, 126.

6. In his efforts to counter the effects of the conquest of Iraq, al-Ḥajjāj devoted considerable attention to the irrigational system. The majority of the slaves had previously been imported from the Red Sea and Zaila'wī coasts, but the need for more labor for the arduous work of land reclamation forced the Arabs to increase the import of slaves; the most accessible source (as compared with Eastern or Western Sudan and given the trading system of the Persian Gulf) was East Africa. Yet the coastal regions do not appear to have been intensively settled at the time. It is not a region that can support a large population, and we know nothing of the political organization involved. The period when the greatest importation took place was between A.D. 833 and 868, when the great revolt began. The wastage by disease and death in the marshlands of Iraq must have been very heavy, and there is no evidence that the slaves were supplied with women for breeding purposes.

7. The Indian Ocean is normally called Baḥr al-Hind and its western part Baḥr az-Zanj, but sometimes the name of a part is applied to the whole as by Iṣṭakhrī, followed by Ibn Ḥawqal, who called it Baḥr Fāris. The geographical school of al-Balkhī, to which these writers belonged, was not concerned with latitudinal climes and practically ignored sub-Saharan Africa. Yet their maps, with their greater perspective, are superior to those of Idrīsī.

8. Mas'ūdī (ed. Adrien Casimir Barbier de Meynard and Pavet de Courteille, revised by Charles Pellat), Muruj (Beirut, 1965), I, 151; (ed. M.J. de Goeje) Kitāb at-Tanbih wa 'l-ishrāf (Leiden, 1894), 51.

was maintained between the Indian Ocean and the "Environing Sea" (al-Baḥr al-Muḥīṭ) by means of a channel; "the sea behind Sufāla of the Zanj is unnavigable. No ship which ventured to go there ever returned."[9] In this respect, the work of later geographers represents a retrogression from al-Bīrūnī's work. Their conception distorted and narrowed the Indian Ocean so as to make the identification of islands difficult. Madagascar and the Indonesian islands are spread over an area stretching from the seventh to the tenth sections of the first clime bands. Sumatra is split into many islands. The island of Qumr (or Malāy) embraces elements from Madagascar, the Malay peninsula, and Burma, as well as parts of Sumatra.

Al-Khwārizmī (d. after 232 [847]), who made a recension of the *Geography* of Ptolemy, translated Ptolemy's Ἀρώματα ἐμπόριον as Madīnat aṭ-Ṭīb and transliterated Ῥαπτά as Rāfāṭā(رافاطا) and πανῶν κώμη as Fanānā(فنانا). But he also included "the island of the anthropagous Zanj," not found in Ptolemy, 4 degrees in length and breadth, with its center at 138° longitude and 3° latitude south of the equator, that is, in the East Indies.[10]

The Arab material which really contributes toward our understanding of the coast begins with al-Masʿūdī, supplemented by valuable information contained in Buzurg ibn Shahriyār's *Kitāb ʿAjaʾib al-Hind* (A.D. 930–947). The next collection of evidence is associated with al-Idrīsī (1154), supplemented by Yāqūt and especially Ibn Saʿīd (both thirteenth century), whose accounts complement and help to elucidate each other. Between these two collections is a hiatus of some two hundred years—a period of change on the East African coast.

Although the Arabs used the term Zanj for the East African peoples in general, the term Bilād az-Zanj was applied to one

9. E.C. Sachau (trans.), *Alberuni's India* (London, 1910), I, 270; and cf. 197.
10. Al-Khwārizmī (ed. H. v. Mžik), *Ṣūrat al-Arḍ* (Leipzig, 1926), 99; repeated by the tenth century Suhrāb, *Kitāb ʿajaʾib al-aqālīm us-sabʿa* (ed. H. v. Mžik) (Leipzig, 1932), 77. Al-Yaʿqūbī considered the Barābara as Zanj in his brief notice that "after [the amber of Shihr] comes that of the Zanj exported from the coasts of the Zanj," *Kitāb al-Buldān* (composed 276 [889]), BGA (Bibliotheca Geographorum Arabicorum) (Leiden, 1892), VII, 367.

particular section of the coast which the Arabs divided into four sections, each with clearly defined characteristics. This sectional distinction is evident even in Mas'ūdī's vague coastal indications and becomes clear in Idrīsī's coastal itinerary.

(1) *Bilād al-Barbarā* (or *Barābara*). "The Land of the Eastern Hamites or Kushites"—now the northern and eastern coasts of Somalia; the latter stretch at a later period was also called the Banādir (Benadir) coast. South of Maqdishū, according to Yāqūt, came a zone of interpenetration of Kushitic and Zanj peoples and, according to Idrīsī, a distinct tribal zone, *Arḍ Kafarat as-Sūdān.*

(2) *Bilād az-Zanj*. "The Land of the Zanj" proper, was organized into town-states, definitely pagan, with an overlord who lived at Mombasa. Opposite this part of the coast are the islands of the Zanj.

(3) *Bilād as-Sufāla*. "The Land of Sufāla," was also referred to as "Sufāla of the Zanj," as well as *Arḍ at-Tibr* or *Arḍ adh-Dhahab*, the "Land of Gold." The ruler had his seat at Ṣayūna, which was also a commercial center.

(4) *Arḍ al-Wāq-Wāq*. "The Land of the Wāq-Wāq." This region, necessary to complete the picture, was made up of mysterious unknown lands stretching from the Sofāla zone eastwards to the far eastern islands. From the first section of this Wāq-Wāq region came the African gold, which meant that the gold region was situated in the interior of Africa. Sufālat adh-Dhahab was simply the coastal trading zone to which the gold was brought for collection. A glance at one of the Arab geographer's maps will make all this clear. There were other Wāq-Wāqs stretching eastwards.[11] Ibn al-Faqīh al-Hamadhānī, for example, said that the gold of the Wāq-Wāq of Yaman, by which term he presumably means "the south" (= "west" on our maps, and so East African gold) was inferior to that of the Wāq-Wāq of Ṣīn (that is, the East Indies).[12]

11. Al-Bīrūnī did not have an African Wāq-Wāq: "The island of Wāq-Wāq forms part of the Qumair (archipelago)," *Alberuni's India*, I, 210.

12. Ibn al-Faqīh al-Hamadhānī (ed. M.J. de Goeje), *Kitāb al-Buldān* (completed *c*. 290/903), BGA, V (1885), 7. The navigator clerks of the fifteenth

According to al-Mas'ūdī, the Zanj were a type of Ethiopian (*Aḥābish*), therefore Kushites (or Eastern Hamites) and not Bantu, who spread southwards along the coast, "extending their settlements (*masākin*) up to Sofāla."[13] There they formed a state center (*dār mamlaka*) over which ruled a king entitled *waflīmī*, who had a great army of soldiers mounted on oxen.[14] (This center would not necessarily be a town if the ruling-class remained nomadic.)

The Zanj controlled the territory around their settlements along the coast by means of organized states, even if these were only trading-town states. They adopted a *lingua franca* and traded with Asiatic ships whose main commercial and southern limit was "the gold country" of Sofāla, from which gold and other metals were exported.

Al-Mas'ūdī does not seem to have sailed south of Qanbalū (probably Pemba). Thus his actual experience would have been with the northern Zanji country, not the Sofālan coast. He did obtain a little information about the more southern coast, but it is difficult to tell whether his information refers to the northern or southern Zanj. He said that Sofāla is "the extreme limit to which the 'Umānīs and Sīrāfīs go on the coasts of the Sea of the Zanj." There was no town called Sofāla, but the word *sufāla* means "shoal" and Arab sailors may have so named that part of the coast as a result of their experience of the navigational dangers of the

and sixteenth centuries, Aḥmad ibn Mājid and Sulaimān al-Mahrī (facsimiles in Gabriel Ferrand, *Instructions Nautiques et Routiers Arabes et Portugais des XVe et XVIe siècles* [Paris, 1921-1925]), had a somewhat similar division with a different terminology and without this Wāq-Wāq section. They were practical specialists who knew that one could reach the Atlantic by sailing around the southern coast of Africa:

(a) *Barr al-'Ajam*, lit. "the non-Arab coast," from the Red Sea to Maqdishū.
(b) *Barr az-Zanj*, the Zanj coast: 3° lat. N. to 4° lat. S.
(c) *Barr as-Sawāḥil*, the Sāhil proper: 4° lat. S. to 8° lat. S.
(d) *Barr ar-Rīm*, the Mrīma coast, from 8° lat. S.

13. (Ed. Adrien Casimir Barbier de Meynard and Pavet de Courteille), *Murūj* (Paris, 1861-1877), III, 5-6.
14. *Ibid.*, III, 6-7; cf. I, 371, and III, 26. *Waflīmī* is naturally taken to be the Swahili *wafalme*, plural of *mfalme*. Mas'ūdī says (III, 29) that this term means "Son of the Great Lord" (*Ibn ar-Rabb al-kabīr*). If read as *Wāqlīmī* the first syllable could be Kushitic *Wāq*, "God."

Moçambique Channel.[15] Later Idrīsī and Ibn Saʿīd showed that there were a number of landing-places and collection-centers known to the Arabs, and this conclusion probably holds for the earlier period also.[16]

We must distinguish between the organizers of the coastal town states in Bilād az-Zanj proper who, if the indications given in Masʿūdī's *Murūj* are of any value, were Kushites, and the actual inhabitants of the coastal regions. Bantu probably arrived on the south Banādir coast during the period A.D. 500–800, settling along the rivers and other cultivable places. In the northern interior, behind Ra's Ḥāfūn, were the Hāwiya nomads, and also inland, between the Berbers and the Zanj, were a type of people whom Idrīsī calls *Kafarat as-Sūdān*, "pagan Blacks."

Islam and the Formation of a Coastal Culture

Evidence of the supposed Shīʿī origins of early immigrants to the African east coast has been based on the vaguest indications from legend, written (e.g. Barros) and oral tradition. But there is no confirmatory evidence from the Arab geographers of any migrations before the twelfth century. On the contrary, they make it quite clear that the coast was under the organized control of the Zanj, who were certainly Africans of some sort, with African religious beliefs and practices. Trade relations formed the only connection of the Arabs and the Persians with the coastal Zanj.

The earlier group of geographers, as well as *adab* writers such as Abū Zaid as-Sīrāfī, Jāḥiz, and Masʿūdī, have left accounts of the religion of the Zanj ruling classes which may provide some indication as to their ethnic affiliation.[17] The only reference to Muslims is to a group on the peninsula of Qanbalū on the island of Pemba, which, as will be shown in the next section, was a staging point for trade between the Persian Gulf and the East African

15.   Cf. Masʿūdī, *Murūj* (Pellat edition, I, 177). The word can also mean low-lying country.

16.   Al-Bīrūnī is the first to treat Sufāla (= Ṣayūna) as a fixed point for the purpose of providing latitude and longitude.

17.   *Adab*, originally "custom," then "civility," Latin *urbanitas*, also acquired the intellectual meaning of profane learning. It was particularly applied to collections of anecdotes and miscellaneous material collected for the purpose of secular entertainment.

coast, and none of the accounts indicate that this was a refugee settlement.

It is true that the Persian Gulf region was, largely because of religious differences, undergoing a period of unrest, change, and upheaval. The history of ʿUmān during this period consists of little but wars, both internal and external, and of revolts and conquests by Qarmatians (Qarāmiṭa), Baghdadi imperialists, and Persian Shīʿī Būyids. In the armies of the Qarmatians there were Negro Zanji contingents (refugees from the ruthless suppression of the Zanji revolt)—those in ʿUmān numbered 6000, forming the main strength of the force—while the imperial (Dailamite) army which next occupied ʿUmān was composed to a considerable extent of Negroes.

These events certainly led to migrations, but it would be much easier to seek refuge with nearby coreligionists than to undertake the difficult journey to East Africa. Qarmatians lived precariously in ʿUmān until 375 (985) when they disappeared from the region. Instead of emigrating overseas, they probably joined their co-sectarians in al-Aḥsā (from A.D. 913 the capital of the Qarmatī state of Baḥrain).[18]

At most we can say that though migrations from the Persian Gulf region were likely, nothing points to the East African coast as a place of refuge, and the religious confusion of the Gulf region does not allow us to say to what sect any migrants are likely to have belonged. It is not really a question of whether some Shīʿī settled on the coast, but whether they arrived in such numbers as to be historically significant through forming Shīʿī congregations or becoming a ruling class. If mosque construction were to show Shīʿī influence, that would be real evidence, but the fact that no mosques built of permanent materials belonging to this early period have yet been found allows us to suppose that there were no permanent communities. If traders, living more or less temporarily on the coast, provided themselves with a mosque, it would have been the usual wattle-and-daub structure.

Had the Zanji coastal centers developed strong connections with Islamic states, one might expect that they would have

18. Today at al-Aḥsā are Ithnāʿasharī Shīʿa, and in al-Qaṭīf are some forty villages inhabited by Qarāmiṭa.

embraced Islam quickly. The fact that they did not clearly indicates that the ruling clan religion was sufficient to maintain the stability of the Zanji states, and the value of belonging to Islam with its overseas links was not yet apparent to the rulers of these states. But once the Banādir coastal towns became Muslim, Islam moved southwards and was possibly a factor in bringing about dynastic changes, such as the foundation of a Kilwan ruling house around A.D. 1150.

The trading system based on the export of ivory, gold, slaves, and other East African products to Asian countries required a secure staging point, a supply center, and a safe haven in which to spend the period between monsoons. Qanbalū, which will be discussed in the next section, was apparently such a center but was supplanted in time by Maqdishū as the intermediary center for trade with Sofāla. Maqdishū was almost certainly one of the places mentioned by Idrīsī in that region (Badūna?),[19] but its prominence and prosperity did not begin until after 554 (1159) when the Banū Majīd, driven out of al-Mundhiriyya district in Yemen, split into three sections, one settling in Zafār, another in Zaila' (Zeila), and the third in Maqdishū.[20] Subsequent references to the role of Maqdishū are fairly numerous. Yāqūt's accounts[21] show it to have been a settlement of immigrants, distinct from the "Berber" (Kushitic) nomads and the Bantu who cultivated the river valleys and formed the general population of the towns. In Maqdishū and similar foreign outposts there developed the civilization which we call "Shirazi," and which was inspirationally non-African but, when blended with African elements, became unique and distinctive.

Ibn al-Mujāwir, a contemporary of Ibn Sa'īd, showed the interrelationship between Aden, Maqdishū, Kilwa, and Qumr [= Madagascar]:

19. Judging by Ibn al-Mujāwir's comment (I, 137) about the tombs (maqābir) of Maqdishū providing sanctuary during the day for the dogs which infested the town by night, the place must have been a fairly old settlement. This is confirmed by epigraphic evidence.
20. Ibn al-Mujāwir, I, 98–99. The same writer also records (I, 130) an influx of merchants into Maqdishū after the destruction of the Yemeni ports of Abyan and Haram.
21. Translated in J.S. Trimingham, Islam in East Africa (Oxford, 1964), 5–6 n.
22. Mawsim can hardly mean "monsoon" in the strict sense, but a period of favorable winds, a voyage not needing an intermediary landfall.

From Aden to Maqdishū is one *mawsim*,[22] from Maqdishū to Kilwa is a second *mawsim*, and from Kilwa to al-Qumr is a third *mawsim*. This people [*al-qawm* = al-Qumr?] used to combine the three *mawsims* into one. A boat made its way from al-Qumr to Aden [directly] by this route in the year 626 [A.D. 1228–1229]; it sailed from al-Qumr aiming for Kilwa but made its landfall at Aden. Their boats have wings [i.e. outriggers] because of the confines, difficult landings and shallows of the seas [around the coasts of al-Qumr].[23]

From Idrīsī's account it is clear that the inhabitants of the settlements on the northern (Zaila'wī) Barābara (Berbera) coast had turned to Islam, but there is no hint that this was true of any of the southern Barābara. Qarfūna, near Cape Guardafui and the country of the Hāwiya, and Bazūna (Bazūa), north of Maqdishū, were pagan. The Hāwiya, presumably ancestors of the Somali tribe of that name, were still pagan. The Zanj, with the exception of the people of the island of Anjaba/Unqūja, were not yet Muslim.[24] He mentioned that Malindi (with its medicine-men called *maqanqā*, Nyika *mganga*?) and Mombasa were pagan and referred specifically to pagan practices at al-Bānas on the mainland opposite Unqūja island. A Jazīrat az-Zanj, with the town of Kahūa or Kahuwa, was mentioned. It may be the Kisimani site on Mafia.[25]

The Zanj of the Sofāla coast were different from those on Bilād az-Zanj proper, and we will not pursue this subject here except for a reference to their outside contacts. They were wholly dependent upon visiting ships for transoceanic trade. Idrīsī wrote:

The Zanj have no ships in which they can travel [the open sea], but ships come to them from 'Umān and other places [concerned with trade with the Zābaj islands] that belong to the islands of Hind.[26] They exchange there [in Zanj country] their goods for those of the

23. Ibn al-Mujāwir, I, 117. I apologize for the English of these translations but prefer to stick closely to the original.
24. "Its people are mixed, the majority at the present time being Muslims" (Rome edition), 33.
25. It would be natural to identify Kahūa with Kua on the island of Juani, but Chittick informs me that the brief archaeological tests he has made at Kua have not brought to light anything there as old as the time of Idrīsī. Hence the conjecture that it is on Mafia.
26. Zābaj/Zānaj, an early Arabic rendering of Java, though actually Zābaj, was also Sumatra.

Zanj. The people of the Zābaj islands [also] travel to the Zanj in both small and large ships [zawāriq wa marākib kubār] and engage in trafficking in their goods because they understand each other's language.

We conjecture, without any sound evidence to support it, that this mutual comprehensibility refers to the Malagasy, in continuous relationship with and exiguous settlement on the Sofalan coast opposite their vast island.[27] And it is said that some "Indians" lived in Ṣayūna, the capital, situated near what seems to be the mouth of the Zambezi.[28] A little later (c. 1210) Yāqūt showed that Islam had been adopted by most of the inhabitants of Unqūja Island and the neighboring island of Tunbātū. The Isle of Verdure with its town of mKanbalu (Qanbalū) was Muslim. Farther north, while Idrīsī described the southern Barābara (Banādir) coast as still pagan, Yāqūt and Ibn Saʿīd confirmed that Maqdishū and Marka (Merca) were Muslim.[29]

27. Another passage reads, "The people of Qumr [Madagascar] and the merchants of the country of the Mahrāj come to them [the inhabitants of Jaḃasṭa of Sofāla] where they are hospitably received and trade with them." In spite of its association with the country of the Mahrāj, Qumr need not necessarily be interpreted as Qimār or Qumair, that is, Khmer or Cambodia, rather than Madagascar, since the passage continues, "From the town of Jabasṭa to the town of Daghūṭa by sea is a journey of three days and nights, and from it [Jabasta?] to the island of Qumr is one majrā. The town of Daghūṭa is the last place of the country of Sufālat at-tibr."

28. "Ṣayūna is medium in size and its inhabitants are a collection of people from Hind, Zunūj, and others. It is situated on the shore of the sea (baḥr) and is the residence of the ruler of this country. He has an army of foot-soldiers for they have no horses. This town is situated on an estuary (khōr) into which the ships of the voyagers can enter. From it to the town of Būkha along the coast (ʿal as-sāḥil) is three majrās"; Idrīsī (Rome edition), 35.

29. The Marka (Merca) of Idrīsī (Nuzha and Uns) and Ibn Saʿīd was north of Maqdishū; if so, then the Hāwiya with their 50 villages (or, if Somali, "encampments") whose center it was, were still in the north and there need be no Somali in the south. Such clustering, however, hardly fits the pattern of Somali life. Yāqūt, on the other hand, believed Marka to be situated to the south of Maqdishū. His notice ([ed. F. Wüstenfeld] Muʿjam al-Buldān [Leipzig, 1866–1873], IV, 502) is brief: "Marka is a town on the coast of the Zanj, belonging to the Berbers of the Blacks, not the Berbers of the Maghrib." (The Arabic is interesting: madīnat bi 'z-Zanzibār li barbar as-sūdān). It is clearly a town of Kushites, not an Arab colony, for instance. Nothing here indicates where it is situated, but his

On his map, Idrīsī began *Arḍ az-Zanj* with Badūna. I have suggested that this be distinguished from a nearby pagan town with a similar-sounding name, and that it may be the later Maqdishū which changed its name with its revival under the Banū Majīd shortly after 1159. A little later (1200), Yāqūt showed it to be an important settlement of foreigners in the midst of nomadic Berbers, "not the Berbers who live in the Maghrib, since these [eastern Berbers] are blacks resembling the Zunūj, [but] a type intermediary between the Ḥabash and the Zunūj."[30] It is conjectured that the Somali had not penetrated so far south at that time but the people in question might have been the Galla. Just to the north of Maqdishū were the people of Idrīsī's *Arḍ Kafarat as-Sūdān*, "the Land of the Pagan Blacks," no doubt inhabiting the banks of Nīl Maqdishū (Webi Shabeli)—we know that Galla as well as Bantu were in this region. The religion of the inhabitants of the two coastal places, Qarnūa and Barūa (or Marūa), seems to have been Kushitic since Idrīsī said that "they have no revealed religion, but take standing stones which they anoint with fish oil and to which they prostrate themselves in worship."[31]

East (i.e. south) of Marka, said Ibn Saʿīd, "is the Islamic center (*madīnat al-Islām*) famous in those parts, whose renown is perpetually on the lips of travellers, I mean, of course, Maqdishū."[32] This attests to the fame of Maqdishū as compared, for example, with Kilwa, whose existence is just barely recognized by Yāqūt and Ibn Fāṭima (quoted by Ibn Saʿīd).[33] Even so, although the existence of Kilwa was first recognized by Yāqūt, Ibn al-Mujāwir shortly afterwards (writing in 630 [1232-1233]), showed that it was an important stage on the route to al-Qumr. He had an interesting

---

notice (V, 272) on Nujah (or so he carefully spells the Najā of Idrīsī) shows Marka to the south of Maqdishū: "Nujah, a town of the land of the Berbers of the Zanj (*Barbarat az-Zanj*), on the shores of the ocean, after a town called Markah, and Markah is after Maqdishū on the Sea of the Zanj."

30. Yāqūt, *Muʿjam*, IV, 602; cf. I, 502.
31. Idrīsī (Rome edition), 32. *Al-aḥjar al-qāʾima*, obelisks, phallic pillars?
32. Ibn Saʿīd (ed. Juán Vernet Ginés), *Kitab Basṭ al-Arḍ fī ʾṭ-ṭūl wa ʾl-ʿarḍ* (Tetouan, 1958), 14.
33. Yāqūt, *Muʿjam* IV, 302; Ibn Saʿīd (see below, 146) situated it in the Laccadives.

note about the legal school to which its inhabitants belonged
—"Kilwa reverted from the Shāfiʿiyya to the Khārijiyya and they
remain attached to this legal school until the present day."[34] This
probably, though not necessarily, points to an influx of ʿUmānīs,
who must have gained control, since we can take any such reference
to refer to the official legal school. But when Ibn Baṭṭūṭa visited
Kilwa in 1329 it was once again officially Shāfiʿī.

Ibn Saʿīd's account shows that the Barābara coastal towns were
all Muslim, but that the Zanji coastal places (including Malindi
and Mombasa) were still religiously traditional African, except for
a few island settlements. Similarly, the inhabitants of the Sofālan
coast were pagan and pagan practices were mentioned in connection
with Ṣayūna.

The term Shirazi, though unfortunate in its implications and
perpetuation, is generally accepted as a convenient term for the
Muslim-oriented civilization which grew up first along the Banādir
coast. This civilization seems most likely to have developed here,
since only on the Benadir coast were there available the full range
of interacting factors: old Kushitic cultural influence, surrounding
nomads, and a strong Bantu influx, on the one hand, and
commerce, South Arabian Islamic culture, and Arab settlement,
on the other. I have suggested that the ruling class in Bilād az-
Zanj (in the narrow territorial sense) was Kushitic rather than
Bantu, though they adopted a Bantu *lingua franca*. The southern
Banādir of today, both coast and inner river valleys, was the
northern limit of the Bantu movement. But because the northern
Bantu dialects spread easily we may suppose that a proto-Swahili
was spoken from Maqdishū southwards. And it is more likely
that Maqdishū's inhabitants spoke such a Bantu *lingua franca* (the
bulk of the population of these places being of Bantu background)
than Somali, the language of nomads, who were not yet numerous
so far south. Full control by Arab clans (represented by the

34.   Ibn al-Mujāwir, II, 278. The only reference to Shiʿa occurs in ad-Dimishqī
(1256–1327) and they were placed in northern Somalia: "The island
[region] of Barbarā is inhabited by Muslim Negroes who follow the Zaidī
and Shāfiʿī rites" (ed. Mehren) *Nukhabat ad-dahr* (St. Petersburg, 1866),
162.

muqaddamūn or "elders" of Yāqūt), which had migrated from Arabia, began on this coast.

It is clear that religion and kingship were bound up together in the Zanji coastal centers. The state religion survived a long time in spite of the obvious attractions of Islam to the ruling class of such centers, but when the change took place around 1150, it occurred rapidly and simultaneously in all of these places and was probably associated with a change of leadership which might have been the result of external or internal stimulus. The centers of commerce were receiving influxes of people from the southern coast of Arabia and the Persian Gulf, and the old Zanji ruling class was either ousted or changed internally through marriage with immigrants. Thus a class grew up which claimed an Arab and Islamic origin. The fact that the rulers of these places do not seem to have followed an indigenous cult simultaneously with Islam implies that the original Zanji ruling class had been displaced by immigrants who were already Muslims and who used Islam both as a cohesive basis for the state and as an important transoceanic link.

A relatively homogeneous urban commercial civilization developed on the Banādir coast which had such force that, in spite of the political diversity and commercial rivalry of the little island-states, it spread along the coast southwards as far as Kilwa. It is possible that the Zanj of Bilād az-Zanj proper were at first Kushites, later they were clearly Islamized Bantu with an Arab ruling class modified through settlement on the coast and intermarriage with its inhabitants. On the other hand, on the Sofalan coast, with which the Arabs had early, strong contacts, no permanent colonization or civilization comparable with that of the Shirazi towns seems to have been formed, nor to have spread there from the north.

Qanbalu

As a writer of *adab* literature rather than a geographer, al-Mas'ūdī, whose experience as a traveler dated from A.H. 304 to 345 [916 to 943], tells little about the East African coast from the more strictly geographical aspect, yet he included much "entertaining" material concerning East Africa which we, thankful for even the slightest reference, accept avidly. His "Golden Pastures" may be taken as the starting point for studies on particular aspects of the East African coast, to be followed with the evidence of succeeding writers and coordinated wherever possible with archaeological evidence. I have chosen to follow up the references to an island or peninsular town named Qanbalū in the hope that such an approach may help clarify what has been, only too often, unsupported conjecture.

Al-Masʿūdī writes of a branch of the Nile as:

> traversing the land of the Negroes (Sūdān) who adjoin the regions of the Zanj. From it there branches out into a gulf (khalīj) which falls into Barr az-Zanj, the sea where the island of Qanbalū is found. Among the inhabitants of the island is a community of Muslims, now speaking Zaḥjiyya [the language of the Zanj], who conquered this island and subjected all the Zanj on it in the same manner as the Muslim conquest of the island of Crete in the Mediterranean.[35] This event [the conquest of Qanbalū] took place around the period of the changeover from the Umayyad to the ʿAbbāsid dynasty. From them [Qanbalū] to ʿUmān is about 500 farsakhs [1415 miles] according to the guess rather than to any exact calculation by the sailors.[36]

Later he writes concerning al-Khalīj al-Barbarī, the Gulf of Aden:

> The ʿUmānī ships' captains cross this sea to the island of Qanbalū in the Sea of the Zanj. In this island are Muslims living among pagan Zanj[37] ...The goal of these [ships' captains] on the Sea of the Zanj, is the island of Qanbalū, as we have mentioned, and [also] the country of Sofāla and the Wāq-Wāq at the extremities of the land of the Zanj and the lower parts of their [the Zanj] sea. The Sīrāfīs [also] cross this sea, and I have myself sailed on it from Suḥār, capital of ʿUmān, in the company of Sīrāfī shipowners who were ships' captains,[38] such as Muḥammad ibn Zaidabūd and Jawhar ibn Aḥmad

35. Ka ghalabat al-Muslimīn ʿalā jazīrat Iqrīṭish. I take the kāf li 't-tashbīh to mean "under similar circumstances" or "in a similar manner,"by independent Muslim adventurers at the time of the dynastic changeover, that is, around A.D. 750. It can hardly mean at the time of the conquest of Crete, for it was not until A.D. 827–8 that ibn Ḥafṣ ʿUmar al-Ballūṭī, a powerful refugee from the unsuccessful revolt against al-Ḥakam at Cordoba, conquered Crete.

36. Murūj (Pellat edition), I, 112; cf. 115.   37. Ibid., I, 124.

38. I take nākhodhāh (pl. nawākhidha) in these passages to mean "shipowner"

called Ibn Sīrah who was lost in this sea with all his company. The last occasion I sailed on it from the island of Qanbalū to ʿUmān was in the year 304 [916–917].[39]

Among these islands is one, situated at a distance of one or two days' journey from the Zanj coast, which has inhabitants who are Muslims (fīhā khalāʾiq min al-Muslimin) among whom the royal authority is transmitted. This is the Qanbalū about which we have written elsewhere in this book.[40]

Another reference to Qanbalū is found in al-Masʿūdī's Tanbīh:

Near this Jabal al-Qamar are found many territories and settlements of the Zanj until that region joins up with Bilād Sufālat az-Zanj, the Island of Qanbalū whose people are Muslims, and Bilād Barābara and Hafūnī.[41]

In this reference Qanbalū is situated in the region of Bilād az-Zanj proper. It cannot be Madagascar, which had not been conquered by Muslims, and which is a much greater distance from ʿUmān than the indications given by Masʿūdī,[42] and which in any case was not mentioned in any identifiable way by the early geographers.[43] It must have been some intermediary collection center for the export trade, not merely for slaves to work in the marshlands of Iraq, but for other things like sāj, the wood from which the houses of the great Persian Gulf port of Sīrāf were built,[44] ivory, leopard skins, iron, and gold from Sofāla.

(or hirer), "merchant-venturer," not "ship's captain" as in later usage, and arbāb (notables) to be the same as rabābina, sing. rubbān, "captain," "master," or "navigator."

39. Murūj, I, 125.   40. Murūj, III, 31.
41. Al-Masʿūdī, At-Tanbīh, 58.
42. Qanbalū would be the name originally given by the South Arabians to their settlement and so to the peninsula. For the term see "qanbal" in Tāj al-ʿArūs, VIII, 88, and Lisān al-ʿArab (Beirut, 1956), XI, 569–570.
43. Wāq-Wāq, is first mentioned under the form (Jazīrat) al-Qumr by Idrīsī (but cf. Khwārizmī's Madīnat al-Qumr, associated with Sarandīb or Ceylon [ed. Mžik, 97]). It then follows Yāqūt, Muʿjam, IV, 174, and Ibn Saʿīd, who has an important account of the migrations of the Qumr in Basṭ al-Arḍ, 18–19.
44. Al-Iṣṭakhrī, Masālik al-mamālik (BGA, Leiden, 1870), 127. Al-Maqdisī Descriptio Imperii Moslemici (BGA, Leiden, 1906), 426, 480, wrote of multistoried houses in Sīrāf. Chittick has suggested that the word sāj in this context probably refers to mangrove wood.

Ibn Ḥawqal, who wrote (c. 943) a little later than Masʿūdī, but whose information goes back to 916, shows an island of Qanbalū on his map of Baḥr Fāris, on the right side of its coast[45] opposite the *mafāza* (wilderness) stretching between Bilād al-Ḥabasha and Bilād az-Zanj.[46] The only likely islands seem to be either Pemba or Unqūja (Zanzibar Island).

To the same period belong the important sailors' tales collected (A.D. 930–947) by a captain of Rāmhormuz called Buzurg ibn Shahriyār.[47] Buzurg said that ships took from six to seven days to traverse the Sea of Barābara en route for Bilād az-Zanj.[48] This Barābara (i.e. Banādir) coast was described as being full of dangers, one was that its inhabitants castrated any strangers who fell into their hands. Traders had to have a local sponsor in order to avoid such a fate[49] (thus linking the objectionable habits of these nomadic tribes with the common custom of sponsorship). From Qanbalū (or Qanbaluh قنبله) to the place the ships normally made for on Bilād az-Zanj was 800 farsakhs (2264 miles), an impossible distance. Further, boats were sometimes carried beyond to what he calls "cannibal country." Buzurg described such a misadventure.[50] In the year 310 (922–923) a boat aiming for Qanbalū was carried by the wind to the country of Sofāla of the Zanj. The captain, Ismāʿilawaih, had a cargo of 200 slaves, and slave trading seemed to be a normal part of his activities. By an act of treachery he sailed off with a Zanji king and his entourage

45. By "right side" we mean "to the east of" since the south is on the upper part of Arab maps. When Yāqūt, for example, writing (*Muʿjam*, IV, 936) of the Far Eastern Wāq-Wāq, said "The Wāq-Wāq is a country situated *above* China" (*bilād fawq aṣ-Ṣīn*) he was looking at an Arab map and he meant that it was *south* of China.
46. Ibn Ḥawqal (ed. J.H. Kramers), *Ṣūrat al-Arḍ* (Leiden, 1939), I, 45, gave the distance from ʿUmān to Bilād az-Zanj as 700 farsakhs or some 1980 miles. A little earlier al-Hamadhānī (*fl.* A.D. 902) had said that the same journey to an unspecified Zanj coast took two months (*Buldān*, 296). Al-Iṣṭakhrī (d. 934), whose book Ibn Ḥawqal revised, did not put Qanbalū on his map.
47. (Ed. P.A. van der Lith, trans. L.M. Devic), *Kitabʿ Ajāʾib al-Hind* (Leiden, 1883–1886), a new translation was published as *Les Merveilles de l'Inde* in *Mémorial Jean Sauvaget* (Damascus, 1954), I, 188–300.
48. *Merveilles*, 261.
49. *Ibid.*
50. *Merveilles*, 221; cf. reference in Masʿūdī, *Murūj* (Pellat edition), I .169.

and sold them in ʿUmān. A few years later he was again driven to the same coast, only to find that the king whom he had carried off had returned and was once again in control. The king's magnanimity toward the slaver is described, as well as an account of his adventures.

Buzurg recorded the invasion of the East African coast and islands by Far Eastern Wāq-Wāq in 1000 ships in the year 334 (945-946).[51] Qanbalū was attacked but was able to resist "since it is surrounded by a strong wall, around which extends an estuary full of water." The Wāq-Wāq had taken a year over the journey—of course including all of their diversions—and had pillaged islands and conquered villages and towns of Sofāla of the Zanj (according to the later Idrīsī, Sofāla country begins at the Pemba region). When Buzurg's informant asked the invaders why they had come this long distance they replied: "because they found [in East Africa] products useful to their country and to China [= East Indian islands], such as ivory, tortoiseshell, leopard skins, and ambergris, and because they sought [to export] Zanj owing to the ease with which they supported the state of slavery and their [strong] physique."[52]

Al-Bīrūnī (A.D. 1030) simply noted that there was a: "Qanbaluh, seat (maqarr) of the kings of the Zanj, situated on an island: longitude 52° and latitude 3°."[53] If it were the residence of Zanji kings then it seems likely that the rule of the Muslim immigrants on this island had come to an end (though one must remember that village-state rule was common on these islands). This latitude, if read in conjunction with a similar reference in Idrīsī, and supplemented by the reference to Zanji kings, would imply that

51. *Merveilles*, 301.
52. As is shown elsewhere, both the term Zanj and African slaves were known in Java. The expeditions and migrations of the Qumr explain this. Java sent four slaves, *seng-k'i*, to the emperor of China in 813, and a little after 860 a Javanese inscription mentions *jengi* slaves.
53. *Al-Qānūn al-Masʿūdī* (composed A.D. 1030), in (ed. V. Togan), *Bīrūnī's Picture of the World* (Delhi, 1937), 9. As transmitted by Abūʾl-Fidā, it is "situated to the south of the first clime in al-Khalīj al-Barbarī," whereas Soqoṭrā, with which, as we shall see, Qanbalū is associated by Idrīsī at 66°30' long. and 9° lat., is situated in the Sea of ʿUmān (ed. Reinaud), *Géographie d'Aboulféda*, 370-371; tr. II. ii. 127-128.

the island was Mombasa.[54] But, of course, there were many Zanji kings.

Inserted in the middle of Ibn Salīm's account of Nilotic Sudan (which has been preserved by Maqrīzī) is a passage concerned with the sea route to Qanbalū. Although displaced and difficult to interpret, it seems reasonable to suppose that it derives from Ibn Salīm, who went on a mission to King George of Maqurra in A.D. 969. It says nothing about Qanbalū itself except that it is in "the country of the Zanj and is the city of their ruler."[55] The route is clearly to Bilād az-Zanj, though the text seems distorted, but one can confirm its relevance to this coast by reference to such sailing indications as those given for a journey to East Africa by al-Hamdānī (334 [945–946]).[56]

Not until Idrīsī (1154) do we have any further references to Qanbalū or the east coast in general. But this period was one of considerable change during which Qanbalū apparently ceased to be a major port of call for Muslim ships. The name, however, was perpetuated on later maps but was moved into the Gulf of Aden where it became a companion island to Soqoṭrā (Socotra).[57] This complete displacement is seen most clearly in Idrīsī's map as compared with that of Ibn Ḥawqal. Idrīsī divided the seven latitudinal climes of the Ptolemaic tradition into ten longitudinal sections and simply put Qanbalū into section six (near the border with section five) of Clime One instead of in section seven. Similarly, in his text he associated it with Soqoṭrā and situated it off Bāqaṭī:

54.   Idrīsī said that Mombasa was the seat of the king of the (northern) Zanj, and Yāqūt (1212–1224) wrote that Lanjūya (= Unqūja) was "a large island in the land of the Zanj in which is the seat of the king of the Zanj; a converging point for ships from all quarters. Its people have now transferred themselves to another island called Tunbātū whose people are Muslims." (Yāqūt, Mu'jam, IV, 366).

55.   Al-Maqrīzī (ed. Gaston Wiet), Khiṭaṭ (Cairo, 1922), III, ii, 261–263.

56.   Al-Hamdānī (ed. D.H. Müller), Ṣifat Jazīrat al-'Arab (Leiden, 1884–1891), 53.

57.   It is, of course, possible that there is some confusion with another island of the Soqoṭrī group also used occasionally by mariners. It is unfortunate that for lack of evidence one cannot think of it as a carry-over of the legendary frankincense island of παγχαια mentioned by Diodorus, Strabo, Pliny, and others as situated in the vicinity of Soqoṭrā.

The fourth island is called the island of Qanbalā, situated on the western side of this section (juz').[58] It is uninhabited but thickly wooded, with rugged mountain chains, various species of wild and dangerous animals, as well as a waterfall which falls into the sea. Sometimes boats carried away [akhrama] from Yemen or vessels from Qulzum or Abyssinia put into this island seeking refuge. It is opposite the strong-point called Mikhlāf Ḥakam on the coast of Yemen.[59] Two stages separate it from Jabal al-Mandab.[60]

The next mention of Qanbalū occurs in Yāqūt's Geographical Dictionary, which was completed in 1224. After Idrīsī this is enlightening, for here it is a town on the Isle of Verdure:

Jazīrat al-Khaḍrā' is also the name of an important island belonging to the Zanj region in the Indian Ocean. It is large and broad, surrounded by the Salt Sea on every side. On it are two cities, the name of the one being mTanby (متنبى) .and that of the other mKanbalū (مكنبلو). In each of these there is a chief, each independent of other. There are also a number of villages and parishes. Their sultan asserts that he is an Arab who emigrated from Kūfa to settle there. That was told me by Shaikh aṣ-Ṣāliḥ ʿAbd al-Malik al-Ḥallāwī al-Baṣrī, a trustworthy first-hand eyewitness of that [place] who had known him [the sultan].[61]

This island is almost certainly Pemba since Unqūja (Zanzibar Island) and Kilwa each have separate notices in Yāqūt's Dictionary.[62] Ras Mkumbuu is the obvious site for mKanbalū, though archaeologists have yet to show that this site was occupied by Zanj-speaking immigrants in the tenth century, and mTanby may be linked with Mtambwe Kuu.

Ibn Saʿīd (1214–1274) situated Qanbalū in Clime One, section four, that is, in the clime-band north of the equator, in the Gulf of Aden, off Sāḥil al-Ḥabasha. After mentioning Zailaʿ at 66° longitude and 11° (less a few minutes) latitude North:

58. The others are the twin islands of Khūriyān and Mūriyān (Kuria Muria) and Soqoṭrā.
59. Idrīsī seemed to use mikhlāf, the Yemeni term for "administrative district" (see Yaʿqūbī, Buldān, 317); Yāqūt (tr. W. Jwaideh), The Introductory Chapters of Yaqut's Muʿjam al-Buldān (Leiden, 1959), 56–57, used "district headquarters," and he had a later note (31) explaining that it meant "castle." Earlier Masʿūdī (Pellat edition, I, 234) used al-makhālif al-qalaʿ for such provincial fortresses.
60. Rome edition, 27.   61. Yāqūt, Muʿjam, II, 75.
62. The name Jazīrat al-Khaḍrā' was used by Ibn Mājid (A.D. 1462) (Ferrand, Instructions Nautiques, I, f°111r.) under the form Ḥaḍrā' and

Among the islands of this sea mentioned in the books [of preceding geographers] as neighboring Sāḥil al-Ḥabasha, is that of Qanbalū separated from Bāqatī by a stretch of $2\frac{1}{2}$ degrees. Its southern point is on the same parallel [as Bāqatī], and its length is about the same as its breadth, around 2 degrees. The distance between its northeastern part and Aden is 4 degrees 30 minutes. It used to be prosperous but is now derelict. Boats that have been carried off their courses[63] and have need of water and firewood take refuge there. It is recorded that the extremity of Baḥr al-Hind, where are located the Abyssinian towns mentioned...situated just a little off the Sawāḥil, consists of reefs and rocky stretches where the water is shallow[64] as far as Bāb al-Mandab where none except small boats can sail.[65]

It is clear from the maps of early geographers and accounts of navigation to the East African coast that Qanbalū could only have been an alien settlement on an island off that coast—Pemba, Zanzibar, or Mafia—and not Madagascar. Buzurg's account of its situation helping its inhabitants to resist Indonesian invaders, linked with Yāqūt's account of an independent town of that name (now Swahilized), fits in with a conjectural identification with Ras Mkumbuu. In Yāqūt's time Qanbalū was no longer a link in the navigational network between the Persian Gulf and East Africa, and the accounts of Idrīsī and Ibn Saʿīd indicate that the position of the original Qanbalū was unknown to their informants. Navigators, if asked about the whereabouts of Masʿūdī's Qanbalū, guessed it to be an island in the Gulf of Aden where they took shelter if driven out of their courses, as on Soqoṭrā.[66]

---

also Ḥaṭrā by Sulaimān al-Mahrī (c. 1512) (ibid. II, f°33r.), and he situated it on 1° Farqadain = 6° lat. = 5°10' lat. by our reckoning, which is near enough to the latitude of Pemba.

63. The printed text has aḥzama, which should perhaps be read akhrama as in the corresponding text of Idrīsī translated above.

64. Reading حُشِّفَ for حِسَفَ and emending يَضْحَر to يَضْحَل following the suggestion of a colleague. This text is full of problems and does not seem to have been well edited.

65. Ibn Saʿid, Basṭ al-Arḍ, 32.

66. Idrīsī's conception of the islands throughout the whole Indian Ocean was very vague and confused. Yet if one examines his maps, one can see that there is really no problem when he says that Soqoṭrā "is adjacent on its northern and western sides with Yemen...Confronting it on the Bilād az-Zanj side are the towns of Malindi and Mombasa" (Rome edition, 27). Similarly, after describing Qarnūa and Bazūna (26), he said that they were opposite the territories of Yemen.

The Coast According to Idrisi and Ibn Sa'id

A detailed investigation of the works of Idrīsī and Ibn Sa'īd is necessary for any study of the Zanji question. One difficulty which immediately arises is that the geographers and astronomers of those times worked independently. The astronomers, from al-Farghānī (A.D. 860) to al-Bīrūnī (A.D. 1030), provided tables of longitudes and latitudes, but the geographers, in their listing of itineraries and topographical descriptions of the places through which they passed, did not incorporate these guides or use them for working out their maps. Idrīsī's work cannot be regarded as a real step toward a reconciliation between geographers and astronomers since, although he gave selective latitudes and longitudes on his maps (though not in the text), he obviously did not use astronomical methods to design them. From my limited observations I would say that he was not acquainted with al-Bīrūnī's work. He gave figures for the latitude and longitude of Soqotrā ($11°/72°$) but not of the Qanbalū that has just been discussed. The 1154 edition of his work has the usual seven latitudinal climes, but the map of 1192, known as "the Lesser Idrīsī," has an extra clime south of the equator. Ibn Sa'īd (perhaps quoting Ibn Fātima) took this up and began his treatise with this "Sub-Equinoctial Line Clime" (*al-ma'mūr khalf khaṭṭ al-istiwā' ilā 'l-janūb*). Into this band he put his south Saharan (very meager) and East African material, the latter showing a considerable advance upon Idrīsī. His new material, including his latitudes and longitudes, was derived from the Book of Ibn Fātima which has not survived independently.

Until Idrīsī, the geographers provide us with practically no names of coastal establishments, but with Idrīsī we obtain a wealth of them and, as with Ibn Fātima/Ibn Sa'īd, many more latitudinal indications. Owing to the peculiar conception of the Indian Ocean which these geographers inherited and used blindly, neither their latitudes nor their longitudes are of much value for plotting the places named, but other information, such as place relationships, can be derived from these directions.[67]

---

67. None of the problems, such as the confusion in the sixth and seventh sections between Bazūa and Bazūna, can be discussed in a short essay.

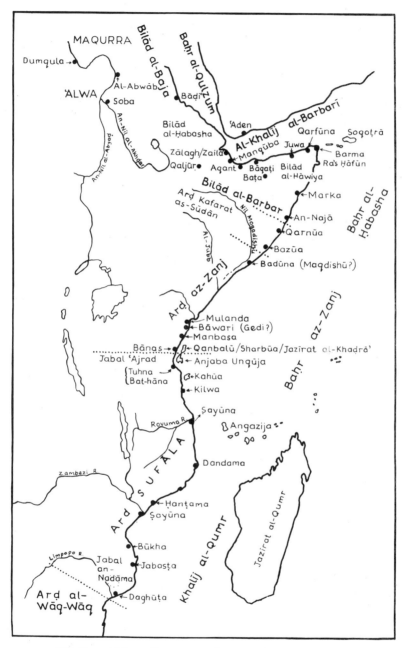

The East African Coast according to Idrīsī's Map of 1154

In making this study one must first examine the manuscripts and then make a comparison between maps and text. Names appear on the maps which in the text appear in a different (and often corrupt) form or do not appear at all. What follows is a rough guide—an outline of coastal itineraries—which indicates the more exhaustive work which needs to be done.

Clime I
    Section 5
        Zālagh = Zailaʿ
        Manqūba/Manqūna = Ptolemy's Cobê Emporion. Ten stages
            inland is Qaljūr/Falḥūn/Faljūn = Harar?
        Aqant(ā) = Ptolemy's Accanae Emporion
        Bāqaṭī/Rāfaṭī and Rāqaṭā (in *Uns al-muhaj*)
            Island of Qanbalā, 2½ degrees from Bāqaṭī
            Inland: Madīnat *Baṭā* fī ṣaḥār wa ramāl khalf khaṭṭ
                    waṣṭ al-arḍ (The town of Baṭā in sandy desert
                    behind the [geographical] center of the earth.)
        Here are villages of Barbarā, the first being:

Juwa/Jūa	
Section 6	
Khaṭṭ al-istiwāʾ	
Qarfūna/Qarfūa: Qarfawa/Qarqūna/	
Qurūnū	
Barma/Tarma	"Regions of Barbar
Jabal Khāqūnī = ⎧ Some 50 villages	below the Ḥabasha"
Raʾs Ḥāfūn[68] ⎨ of Hāwiya on a	
⎩ river of the same	
name[69]	
Marka	
An-Najā: the last of the land of	
Barbarā	

68. Mentioned first by Masʿūdī (Pellat edition), i, 124, and in *Tanbīh*, 58.
69. In Idrīsī's *Uns*, Marka, an-Najā, and Qarnūa are all associated with the Hāwiya. Jaubert, *Géographie d'Idrisi*, (Paris, 1836), I, 44 has a reading Hādiya.

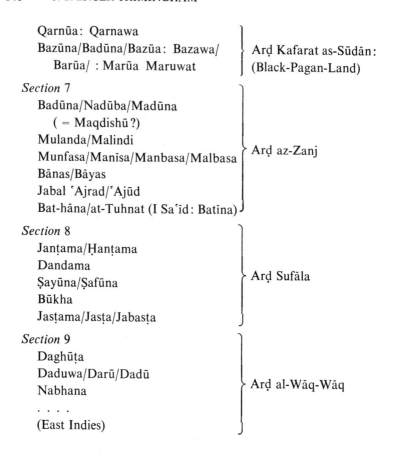

Qarnūa: Qarnawa
Bazūna/Badūna/Bazūa: Bazawa/ Barūa/ : Marūa Maruwat
} Arḍ Kafarat as-Sūdān: (Black-Pagan-Land)

Section 7
Badūna/Nadūba/Madūna
(= Maqdishū?)
Mulanda/Malindi
Munfasa/Manīsa/Manbasa/Malbasa
Bānas/Bāyas
Jabal ʿAjrad/ʿAjūd
Bat-hāna/at-Tuhnat (I Saʿīd: Batīna)
} Arḍ az-Zanj

Section 8
Janṭama/Ḥanṭama
Dandama
Ṣayūna/Ṣafūna
Būkha
Jasṭama/Jasṭa/Jabasṭa
} Arḍ Sufāla

Section 9
Daghūṭa
Daduwa/Darū/Dadū
Nabhana
. . . .
(East Indies)
} Arḍ al-Wāq-Wāq

Islands off Mombasa and Bānas

The following are bunched together and clearly associated on Idrīsī's map. Two have no indications other than the phrase *jazīrat min az-Zanj*, "an island belonging to the Zanj." The others are:

1. Jazīrat min az-Zanj, with the town of Kahūa (Kua on Juani Island?). Is this the same as the island of Karmūa (see Map and Rome edition, 34); Karmadat, Karmūa, Karmaba (Jaubert, I, 61)? "It is separated from Sāḥil az-Zanj by a *majrā* of a day and a night. Between it and the island of Rānih [Rome text, but in Jaubert it is Zānaj, might it be

Zanj?] called Unfūja [Jaubert: al-Unfaranja] is a *majrā* of a day."

2. Jazīrat min az-Zanj, with Jabal an-Nār (Angazija or Grand Comoro?)

3. Aqjiya/Anjaba, with the town of al-Unfūja/Unqūja, with Jabal Wabra/Dīra/Rīra. Although in the text Unqūja is included in the islands of Zābaj, it clearly belongs to the East African coast since it is described as being "separated from the town of al-Bānas which is on the coast of Bilād az-Zanj by one *majrā*" (Rome edition, 33–34). This supports my plea for a close and coordinated study of maps and text. We have also to allow for confusion with Anbariya (ابونه انبونه انبوبه انبريه), the largest of the Dībajāt group (Laccadives, etc.).

4. Jazīrat Sharbūa/Sharbuwa/Sharbada/Saranda *min az-Zanj*. This has naturally been taken to be Sarbuya = Sribuza = Palamban, but there is a possibility that there was actually an East African Saryūa/Sharbūa, as mentioned by Sulaimān

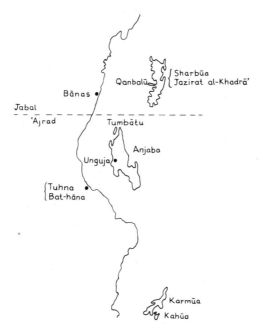

Pemba and Zanzibar on Idrīsī's Map of 1154

al-Mahrī much later.[70] On the map the island is situated right off Mount Naked (Jabal ʿAjrad) between al-Bānas and Bat-hāna.

Ibn Saʿīd, Kitāb Basṭ al-Arḍ fī ʼṭ-ṭūl wa ʼl-ʿarḍ ("The Expanse of the Earth in Length and Breadth")

Sections of the Clime Band Behind the Equator

Section 4	Longitude	Latitude
Jabal al-Qamar (p. 3, 11.5–6)[71]	51°50'	11°
Dandama/Damādim	54°20'	9°30'
Qaljūr, near which are iron mines (*maʿdin ḥadīd fāʼiq*), source of the material from which the Qaljūriyya swords are made	– 56°	– 2°30'
Barbarā: Qāʿidat al-Barābar	68°	6°30'
Nīl Maqdishū continues ascending in this section up to 11° lat. N. and 66° long., then swings round to the east (south) of Barbarā from which it is separated by a degree; then curves to the east (south) of Maqdishū	66°	11° N
Qarqūna/Farfūna, first of the cities of Barbarā on the shore of the Indian Ocean	64°30'	0 20'
Barma	66°	1°
Ḥāfūnī = Raʼs Ḥāfūn		
Marka, east (i.e. south) of Ḥāfūnī. Capital of the Hāwiya on the banks of the river branching out from Nīl Maqdishū	69°30' (42°34')	1°10' N (1°42')
Maqdishū, east (i.e. south) of Marka (the Merka of our maps is south of Maqdishū)	72°	2° (2°02'18 N)

70. See *Al-ʿUmdat al-Mahriyya* in Ferrand, *Instructions Nautiques*, II, folio 20 v. (Sarnūa), and folio 30 r. (Jazīrat Saryūa and Sharbūa).

71. I distinguish between Jazīrat al-Qumr and Jabal al-Qamar; the latter seems a natural translation of Ptolemy's ὄρη σεληνᾶτα, where the Nile was supposed to rise.

	Longitude	Latitude
Section 5		
Mouth of Nīl Maqdishū, "at 0°12" (of long.) from 4th section	72°12'	2°

East (south) of this is the boundary
between Bilād al-Barbariyya and Bilād
az-Zanj

Mulanda = Malindi (p. 15)	81°30'	2°50'

West (north) of it is a *khor* (estuary)
from Jabal al-Qamar, on its banks are
habitations of the Zanj and to the south
(i.e. west, inland) those of the Qamar
Kharānī, a *jabal* (mountain) known to
travelers

Manbasa = Mombasa, a degree from
Malindi. Capital of the king of the Zanj

Mafāza, uninhabited stretch, between the
Zanj and Sofāla (Ibn Ḥawqal located
Qanbalū opposite Mafāza)

Batīna, in Sofāla country	87°10'	2°30' S

(Idrīsī's Bat-hāna/at-Tuhnat)

Jabal 'Ajrad

Qubbat Arīn for *Qubbat Uzain*—the	90°	

geographical (not the geometric) center
of the earth, the point where a central
meridian cuts the equator. This serves
to determine the longitude

Section 6: In this section are the
inhabited regions of the Sofālans.

Ṣayūna, on a large estuary (*khor*) into	99°	2°30' S

which flows a river coming from Jabal
al-Qamar. On a gulf (*jūn* = Mozambique
Channel?) whose length on the
equator is 5°30'

Ṣayūna is the capital of the Sufāliyyūn,
who are pagan Zanj

East of this town begins:

Khalīj al-Qumr = Mozambique Channel,
"which comes from the Indian Ocean
and prolongs itself up to the farthest
extent of the inhabited world to the
south. Its width (?) is 200 miles." It
describes a curve until it arrives at
Jabal an-Nadāma (Mount Repentance)
    East (i.e. south) of Ṣayūna is
Jabal al-Mulaṭṭam, stretching along the
shore of the channel (khalīj) for 260
miles
The inhabited regions of the Qamar are to
the south of this juz' ("section" 6),
contiguous with the mountain, Jabal
al-Qamar
Island of Qumr (= Madagascar and other
islands) with the town of Layrāna   102° less   0°32'
which is Muslim, an important port.   a few min.
The shaykhs who govern it (the town)
maintain relations with the ruler of
Malāy = Malabar. Towns of Qumr
are also mentioned in sections 7, 8, and
9, most of which are foreign to
Madagascar. This is because Qumr
includes a number of islands

Section 7

Daghūṭa, on the northern side of and at   109°   12° lat. S.
the foot of Jabal an-Nadāma and on
Khalīj al-Qumr. It is the last town of
the Sofāla. It has on the north an
estuary (khor) to which descends a
river coming from Jabal al-Qamar
sharing a common origin with the river
of Ṣayūna
(Towns of Jazīrat al-Qumr: Dahmā,
capital of its kings, long. 112°30', lat. 3°;

Balbaq/Balīq, at long. 118°30', lat. 1°.
Not Madagascar)

Section 8
Towns of Qumr, continued

Section 9
Towns of Qumr, continued. Old capital
  Qumriyya
Account of the migrations of the Qumr
Account of the Qumurians, boats,
  buildings and so forth

Clime I

	Longitude	Latitude
Section 4		
Donqola, qāʿidat an-Nūba	58° +	14°15'
Nawāba	58°30'	9°
Kūsha, (كوشه) capital of *Majālāt Zanj an-Nūba*; *khalf al-istiwā*, situated behind the equator		
ʿAlwa = capital Soba	57°	16°
Tājawa: Qāʿidat az-Zaghāwiyyīn. Muslims under the control of Kānem	55°	14°
Madīnat Zaghāwa	54°	11°30'
"Among the Abyssinian towns in this 4th section are..." (p. 30):		
Junbaita	58°	3°
Country of the Kazla (read Karla, Karka?) Jabal Mawrus/Mawrīs		
Buḥairat al-Ḥāwrus/Ḥādrus, named after a tribe of Zunūj al-Ḥabasha (Abyssinian Zanj)	62°	2°
An-Najāʿat, to the east of Nīl al-Ḥabasha (the Abyssinian Nile), beside the lake	(61°	2°)
Markaza/Markaṭa, on this Nīl	62°	6°
Bilād Saharta		
Kalghūr	63°	10°
Bilād al-Khāsa, to the north of Saharta		

between the Nile and the sea
Samar, read Samhar

Bakhta, east of Kalghūr	65°	12°
Jabal al-Khamāhin, west of Bakhta		
Baṭā (p. 32), the first place on the Indian Ocean, marking the boundary between Bilād al-Ḥabasha and Bilād al-Barbarā, and situated just behind Khaṭṭ al-Istiwā'[72]	64°30'	
Bāqaṭī/Bāqaṭā, north (i.e. east of Baṭā, 100 miles		
Mount Manqūba	65°	8°30'
Mount Maqūrus	66°	11°

Jazīrat Qanbalū: "Among the islands of this sea mentioned in the books neighboring the coasts of al-Ḥabasha is the island of Qanbalū. Between it and Bāqaṭī are 2°30'."

Section 5
South Arabia

. . . .

Jazā'ir al-Hind/Mand: among them

Kilwa (p. 36) } situated among	84°30'	7°55'
Jazīrat Unqūja (p. 37) } the Dībajāt Isles		

---

72. Ibn Saʿīd said a little farther on that Baṭā is situated 2 degrees from the *khaṭṭ*. In this case *khaṭṭ* indicates the line of clime (*iqlīm*), not the equator which he had just mentioned.

THE DATING AND THE SIGNIFICANCE
OF THE *PERIPLUS OF THE ERYTHREAN SEA*

Gervase Mathew

Any detailed consideration of the *Periplus* should begin with a close examination of the text. It has been preserved in two Byzantine manuscripts, the Codex Palatinus Gr. 398, which is in Heidelberg and Add. MS. 19391, at the British Museum. It is only through working on these manuscripts that I have become aware of the complexity of the textual problems.

Most American and English scholars have been introduced to the *Periplus* in W.H. Schoff's translation, published in New York in 1912. This is a very readable, rather free, translation of the thoroughly unsatisfactory text emended by Carl Müller and published at Paris in 1853. Much use has also been made of readings suggested by B. Fabricius in his edition of 1849. Every student of classical geography is indebted to Müller. He possessed an intense industry and a passion for research. If he worked very rapidly it was because he had so much ground to cover—he had taken all of the Graeco-Roman geographers as his field of study. But he belonged to a period when Greek texts were emended lightheartedly, and he was handicapped by his ignorance of the language of the *Periplus*. In 1853 the science of papyrology had not yet been developed, and the syntax, the grammar, and even the vocabulary of postclassical Greek were hardly known. Müller would

seem to have treated the *Periplus of the Erythrean Sea* as if it had
been written by a relatively illiterate author in a poor form of
classical Greek. As has since been proved, it was deliberately
written in postclassical Greek, probably by an educated man.

The other nineteenth-century edition, that of Fabricius (published at Dresden in 1849 and at Leipzig in 1883), combined the
defects of Müller with a carelessness that was Fabricius' own. The
first scientific edition of the text was by Hjalmar Frisk, published
at Goteborg in 1927. Frisk was a Swedish philologist of distinction
who possessed precisely that knowledge of postclassical Greek
which Müller had lacked. He was a careful and meticulous scholar
who spent four years in the preparation of his edition. He provided
a clean, convincing rendering of the main text as found in the
Codex Palatinus. Any future translation could be based on his
work. In fact, three English translations of his edition are already
known to me. I regret that none of them has as yet been published.

But it would be a mistake to regard the Frisk edition as definitive.
Frisk was primarily a philologist and was not so much interested
in the textual history of the *Periplus* as in its syntax and grammar.
And in this field, the last forty years have brought great advances
in knowledge of postclassical Greek. More serious is the fact that
he practically ignored the British Museum manuscript, which has
its own clusters of textual problems. But Frisk's most serious defect
lies in his critical apparatus, so much of which was devoted to
emendations suggested by Müller, Fabricius, and even Stuck.[1] The
definitive critical edition of the *Periplus of the Erythrean Sea* should
record not only the variants between Codex Palatinus Gr. 398 and
B.M. Add. MS. 19391, but the varying readings noted in the
margins of both manuscripts.

As all of our knowledge of the *Periplus* is based upon these
manuscripts, they should be closely compared and analyzed. Codex
Palatinus Gr. 398 was written by three hands, the main scribe
working in early Macedonian minuscule. On the basis of my own
work on Byzantine manuscripts of this period, I believe that he
was writing at Constantinople and in the workshop of Constantine

---

1. Joannus Stuckius Tigurinus published his edition of the *Periplus* in Geneva
   in 1577.

Porphyrogenitos (A.D. 912–959). It is characteristic of this workshop that the original is treated with extreme reverence, and this scribe copied out words that must have been unintelligible to him; twice he marked lacunae where he could not read the text (at 1, 11 and at 19, 14). Almost certainly he occasionally misread proper names; thus "Limerike" was probably "Damarika." But he tried to repeat the letters before him, thus, for example, always writing Bernike, obviously a contraction for Berenike. A likely hypothesis is that he was copying a much older ms. written in cursive script with all of the conventional contractions and, of course, unaccented. Some of these contractions must have been unknown to him; it it is likely that he never realized that his "Barike" was really "Barbarike." His system of accents suggests that he was a well-trained scribe but not a geographer. Thus he evolved a scheme of placing an accent on the final syllable of a foreign proper name ending with a vowel, ignoring the common usage of geographers; Adouli and Rhapta are African examples. But though he was probably not familiar with Ptolemy, it is certain that the works before him also included the *Periplus of the Euxine Sea* ascribed to Arrian since we find this ms. dealt with in an identical fashion by the same hand. It is likely that he treated the *Periplus of the Erythrean Sea* with respect because he found it ascribed to "Arrianos," and he assumed this was the same great Arrian who was reputed to be the Xenophon of the second century A.D. and was the author of the *Indika*.[2]

The scribe made a number of alterations and erasures in the *Periplus* manuscript; these are presumably only corrections of a copyist's errors. He then made thirty-five additions on the margin, sometimes whole words and sometimes letters. It is possible that he was suggesting emendations to the text but, if so, he followed no consistent plan. I think it is also possible that he was collating from another manuscript.

There is a second hand in the margin, written not in minuscule but in uncial. This I would also place in the tenth century, though probably later than the first hand. Sometimes it consists of whole

2. The *Indika* is the description of India written as a supplement to Arrian's *Anabasis of Alexander*. Since it incorporates the "Voyage of Nearchus" it might have suggested some association with the *Periplus*.

sentences, sometimes of proper names. This scribe seems particularly interested in place names and in forms of merchandise. I have noted twenty-six of these additions. The variants from the main text tend to be more classical and more Attic. It is possible that the uncial scribe paraphrased the original, or again that he collated from another manuscript. Thus far the whole text is written in brown ink. But there is a third hand written in black ink. There are forty-four words written in the margin in this hand. In twelve cases they have been corrected, perhaps by a fourth hand.

Codex Palatinus contains 321 leaves of parchment of good quality; there are thirty-three lines to the leaf. The main hand is very similar to that of the Paris copy of Plato, and it has been stated that they were by the same scribe.[3] If that were so, the earliest text of the *Periplus* might be about fifty years older than I have suggested, for the Paris Plato is commonly held to be of the tenth century.

On the most likely hypothesis the *Periplus* manuscript now at Heidelberg was bought at Constantinople in 1436 by the Dominican Cardinal John of Ragusa and left by him to the library of the Dominican priory at Basel in 1443—it was certainly at Basel in 1533 when it was first published by Frobenius, the Renaissance scholar.[4] In 1553 it was probably among the Greek manuscripts given by Frobenius to the Elector Palatine's new library at Heidelberg.

The history of the manuscript of the *Periplus* found in the British Museum seems still more complicated. It was practically ignored by Frisk, who merely stated that it was a fourteenth- or fifteenth-century manuscript and a very bad copy of the Codex Palatinus. It had been bought for the British Museum in 1853, by M.W. Barker of the Museum, who acquired detached portions of manuscript from a certain M.C. Simonides, who had abstracted them from the monastery of Vatopedi on Mount Athos. They were bound together at the Museum and proved to be fragments written in the same hand. They contained sheets and maps from the

3. T.W. Allen, "A Group of Ninth Century Greek Manuscripts," *Journal of Philology*, XXI (1893), 48–53.
4. Aubrey Diller, *The Tradition of the Minor Greek Geographers*, (Lancaster, Pa., 1952), 9.

Geography of Ptolemy; other items including a description of Constantinople and a description of the Bosporus; and the only complete text of the *Periplus of the Euxine Sea* as well as the *Periplus of the Erythrean Sea*. It has been established that these were torn from Codex Vatopedinus 655. Perhaps, like other manuscripts from Vatopedi, it had been brought to Mount Athos after the fall of Constantinople in 1453.

The main hand is early fourteenth-century Palaiologan. I am inclined to hold that it was written in Constantinople in the circle of the Grand Logothete Theodore Metochites since, about 1322, he was the patron of a group of scholars who were intent on a revival of geography and the sciences. Codex Vatopedinus derives from a good text of Ptolemy illustrated with maps and from a volume descended from the Codex Palatinus.

The descent of this volume from the Codex Palatinus can be proved by a comparison of the lists of contents. It cannot be coincidence that both manuscripts have included among the minor geographers a treatise on the Olympic games, and in both there are identical mutilations in the treatise by Philo of Byzantium. But a comparison of the two existing texts of the *Periplus of the Erythrean Sea* suggests that there was an intermediary in the course of the descent.

Let us name this hypothetic intermediary Codex B. Codex B is based on the text in Codex Palatinus but it incorporates the notes in uncials and the other marginalia that are in brown ink. It does not use the variants written in the margin in black ink. It was therefore copied before the variants in that third hand had been added. But there is another element in Codex B which is most easily explained if the scribe collated Codex Palatinus and its first group of marginalia with a manuscript of a different tradition.

On this hypothesis the British Museum *Periplus*, far from being the work of a grossly inaccurate scribe, was a good clear copy of Codex B. There is evidence that it was worked on much more closely by Byzantine geographers than Codex Palatinus, probably because it was a companion to Ptolemy. I thought that I could distinguish four hands in the annotations, all Palaiologan, all minute, and frequently using contractions that baffled me.

This section therefore may be taken as a report on work in progress. I regret that the progress has been so slow and the results so inconclusive. I am not sure how many of these variants and marginalia will prove to be of importance; I am sure, however, that none of them should be ignored. Any variations in proper names are particularly noteworthy.

Authorship of the Periplus

The next problem is the extent to which the *Periplus* is a composite document. Here I feel more assurance. During the last ten years I have often had occasion to work on Byzantine "cumulative" texts. These are Hellenistic or early Graeco-Roman treatises that were considered as encyclopedic and therefore had none of the sacrosanct quality of a classic.[5] They were re-edited, altered, and persistently added to. Thus the *Optics* of Euclid has come to us in a late fourth-century recension by Theon of Alexandria, containing third-century additions and with a preface added by one of his disciples. The *Mechanics* of Hero of Alexandria was added to in the fourth century and reached its final form in the fifth. The geometrical treatise of Pappus, the *Synagoge*, is basically a second-century document. It was added to during 400 years and probably reached its present shape under Justinian. I have no doubt that the *Geography* of Ptolemy is a cumulative text of this character: much of it is basically second century and by Claudius Ptolemaeus of Alexandria, notably the theoretics, but it was freely edited until the ninth century, with fresh facts being continually added. The account of India may still be basically second century, but the descriptions of Malaya and East Africa were most likely the work of geographers in late fourth-century Alexandria.

It might have been expected that the *Periplus* would have received the same treatment as the *Geography*, but in fact the text seems to have possessed the sacrosanct quality of a classic. Throughout it retains its own distinctive style—a very technical vocabulary, occasional Latin loan words, and characteristic uses of the genitive. I do not think that it can be doubted that it is the work of a single

5. Gervase Mathew, *Byzantine Aesthetics* (London, 1963), 31, 167.

author. Presumably it was treated as a classic since it was held to have been written by Arrian. If the ascription to Arrian was already in the manuscript used by the scribe of Codex Palatinus, this will explain why he placed it among Arrian's writings next to his *Cynegetikos* (the treatise on hunting), his letter to Trajan, and the epitome of his *Periplus of the Euxine Sea*. A simple explanation of the ascription to "Arrianos" is that the author was in fact named Arrianos and so came to be confused with Flavius Arrianus, Legate in Cappadocia from A.D. 131 to 137 and Archon of Athens in 147 and 148. To that confusion we may owe the document as it now stands.

If the *Periplus* had a single author, how far was it based on his personal experience? Here there must be a subjective element in the answer. During my attempts to identify the sites in the *Periplus*, I have traveled over a fair amount of the area described in it, and I have read widely in Graeco-Roman geography. On both grounds I believe that the *Periplus* is basically the account of an eyewitness. I felt this strongly when I was in South Arabia and looked out from the site of Cana toward the island called the Birds and the island called the Dome.[6] But there are so many details that support this conclusion; the account of the anchorage off Papike, of the entry into Barugaza, and of the wicker baskets used for fishing off Menouthias. The difference between the author of the *Periplus* and the other Graeco-Roman geographers is one of kind, not of degree; that will be brought home vividly to anyone who reads that arid epitome, the *Periplus of the Euxine Sea*. I doubt if the author of the first *Periplus* went further than Nelcynda on the Malabar coast; certainly he never visited Ceylon and seems to have gathered only hearsay on the "voyage to Chryse and the Ganges."

If the *Periplus* is the work of a single author who had traveled on the trade routes of the Indian Ocean, the next problem is the purpose of its composition. There are three theories. The first is that it was the work of a sea captain and was intended as a navigator's guide. This cannot be sustained; the *Periplus* would be of little use as a navigator's handbook. The second is that it is a

6. *Periplus*, §27.

report on the state of the markets intended for some firm in Egypt and written by a supercargo who traveled from Berenice. I proposed this in 1963.[7] I still think this theory ingenious and tenable, but I no longer support it. The third possibility is that it is an official report sent by an agent of the Imperial Roman Government. This is the hypothesis I now hold. It will explain so much: the limited, repetitive but technical vocabulary still so characteristic of official jargon, the use of "emporium" as a technical term implying a fixed commercial organization and regular customs dues,[8] the use of the phrase "designated port," the technical sense given to the word tyrant—here it is always a subordinate governor under a king—and perhaps also the interest in the centurion at Leuke Kome and in the friendship of Charibael for the Caesars. It has already been suggested that the postclassical Greek of the author was that of an educated man. It has Attic and Ionian echoes,[9] and there was a preference for the more solemn word; Theos is used for goddess instead of Thea.[10] It is likely that the author could have used classical Greek in a literary composition. But an official report has never been a form of literature.

The Date of the Periplus

If the *Periplus* is an official dispatch on the traffic in the Erythrean Sea, it was probably sent to the Prefect's Office in Alexandria and was preserved in its archives. But what was the date of its composition? How far can this be determined by comparison with other geographers? How far can it be demonstrated from the text? What are the possibilities that future excavations may shed some light on the problem?

A comparison of texts suggests that the *Periplus* is probably later than the *Natural History* of Pliny and certainly earlier than the *Geography* of Ptolemy. It was probably written later than the

7. Gervase Mathew, "The East African Coast Until the Coming of the Portuguese," in Roland Oliver and Gervase Mathew (eds.), *History of East Africa* (Oxford, 1963), I, 94.

8. Mortimer Wheeler, *Rome Beyond the Imperial Frontiers* (London, 1955), 151.

9. E.g. *Periplus*, §8, 5; §8, 18; §12, 55; §13, 18; §18, 21; §20, 1.

10. *Periplus*, §58, 21.

Natural History, for Pliny's knowledge of the East African shore ends at Mosyllum (which has not yet been given a modern identity) but the *Periplus* mentions thirteen place names farther south. Unlike Pliny, who was primarily an antiquarian and an anecdotist, Ptolemy was a professional geographer. It is worth noting the contrast between the description of East Africa in the *Geography* and that in the *Periplus*. By the time of the *Geography* there was a new emporium in Somalia named Essina, not yet given a modern identity, and there are several references to the harbor at Serapion, probably a few miles north of Merca. Nikon, possibly the modern Port Durnford, had become an emporium. Ships sailed directly from there to Rhapta. Rhapta, also not yet given a modern identity, had become a metropolis. There no longer were references to any Arab suzerainty, and the term *metropolis* suggests that it was conceived as the capital of a state. It seems to have been the center of trade contacts that stretched far southwards and far inland. To the author of the *Periplus*, Rhapta is the end of the known world: "Beyond it the unexplored ocean curves round towards the west." But Ptolemy knew that to the south there were another people— "man-eating Barbarians" or "man-eating Ethiopians"—who lived near a wide shallow bay. By sailing southeast it was possible to reach Prason which, with its promontory, is most likely Cape Delgado. A great snow mountain is described as lying inland from Rhapta; this surely was Kilimanjaro. Beyond it and far inland were the great lakes that form the sources of the Nile.

Such changes could hardly have taken place in fewer than several generations. Then there is the new, detailed knowledge of Ceylon and of the Far East, Malaya, and the Golden Chersonnese. If Ptolemy wrote his *Geography* about 156, the *Periplus* cannot be later than the end of the first century and, since it was probably written after the *Natural History*, it may be dated between A.D. 76 and 100.

But did Ptolemy write his *Geography* about A.D. 156? I think that he did but that the text that has reached us is a "cumulative" one and that, as I have already suggested, new sections were added by later geographers. It seems safest to treat the East African and Malayan sections as representing the sum of knowledge acquired by the Mediterranean world by the close of the fourth century A.D. If this is so, all that can be argued is that the *Periplus* was written not later than the third century.

The evidence derived from the comparison of geographical texts therefore seems to be inconclusive. But the text of the *Periplus* itself contains a number of indications of its date. By the beginning of 1966 these indications had led to the formulation of four distinct theories. Schoff wrote that "the nearest single year that suggests itself as the date of the Periplus is therefore 60 A.D."[11] Wheeler placed the *Periplus* "in the latter half of the first century A.D."[12] In 1963 I wrote that the *Periplus* belonged "to the late first or early second century," and that "its most likely date is approximately A.D. 110."[13] In reaching this conclusion I drew on some evidence found in an article by J.A.B. Palmer.[14] He identified the Mambanos of section 41 of the *Periplus* with the Saka king Nahapana, whose reign he dated approximately between A.D. 90 and 124. Meanwhile Jacqueline Pirenne had followed quite a different line of research with stimulating scholarship. As a result, she revived the theory that the *Periplus* was a third-century document. This had already been proposed in 1861 by Marcel-Toussaint Renaud, who had suggested A.D. 246 as its most likely date, but his suggestion had been forgotten. Pirenne modified his theory by twenty years and placed the composition of the *Periplus* about 226.[15] She used great skill to maintain this position. She accepted the identification of Mambanos as Nahapana but placed him in the third century. She identified Charibael with Karib'il Watar Yuhanim, King of Saba', and dated him about the year 220. She decided that the reference to the Nabateans was a sixteenth-century addition to the text and that the reference to Caesar in section 26 was merely the error of a scribe.

11. W.H. Schoff, *The Periplus of the Erythrean Sea* (New York, 1912), 15.
12. Wheeler, *Rome Beyond the Imperial Frontiers*, 138.
13. Mathew, "The East African Coast," 94.
14. J.A.B. Palmer, "Periplus Maris Erythraei, The Indian Evidence as to the Date," *The Classical Quarterly*, XLI (1947), 136–140. I also owed much to a consultation with David Barrett of the British Museum.
15. Jacqueline Pirenne, "La Date du Périple de la Mer Erythrée," *Journal Asiatique*, CCXLIX (1961), 441–459.

Any such summary must be unjust since it makes Pirenne's decisions appear arbitrary. Perhaps it would be simplest if I were to state which of her conclusions had by 1965 convinced me. I had been greatly impressed by her study, *Le Royaume Sud Arabe de Qataban*,[16] and was ready to agree that Karib'il Watar Yuhanim belonged to the early third century, but I saw nothing that necessarily identified him with the Charibael of the *Periplus;* Karib'il seemed a suitable dynastic name for a Sabaean King. I also accepted the identification of Mambanos as Nahabana, but I continued to place him in the late first and early second century. I could not be persuaded that Ptolemy's *Geography* was earlier than the *Periplus*, and I could find no textual reason for altering the phrase on Eudaimon in section 26: "Now not long ago in our own time Caesar subjected it to himself."[17] I think it quite possible that the words "the Nabateans" entered section 19 from a marginal gloss, though the Nabatean textual history is very complicated. At any rate, I do not regard this as very significant since we are anyway left with the statement that the hinterland of Leuke Kome, precisely the area of the Nabateans, was ruled by King Malichas. I agreed that too much had been based on the suggested identification of the king, Ali Azzu Ialit, with the Ethiopian ruler, Zoskales: Even if this were established it is doubtful that any Axumite ruler can be dated with any precision before the third century. I was very impressed with Pirenne's reflections on the Persian Gulf and would agree that the description of Ommana as Persian in section 36 suggests the period 225–230. I still held to my own theory that the date of the *Periplus* was late first or early second century, but I did so as a matter of opinion only.

But in 1966 the whole case was altered by the publication of David Macdowall's, "The Early Western Satraps and the Date of the Periplus," which appeared in the 1964 volume of the journal of the Royal Numismatic Society (which was two years overdue).[18]

16. (Louvain, 1961).
17. It would not be impossible that this happened under Trajan after the annexation of Petra in 106.
18. David M. Macdowall, "The Early Western Satraps and the Date of the Periplus," *The Numismatic Chronicle*, IV (1964), 271–280.

He concluded that "the *Periplus* may therefore confidently be dated c. A.D. 120–130 on the evidence of its reference to Nahapana and of its description of the state of affairs in Western India when Nahapana held the Western Ghats and the customary Andhra ports but when the Andhras had secured an alternative outlet to the west through Barygaza to which any Greek ships arriving by chance at Kalliena were escorted under guard."[19]

It will be noted that Macdowall's argument rests on combining sections 41, 51, and 52 of the *Periplus* with specialized numismatic knowledge and, that if his conclusions are accepted, we have passed from a state of varying opinion into a state of certainty. Such numismatists and Indianists as I have consulted have assured me that they consider his finding to be definitive. If I do not quite share their conviction, it is probably because I have worked so long upon the *Periplus* that I find it hard to conceive that anything can be demonstrated from the text alone.

Much labor and ingenuity have been expended on the *Periplus* as a document. The present need is for fresh archaeological research in the Indian Ocean area. This can never establish the year in which the *Periplus* was written but it could establish with certainty the period to which it belongs—and this is equally true for the varying sections of the *Geography* of Ptolemy. Perhaps the fundamental reason why I have never accepted a third century date for the *Periplus* is that it seemed to conflict with the little archaeological evidence that we now possess. Only once has there been a scientific excavation at a site referred to in the *Periplus*. That was at Podouke in 1945, and the quantity of Arretine ware discovered there primarily suggests the first century. Adulis has not yet been excavated adequately. From A.D. 300 to 600 it was clearly a great seaport, and it seems incredible that as late as the third century it could be described as only "a fair sized village."[20]

The most important contribution that could be made to the knowledge of Graeco-Roman trade in the Indian Ocean would be

19. *Ibid.*, 180.
20. *Periplus*, §4.

the discovery and excavation of Muziris, which is likely to have been the chief entrepôt for the pepper trade and the most important Roman "factory" in India. The map called the Peutinger Table records that there was a temple of Augustus there. The site should not be too difficult to find. "Muziris is of the same kingdom [Keprobotos] and abounds in ships that come there from Ariake and also with Greek ships. It lies beside a river. By river and by sea it is five hundred stades distant from Tundis. It is twenty stadia."[21] Schoff added here the words "up the river," and it is quite possible that he was right. It is most likely to be found close to Cranangore.

But Muziris has not yet been discovered, while there are two key sites that are already identified and relatively accessible— Adulis and Kane. The great Adulis site will be very complicated to excavate; Kane is a much simpler proposition. It is situated on the Indian Ocean shore of southern Arabia in the Wahidi Sultanate. It is $3\frac{1}{2}$ kilometers to the southwest of the village of Bir 'Ali, which with its fresh water springs would be well suited to be a base camp. The name, Qana, is recorded in an inscription on its acropolis, Husn al-Ghurab. There are five terraces on the slope of the citadel, but I would suggest that the site to be excavated should be that of the small harbor town at its foot. During a brief survey in the spring of 1961 I noted the remains of houses of black basalt under a light covering of sand and also that on the western edge of the site there was a large rectangular building lying north and south, with small rectangular rooms in its northwest and northeast corners. This is reminiscent of the store rooms and customs depot which were discovered by Hackin at Begram.[22] Many sherds and some fragments of glass are scattered across the surface of the harbor town, the earliest to be identified being some Rhodian ware which is possibly of the second century B.C. The *Periplus* states that "all the frankincense produced in this country is sent to it" and that the port of Kane also traded with emporia on the far side of the Indian Ocean, with Barugaza, Skuthis, and

21. *Periplus*, §54.
22. Wheeler, *Imperial Frontiers*, 193–194.

with Omanos and its neighbor Persia.[23] It also lists the goods brought to Kane from Egypt.

According to the *Periplus*, Kane was in the kingdom of Eleazos and close to it, on the inland side, was the metropolis where the king lived. This I would identify with the deserted walled city of Naqb al-Hajar in the Wadi Maifaah. I spent only two days there but it seemed a very manageable site at which to excavate.

There is a depression within the high town walls which leads directly from the southern to the northern gates and perhaps marks the main street. The crowded rooms that cover the western slope above the depression often seem interconnected. They were dressed in soft limestone and perhaps all formed part of a palace complex. In that case the ordinary buildings of the town would be represented by the ruins to the east of the depression. But there was also a considerable suburb outside the southwest wall served by the southern gate; a cemetery seems to lie a little to the west of it. Close to the northern gate there are two very promising middens against the city walls. It has been suggested that the site belongs to the last century B.C. and the first centuries A.D., and, in case it should be worked on, these facts are worth recording. Images and embossed silver are mentioned among the goods that were brought to the king who lived in the metropolis inland, close behind Kane. An inscription built into the east face beside the south gate of Naqb al-Hajar gives Maifat as the name of the kingdom. It is possible that it might be the capital of the Mopharitic king who exercised suzerainty over Rhapta.[24]

If there were to be an expedition to Bir 'Ali (Kane) and Naqb al-Hajar, there should also be some effort to determine the trade route that led to them from the north. I have worked on the palace acropolis of Husn al-Urr at the western end of the Wadi Hadramaut beyond Tarim, and I think that this will prove a vital link. It is built of carefully dressed blocks of fine white limestone; Graeco-Roman art motifs are dominant in the elaborate carvings on its capitals and door jambs with their crowded vine tendrils and the

23. *Periplus*, §27.
24. *Periplus*, §16. The Mopharitic king is commonly identified with the district of Mopharitis high up the Red Sea coast.

windblown acanthus. It is perhaps the furthest trace of Graeco-Roman influences emanating from Kane.

Opone was clearly an important emporium: "Past a peninsula at a place where a river rushes down there is another market town called Opone into which all the things aforesaid are imported. In it is produced a very great quantity of cassia, cinammon, spices and the better sort of slaves which are increasingly imported into Egypt and very much tortoise shell of better quality than elsewhere."[25] The list of exports suggests that it was an entrepôt where cargoes coming from the east were transshipped to the Red Sea trade route. (John Bradford and I have examined detailed air photographs of the area round Ras Hafun. Bradford pointed out to me a large rectangular building covered by sand close to the shore.) In the time of the *Periplus* Opone was the last emporium before the ships reached Rhapta, and a comparison of the list of imports to the two ports suggests that Opone had the more developed economy.

The *Periplus* refers to six sites south of Opone, and all may have archaeological possibilities. Two on the coast of what is now southern Somalia were called Sarapion and Nikon. Sarapion is clearly the haven of Serapion recorded in the *Geography* of Ptolemy. It is probable that, like Neiloptolemais to the north of Opone, it owed its name to merchants from Ptolemaic Egypt; Greek ships may have first pressed round Cape Guardafui in the reign of Ptolemy III as part of the search for ivory. There are not many harbors on the shore of southern Somalia, and the haven of Gonderscia is a possible site. This begins about 6 kilometers north of Merca and is sheltered by the Gonderscia headland and the little island of Au Garuin. It seemed a palimpsest of a site when I surveyed it, with masses of broken masonry; and the ruined houses crammed upon Au Garuin are probably not earlier than the fifteenth to seventeenth century. But at least it needs further investigation.[26]

25. *Periplus*, §13.
26. This site, the name of which is better spelled Gandershe, has since been further examined. No stratification was observed and the village seems to date from before the eighteenth century. See Neville Chittick, "An Archaeological Reconnaissance of the Southern Somali Coast," *Azania*, IV (1969), 118.

Nikon was to the south of Serapion; by Ptolemy's time it had become the emporium of Niki. Port Durnford (also called Bur Gao or Birikao) is the only site in this area from which Graeco-Roman remains have been reported. These included forty-six Roman coins of the first half of the fourth century A.D., struck at the mints of Alexandria, Rome, Thessalonica, Antioch, Cyzicus, Nicomedia, and Constantinople. But there were also six coins of Roman emperors from Nero to Antoninus Pius struck at the Alexandrian mint, and seventeen Ptolemaic coins from Egypt, six of which date from Ptolemy III.

It is perhaps significant that an analysis of this find largely corresponds with reports on coins from India. There again, fourth-century coins of the house of Constantine are very numerous, there is a well established sequence from Nero to Antoninus Pius, and there is a curious scarcity from the late second to the late third century, a period which perhaps coincided with the development of overland routes from the Far East. Only the Ptolemaic coins found in Nikon are unique.

These coins were examined and a report published by the great numismatist Harold Mattingley in 1932. They were brought to him by Captain C.W. Haywood who stated that in 1912 he had "found in the neighbourhood of Port Durnford, some 300 miles north of Mombasa, a walled in fortress enclosing about five acres of ground. He caused his native servants to dig over the top soil in places and was rewarded with the discovery of...copper coins."[27] It is oddly convincing that he also recorded that he had found a Greek amphora but had thrown it away when it became broken. The fact that he also brought in thirteen Egyptian coins from the fifteenth to the eighteenth centuries only suggests that Port Durnford continued to be in use as a coastal harbor until 200 years ago. Probably it was finally replaced by Kisimayu.

My own knowledge of Port Durnford is slight—I first saw it from an airplane circling low over the site. Later I spent a few hours there with Sir Mortimer Wheeler after a rather arduous

27. Harold Mattingly, "Coins from a Site Find in British East Africa," *Numismatic Chronicle*, XLII (1932), 175. (Grotanelli and Chittick doubt the genuineness of this find.)

journey. But it is clear that it lies on both sides of the mouth of an estuary and continues for perhaps three miles up its south bank. There is so much there of so many periods, the derelict house of a British assistant commissioner, a ruined shrine, high pillar tombs, fragments of many walls—but excavation might also uncover the Nikon of the *Periplus*.[28]

South of Nikon, says the *Periplus*, "passing other harbors and numerous rivers" there are the "Puralaoi islands and that called Diorux." The Puralaoi seem to be the Lamu group; it might be recorded that when I was working there in 1952 I became convinced that any search for an early site should take place on Manda. Diorux seems to be another island contrasted with them. Probably it is Mombasa as Vincent suggested long ago.[29] Diorux means primarily a water conduit, but it can also mean a canal; perhaps there was a watering place on the western shore of the island.

The island Menouthias is "two runs southwest by day and night." Here perhaps "island" is a collective and covers the whole group Pemba and Zanzibar, to Mafia. The emporium of Rhapta was two days' sail further on. Ptolemy records that it lay up a river. Possibly it was up the old course of the Pangani which an aerial survey suggested was some distance to the south of the present riverbed. Much more probably it lies in the delta of the Rufiji River.[30]

It is fitting that so much space should be given to the possibilities of archaeological research in the course of a paper on the date and significance of the *Periplus*. For only archaeology can finally determine the date and the significance of the Graeco-Roman geographers. Much ingenuity has been spent on the elucidation of a printed text, but a printed text has only the authority of the manuscripts it represents. There can be no equivalent to the certainty of a scientific excavation.

28. Chittick, "Somali Coast," 124–129.
29. William Vincent, *The Voyage of Nearchus and the Periplus of the Erythrean Sea* (Oxford, 1809), 80.
30. During the course of my unsuccessful search for Rhapta I visited Pangani with Sir Mortimer Wheeler in the summer of 1955 and made a brief aerial survey south from Tanga.

AUSTRONESIAN CONTRIBUTIONS TO THE CULTURE OF MADAGASCAR: SOME ARCHAEOLOGICAL PROBLEMS

Pierre Vérin

The existence of Austronesian influences on the east coast of Africa continues to be a matter for conjecture and discussion. Yet there is little doubt that in the past Madagascar received migrations originating in Southeast Asia or in the Indonesian archipelago. The data of linguistics, physical anthropology, and comparative ethnography are sufficiently in accord to suggest this point of view. One might therefore hope that this article could, with the aid of archaeological data, provide a description of the Austronesian protoculture, and a chronology of the departure of the Austronesians toward the western edge of the Indian Ocean, their sojourn in intervening territories, their arrival in Madagascar, and their subsequent occupation of the island. Unfortunately such an enterprise is unlikely to be realized in the near future.

Before embarking on the archaeological problems involved, it is essential to appraise the linguistic, physical anthropological, and cultural parallels which justify the consideration of Madagascar as an outpost of Austronesian migrations in the western Indian Ocean. This effort will be concerned with confirming various theories which, with the assistance of the views of my predecessors, I shall deduce from the assemblage of facts at my disposal.[1]

1. Methodologically we are in about the same situation as the scholars of the Bishop Museum in Honolulu who, in 1960, sought the origins of the Hawaiians. Evidence furnished by tradition pointed to a Tahitian origin.

An Appraisal of Non-archaeological Research into the Malagasy Past

Linguistics

Nothing can deny Malagasy's membership in the Malayo-Polynesian linguistic group. Foreseen by Houtman, who in 1603 published some dialogues and a Malayo-Malagasy dictionary,[2] this membership was reaffirmed by Luis Mariano, a Portuguese who, a decade later, recognized the existence of a "Kaffir" language (Swahili) on the northwestern coast of Madagascar. He distinguished it from a Bouki language (Malagasy) which he found to be present "throughout the interior of the island and on the other coasts...which is peculiar to the natives and completely different from the Kaffir language, but which is very similar to Malay, proving almost definitely that the first inhabitants came from ports of Malacca."[3]

It is to the works of Van der Tuuk that we owe a scientific confirmation of the relation between Malagasy and other Indonesian languages.[4] His studies were followed by those of Brandstetter and Ferrand—to the latter we also owe remarkable works on the Islamic aspects of Malagasy culture.[5] In addition, Ferrand pointed out the existence of Bantu words in the Malagasy vocabulary. Yet the essential fact of Malagasy's membership in the Indonesian

---

Yet archaeological research conducted under the direction of K.P. Emory and Y. Sinoto in the Society Islands and in the Marquesas showed that a Tahitian migration toward Hawaii dating from the end of the first millennium A.D. had been preceded by a migration coming from the Marquesas.

2. Frederic de Houtman van Gouda, "Dialogues et dictionnaire malais et malgaches avec de nombreux mots arabes et turcs" (translation of the 1603 Dutch edition) in Alfred Grandidier *et al*, (eds.), *Collection des ouvrages anciens concernant Madagascar* (Paris, 1903), I, 323–392.

3. Luis Mariano, "Relation du voyage de découverte fait à l'Ile Saint-Laurent dans les années 1613–1614," in *ibid.*, II, 1–64.

4. H.N. Van der Tuuk, "Outlines of a Grammar of the Malagasy Language," *Journal of the Royal Asiatic Society*, I (1864), 419–446.

5. Renward Brandstetter, *Malayo Polynesischen Forschungen: I. Malay und Madagascar; II. Tagalen und Madagascar* (Lucerne, 1893 and 1902), 86; Gabriel Ferrand, "L'origine africaine des Malgaches," *Journal Asiatique*, X (1908), 333–500.

subgroup of the Malayo-Polynesian linguistic family should not lead us to disregard other influences (Indian, Arabic, and African) which have been grafted onto the Malagasy linguistic corpus.[6] The contacts which such grafts suppose are of great assistance in understanding the nature of the diaspora of the proto-Malagasy among other groups.

In this area, Dahl has shown how the proto-Malagasy phonological system indicates the influence of a Bantu substratum on the evolution of the Malagasy language after its divergence from proto-Indonesian.[7] With regard to Arabic influences, Dez has demonstrated the extent to which the Arabico-Malagasy alphabet was an independent invention and the manner in which the Malagasy vocabulary is connected to Swahili through navigational names and to Arabic through esoteric and astronomical terms.[8]

In his study of the vocabulary and the grammar of proto-Indonesian, Dempwolff has accomplished for the Malayo-Polynesian group what his German predecessors did for Indo-European and proto-Bantu: a reconstruction of the protolanguage, obtained by rigorously following the rules of the comparative method.[9] It is important for us to note that Malagasy (that is, the Hova, or Merina, dialect) is included in his comparison, and that this language, when compared to the common trunk, can hardly be said to have acted in a more divergent way than other languages of the Indonesian subgroup. In fact, Malagasy retains certain forms and terms which have often virtually disappeared among the languages which are currently spoken in areas closer to the geographical center of the proto-language. Such survival results

6. Recently there have been European grafts. However, these are too recent to be of interest to the study of early cultural history. On this subject see the articles of Jacques Dez on the Malagasization of borrowings from Indo-European languages, "La malgachisation des emprunts aux langues européenes," *Annales de l'Université de Madagascar*, III (1964), 19–46; "Lexique des mots européens malgachises," *ibid.*, IV (1965), 63–86.

7. Otto Christian Dahl, "Le système phonologique du Proto-Malgache," *Norsk Tidsskrift for Sprogvidenskap*, X (1938), 189–235.

8. Jacques Dez, "De l'influence arabe à Madagascar à l'aide de faits de linguistique," in *Arabes et Islamisés à Madagascar et dans l'Océan Indien* (Tananarive, 1967), 1–20.

9. Otto Dempwolff, *Vergleichende Lautlehre des Austronesischen Wortschatzes* (Berlin, 1934–1938), I, 124; II, 194; III, 192.

from Madagascar's insularity and its distance from the parental area.[10]

The last phase of the comparison consists in determining the language or languages of the Indonesian branch which are closest to Malagasy. Here Dahl has shed light on the close affinity of Malagasy and the Maanyan language of Borneo.[11] This relationship was subsequently confirmed by Dyen's glottochronological calculations, which indicate a larger number of shared retentions in basic vocabulary for the couple Malagasy-Maanyan than for Malagasy-Malay.[12] This is not to say that Malagasy originated in Borneo. Dahl's efforts simply indicate a direction for the comparativists; parallel studies for several other Indonesian languages will be indispensable.

In addition, even though it will be necessary to consider a large number of comparative Indonesian cases, it is also evident that use will have to be made of other Malagasy dialects. It is now becoming apparent that the differences within the linguistic ensemble of the island are considerably more notable than had previously been thought. Preliminary calculations made by Kottak, Gorlin, and myself indicate that between Antandroy, on the one hand, and the dialects of the highlands, on the other, there is a chronological divergence which may approach some 1,300 years.

Examination of those words based on Sanskrit has permitted certain researchers to refine their speculations about the date of ancient Malagasy migrations. After Thierry's eloquent demonstration that the percentage of words in Malagasy bearing a Sanskrit origin is very small, it is no longer possible to give credence to the opinion of Razafintsalama (Damantsoa) who, in 1928, attempted to show the ancient colonization of Madagascar by Buddhist

10. The same applies to phonological and lexical elements deriving from the Paleo-Tahitian trunk. The current Tahitian dialect has suppressed and replaced a much larger number of the phonemes and words of the mother language than the dialects of the marginal zones (Australs, Cooks), where external influences have not figured so prominently.
11. Otto Christian Dahl, "Malgache et Maanjan, une comparaison linguistique," *Egede Institutett*, III (1951), 408.
12. Isidore Dyen, Review of *Malgache and Maanjan, Language*, XXIX (1953), 578–591. The divergence of Malagasy and Maanyan, according to Dyen's calculations, is of an order of 1900 years.

monks.[13] Of even greater importance is the opinion of Dahl, who noted that the corpus of words coming from Sanskrit is much less significant for Malagasy than for closely related languages, such as Maanyan.[14] Therefore, Dahl concluded that the migrations of the ancestors of the Malagasy must have taken place at the beginning of Hindu influence in Indonesia.

The deductions about Sanskrit contacts which Hébert made from an examination of traditional Malagasy calendars are particularly stimulating.[15] He demonstrated that these calendars were, to a more or less significant extent, of Sanskrit origin. He estimated that if the assumption of this terminology took place in the country where these migrations originated (Indonesia-Malaysia), they could not have taken place more than two thousand years ago. Hébert believed that he had also revealed the substratum of a seasonal calendar and the terms of a duodecimal system, which would accord with two distinct migratory waves. The Sakalava would be included in the first migratory wave from Indonesia.[16]

13. Solange Thierry, "A propos des emprunts sanscrits en malgache," *Journal Asiatique*, CCXLVII (1959), 311–348; Gabriel Razafintsalama, *La langue malgache et ses origines malgaches* CCXLVII, (Tananarive, 1928), I, 171.
14. Dahl, "Malgache et Maanjan," 66 ff.
15. Jean-Claude Hébert, "Recherches sur l'histoire et la civilisation malgaches," *Bulletin de Madagascar*, 172 (1960), 809–820; Hébert, "Recherches sur l'histoire et la civilisation malgaches: documents pour un atlas linguistique des calendriers provinciaux malgaches," *Bulletin de Madagascar*, 191 (1962), 339–352.
16. These views have caused reservations, to which Hébert has replied in the following terms (my translation):

    No doubt you are correct in reproaching me for connecting the existence of the calendar of Sanskrit origin with the very origin of the Malagasy. My answer is that there are no more arguments for than against. I admit that the hypothesis is hazardous, but, after all, I could very well be right. Therefore, I do not see, for the moment, any serious reason to modify my conclusion.

    As you have seen, I base my contentions on the fact that the seasonal terms of the west coast (contrary to the Merina terms, which are, from all evidence, posterior) are of Sanskrit origin. I think that I shall be able to show that they are not derived from a 'Sanskrit-Malagasy calendar,' but that they are anterior, which to my mind proves two waves of peopling, the first having undergone less Sanskrit influence than the second. I do not think that this influence would have been felt directly in Madagascar; I believe in an Indonesian stage. I see no major impediment to the possession by the first Malagasy coming from Indonesia of rudiments of a Sanskrit calendar. "Recherches sur l'histoire," 353.

The application of the techniques of *Wörter und Sachen* to the Malagasy linguistic corpus has contributed valuable inferences about the cultural history of Madagascar. Dahl discovered that the terminology for directions in Malagasy and in other Indonesian languages is closely related, but that in order to make the terms coincide exactly, it is necessary to rotate the directions of the Malagasy winds ninety degrees. Thus, while in Maanyan *barat* signifies the west, and *timor* the east, the corresponding Malagasy words, *avaratra* and *atsimo*, signify respectively the north and south. The discrepancy is explained when one takes into account the fact that for maritime peoples, directions are usually defined with reference to the winds. The north wind which brings the rains to the northwest coast of Madagascar corresponds to the humid west wind of Indonesia, while the dry south wind in Madagascar has been identified with the dry trade wind from eastern Indonesia.[17] Dahl's explanation is valid only for the northwestern coast of Madagascar, where he thinks that the first immigrants landed.

But, more important, linguistics may furnish solid contributions to knowledge about the origins of material culture. Dez has observed that objects are frequently loaned from one culture to another with their names remaining in the language of the lending culture.[18] With the aid of reconstructed vocabularies, he had been able to show the extent to which the traditional culture was of Indonesian origin, in a cultural rather than a racial sense. This culture included such essential techniques as hunting, fishing, slash and burn agriculture, navigation, the construction of houses, iron smelting, pottery, basketry, and food; but the technical level was fairly rudimentary because, initially, the irrigated rice field and cattle pastoralism were largely absent. Clothing, finery, music, and the measuring system have been influenced by very numerous later borrowings from African and Arabic sources. The same is true of grazing, while the irrigated rice field could have come from India.[19] Naturally, we are dealing here only with suggestions

17. Dahl, "Malgaches et Maanjan," 376, 865. See also Southall, below, 203.
18. Jacques Dez, "Quelques hypothèses formulées par la linguistique comparée à l'usage de l'archéologie," *Taloha*, I (1965), 197–213.
19. I believe that this innovation, of Indian origin, could easily have been

proposed by comparative linguistics. This technique is just as interesting when used to consider the words for the expression of religious sentiments and that portion of the Malagasy vocabulary which permits man to describe himself, his actions, and the world which surrounds him,[20] areas attested in proto-Indonesian.

Here again we lack the means of linking Malagasy specifically with any other particular population speaking an Indonesian language. The proto-Malagasy population could have come from several regions of this linguistic area, or, equally well, from a single region where a certain dialectal heterogeneity prevailed. Hébert has shown that, among the Malagasy terms designating *sea* and *fish* which came from the southeastern region of the Indian Ocean, the ancient forms, *tasi(k)* or *taiki* (sea) and *fia(na)* (fish), are current in an area west of a line running from Vangaindrano to the Comoros, while the more recent terms are found to its east.[21] This is true to such an extent that Hébert considers that this cleavage indicates the populations of the west were established in Madagascar at an earlier date, while those to the east mixed with new arrivals. Although he admits that this conclusion is still tenuous, he hopes that other subjects of study and, particularly, that of the calendar of Sanskrit origin, will confirm his opinion.[22]

Malagasy cosmography also figures among Hébert's interests. In the distribution of the word for star, we once again find the cleavage between two groups of terms: *vasia* in the west and south, *kintana* in the center and north. Both of these forms are Indonesian. Even though, in this instance, the line of separation includes the northwest and excludes a portion of the south, the

---

adopted. The first Malagasy, of Indonesian origin, had for a long time probably been familiar with the cultivation of taro (Malagasy *saonjo*, *Colocasia esculenta L.*), which requires terracing and water control.

20. Jacques Dez, "L'apport lexical de l'Indonésien commun à la langue malgache," *Bulletin de Madagascar*, 200 (1963), 71–82.

21. Jean-Claude Hébert, "Les mots 'mer et poisson' en malgache," *Bulletin de Madagascar*, 186 (1961), 899–916.

22. It should, however, be specified that *taiki* or *tasik* is obsolete as an everyday word, being present only in toponyms such as *Itasy* (a large lake). I accept the body of the conclusions of this work which sheds light on the existence of different areas of population, but I doubt that there was anything in the first migration to connect it with Melanesia.

existence of these two groups still remains very distinct.[23] Thus, a dialectal map, such as the one worked out by Dez, shows a separation between a western and an eastern group, with the territories of Antanosy, Antaisaka, Betsileo, and Sakalava of Sambirano occupied by intermediate dialects.[24]

Physical Anthropology

To understand the cultural history of Madagascar, it has been necessary to bring out certain heterogeneous aspects of its unifying linguistic corpus. Deschamps compared this unity to the diversity of Madagascar's physical types.[25] Thus to answer the question of Malagasy origins it is necessary to find out when, where, and how the Indonesians taught their language to those Africans who must have constituted a very important segment of Malagasy ancestry. The Grandidiers posited an Indo-Melanesian immigration, and, supporting them, Rakoto Ratsimamanga, to whom we owe a remarkable study of the Mongoloid spot, has spoken of a Negro-Oceanic contribution appearing with the types which he calls Indonesian-Mongoloid (60 percent of the population of the Merina, the ruling tribe), Europoid, and Negroid.[26] (With the exception of the Makoa, the Negroid type is said to be proportionally very weak.) Chamla has clarified the matter, despite the fact that, according to Deschamps, her thesis had for basic material only some skulls at the Musée de l'homme and some photos. In distinguishing among an Asiatic type, frequently encountered among the Merina (44 percent), an African type, and, finally, a mixed type common in all regions of the island, she has destroyed

23. Jean-Claude Hébert, "La cosmographie malgache," *Taloha*, I (1965) 83–195.
24. Jacques Dez, "Aperçus pour une dialectologie de la langue malgache," *Bulletin de Madagascar*, 210 (1963), 973–994. I do not as yet know the extent to which these results will coincide with those obtained from the study of the basic vocabulary.
25. Hubert Deschamps, *Histoire de Madagascar* (Paris, 1960), 19.
26. Alfred and Guillaume Grandidier, *Histoire physique, naturelle et politique de Madagascar, Ethnographie*, I (Paris, 1908); Alfred Rakoto Ratsimamanga, "Tâche pigmentaire héréditaire et origine des Malgaches," *Revue Anthropologique*, L (1940), 5–130.

Grandidier's Melanesian hypothesis.[27] Blood group determinations (the study of the Rhesus and sickle-cell factors) also confirm the mixture and juxtaposition of Africans and Indonesians.

Despite the valuable contribution physical anthropological research can make in using statistical samplings, above all among the groups about whom nothing is known,[28] archaeology may be even more useful in resolving the African-Indonesian enigma of the proto-Malagasy population once skeletal materials found in Madagascar and elsewhere are studied.

Ethnography

Comparative ethnography and linguistics have traditionally been brought to bear on the study of that portion of the population which physical anthropology has revealed to have Indonesian attributes (principally the Merina). Ethnography is a domain which has been very slightly studied, and the gaps concern above all the lack of information about the marginal areas of the Indian Ocean, most importantly in the area of cultural history. These zones are of a very particular interest for scholars concerned with Madagascar, for Indonesia is the great cultural matrix from which the major themes in traditional Malagasy civilization originate.[29] In addition, as the diffusion of Southeast Asian culture traits took place at a very remote time (see the influences and echoes noted in East Africa by Hornell and Culwick[30]), comparisons become hazardous.

27. Hubert Deschamps, "Les tâches de l'archéologie à Madagascar," *Taloha*, I (1965), 11–14; Marie Claude Chamla, "Recherches anthropologiques sur l'origine des Malgaches," *Mémoires du Musée National d'Histoire Naturelle*, XIX (1958), 165.

28. There is a certain urgency since the consolidation of national unity is precipitating the mixtures of Merina with former captives described by Jeanine Razafindratovo in her work on Ilafy, "Etude sur Ilafy," (Tananarive, 1966), mimeo.

29. Jean Poirier, "Les origines du peuple et de la civilisation malgaches. Madagascar avant l'histoire," *Bulletin de Madagascar*, 247 (1966), 1171–1185. However I do not necessarily agree that the essential part of the Malagasy population derives from Indonesia. (See *ibid.*, 1181) To me the present level of research indicates that while the essentials of the language and a large part of the culture did indeed have their origins in this Indonesian area, an African contribution to the Malagasy population cannot be denied.

30. James Hornell, "Indonesian Influence on East African Culture," *Journal of the Royal Anthropological Institute*, LXIV (1934), 305–332. A.T. and

Thus, bark is beaten in the same way on the eastern as it is on the western shores of the Indian Ocean, and here and there the same artistic motifs (the branched cross, wavy decoration, and the spiral) are encountered. However, in Madagascar, the existence of two artistic provinces, in one of which the use of anthropomorphic motifs predominates (west and south), in the other of which geometric motifs are almost exclusively employed,[31] seems to be important because it coincides to a certain extent with the cleavage in dialects mentioned above.

Despite these reservations, we find in the traditional Malagasy material culture the essentials of those Southeast Asian techniques which the analysis contained in *Wörter und Sachen* has connected to a proto-Indonesian culture: the construction and orientation of rectangular houses, means of navigation, the use of the blowgun in hunting, weaving of plaited basketry, iron smelting (double tuyère bellows), pottery of Indonesian decoration and form, musical instruments (above all the tube zither), etc.[32] Deschamps has compiled the only detailed inventory of the technological contributions of Austronesia (and other areas) to Malagasy culture.[33] Comparisons of religious and sociological contributions are naturally more difficult because there is no use whatsoever in comparing, as the first ethnographers of the nineteenth century did rather generally, this or that isolated trait. One must describe coherent groups of phenomena, rites, and conceptions. In this connection, I believe that the comparison of funerary themes and ancestor cults would prove heuristic.

Ethnohistorical traditions will aid in preserving traits from Austronesia and other cultures which are threatened with extinction in Madagascar. Ethnohistory is also extremely valuable for help in the placement of certain Malagasy population groups. However, because of the temporal limitations of "cumulative memory," and

---

G.M. Culwick, "Indonesian Echoes in Central Tanganyika," *Tanganyika Notes and Records*, 2 (1936), 60–66.

31. E.E. Gauthier, *Madagascar: Essai de géographie physique* (Paris, 1902). On sculpture, see 384.

32. Kurt Sachs, "Les instruments de musique à Madagascar," *Travaux et mémoires de l'Institut d'Ethnologie*, XXVIII (1938), 1–96.

33. Deschamps, *Histoire*, 21–23.

because of the desire of the latest arrivals to the area to justify their position historically, ethnohistory should be handled with caution. The mention of displacements of dynasties (Antaisaka, Sakalava, and even Merina) does not necessarily signify the movement of whole peoples, because rulers and their supporters have often simply extended their domination over other, previously settled, groups. For example, the transfer of the capital of the Sakalava from Bengy to Mañefa, then to Marovoay, signifies that a loosely organized ethnic group had come under political hegemony. It does not, however, represent an important migration from the southwest toward the northwest of Madagascar. And the succession of capitals attested in the *Tantara*[34] moving from the southeast to the north of Imerina, and encircling the rice plain of the Betsimitatatra, is also an extension of a hegemony over already installed populations.

We should not neglect the information about actual migrations which the traditions report; thus, the odyssey of the ancestors of the Merina, their landing and their ascent to the highlands are evoked in the *Tantara*, but in a confusing manner.[35] The allusion to a "low country" where they were weakened by the climate and where they entered into war with the indigenous people before forcing their way into the interior of the country seems to me to be very important.[36] Some passages of the *Tantara* recount the contacts between the area east of the highlands (Angavo) and the region of Maroantsetra where the Vazimba Andrianoranorana is supposed to have returned.[37] It is also from Maroantsetra that, according to the historian Ramilison, the ancestors of the Andriamamilaza or Zafimamy originated.[38] We see by these accounts that all that can be furnished by the "heritage of the ears" (*Lovan-*

34. François Callet (trans. by G.S. Chapus and Emmanuel Ratsimba as *Histoire des rois*), *Tantaran'ny Andriana* (Tananarive, 1953–1958), 4v. These are traditions concerning Merina history collected by Callet in the second half of the nineteenth century.
35. *Ibid.* (1953), I, 118–120.
36. But from which coastal region did they depart? Deschamps (*Histoire*, 56–57, n. 3) makes the tour of the hypothetical locations which have been proposed: the southeast, the Mangoro Valley (Savaron), the region of Maroantsetra, and the region of Alaotra.
37. Callet (Chapus and Ratsimba), *Histoire des rois* (1953), I, 16.
38. Emmanuel Ramilison, *Tantara ny Andriamamilaza* (Tananarive, 1951, 1952), 2v.

tsofina) in Madagascar concerns interior migrations. No one has discovered recollections of previous homelands among the Malagasy.[39]

The Vazimba problem has considerably obscured many probable theories about the ancient peopling of Madagascar. The phonetic analogy with "Wazimba," a tribe of the East African coast, has made certain students of Madagascar, including Julien, think that there was an ancient African layer in Madagascar.[40] Nevertheless, there is nothing which seems to distinguish the Vazimba and other Malagasy. The Vazimba do not carry Bantu names, and their descendants, still called Vazimba in western Madagascar, are a part of the Sakalava ethnic group from which they cannot, from a physical point of view, be distinguished. Hébert states that

...the Vazimba area, that is to say, the area where, according to the traditions, the Vazimba existed and where, in the western region, there still are Vazimba, corresponds in an approximate fashion to the region in which light-skinned populations are encountered today.[41] These light peoples would have supplanted the original settlers, peoples of a darker hue, to whom would have been given the name "partners in a joking relationship," *voa-ziva*, that is to say, Vazimba.[42] According to the theory which is commonly accepted today, the proto-Malagasy Vazimba were not Africans but proto-Malays, of a darker tint than the Hova who were part of a second Malayan migration in which the deutero-Malayan element predominated. These deutero-Malayans were at first welcomed with

39. In the evocation of the Malagasy past, unlike the Polynesian, there are no references to a direction from which the early ancestors are said to have come. The question of the origin of the Malagasy is one which has been raised by foreign researchers. The majority of the inhabitants of Madagascar think that their ancestors have always occupied the island. In the interior the old Indonesian terms designating the sea have been forgotten. Such a disappearance of the memory of transoceanic migrations endows these migrations with a certain age.

40. Gustave Julien, *Institutions politiques et sociales de Madagascar* (Paris, 1908), 2v. On this subject, see Jean Valette, "De l'origine des Malgaches," *Taloha*, I (1965), 15–32.

41. That is to say, the Merina, Sihanaka, Bezanozano, Vakinankaratra, and Betsileo.

42. As the author has pointed out elsewhere, this transformation of *voazimba* into *vazimba* does not contradict the normal rules of the Malagasy language. I cite "linguistic relics" in which the prefix *voa* has become *va*. As to the alternance v_mb, it is normal in composition. See also Southall, below, page 194–195.

good will, because the Vazimba accepted the creation of joking relationships with the newcomers. Afterward, one part was chased toward the west, while another part mixed with the new arrivals.[43] Nowadays considered on the high plateau to be legendary beings, they are, nonetheless, the pre-eminent masters of the soil, and worship is rendered them on many occasions.[44]

Ethnobotany and Ethnozoology

Ethnobotanical data, which should also furnish valuable evidence for the archaeologist, have been used only superficially in Madagascar. In terms of knowledge of ancient migrations, the study of the diffusion of the cultivated plants belonging to the "Malayan botanical complex," on which Murdock has insisted, seems of great interest.[45] Murdock's complex includes plants introduced at a distant date from a center of diffusion in Southeast Asia, including the following: rice (*Oryza Sativa*), Polynesian arrowroot (*Tacca pinnatifida*), taro (*Colocasia antiquorum*), yam (*Dioscorea alata, D. bulbifera*, and *D. esculenta*), banana (*Musa paridisiaca* and *M. sapientum*), breadfruit (*Artocarpus incisa*), coconut (*Cocos nucifera*), and sugarcane (*Saccharum officinarum*). According to Murdock, the Austronesian migrations which transported this complex took place during the first millennium of the Christian era.

To return to the techniques of *Wörter und Sachen*, Deschamps

43. The first queens of the Merina dynasty (Rafohy and Rangita) were, without doubt, Vazimba or their descendants. Deschamps notes that "The families of the noble *Andriana* married Vazimba in order to be able to settle in peace." (*Histoire*, 56). From such unions comes the result that certain *Andriana* are still today of a physical type more remote from the "Malay" than their *Hova* subjects. (*Andriana* and *Hova* are classes of Merina.)
44. Jean-Claude Hébert, "La parenté à plaisanterie à Madagascar," *Bulletin de Madagascar*, 142, 143 (1958), 175–216, 267–329. Concerning this passage see 296. Hébert is right in thinking that "the *ziva* alliances go back into Malagasy proto-history" and that a complete inventory of these alliances is necessary. We ourselves were able to find out that among the Tanala Ikongo, the oldest groups were linked through joking relationships to the later arrivals (Vérin, "Quelques aspects de la vie sociale et juridique des Tanala Ikongo," *Etudes de droit africain et de droit malgache* [Paris, 1965], 151–168).
45. George Peter Murdock, *Africa: Its People and Their Culture History* (New York, 1959). See also Gwynne, below, 250–268.

and Hébert have verified that certain plants imported to Madagascar in the distant past sometimes bear an Indonesian, sometimes
an African, name, sometimes both at once.[46] Hébert insists that
the use of identical names in different lands does not constitute
proof that a borrowing has taken place. He cites as an example
the fact that the designation of the banana tree by an Indonesian
name (*fontsy*) on the Malagasy west coast does not prove that it
was brought by Indonesian migrants since in the highlands the
banana tree has a Bantu name (*akondro*). He claims therefore that
both origins can be defended with valid arguments.[47] Hébert goes
on to cite Haudricourt's even more explicit point of view that a
name of Indonesian origin is not a certain sign that a given plant
originated in Indonesia, because the emigrants may have recognized
in the indigenous flora plants analogous to those of their homeland and have given them the same names.[48] These examples
illustrate the necessity for the inclusion of pollen analyses in
ethnobotanical research.

The field of ethnozoology contains similar problems. For
instance, even though we are more or less sure that zebu cattle
were introduced to Madagascar from Africa, the species involved
may still be obscure. Grandidier raised this problem apropos of
the bovid traces found at the site of Lamboharana.[49]

HISTORICAL DOCUMENTATION AND PHYSICAL GEOGRAPHY

Actual historical documentation is very rare. The Chinese and
Arabic texts on navigation between 800 and 1500 are sparse and
imprecise. However, we do encounter references to a land of
Waqwaq, sometimes situated to the east, sometimes to the west,
of the Indian Ocean. Deschamps thinks that (1) Indonesian
navigations (for colonization or piracy) continued through the
twelfth century; (2) the early settlers had centers in Madagascar

46. Deschamps, *Histoire*, 36; Jean-Claude Hébert, "Les noms de plantes
    vernaculaires malgaches," (1962), unpub. manuscript.
47. Hébert, "Les noms de plantes," 4.
48. André Haudricourt, *L'origine des plantes cultivées* (Paris, 1946).
49. Guillaume Grandidier, "Les animaux disparus de Madagascar, gisements,
    époques et causes de leur disparition," *La Revue de Madagascar* (August,
    1905), 111–128.

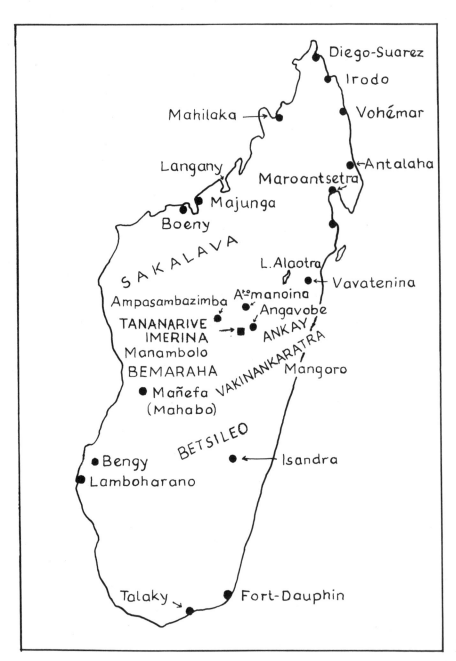

Prehistoric Sites on Madagascar

and used them as bases for expeditions of pillage; and (3) the distinctions between the Malagasy and Indonesians must have been rather slight at that time since they were able to understand each other's speech.[50]

All of the indications bearing on the relationship of Malagasy and Indonesians which have been enumerated above should naturally be judged in the light of physical geography. Donque has discussed the maritime context and thinks that geography did not determine how the Indonesians came to Madagascar.[51] One cannot assume that the immigrants came from Indonesia via the great south-equatorial current because the Mascarenes were not inhabited by humans until the coming of the Europeans in the sixteenth century. By the same token it would be an exaggeration to say, as does Grandidier, that wind directions and the currents of the Moçambique Channel could have prevented Africans from migrating to Madagascar in the remote past.[52]

I believe, as does Deschamps, in the importance of the northern route, passing to the south of India, and veering off to the East African coast, because this is also the pattern of distribution of the outrigger canoe in the Indian Ocean.[53] But I am more inclined to believe that the second phase of Austronesian migrations, which Hébert calls "deutero-Malay," was made directly between the area which includes India, southern Sri Lanka, the Maldives, and the Laccadives, on the one hand, and the northeast or northwest of Madagascar on the other. Sea-going craft from the vicinity of southern India are known to have arrived in Madagascar at various times. Around 1930 Vernier saw fishermen from the Laccadives come ashore in the area of Antalaha, after having drifted for several weeks. Farther in the past, we know from the testimony of Pyrard de Laval that Javanese engaged in commerce in the Maldives, and there is the testimony of Vasconcellos that in 1559

---

50. On this matter see also Jacques and Marcelle Faublée, "Madagascar vu par les auteurs Arabes avant le XIᵉ siècle," *Studia*, II (1963), 445–462; Deschamps, *Histoire*, 41; the article by Trimingham, below, 115, 126.

51. Gérald Donque, "Le contexte océanique des anciennes migrations," *Taloha*, I (1965), 43–69.

52. Grandidier, *Histoire physique*, I.

53. Deschamps, *Histoire*, 26–29.

he saw Javanese in the southeast of Madagascar.[54] There is no reason to assume that they had come there via a direct route.

The fact that accidental voyages took place is interesting, for they could have prepared the way for organized expeditions. As Sharp has shown for the Pacific, the ancient travelers, unwillingly drawn toward unknown islands, were able, thanks to their knowledge of astronomy, to mark the location of the newly discovered territory, return to their point of departure, and guide companions there on a voyage of colonization.[55]

The nonarchaeological proofs for the Austronesian origin of the Malagasy have not always been interpreted in the same way by different authors. It is possible, however, to set up a table of the results which have been obtained, if only to demonstrate the gaps in our knowledge which remain to be filled. (See Table 1.)

The Testimony of Archaeology

I shall deal here only with archaeological materials directly relevant to the study of Madagascar. However, it would be a great addition to our knowledge of the peopling of Madagascar if archaeological remains testifying to the former presence of Austronesians in the Indian subcontinent and in the archipelagos or islands to the south of India were discovered. Similarly, those interested in Madagascar impatiently await the discovery of pre-Islamic sites on the East African coast where the still hypothetical influences of the paleo-Austronesians might be seen. Proper archaeological research in Madagascar began only in 1962. Thus far a certain number of sites have been discovered which provide information both about the epoch of certain populations and also about their mode of life. In this context the chronological placement of the sites studied before 1962, above all Vohémar, should be reconsidered.

Table 2, indicating sites and discoveries dating to before 1500, recapitulates the results which have been obtained so far. In spite of the gaps, we immediately see that the first Malagasy coexisted

54. In particular, see Grandidier, *Histoire physique*, III, 82.
55. Andrew Sharp, *Ancient Voyagers in Polynesia* (Los Angeles, 1964), 159.

Table 1. Non-Archaeological Proofs for the Austronesian Origin of the Malagasy

Dates	Sources	Events and Regions of Their Occurence	State of Civilization
A.D. 300—900	*Linguistics* (Lexico-statistical, calendar, Wörter und Sachen, Bantu substratum, dialectal map, traditional system of orientation; *Ethnography* (African and Asian traits; ethnozoology, and botany) *Toponymy* (Comoros and Madagascar), *Physical Anthropology, Navigation Studies.*	1. Proto-Madagascans of Austronesian origin (paleo-austronesians) leave Southeast Asia or Indonesia; weak Hindu influence. 2. Arrival on the African coast. 3. Possible stops in South India and the Comoros. 4. Arrival in the West and Northwest of Madagascar 5. Progressive occupation of the greater part of the island (encounter with African migrants simultaneous).	1. Maritime populations were familiar with "slash and burn" agriculture, pottery, stone or bronze tools (iron discovered from the last migrants or en route to the island). 2. Acquisition of African traits; physical hybridization, African adoption of the Austronesian language. 3. First intensive clearing of land for tillage, fishing and hunting.
900—1300	*Linguistics* (duality of the lexical corpus, Indian words), *Traditions* (Merina: Tantara) *Historical References* (Arab, Indian), *Physical Anthropology* of the Neo-Austronesians, *Navigation* (drift, unpopulated Mascarenes).	1. Proto-Madagascans of Austronesian origin (neo-Austronesians) pursue navigations toward the West. 2. Contacts with Indian civilizations. 3. Settlements in the East and (or) Northwest. 4. Waq-waq expeditions into Africa. 5. Swahili immigrations from the ninth century onward.	1. Civilization and language close to those of the Paleo-Austronesians. 2. Iron and inundated rice culture are utilized. 3. Adaptation difficult in the East (climate, hostility of original occupants), relations with the "Islamicized" (population). (?)
1300—1500	*Ethnolinguistics, Traditions of the Vazimba* (Merina, Sihanaka, Betsileo), *Oral history* of the tribes, *Sorabe.*	*Highlands:* Progressive establishment of the Neo-Austronesians; alliance, then expulsion or absorption of the Vazimba. *Coasts:* Visits or immigrations from Africa. *On the margins:* Linguistic and cultural interpenetrations of the Paleo- and Neo-Austronesians.	*Highlands:* Building of fortified villages spreading of inundated rice culture. *Coasts:* Navigation and Commerce. *Throughout:* Pursuit of destruction of flora and fauna (burning and hunting), pastoral economy important.

Table 2. Archaeological Sites and Discoveries between 500 and 1500

Year					
500	Dating from Sarodrano(?) Adze from				
600	Ambatomanoina. Lithic traces of Manambolo(?). Adzes (?)				Mahilaka (yellow and black and sgraffiato pottery)
700	from sites of subfossils studied by Grandidier. Axe in Mullerornis and pottery from Ampasambazimba	Tafiampatsa Irodo Remains of eggs from Aepyornis Rc 800±90		Antanimenabe Irodo Rc 970±100 Archaeological primordial soil	
800	Remains of Hippopotamus lemerlei of Itampolo; perhaps destroyed by man Rc 970±20		Tafiantsirebika Irodo Rc 860±90 Remains of habitat		
900	Men of Talaky Rc 1110 ±80	Tafiampatsa Irodo Remains of habitat; and sherds of pottery ranging from Sassano-Islamic through 15th-century celadon; beads from before 1600			
1000					
1100					
1200					
1300					
1400					Necropolis of Vohémar
1500					

with fauna which has subsequently disappeared. It is reasonable to suppose that man himself was, either directly or indirectly, the primary factor in this extinction.[56] However, there are no accurately dated or thoroughly studied sites for the archaic period of Malagasy prehistory. We only have indications. In particular, it would be very important to know with what set of tools the paleo-Austronesians arrived in Madagascar. Since the stone or metal adze is the tool commonly encountered among Austronesian cultures, special attention has been accorded to this kind of object. Although You indicates that "visits to the grottoes of Bemaraha have recently been the occasion for the discovery of some traces of lithic industry though these traces are very embryonic and non-definitive," he does not offer further elaboration.[57]

Grandidier observes, to the contrary, that in the beds of extinct animal subfossils "one finds such ornaments as brilliant stones; teeth of the Aye-Aye (*chiromys madagascariensis*) which have been pierced so as to be worn in a necklace; pottery; and finally flints of exactly the same size and form as those which the indigenous people employed for the guns involved in the trade that the Arabs and the first Europeans introduced to the island."[58] It is not impossible that the "gunflints" which Grandidier has described are in reality small adzes in jasper. The similarity of the forms and the fact that analogous materials, flint and jasper, were used could have led Grandidier to this error.[59]

The adze fragment found by Bloch at Ambatomanoina is also of jasper. I have associated this piece with Indonesian artifacts of the same type and the same materials. But I have also pointed out that the isolated nature of this discovery makes it inconclusive, just as is the radiocarbon date for Sarodrano which it has been impossible to crosscheck by stratigraphic or other considerations.[60]

56. René Battistini and Pierre Vérin, "Les transformations écologiques à Madagascar à l'époque protohistorique," *Bulletin de Madagascar*, 244 (1966), 841–856.
57. André You, "Les populations de Madagascar," *L'Ethnographie*, 25 (1932), 91–105.
58. Grandidier, "Les animaux disparus de Madagascar," 127.
59. In addition, the introduction of the gun trade is much later than the extinction of the subfossils.
60. Maurice Bloch and Pierre Vérin, "Discovery of an Apparently Neolithic

The axe in Mullerornis bone and the pottery discovered in the subfossil site of Ampasambazimba are still other indications of the presence of man in Madagascar during the first millennium A.D., but they do not tell us much about whether these men were Africans or Indonesians.[61] In the present stage of archaeological research one can affirm merely that there was a population in Madagascar at the end of the first millennium A.D.

Since the ninth century the inhabitants of the region of Irodo have been in contact with Islamized peoples or at least with people coming from the East African coast. Carbon-14 datings and the presence of the Sassanian-Islamic type of pottery, a glazed blue-green, confirm settlement at a distant date.[62] At the beginning of the twelfth century a maritime population at Talaky possessed iron, knew how to weave cotton, and used spoons made of the shell *turbo*. As at Irodo, their pottery is decorated with motifs of stripes or dots disposed around the neck of the receptacle.[63]

Beginning in the ninth century, the coming of Islamized peoples, as in East Africa, constituted a major event in the ancient history of the coasts. Irodo was occupied between the ninth and the sixteenth centuries. At Mahilaka, the existence of *sgraffiato* and South Arabian pottery strongly suggests an occupation between the eleventh and fourteenth centuries. Later on—both before and after the arrival of European traders—the hinterland depended on and thus was controlled by the port cities of Vohémar, Langany, and Boeny, the only outlets for commerce. (See Table 3.)

Artifact in Madagascar," *Man*, I (1966), 240–241. The date for Sarodrano is 490 A.D. (+90). Analysis of Gekushuin Laboratory, Tokyo, 1966.

61. A jar from Ampasambazimba has a form which rather closely resembles the ovoid pieces of the Sa-Huynh culture.

62. René Battistini and Pierre Vérin, "Irodo et la tradition vohémarienne," *Arabes et Islamisés*, 17–32. The glazed Islamic pottery from Irodo has also been found in a few sites on the African coast. Neville Chittick, in a personal communication, states that this ware dates through the tenth century.

63. René Battistini, Pierre Vérin, and René Rason, "Le site archéologique de Talaky, cadre géographique et géologique; premiers travaux de fouille; notes ethnographiques sur le village actuel proche du site," *Annales de l'Université de Madagascar*, I (1963), 111–134. Chittick has suggested that the abraded shells may be explained by the custom of cutting off the shell to get at the meat. Without ruling out this explanation, we believe that this is not the case for Talaky specimens.

Table 3. Archaeological Sites between 1400 and 1700

	Coasts			Interior			
1400	Necropolis of *Vohémar* *Langany* in full vigor Abundance of late-Ming and post-Ming Chinese pottery						
1500	Portuguese intrusion does not interrupt activities *Boeny* At first daughter city of Langany Destroyed by the Sakalavas						
1600	Langany continues to prosper after the destruction of Langany. Flourishes until the rise of Majunga	*Sarodrano* Pre-Vezo, then Vezo establishment of cities			*Lake Alaotra* Civilization of Vohitrandriana (Sihanaka pre-Merina)	R. 1600 Ancient Vakinihadianan village of *Angavobe*	
1700			*Nosy Lolo* and neighboring islands	Tombs said to be Vazimba of the *Manambolo*			
1800	*Majunga* Last Antalaotran city Expulsion or subjection of the last Antalaotrans						Civilization of the Isandras. Abandonment of caves at the end of Madagascan period
1900							

Elsewhere I have briefly traced the history of these Islamic settlements, and their past interests us here only insofar as it might link up with the Austronesian migrations.[64] Suffice it to note that these Islamized peoples produced a Malagasy-African mixture, and also that the presence of Islamized groups in the Malagasy northeast could very well have been contemporaneous with the neo-Austronesian migrations of the beginning of the second millennium.

The gaps in our knowledge caused by the lack of sites for the first millennium also extend to the period of neo-Austronesian migrations of the second millennium. However, the sites discovered near Mananara by Battistini, and in the hinterland of Vavatenina by Dandoy, will perhaps furnish the evidence for the arrival in the highlands of the ancestors of the Merina and Sihanaka.[65] Except for the upper levels of Ampasambazimba, whose dates are still in question, we do not yet have at our disposal highland sites which date back further than the fifteenth century. Field work in Isandra has brought to light a civilization dating from the seventeenth to the nineteenth centuries which corresponds to the known history of the Betsileo groups. But the deepest levels at Isandra did not furnish traces of either the Vazimba or the Ngola (pre-Vazimba inhabitants according to tradition).[66]

At Angavobe, at the beginning of the seventeenth century, there lived a people with a knowledge of iron who made graphite pottery. Graphite is characteristic of Merina pottery, and this distinctive trait will no doubt aid in its identification in the oldest sites which produced it.[67] The Merina civilization of the eighteenth century possesses fairly conspicuous Indonesian traits, including the architecture of stone gates and tombs. The latter

64. Pierre Vérin, "Les anciens établissements islamiques à Madagascar," *Sociétés et Compagnies de Commerce en Orient et l'Océan Indien* (Paris, 1970), 255–259.
65. Both Battistini and Dandoy have written to me concerning their finds.
66. Pierre Vérin, René Battistini, and Daniel Chabouis, "L'ancienne civilisation de l'Isandra," *Taloha*, I (1965), 249–285. It was hoped that the excavations would disclose the strata of earlier inhabitants beneath those of the historical Betsileo from Isandra.
67. Pierre Vérin and Christian Gachet, "Les sites naturels et archéologiques de la réserve forestière d'Angavokely," *Revue de Madagascar*, 28 (1964), 53–58.

are often characterized by a stepped structure, with walls made of original courses of stones interrupted in corners and at regular intervals by vertical slabs, a practice common in Indonesia.[68] This mode of construction has been described for the island of Nias (Sumatra); it would be interesting to know its distribution in Southeast Asia.

I suggest that the imprecision of the affinities results essentially from disparity in the time of the documentation. For Madagascar we have ethnographic documents dating from the sixteenth century whose *rapprochement* with the archaeological traits of Austronesian cultures is tempting, but which actually constitute only indications that a cultural affiliation could be established. For instance, the burial sites in tree trunks in Niah recall the canoe tombs of the early Merina queens and those of the Betsimisaraka of the Vatomandry region; the megalithic tradition of Southeast Asia calls for comparison with the raised stones so common in a large part of Madagascar; and the fact that such peculiar elements as the outrigger canoe, the pump drill, the toothed coconut grater, etc. are found in Southeast Asian, East African, and Malagasy culture is suggestive. These all represent a series of indications to be borne in mind, but only archaeological research will be able to show whether these traits were transported from one region to another. It will still be necessary to compare in detail the objects involved and the periods to which they belong in order to determine if there has been diffusion or independent invention. Do the shell spoons of the Kalanay complex have anything in common with the spoons of Kilwa in East Africa and with those of Vohémar or Talaky in Madagascar? Each type possesses differences in material and important divergences in appearance through time.

For the kind of problem which concerns us here I should like to single out two especially important aspects of early Malagasy culture: fortifications and pottery complexes. Adrien Mille is currently investigating the areas from which the Vazimba were deposed (Antsihanaka, Ankay, Imerina, Vakinankaratra, and Betsileo). He has found deep moats constructed on hilltops as defenses for human settlements. It seems that nowhere in the

68. Deschamps, *Histoire*, photograph 65.

coastal regions of Africa do we find this type of protective device. Its existence in Indonesia, however, has been pointed out by Deschamps, who speaks of the "hill-top village surrounded by a trench."[69] On the other hand, the systems of protection in western Madagascar (wooden palisades or those formed by the growth of plants) are typically African. A point-by-point comparison between the construction of fortified villages of Indonesia and the same kind of construction in the highlands of Madagascar (which, in addition, also have in common elements of lithic architecture, mentioned above) would be of the greatest interest. The connections which might be adduced from this correspondence would confirm the more markedly Southeast Asian character of the culture of the neo-Austronesians.

As far as pottery goes, we have not yet gone far enough to be able to divide the styles between two traditions: paleo- versus neo-Austronesian. However, overall, it is useful to formulate similarities, notably with what is known of the complex called Sa-Huynh Kalanay, after the two towns of the same name in Indonesia. Solheim was the first to suggest an affinity. Commenting, in a review of a pamphlet concerning an exhibition of Malagasy pottery, he wrote:

> The archaeological material illustrated ... does not bear specific resemblance to pottery from sites in Southeast Asia but it does show a resemblance to some of the pottery associated with iron in Indonesia. The present day pottery shown in the first three plates is generally similar to Indonesian pottery, particularly the form of the three multiple-necked jars in the third plate. The double-necked jar in the lower right hand corner of the third plate shares several specific elements of form and decoration with two earthenware jars from South Sumatra.[70]

One can usefully compare the types of pottery, both archaeological and contemporary, found in Madagascar with the plates in the volume entitled *Sa-huynh Pottery Relationships in Southeast Asia*.[71] Madagascar possesses all of the types of the Sa-Huynh

69. *Ibid.*, 21.
70. Wilhelm G. Solheim, "Review of La Poterie Malgache," *Asian Perspectives*, VIII (1966), 132–133.
71. Wilhelm G. Solheim (ed.), "Sa-Huynh Pottery Relationships in Southeast Asia," *Asian Perspectives*, III (1961), 97–108.

Kalanay complex with the exception of the funerary jar, which the archaeological sites of the first millennium may eventually reveal.

Among the cooking pots are fairly deep rounded receptacles. In Imerina the rice pot is very broad but pots for other foods are globe-shaped; this contrast is less marked elsewhere. In Southeast Asia we encounter the same varieties of cooking pots, and this also subsumes, as in Madagascar and in Anjouan (Comoros), those with an angle between the lateral wall and the base. The Malagasy jars and jugs are ovoid (with or without neck), round, or with a very broad diameter, and more or less carinated. These differentiations parallel fairly closely those encountered in the cooking pots. The base can be either flat, pointed, or associated with a light support.

The footed vessels (supported bowls, lamps, or incense burners) most closely approach those found in Southeast Asia. For the time being, our archaeological finds of footed bowls are limited to the highlands (Antsihanaka, Imerina, and Betsileo). The Betsileo examples are shorter with a very broad base, while the Sihanaka and Merina plates have a narrower and more slender foot. However, the Merina tradition (those of the *Tantara* in particular) attests to a multiplicity of types of plate.

The lids seem to me to derive from these truncated forms. Dez has noted that their handle is, in Vakinankaratra, called *tongotra* (foot), as a result of the fact that one can turn them over so as to use them as containers.[72] Formerly in Betsileo when the lid was turned with the handle toward the top, the internal cavity could serve as a lamp. This use points up the resemblance of these lids to the footed vessels, and, moreover, it is not easy to distinguish between them in archaeological sites.[73] The truncated lid of the "Thailand hat type" has been encountered on one occasion in the form of a Sakalava vessel.

We shall not concern ourselves with descriptions of the bowls

72. Jacques Dez, "La poterie de Soamanandrariny," *Revue de Madagascar*, 30 (1965), 52–56.
73. Pierre Vérin, "Several Types of Obsolete Madagascar Pottery," *Asian Perspectives*, XI (1968), 111–118.

with and without bases, because it seems to me that they could as easily derive from Islamic or African prototypes. On the other hand, stone cooking pots from Vohémar have a form similar to tripedal pottery cooking pots known in Malaya. Moreover, pottery cooking pots have also been found in Irodo and Vohémar. The comparison with the Chinese bronze vessels may remain valid, since Malayan, Chinese, and Malagasy tripedal pieces could derive from a common Asiatic origin. Finally, the morphological plates include cylindrical vases with a bulging lower part and a wide opening. Perhaps these are related to those wide-necked vases for which Malleret shows an early Chinese influence which reverberated to Sa-Huynh.[74] This preliminary comparison of Malagasy pottery with the Southeast Asian pottery of the Sa-Huynh Kalanay complex should also include the processes of decoration, but this is a more complicated question. For the moment I can offer only certain generalities: In both the motifs are ordinarily made by incision, impression, and slipping, in the two cultural areas where red and black slips are preferred. Malagasy *peignage* corresponds to Solheim's description of Sa-Huynh as "paddle impressed." Solheim's observation that "the patterns of decoration are commonly in horizontal bands, and include vertical or diagonal rectangular elements, curvilinear scrolls, rectangular scrolls, or meanders, zigzags, triangles and chevrons,"[75] could apply, as a whole, to the decorative motifs of Malagasy pottery.

This review of the first archaeological results reveals that the theory of the Austronesian origin of the Malagasy still has been no more than formulated. A solution seems possible only if three conditions are met: (1) there is a discovery of numerous sites of the first millennium on the Malagasy coasts; (2) there is an intensive utilization of disciplines complementary to archaeology, notably palynology and, above all, physical anthropology, which alone will determine the Austronesian characteristics of the skeletons

74. Louis Malleret, "Quelques poteries de Sa-Huynh dans leurs rapports avec divers sites du Sud-Est de l'Asie," *Asian Perspectives*, III (1961), 113–120.
75. Wilhelm G. Solheim, "Indonesian Culture and Malagasy Origins," *Taloha*, I (1965), 33–42.

found in the oldest sites;[76] and (3) sites on the African coast anterior to the ninth century are discovered and studied.

76. In this connection the only studies which have been made to date are of Vohémar, and they concern a fairly recent period (fifteenth through eighteenth centuries). These studies indicate the extent to which the Iharanians were of mixed racial origins.

THE PROBLEM OF MALAGASY ORIGINS

Aidan Southall

Everyone interested in the problems of Malagasy origins has addressed himself to the reasons for the fundamental relative linguistic homogeneity of Madagascar, expressed in an array of cultures which, though varying considerably, are striking variations on a set of common themes and yet are carried by human groups of astonishingly diverse physical types. It has been pointed out often enough that linguistic homogeneity cannot have been imposed by conquest; certainly not by the only known widespread conquest—that of the Merina during the last two centuries. Furthermore, there is a great deal of comparative evidence to show how easily conquerors adopt the language of the conquered rather than the other way round.

Some examples from East Africa will help to illustrate the structural circumstances in which this may occur. The Bito dynasty of Bunyoro abandoned its Nilotic speech and adopted that of the conquered Bantu, keeping only their Nilotic "drum-names" and a few other scattered words. Similarly the Tutsi of Rwanda, whose distinctive physical type makes it impossible to assume that they are descended from Bantu speakers, show no acceptable sign of language other than that of their Bantu subjects. There are other instances of both Bantu-derived and Nilotic-derived dynasties

I wish to express my appreciation for grant award GS–1301 from the National Science Foundation which made possible my work in Madagascar.

adopting the speech of their Sudanic subjects, and so forth. But an example nearer to the sphere which is our immediate concern is that of the Kilindi dynasty of Usambara, who may well be of Arabic origin but who retain no Arab speech. Even more recently, the Omani sultans of Zanzibar, in little more than a century, lost all but a nominal adherence to Arabic speech, for most purposes adopting the Swahili of their Bantu subjects. A further striking example is, of course, the remarkable retention of Arabic script, without any knowledge of Arabic speech, by many high-caste groups on the southeastern coast of Madagascar.

All of these cases concern the contacts of agricultural peoples, not fundamentally different from each other in their levels of technical mastery. But because the question of Malagasy origins involves much longer periods, other factors have to be taken into account, more particularly the possibility of confrontation between peoples with and without the knowledge of agriculture and possibly even with and without the knowledge of ironworking. In these circumstances, I suggest, there is a good deal of evidence to show that the language of the group with the simpler technology, and necessarily much lower possible population density, may well disappear. Cases in point are the Pygmies, speaking Bantu languages, or the Ndorobo, Boni, and other hunting and collecting remnants in East Africa, who speak the Nilo-Hamitic or Kushitic languages of their economically superior neighbors, although some of their components certainly did not earlier belong to these speech communities.

Early Inhabitants

This conclusion that peoples with simpler technology and lower density may adopt the language of those with more advanced technology and higher population density may or may not prove to be relevant to the peopling of Madagascar, but it cannot be ignored. For example, Dez properly points out that the Vazimba of Madagascar did not necessarily speak Malagasy.[1] But if not, certain considerations have to be kept clearly in mind. Let us

---

1. Jacques Dez, "Quelques hypothèses formulées par la linguistique comparée à l'usage de l'archéologie," *Taloha*, I (1965), 200.

suppose, for the sake of argument, that they spoke a Bantu language. This is not so far-fetched, for it seems that their possible connection with the presumably Bantu-speaking Zimba of Moçambique has never been seriously explored. Deschamps refers to the sixteenth century sacking of Kilwa by Zimba, who thereafter supposedly fought their way up the eastern coast of Africa to Malindi.[2] Subsequently they disappeared, mysteriously. Nor has any suggestion ever been made as to where they came from except, equally mysteriously, "the interior." (Since today the Zimba groups of western Moçambique are certainly nearest to the scene of that sixteenth century action, it is strange that few attempts have been made to relate them to the earlier Zimba.)[3] Even in the light of Idrisi's twelfth-century statement that the Zanj had no boats, one can assume that the southeastern Bantu could have acquired boats not long after that, if only from the Arabo-Shirazi people of the coast. But, in fact, since the boats of the East African coast are mostly of Indonesian and not of an Arab type, it is likely that they acquired them earlier than this time from Indonesian sources. The Vazimba could thus have made their way to Madagascar and occupied the central part of the island for several centuries before their eclipse by the Merina and other Malagasy groups. However, I do not wish to add yet another undemonstrable hypothesis; on the contrary, I think it difficult to accept that the Vazimba were non-Malagasy speakers. If we could regard them as bearers of a culture with a very simple technology, perhaps pre-agricultural, and with a very low degree of political centralization, it would be easy to understand, in the light of comparable situations elsewhere, the disappearance of their language before the impact of the superior technology and denser population of subsequent invaders. But the Vazimba are represented

2. Hubert Deschamps, *Histoire de Madagascar* (Paris, 1960), 25.
3. For a discussion of the Zimba, see René Avelot, "Les grands mouvements de peuples en Afrique: Jaga et Zimba," *Bulletin de Géographie Historique et Descriptive*, I (1912), 115–135, 188–191; Joâo dos Santos (trans. Gaëtan Charpy), *Histoire de l'Ethiopie orientale* (Paris, 1688), 149–157; E.C. Baker, "Notes on the History of the Wasageju," *Tanganyika Notes and Records*, 27 (1949), 24–26; John Milner Gray, "A Journey by Land from Tete to Kilwa in 1616," *ibid.*, 25 (1948), 46–47; Roger Summers, *Inyanga* (Cambridge, 1958), 255. Cf. Ptolemy, i, 9, iv, 1–8.

in the oral tradition as former rulers, gradually absorbed, obliterated, or driven to the west. This makes it difficult to understand why, if they spoke a different language, it disappeared. At the same time, it is strange that no hint of a different language is given by recorded oral tradition. If the Vazimba rulers of early Merina tradition had been speaking a different language, it would surely have been noted, and if they were indeed independent rulers, there was no easily discernible reason for them to have lost their former language. Nonetheless, it is hard to forget the close correspondence of the name of the Vazimba to that of the ethnic group in Moçambique, especially in view of the retention of the name Makoa by Moçambiquan Africans in Madagascar—as Julien remarked long ago.[4]

Perhaps the Vazimba who were in contact with the early Merina were not really rulers at all, but simply prominent persons in the aboriginal communities with whom the Merina inter-married because of their importance as long-established guardians of the shrines of the supernatural beings of the country without whose favor the fertility and prosperity of newcomers could not be assured. Such an assumption is certainly supported by the general nature of the Vazimba communities which have survived in western Madagascar.[5] The superior technology and population density of the Merina would have favored the adoption of Merina speech by those Vazimba who were incorporated into Merina society, while the remnants of Vazimba who escaped or were driven away would similarly, in the course of time, have absorbed the speech of other Malagasy peoples of superior technology by whom they were surrounded or infiltrated. (The derivation of Vazimba from the early Malagasy word *ziva* [joking relation] proposed by Hébert, and since adopted by other writers, is ingenious, like so many other suggestions in this field, but completely unconvincing from a linguistic point of view.[6]) It is simpler to

4. Gustave Julien, *Institutions politiques et sociales de Madagascar* (Paris, 1908), I, 11.
5. Alfred Grandidier, *Histoire physique, naturelle et politique de Madagascar, l'origine des Malgaches* (Paris, 1901); E. Birkeli, "Les Vazimba de la Côte Ouest, "*Mémoire de l'Académie Malgache*, XXII (1936), 15–45.
6. Jean-Claude Hébert, "La parenté à plaisanterie à Madagascar," *Bulletin de Madagascar*, 142, 143 (1958), 175–216, 267–329.

consider the homogeneity of the Malagasy language as being due to the spread of the first people to settle in the island, while recognizing the possibility that an earlier population, of markedly lower technical equipment and density, could easily have disappeared or been absorbed without linguistic trace.

Early settlers

One of the premises in arriving at the most approximate dating for the arrival of the first settlers and Malagasy speakers has hitherto often been the assumption that they brought with them the knowledge of ironworking, but with the discovery in 1965 of a possible stone adze head and the likelihood of further such discoveries, this assumption has to be modified.[7] Of course it is conceivable for stone and iron tools (and, still more, stone and bronze tools) to coexist in the same culture for a certain intermediate period, but it would be stretching credibility unnecessarily to assume that stone adzes indicate anything other than a stone culture. Again, we can either relate the possible bearers of a stone-using culture of Madagascar to an earlier sparse population having very simple technical equipment, easily overwhelmed linguistically by later arrivals, or consider the possibility that the seafarers who brought the first Malagasy speech came from a pre-Iron Age culture. Deschamps, for example, assumed a date of about A.D. 1000, plus or minus two or three hundred years, for the first voyages, because he thought that these immigrants must have left Indonesia after the coming of iron and before the coming of Hinduism.[8] Obviously, if they left before the coming of iron, the date must have been considerably earlier.

To account for the linguistic homogeneity of the island, it is necessary to assume that it was at some stage effectively peopled by persons of the same speech community. But any mass immigration seems highly improbable. Even the repeated arrival of parties of people of the same speech community seems rather unlikely, given the difficulties of travel and the hardships encountered along the route. Solheim suggests that, particularly

---

7. Maurice Bloch and Pierre Vérin, "Discovery of an Apparently Neolithic Artifact in Madagascar," *Man*, I (1966), 240.
8. Deschamps, *Histoire*, 29.

during the first five centuries B.C., sailor traders from Indonesia might have passed from Indonesia via the Malabar coast and possibly also East Africa to Madagascar.[9] He assumes that they spoke a trading *lingua franca* and took several generations to reach Madagascar. One would like to have some evidence on both these points. Did they have iron tools and weapons or not? Without them, could they have made successful attacks and settlements on the Malabar coast as suggested? If the process took several generations, what attracted them all the way to Madagascar, and why did not the same attractions bring other immigrants from Malabar, Arabia, and even East Africa to Madagascar at much the same time, with the inevitable result of a heterogenous, not homogenous, language base?

On the other hand, it is easy to imagine Indonesian traders on their way to or from Malabar being driven off course— eventually to Madagascar. It is even conceivable that parties of Indonesian sailors were driven directly across from Indonesia to Madagascar on the southern currents, but we have to assume that such accidents occured first and only to Indonesians. Given certain assumptions this is quite likely, but the more the hypothesis depends upon a repetition of similar accidents, the more unlikely it becomes.

Most evidence points to the crucial first landings having taken place on the east coast of Madagascar. The ecological evidence amassed by Poirier points to the extension of settlement from the southeast to the northwest. The whole burden of oral tradition also emphasizes an extension from the southeast.[10] This applies to the spread of the Antemoro diviners and the founders of ruling lines: the spread of ruling lines to the Betsileo and the Bara, and from the Tanosy and Tandroy through the Mahafaly and the Masikoro to the Sakalava and right up the western half of the island. Although it is wrong to confound the migrations of rulers with mass migrations of common people, and much oral tradition naturally refers to the former rather than the latter, there are many

9.   Wilhelm Solheim, "Indonesian Culture and Malagasy Origins," *Taloha,* I (1965), 33–42.
10. Jean Poirier, "Données écologiques et démographiques de la mise en place des Proto-Malgaches," *Taloha,* I (1965), 61–82.

signs that a certain general movement of population did take place in the same direction. It is true that one must assume that oral tradition refers at most to the past millennium and proves little for any previous period, but to assume a precisely contrary situation in the previous millennium seems uneconomical. Sailors arriving from East Africa would certainly have come most easily, via the Comoros, to the northwest coast of Madagascar. Therefore, if it is thought more likely that the landings were in the east or southeast, then it is also more likely that the early settlers were seafarers brought by storms from the northeast or by currents directly from the east, rather than that they arrived by way of the East African coast.

The question of what boats were used also remains confused. Poirier argues that outrigger canoes were unknown on the east coast of Madagascar and that dugouts and, above all, rafts were used.[11] This is difficult to reconcile with Grandidier's statement that the Betsimisaraka of the east coast raided the Comoros and even the towns of the East African coasts in fleets of hundreds of canoes, which he implies were single outriggers.[12] Indeed, there is abundant evidence for the presence of outrigger canoes on the east coast of Africa and even for the possibility that some were of quite large size.

Poirier argues for a late arrival of the first inhabitants of Madagascar—during the second half of the first millennium A.D.—on the basis of the relation between population growth and deforestation.[13] The thesis is important; but it seems to me that the precise value of a number of the factors concerned is highly debatable. It depends, for example, upon assumptions, some stated and some not—which must in the nature of the case be arbitrary—about population growth; the balance between fishing and agriculture and other forms of subsistence; the dating and relative importance of different types of exploitation of forest lands, such as various kinds of slash and burn cultivation, or burning as a preparation for cattle pasture. None of these values can possibly be absolute, and a slight shift in them would easily push back the

11. *Ibid.*, 65.
12. Grandidier, *Histoire*, 61.
13. Poirier, "Données écologiques et démographiques," 61–82.

peopling of the island to a thousand years earlier than the author assumes. Above all, there could have been—and the unfolding archaeological, linguistic, and other cultural evidence makes it look increasingly likely that there were—long periods of coastal occupation by peoples whose primary food was shellfish before the agricultural exploitation and deforestation of the interior began. Although this factor seems only indirectly connected to the question of first arrivals, Poirier's work nonetheless provides a valuable basis of calculation for the progressive occupation of the interior.

It is not necessary to account for the East African elements (such as cattle, goats, dogs, and sorghum) in Malagasy culture by assuming, as Deschamps does, that the first Indonesian immigrants picked up these elements in East Africa on their way to Madagascar. Once the basic linguistic homogeneity is explained, the accretion of other linguistic and cultural elements, from African, Arabic, and other sources, is very easily accounted for by the later arrival of traders and settlers. We have to assume that the first Indonesian immigrants had a considerable period, probably centuries, during which to increase and disperse themselves in Madagascar before any rivals bearing other languages and cultures had a chance to establish themselves effectively in the island. This, I believe, was the logical argument of Malzac, though it was combined with other untenable suggestions.[14] If Indian traders from Malabar, and Arab, Persian, or Swahili traders from Arabia, the Persian Gulf, or East Africa had been able to establish communities in Madagascar before the Indonesian cultural base was firmly rooted, the result would almost inevitably have been a greater diversity of language and culture than is actually the case. Furthermore, it is rather doubtful whether such traders would ever have been attracted to Madagascar either as an uninhabited island, or even as one sparsely peopled by scattered hunters and gatherers, without the existence of a disposable surplus. From this point of view, our earlier hypothesis about the involuntary arrival of immigrants by storm, or adverse current and shipwreck, is more plausible.

Although it is idle to speculate upon the population dynamics

14. R.P. Malzac, *Histoire du Royaume Hova* (Tananarive, 1912).

of a hypothetical group of possibly shipwrecked men and women, there can be no doubt that as little as three centuries would have been quite sufficient to distribute a number of small communities around the coast of Madagascar to the more favorable points. Seafarers, even if shipwrecked, could easily have constructed boats. Once the spread had occured, all subsequent chance arrivals would eventually have been absorbed into extant polities; they would not have affected the basic linguistic structure, but they could have introduced variations of physical and genetic composition and exerted a selective influence here and there on particular elements of the culture.

It is now universally accepted that Malagasy is connected to the Indonesian languages, but the identification of its closest connections is still elusive. The most complete and adequate study is that of Dahl, but, according to the author himself, the choice of Maanyan as a specific comparison was almost a coincidence.[15] There are many Indonesian languages which remain little known; it would therefore be rash to assume that the point of origin of the proto-Malagasy was either the present or any past country occupied by the Maanyan or their ancestors. The time elapsed, the migrations of Indonesian peoples, and the fact that Malagasy has not yet been compared to many other Indonesian languages, make such an assumption impossible. Dahl himself notes other characteristics of Malagasy which suggest comparisons with the languages of the Celebes and the Philippines respectively. Thus the choice, although limited to a certain area, still remains fairly wide.

Incomplete as is the search for those current languages and their predecessors which might be closest to Malagasy, the study of Malagasy dialects is even more so. Earlier studies suffered from the extreme poverty of data, so that few terms could be effectively compared across the whole range of dialects; nor was the interrelation and clustering of dialects made clear. The recent work of Dez and Hébert is particularly interesting because the objectives are narrowed and the data are correspondingly more adequate.[16]

15. Otto Dahl, *Malgache et Maanjan* (Oslo, 1951), 2, 23, 371.
16. Dez, "Quelques hypothèses," 200; Jean Claude Hébert, "Les mots 'mer' et 'poisson' en malgache," *Bulletin de Madagascar*, 185 (1961), 899–916. See also his "Recherches sur l'histoire et la civilization Malgaches:

In the fields of agriculture, food preparation, hunting, fishing, pottery, metallurgy, basketry, weaving, housebuilding, and navigation Dez finds a largely Indonesian vocabulary.[17] On the other hand an appreciable number of domestic animals and some plants have Bantu-derived names, some words for musical instruments and measures are of Arabic derivation, as are the terms for paper and ink, while he finds some Indian connections for the word for rice (though Dahl is able to relate it to a Maanyan term).[18]

Hébert's work is even more relevant to the attempt to amplify evidence for the successive peopling of Madagascar. From a study of the dialectal distribution of Malagasy terms for fish, he further confirms the general division of Malagasy dialects already arrived at by a number of others into those of the west coast, those of the east coast, and those of the central plateau.[19] There also is confirmation of much other evidence suggesting that the culture of the west coast peoples represents the oldest stratum, that of the east coast a later intrusion, and that of the central plateau the most recent of all. The parallel study of terms for the sea leads to the same conclusions. What is still more intriguing is that the closest Indonesian cognates of terms used on the east and north coast, on the central plateau or on certain mid-points of the east coast, and finally in the south and west, are found in corresponding relative latitudes, north, midway, and south in Indonesia and beyond. Thus the eastern and northern Malagasy word for the sea is linked closely to Malayan usage, the term used at two midpoints on the east coast to that of Borneo, and the term of the south and west to that of Melanesia or Polynesia. Although a much more broadly based inquiry is needed to go beyond the realm of fascinating hypothesis, this study is already highly suggestive in view of the attribution by some authorities of the darker skin and curlier hair of the coastal Malagasy to Melanesian origin.

---

documents pour un atlas linguistique des calendriers provinciaux malgaches," *Bulletin de Madagascar*, 191 (1962), 339–352; *idem*. "La cosmographie ancienne malgache suivie de l'énumération des points cardinaux et l'importance du Nord-Est," *Taloha*, II (1965), 83–195.
17. Dez, "Quelques hypothèses," 197–213.
18. Dahl, *Malgache et Maanjan*, 322.
19. Hébert, "Les mots," 899–916.

The distribution of calendrical and cosmographical systems in Madagascar leads to remarkably consistent indications.[20] Because the peoples of the southern and western regions have only three of the Sanskrit names for months, which they apply instead to seasons, it is reasonable to assume that the Sanskrit monthly calendar which reached the east arrived later than the first wave of Indonesian migration. The Sanskrit calendar presumably became modified as knowledge passed from the east to the south and west, resulting in the retention there of only the three names, transferred from their former monthly significance to apply to seasons. Hébert's evidence suggests that the first wave of migrants must have left Indonesia about the beginning of the Christian era in order to have escaped a stronger Hindu and Sanskrit influence, while the second wave must have been, according to which part of Indonesia was their point of departure, at least after the second or fifth century A.D. Later still, the Arabo-Swahili calendar reached the northwest and east coasts, spreading to Merina and Betsileo on the plateau probably through the wanderings of Antemoro diviners. These first serious essays in ethnolinguistics suggest a promising field for further work.

The most vexing question is: On which coast did the founders of the Malagasy culture arrive? For the reasons stated above, my first logical conclusion was that it must have been the east coast and that the first wave of settlers moved to the west when the second wave of settlers came three or four hundred years later. All of the evidence that we have of cultural accumulation is of successive cultural pressures moving, in general, from east to west. It is generally accepted that the peoples of the west and south (the Southern Sakalava, Vezo, Mahafaly, and parts of the Bara) represent the oldest stratum of Malagasy culture. This is to neglect remnants such as the western Vazimba and the Mikeha, but their evidence would not alter the argument. However, Deschamps, following Dahl and supported in turn by Vérin, argues forcefully for a landfall on the northwestern coast. Deschamps and Vérin assume that the immigrants came by way of India, East Africa,

20. Hébert, "Recherches sur l'histoire," 339–352; *idem*, "La cosmographie ancienne," 83–195.

and the Comoros, a position which I find untenable.[21]

The strongest argument is that of Dahl. He discovered that in Maanyan and in common Indonesian the Malagasy terms for north and south refer to west and east.[22] He explains that this is due to the fact that the terms refer fundamentally to the regime of wind and weather and that the west and east winds of much of Indonesia are the counterpart of the north and south winds found only on the west coast of Madagascar. However, Dahl points out that there also are other Indonesian languages in which, because of a similar wind and weather regime, the terms concerned refer to north and south as in Malagasy.[23] I find two possible solutions to this dilemma. Either the first arrivals came from a part of Indonesia where these terms in fact referred to north and south as in Malagasy, and they landed on the east coast as I have assumed; or as they came from the east they were driven by the winds and currents down on to the northwest coast (an appreciable part of which in fact faces almost north), but without passing by way of East Africa or India. They may very well have touched the Comoros, which were probably uninhabited at the time. Comoro culture is very little known to us, but almost certainly has a considerable Indonesian stratum under its predominantly Arab and Swahili elements.

We must assume that, wherever the first landings were made, small, autonomous communities were established and spread around the coast of Madagascar and that their inhabitants lived by fishing and shell collecting, gathering wild roots and fruits, and, where possible, dry rice cultivation, though this trait may have arrived somewhat later. Any subsequent arrivals, whether driven involuntarily and shipwrecked or coming in the hope of trade, if they survived and stayed for any length of time, must have been absorbed by the original settlers. One assumes that some three to six centuries or more after the first arrivals, an important second wave of immigrants came, perhaps the first to

21. Pierre Vérin, "Austronesian Contributions to the Culture of Madagascar and Some Archaeological Problems," above, 169; Dahl, *Malgache et Maanjan*, 326; Deschamps, *Histoire*, 28.
22. Dahl, *Malgache et Maanjan*, 326.
23. *Ibid.*

bring with them the knowledge of ironworking and irrigated rice cultivation. They may also have brought with them elements of the Hindu and Sanskrit culture which had been earlier incorporated into their Indonesian culture. They cannot have settled mainly on the west coast; if they had, the distribution of cultural elements in Madagascar would be incomprehensible. If they did not land in the east but rather in the far northwest or north, they must have proceeded around the east coast rather than the west.

My present hypothesis is that the southern and western peoples of Madagascar represent, in certain linguistic and cultural respects —overlaid by many subsequent transformations—the first proto-Malagasy Indonesian immigrants. The eastern and northern peoples similarly represent subsequent arrivals, and the Merina represent later arrivals still. These three phases are of course only a roughly schematic way of representing what must have been a much more complicated process. My assumption is that the western peoples were originally distributed all around the coast but were not found inland. When the second wave of immigrants occupied the east coast the peoples of the first phase partly mingled with them and partly withdrew westward, just as occurred later when the Vazimba withdrew before the Merina. Given the structural homogeneity of the Malagasy dialects, it is necessary to make this assumption rather than to posit that the first phase peoples occupied the west and the second phase peoples found the east unoccupied.

My chief concern has been to find the connecting links among the known, or most reasonably supposed, data. The chief virtue in setting up a speculative hypothesis is that as soon as an attempt is made to substantiate the necessary elements in an integrated statement, the weaknesses in the arguments appear. I therefore offer a statement, in skeletal form, not in the naive hope of easily attaining the truth which has eluded others but as a necessary exercise to expose the weaknesses in my own arguments.

The hypothesis to which I am logically driven by consideration of the major evidence, produced by those more expert in this field than I, runs as follows. Once the basis of Indonesian settlement and language was laid widely but sparsely round the coasts of

Madagascar, with gradual penetration inland, any subsequent arrivals of small groups could have been largely absorbed into the existing populations without leaving very distinct traces. This could have occured with subsequent arrivals of Indonesian language and culture, or of persons of other derivations. Some rather indistinct traces of other derivations are suggested by the presence of Arabic and Islamic elements in the language, culture, and traditions of both the nothern and southeastern coasts.

It is generally assumed that it was a second or subsequent wave of Indonesian immigrants which brought more advanced technology and agricultural methods, including iron tools and irrigated rice cultivation, along with the Hindu and Sanskrit elements picked up along the way. It is logical to assume that a significant part of this second phase of Indonesian immigration occurred before the arrival of the bearers of the main Arabic and Islamic elements.

This remains hypothetical and speculative. Many alternative possibilities can be envisaged, but given the overall components of the situation to be reconciled, there are not so many consistent alternatives which account comprehensively and economically for the facts. However, it certainly cannot be proved that irrigated rice cultivation was not evolved within Madagascar itself, in response to favorable ecological niches combined with increasing local pressures of population, deforestation, and erosion of hillsides which may have offered adequate possibilities of dry rice production before their deterioration.

The next assumption is that about the time of Muhammad—or even a century or two later, after undocumented wanderings—refugees of dissident sects or anti-Islamic groups found their way to the southeast coast. Here, they lost their Arabic speech (if they had possessed it) and adopted the Malagasy language while religiously preserving their Arabic script and their elaborate system of divination. They were able to insinuate themselves as high caste or ruling elements into a number of other communities. As well as being the progenitors of the Antemoro, Antesaka, Antambahoaka and other southeastern Malagasy communities, they were responsible for introducing Arabic systems of divination, the Arabic reckoning of days of the week and months of the year, the Arabic nomenclature for heavenly bodies, and the Arabic orientation of ritual directions. Slowly, these systems spread through the island.

Arab and Shirazi Settlers

By about the tenth century A.D. the Arab and Shirazi settlement of the East African coast had penetrated southward to Kilwa, Sofala, and the Comoro Islands. Visits to Madagascar became frequent, and, eventually, trading posts were established on the northwest and northeast coasts. These Arabo-Shirazi traders had already mingled extensively with Negro Africans and had acquired a heavy intrusion of Negro blood. And it is assumed that their following included large numbers of Negro slaves. This assumption is based on the fact that all of the Arab or Swahili settlements in eastern Africa for which there is any relevant evidence consisted either of relatively "pure" Arabs, and possibly other Persian Gulf peoples, together with African Negro slaves, or of mixed dominant groups (Afro-Arab) already of largely Negro blood, also possessing African slaves. It is impossible to conceive of this population without a slave element, or of a slave element which was anything but African Negro.

Thus both Arabo-Caucasian and Negroid gene types were added to the Malagasy pool. These traders may also have brought cattle, dogs, and other material elements to Madagascar, or at least to some parts of it, for the first time. This may explain why the words for these elements were adopted into Malagasy speech in their Bantu-Swahili form. We also attribute to this population movement the cultures revealed by excavation at Vohémar and other sites on the northeast and northwest coasts traditionally linked with the Malagasy—the Antalaotra and Iharanian peoples.[24] It would be interesting to study the possible links between the

24. Deschamps, *Histoire*, 47–48. The Vohémar culture is similar in most respects to the range of Afro-Arab-Swahili cultures of the East African coast and most likely to have flourished from early in the present millennium until it declined under Portuguese attack. It is necessary to add that the Malagasy and Comorian versions of the Afro-Arab-Swahili coast and island culture seem to have incorporated an antecedent Indonesian element, as indicated by the Indonesian derived term Antalaotra,

three-legged stone pots of Vohémar, carved in chloriteschist, and the big three-legged wooden drums of the Swahili on the East African coast. The Arabo-Swahili trading settlements of the northwest, which were nearest to their counterparts on the East African coast, seem to have flourished much like the latter until they were attacked by the Portuguese in the sixteenth century. Linguistically, while the Arabs of the East African coast were continuously dropping their language in favor of Swahili in spite of the fact that the Arabic influence was constantly being renewed by new immigration, it must be assumed that the Arabo-Swahili traders and settlers arrived on the coast of Madagascar with various mixtures of Semitic and Bantu speech which they likewise lost the longer they stayed in favor of the Indonesian or Malay speech of the Malagasy. These trading settlements were either obliterated or driven into decline and eventual extinction by the Portuguese attacks of the sixteenth century, or survived in greatly modified Malagasy form.

There may well have been further arrivals of Indonesian migrants, but they did not affect the basic language, except that they may have brought new and sometimes improved elements which were permanently adopted with their names into the existing culture. These new arrivals may have come from widely different parts of the vast Indonesian region. One can assume that in no single case did any party arrive in sufficient strength and number to establish itself as a distinct, autonomous social group. However, the immigration which gave rise to the Hova, or Merina, populations of the plateau must have been one of the largest. Their technical skills and sense of superiority gave them great influence among the populations with which they mingled, while at the same time their endogamous practices maintained their physical distinctiveness. (The Merina are, by common consent, more Indonesian in physical type than any other contemporary Malagasy group.) It has been popular to date their arrival in the plateau from about A.D. 1500. While no firm suggestions are made as

---

applied to these peoples in the tradition of the Comoro Islands and the northern coasts of Madagascar (Deschamps, 44–46), and as mentioned above, 185.

to the date of their actual arrival in Madagascar, I would only comment that this date should be placed beyond the range of oral history, since the latter seems to retain no echo of the direction of their origin from across the seas—the one short relevant passage in the *Tantaran'ny Andriana* is very vague and its source dubious.[25] The phrase "beyond the range of oral history" is precise in meaning but ambiguous in definition, depending upon techniques and practices of preserving social tradition and upon the social structure which alone gives it relevance. The Antemoro appear to have preserved their social tradition jealously for more than a thousand years. Even given the fact that the Antemoro could write, it seems to me that to account for the Hova of Imerina lacking any strong tradition about their direction of origin, however legendary (especially when they are so proud of their Asiatic origins), their arrival must be assumed to have occured at least several centuries before 1500 A.D. Otherwise these dramatic events would surely be reflected much more prominently in their tradition and mythology.

Additional Notes

There are a number of miscellaneous comments which must be added to this skeletal account. A perennial focus of speculation has been the origin of supposedly Negroid physical traits such as dark skin and tightly curled hair. Recent studies have swung the pendulum once again in favor of an African origin for these elements.[26] But it is necessary to distinguish the present gene pool—to which undoubtedly a major African Negroid contribution has been made in recent centuries through immigration, enslavement, and accelerated internal migration and miscegenation—from the hypothetical gene pool of three or four centuries ago. Though at that time it could not yet have received this modern African contribution, it produced a population which, whether of African or Asiatic origin, struck the earliest European travellers as being

25. François Callet (trans. G.S. Chapus and Emmanuel Ratsimba as *Histoire des Rois*), *Tantaran'ny Andriana* (Tananarive, 1953), I.
26. Marie-Claude Chamla, "Recherches anthropologiques sur l'origine des Malgaches," *Mémoires du Musée*, XIX (1958), 1–205.

(in superficial and popular terms) predominantly Negro.

Furthermore, African Negroid genes have probably been continuously implanted by the partly Negroid Arabo-Swahili groups since at least A.D. 1000. We obviously cannot make any precise identifications between language and physical type for one or two millennia ago—even if some language antecedent to Maanyan was the closest relative to proto-Malagasy, we cannot be sure exactly where it was spoken or what were the physical types of the speakers. Similarly if the suggestions of Melanesian linguistic links put forward by Hébert should be confirmed, we would not be certain that this indicated a physical type similar to present-day Melanesians. Despite such elaborate cautions, the possibility of a Melanesian origin for the Negroid element in the proto-Malagasy remains open and seems the simplest explanation for the Negroid characteristics remarked in the populations of the south and west of Madagascar by European travelers of the seventeenth century. And Linton claimed in 1943 that the aboriginal Teriandroka in South Tanala at that time still included individuals resembling Oceanic Negritos.[27]

As Solheim points out, although Malagasy links with Indonesia during the general period of the Sa-Huynh culture complex (1000 B.C.–A.D. 500) seem plausible, there is much too little systematic detail on timing and distribution for any precision to be possible. The same applies to the study of linguistic connections. Although Dahl's Maanyan-Malagasy comparison is the most impressive yet made, we do not know for certain whether Maanyan is the nearest of all contemporary Indonesian languages to Malagasy, let alone where the most closely related speech community to the original bearers of the Malagasy language may have lived at the time when it was brought to Madagascar. Furthermore, a systematic lexico-statistical study of contemporary, or at least nineteenth-century, Malagasy dialects would add strength to any analysis of the basic distribution and spread of population in the island. For example, working in northern Betsileo I found a five percent divergence between the dialect of that area and standard Merina—that form

27. Ralph Linton, "Culture Sequences in Madagascar," *Peabody Museum Papers*, XX (1943), 72–80.

of Merina which was spread first by missionaries and later by Merina traders, administrators, teachers, and clergy. Given the proximity of the two speech areas and the intensity of Merina influence during the last century and a half, this is a striking demonstration of the fact that despite the underlying linguistic homogeneity, local dialects have been developing for many centuries in Madagascar.[28]

It has usually, I think, been assumed that the first Indonesian arrivals were slash-and-burn hill-rice cultivators, as well as fishermen. How does this accord with what is known of Indonesian material culture and ecology at the relevant period? Both fishing and slash-and-burn rice cultivation would in time have encouraged the spread of the immigrants around the coastal regions of the island seeking new fishing grounds and new areas for their rice cultivation. I see no great difficulty in explaining the subsequent adoption of irrigated wet rice farming as a technique acquired from later Indonesian visitors. For I assume that, especially as seafaring techniques improved, there may have been a number of later Indonesian arrivals, whether voluntary or involuntary. Although the historical records are so ambiguous and fragmentary, they do suggest a later period of direct Indonesian trading with the East African coast. To account for the Malagasy situation this must have been after the first settlement of the island by the proto-Malagasy but before the period of Arabo-Swahili trading and settlement began. It could thus have coincided with the second phase of Indonesian settlement. As this period also coincides with the Sassanian period of expansion and vigorous trade, one can assume that the early connections of Persia and East Africa with Madagascar came at this time. Any of these seafarers reaching Madagascar during the first millennium of our era, but after the first establishment of the proto-Malagasy, might have been respon-

28. Since this was written, the excellent Pierre Vérin, C.P. Kottak, and P. Gorlin, "The Glottochronology of Malagasy Speech Communities," *Oceanic Linguistics*, VIII, 1 (1969), 26–83, has appeared. It supports the general unity of all Malagasy dialects, but also a period of divergence between them of approximately two millennia, thus further strengthening the assumption of that time period since the first arrival of the original speakers in Madagascar.

sible for bringing East African elements to the island. However, if the existence of a Bantu substratum in the Malagasy language could be satisfactorily demonstrated, it might strengthen the supposition that these elements were brought by the second phase of Indonesian immigrants. But it is perhaps simpler to assume, as I have, that they were brought by the earliest Swahili traders, for there is as yet no clear evidence of the influence of any Bantu languages other than Swahili at this early period.

Indonesian influence on East Africa is markedly different from that on Madagascar. In the latter case this influence must be assumed to have laid the foundations of all languages spoken and all organized societies; in the former no traces of Indonesian languages or social organization survived. However, to explain the Indonesian derivation of East African outrigger canoes, the sewn-plank boats of Lake Victoria, the square two-gabled coastal house design, perhaps the collective cave burials of some of the Nyika peoples, and even the controversial banana and xylophone, one presumes that the Indonesian influences in East Africa, however sporadic, must have spread over a considerable period before the Arabo-Swahili supremacy on the coast and must also probably have continued beyond the arrival of Bantu-speaking Negroes in the coastal regions.

Suggestions for Further Research

In the search for origins and Indonesian influences, little systematic attention has been paid to features of Malagasy society other than the language and physical composition of the people. It is true that Grandidier, to whom one must pay homage as the founder of serious Malagasy ethnology, in 1908 did seek parallels to Malagasy socio-cultural features everywhere. He compared vaguely defined cultural and behavioral items from all over Southeast Asia and the Pacific with supposedly similar items in Madagascar.[29] Examples were picked randomly, or rather, one supposes, wherever they could be found, from Burma and Siam

29. Alfred Grandidier, "Etude comparative des Malgaches et des Indo-Océaniens," in Alfred and Guillaume Grandidier, *Ethnographie de Madagascar* (Paris, 1908), I, 13–71.

to New Zealand, and from Ceylon to Hawaii. In many cases examples could just as well have been found in Africa, thus over-turning Grandidier's main argument, or even in America or ancient Europe, proving nothing at all except the psychic unity of mankind. It is impossible to understand what scientific purpose could have been served by this method. It can only be excused as following the anthropological conventions of the day, but it has provided a very bad example to subsequent enquirers.

First Grandidier said that the travelers' reports show an almost complete similarity between these peoples; then he recognized that there are many and numerous divergences among them, yet he unaccountably concluded that from the synthetic exposition arises "a coherent whole of facts which, when taken in isolation, would have little significance; but which considered in the mass are typical." It is this belief and this approach which must be utterly rejected. There is no space or necessity to go over the well-known articles in detail. It can never be assumed that apparent likenesses between cultures are fundamental, while obvious differences are coincidental and due to special local circumstances. The selection of similar elements from different cultures and the dismissal of differences must always be justified logically, in detail, and in both historical and functional terms. As in any scientific enterprise, we must not simply choose our facts to suit our theories but must demonstrate that the cultural similarities considered to be funda-mental are similar in detail and durable, while dissimilarities must be logically explicable as easily changeable cultural features.

It is always necessary to distinguish Polynesia, Melanesia, and Indonesia, and preferably to make more refined geographical, historical, and socio-cultural distinctions within these vast regions. Given such refinement, renewed interest would attach to detailed and systematic studies of the more striking social institutions and structural features of the Malagasy peoples and their comparison with demonstrably similar institutional complexes elsewhere. The lack of detailed, reliable, and scholarly socio-cultural analyses of the peoples of Moçambique is a serious gap. Historians are inevitably tempted to look for links with Mwanamutapa, but our knowledge of Mwanamutapan institutions is so poor that useful comparisons cannot be made. Lavondès makes a striking comparison between the kinship system of the Masikoro of southwestern Madagascar and that of the Lozi of western Zambia, but it is hard to think of a plausible historical link between these otherwise dissimilar peoples separated by a thousand miles of land and ocean.[30]

It is surprising that so little comparative study has been made of the tomb complex for which the Malagasy are above all famous.[31] Other structural features calling for further study are the system of descent endogamy, preferential cousin marriages, and the traditional role of the chief. In all these respects there are contrasts with the characteristic institutional forms of East Africa. But we only need to remember the bilateral Iban of Borneo, or the Kalinga and Ifugao of the Philippines, the matrilineal Menangkabao of Sumatra and the Negri Sembilan of Malaya, or the patrilineal Toba Batak with their polysegmentary lineages, to realize how careful we must be in framing Indonesian similarities. We must also remember that races are constructs of the observer and do not exist empirically. Many physical characteristics are not as durable over long periods as is often supposed, and, as Linton pointed out, it is possible that the less Negroid physical elements may have been bred out by malaria over long periods in the lowlands of Madagascar, leaving an apparently Negroid type more dominant.[32]

In conclusion, it may be said that Madagascar remains an ethnological enigma in part because of its marginal situation. This marginality is expressed not only in the divisions of continental geography but in the organization of scholarship. Marginality may, perhaps, be either positive or negative. Neither the Africanist nor the Orientalist usually thinks of Madagascar as belonging to his field. Restricting fields of scholarship geographically may result in some loss of depth and understanding and may entail the danger of mistaking particularities for universals. Scholarly interest

30. Henri Lavondès, *Bekoropoka, quelques aspects de la vie familiale et sociale d'un village malgache* (The Hague, 1967), 52.
31. Except for the useful beginning made by Raymond Decary, *La mort et les coutumes funéraires à Madagascar* (Paris, 1962).
32. Linton, "Culture Sequences," 72–80.

in Madagascar provides a healthy challenge to such intellectual parochialism. The cultures of Indonesia, Islam, and Africa have all made their contributions, and if the major crystallization appears to be Indonesian, the other elements are of great significance. No individual or even group of anthropologists as yet controls these diverse ethnographic fields with sufficient depth and confidence to be able to make the immense effort of extensive, detailed, comparative analysis and synthetic interpretation which is required. When the interdisciplinary requirements are also considered, the possibility of achieving such a sustained cooperative effort seems remote. Yet marginal studies of this sort may be the most important of all in revealing fundamental cultural processes.[33]

33. Raymond Kent's *Early Kingdoms in Madagascar* 1500–1700 (New York, 1970) and his previous articles in the *Journal of African History* ("Madagascar and Africa: I. The Problem of the Bara," IX [1968], 387–408; II. "The Sakalava, Maroserana, Dady and Tromba before 1700," IX [1968], 517–546; III. "The Anteimoro, a Theocracy in Southeastern Madagascar," X [1969], 45–65) provide the most impressive analysis and reassessment of Malagasy history which has appeared in English. The amount and detail of evidence marshalled from extremely varied and often highly recondite sources is overwhelming and indeed self-defeating, as the author's interpretation is often unclear except for the general theme of redressing the balance in favor of an acceptance of the heavy African cultural and even political influence on Madagascar. Sometimes it is almost emotional. What he objects to most is the tendency of past writers to assume that the founders of ruling lines were whites or Arabs. This feeling is justified and reminiscent of the havoc wrought by the Hamitic myth in Africa. Yet, after all the build up, his most important string of evidence is disappointing. It amounts to this: There is one written record of the verbal account by one elder of his recollections of a manuscript version of Sakalava tradition which was burnt which "states that the Maroserana came from Mijomby or Midzomby with a shipload of gold, landed at present day Tulear, and gained supremacy over local people very gradually." Kent assumes that Midzomby means Moçambique, without giving any further evidence. This would obviously imply the Swahili speaking Afro-Arabs of the coast settlements rather than Africans from the interior. Kent seems to assume this too, but the mention of gold irresistibly suggests Mwanamutapa to him so he tries to insinuate a connection by the incredibly far-fetched identification of Rabaratavokoka (a very shadowy Maroserana ancestor whose name can be interpreted etymologically in Malagasy to mean "great stone unequalled") with the account of a striking rock in the heart of the Mwanamutapa Empire (J.T. Bent, *Ruined Cities of Mashonaland* [London, 1893], 85) near which stood a "fantastic kraal" called Baramazimba ruled by Umgabe. This carries overtones of Bara and Vazimba for Kent, though no association

between Bara and Vazimba is mentioned or relevant here. Umgabe is then equated with Ngabe, which Kent says is an honorific title for Malagasy elders, with *angabe* the Bara ancestor spirits and Monongabe one of the Bara capitals. This seems to be an elementary linguistic confusion between Umgabe, which derives from a very widespread Bantu root, and the Malagasy terms *inga* or *ainga* (with the general sense of elevation), -*be* (great), or *ingahy* (venerable). It is one of many cases of fortuitous phonetic convergence which Kent takes as evidence of Bantu borrowing in Malagasy. The Maroserana then became indigenous Malagasy through intermarriage. Kent's further argument for the African origins of Malagasy kingdoms is that the Maroserana used Sakalava warriors to conquer and establish the kingdoms of Menabe and Boina. This rests entirely on his identification of the Succulambes with Sakalava, which is tempting but unconvincing. The Succulambes were Bambala who "were an important African colony in Western Madagascar." However, Luis Mariano, the sole authority, wrote that the Bambala "descend from Malindi Cafres." This can only mean, once again, that they were Afro-Arabs from the mixed population of Malindi. While one gladly accepts Kent's evidence for the fact that these early rulers were neither whites nor pure Arabs, the conclusion is something of an anticlimax, hardly commensurate with the categorical statement that "the first Malagasy empire was an African creation." Even more tendentious is the ensuing assertion that "many features of the old African culture which vanished in Western Madagascar penetrated the Merina highlands." There are many known African elements in Madagascar and perhaps many more to be demonstrated, but this cannot be done by shoddy linguistics and far-fetched speculation.

Kent assumes a movement "from the general direction of Indonesia in the early centuries of the first millennium of our era." He assumes such a movement into eastern Africa before the arrival of the Bantu, and that these Indonesians met and mingled with the Bantu in the interior, by implication as far away as Zaire! From such a meeting an "Afro-Malagasy race should have resulted." Bantu pressure later impelled the Indonesians to migrate to Madagascar, providing the island with its permanent Indonesian linguistic matrix together with agriculture and rice, megaliths, terracing, stone walled villages, cattle and pens, ancestral cults, and village chiefdoms. In the second millennium the Bantu expansion and the Swahili commercial empire produced a further migration to Madagascar, bringing iron and paving the way for the Maroserana, Temur, "and their Anteony, both from the mainland as well." This is a bold and interesting theory, but there is little specific evidence to support it. It still seems more logical and economical to assume a first migration to Madagascar direct from Indonesia, laying the indelible foundations of Malagasy Indonesian speech, followed by migrations of Indonesians to the East African coast, who later brought domestic animals, customs and vocabulary items from Africa to Madagascar. Later still, Afro-Arabs from the East African coast established Islamic and Swahili speaking settlements around the coasts of Madagascar. Their influential diviners provided powerful mystical support to the princelings whose courts they graced and came to be in such demand that they moved far into the interior and were instrumental in the emergence of the ruling dynasties of Maroserana, Sakalava, and finally Imerina.

CONNECTIONS BETWEEN THE LACUSTRINE
PEOPLES AND THE COAST

Merrick Posnansky

Though intensive research on the Iron Age of western Uganda has been conducted for the past ten years[1] and has been tied closely to parallel work on the interpretation of the traditional history,[2] little information on the contacts between the east coast and the interior has been gathered beyond that presented by Gray in 1957.[3] However, I have indicated the wider contacts of the interlacustrine area and in particular demonstrated some links between the Ugandan area and the southern Sudan.[4]

The meager data that can be presented to indicate possible contact falls within five categories: historical, traditional, archaeological, ethnographical, and ethnobotanical. The last three sources

1. Merrick Posnansky, "The Iron Age in East Africa," in Walter W. Bishop and J. Desmond Clark (eds.), *Background to Evolution in Africa* (Chicago, 1967), 629–649.
2. Merrick Posnansky, "The Traditional History of the Hereditary Kingdoms of the Western Lacustrine Bantu and Rwanda," in "Proceedings of the 17th Conference of the Rhodes-Livingstone Institute" (Lusaka, 1963), 13, mimeo.
3. John M. Gray, "Trading Expeditions from the Coast to Lakes Tanganyika and Victoria before 1857," *Tanganyika Notes and Records*, 49 (1957), 226–246.
4. Merrick Posnansky, "Iron Age East Africa and Outside Contacts," in *Actes du premier colloque international d'archéologie Africaine* (Fort Lamy, 1969), 334–335 and as "East Africa and the Nile Valley in Early Times" in Y.F. Hassan (ed.), *Sudan in Africa* (Khartoum, 1971), 51–61.

suggest possible contacts before the eighteenth century, but inadequately indicate scale or diffusion patterns; the former indicate an intensifying of what little contact there was from the mid-eighteenth century to a peak at the time of the first European contacts after the explorer John H. Speke's journey of 1862. This movement from the south coincided with the first penetration from the north, by Andrea de Bono, a Maltese trader, into the Acholi area of Uganda in 1861.[5]

Before considering in detail the evidence that does exist for the connections, it is important to decide why they were so slight before the colonial period. Basically, the interior of East Africa had little to offer the coast. No gold or copper is found in surface outcrops, and until the early nineteenth century, ivory was abundant much closer to or along the coast itself. At the same time there were insufficient attractions found solely between the interlacustrine area and the coast to entice the peoples of the interior toward the coastal area, so that even in the nineteenth century trade was in the hands of intermediaries. This lack of incentive for buyers or sellers was certainly more important than any problems of communication, difficult though they may have been, across the Nyika semi-desert of Kenya. A greater number of natural routes led inland to Malawi farther south. In East Africa the Tana River leads to desert regions, and the Ruvuma and Rufiji Rivers are not natural routes because of their coastal swamps and meandering streams. Thus journeys upstream depended completely on the attractiveness and value of trade goods in the interior.

The population in the interior was concentrated on the plateaux of the Kenya Highlands and especially around Lake Victoria, both agriculturally self-sufficient areas. Movement was more often undertaken in conjunction with cattle raids to the west and south. To the east the area was unsuited to cattle. (The myth of the Masai ferocity has been overstated. They did not form a warlike wedge into the Rift Valley until the eighteenth century at the earliest.) It was the conditions on the coast, particularly the consequences

5. John M. Gray, "Acholi History, 1860–1901," *Uganda Journal*, XV (1951), 123.

of the more settled political conditions of the nineteenth century and the growth of the trade in the Indian Ocean and through the Red Sea, together with the slow expansion of the peoples of central Tanzania towards the coast, which eventually dictated change.

Historical and Traditional Evidence

Historical evidence is limited to the brief references which concern the Islamic traders from the coast who had settled in the Tabora region by 1825, were already trading in Koki in southern Buganda sometime before 1832, reached the *Kabaka*'s court by 1844,[6] and penetrated into Busoga from the east by 1853.[7] Though their penetration of the direct route to Buganda was rapid and presumably followed that pioneered by the Nyamwezi[8] traders of the eighteenth century, their penetration into the surrounding areas of the interior was late. In Ankole there is no indication of contact before 1852, while in Rwanda the first "Arabs" did not appear before 1876.[9]

The traditions provide clues to earlier contacts. In the late eighteenth century *Kabaka* Kyabagu is said to have had plates and drinking cups. Later *kabakas* established monopolies of blue beads (*nsinda*), and when cowries were introduced during Semakokiro's reign in the last quarter of the eighteenth century, two would buy a woman; even as late as the mid-nineteenth century, during Suna's reign, 2500 cowries would buy a cow.[10] It would appear from all traditions that cotton cloth was readily available in pre-European times (cotton cloth, possibly of the blue

6. John M. Gray, "Ahmed bin Ibrahim—the First Arab to Reach Buganda," *Uganda Journal*, XI (1947), 80–97.
7. Gray, "Trading Expeditions," 238.
8. A term which probably covers many other kindred peoples engaging in trade in central Tanzania. Similarly, the word "Arab" as used in this paper includes all Muslim people of coastal origin engaging in trade, since they were all so described in Uganda, cf. note 6 above.
9. Jan Vansina, *L'évolution du royaume rwanda des origines à* 1900 (Bruxelles, 1961), 15; Gray, "Trading Expeditions," 240.
10. Apolo Kagwa, *Basekabaka b'e Buganda* (Kampala, 1902) and the translation of the 1912 edition by Simon Musoke (Makerere Institute of Social Research, typescript, undated) provide most of the evidence for early trade.

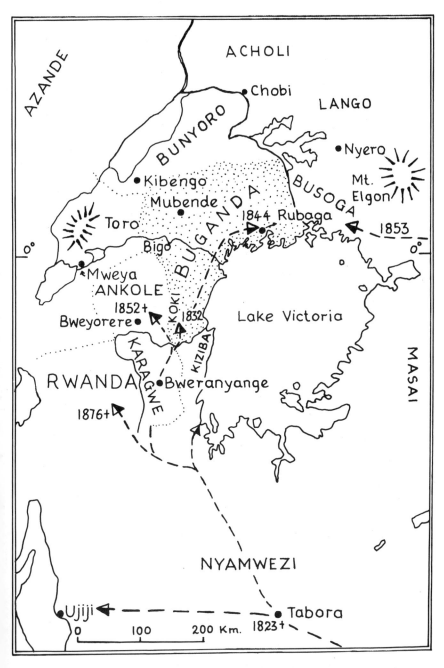

Interlacustrine Kingdoms in the Mid-Nineteenth Century Showing
Penetration by Coastal Traders

kaniki variety, was forbidden to all but palace nobility by *Kabaka* Semakokiro), but on the mechanics and scale of the trade, and on the depth of penetration of the Nyamwezi, the traditions are unhelpful. It is said of Semakokiro, however, that he traded his ivory in Karagwe, to the south of Lake Victoria, from whence he obtained silk goods.[11] The traders reportedly did not bring their goods directly to Buganda. The first mention of copper (a ring) dates from the eighteenth century. Several items which are certainly of later importation, such as the maize sent by Semakokiro to Junju, are credited by tradition to earlier rulers. Little is said about the nature of the trade or traders before the nineteenth century. The chief result of this early commerce was to stimulate Bugandan trade by canoes to the southern region of Lake Victoria when the "Arabs" were beginning to trade there from their base in Tabora region.

The intensification of trade took place when the frontiers of Buganda stretched into Kiziba in northern Tanzania, and it was Buganda, not Bunyoro, which drew the ultimate profit. There is clear evidence from the traditions that ivory was the chief export from the kingdoms, together with the slaves to carry it. Both commodities were obtained largely by raiding, with ivory coming from Lango and southern Busoga. The slaves, who probably rarely exceeded 1000 a year, derived from internecine wars, tribute, and raids on other kingdoms.[12]

Archaeological Evidence

Archaeologically the evidence of contact is slighter and more ambiguous than that provided by the oral traditions. A pierced cowrie shell has been found at the Nyero 2 rock shelter site in eastern Uganda in a disturbed occupation layer which also contains a quartz industry, pottery bearing incised decoration, and ochre pencils which were probably used to provide the red paint for the concentric circles on the overhanging rock face. The pottery, on analogy with sequences from Buganda and Busoga, would appear to date within the last half millennium, but the

11. V.C.R. Ford, *The Trade of Lake Victoria* (Kampala, 1955), 18.
12. *Ibid.*

evidence is inconclusive. The quartz industry is of an undiagnostic nature which characterizes a large number of cave occupations in which pottery is also found and for which the only identifiable tool forms are microliths with U-shaped backs and straight unretouched chords. The occupation almost certainly predates the eighteenth-century movement into the area by the Teso. Cowries have similarly been found in burials eroding out of the banks along the Nile River at Chobi on the present border of Bunyoro and at Mweya on the Kazinga Channel connecting Lakes George and Edward.[13] At both sites precise dating is impossible; however, from the little that is known of the associated pottery from the western region of Uganda, a date in the eighteenth century or slightly earlier is feasible.

The only site which has produced firmly dated evidence of imports is that of Bweyorere in Ankole,[14] a capital site of the *abagabe* of Ankole who ruled, according to tradition, in the seventeenth and eighteenth centuries. During the 1959 excavations at Bweyorere a blue glass bead and two small, white spheroid glass beads were recovered from an horizon for which a radiocarbon date of A.D. 1640 ± 95 was obtained. However, the origin of the beads is uncertain. It is conceivable that they could have come from the West into the Congo basin from Portuguese contacts. A salt trade from western Bunyoro into Zaïre existed well before the earliest Arab contacts and well-defined routes have been traced from the frequent occurence of circular depressions (for grinding simsim and millet) in rocks presumably used by generations of porters.

The same horizon at Bweyorere also produced parts of several smoking pipes of the angled form which are still in use in western Uganda and which, from their affinities throughout Africa, must be assumed to have been for tobacco. Little is known about the

13. Merrick Posnansky, "Rock Painting Survey at Ngora," *Annual Report of Brathay Exploration Group, Uganda Supplement* (Brathay, 1963), 24–25; Merrick Posnansky and Charles M. Nelson, "Rock Paintings and Excavations at Nyero, Uganda," *Azania*, III (1968), 147–166. For Chobi, Brian M. Fagan and Laurel Lofgren, "Archaeological Sites on the Nile-Chobi Confluence," *Uganda Journal*, XXX (1966), 203.
14. Posnansky, "Iron Age," 334–335.

earliest spread of tobacco in the interior of East Africa, but pipes do occur and appear to have been used for tobacco for a considerable period of time. Unlike the pipes from Hyrax Hill in Kenya or Engaruka[15] in Tanzania, consisting of a large tubular bowl of stone or pottery without stems, which could have been used for *bhang* (Indian hemp) or something similar, the Ugandan examples all consist of pipes in which the bowl and short stems are made of one piece, similar to the European type, of Portuguese or Dutch introduction. Several have come from the Gandan shrines, and one is even attributed to Kintu, the first *kabaka*, but it may have been placed in his shrine at a later date as must certainly have been the case with the cowries and beads which adorn the regalia of the early rulers of both Bunyoro and Buganda and the drums of Ankole. There are no smoking pipes among the finds from the Bigo culture sites in western Uganda,[16] which means that tobacco smoking entered the interlacustrine region sometime between the sixteenth and seventeenth centuries.

Beads have emerged as surface and subsurface finds on several sites of a ritual nature which follow the Bigo culture, such as Mubende,[17] but the findings from these sites are mixed with nineteenth-century material and the beads are too undiagnostic for dating purposes. Several surface finds of beads have come from Bigo, and at Kibengo Lanning found a turquoise colored glass bead, associated with a nineteenth-century glass bottle stopper, on a stone floor which also contained Bigo pottery.[18] But though beads have been found they are neither numerous nor widespread before contexts dating to the nineteenth century, a finding which would substantiate impressions gained from the traditions that,

15. Mary D. Leakey, "Report on the Excavations at Hyrax Hill, Nakuru, Kenya Colony 1937–38," *Transactions of the Royal Society of South Africa*, XXX (1945), 345–347; Hamo Sassoon, "New Views on Engaruka, Northern Tanzania," *Journal of African History*, VIII (1967), 207.

16. Merrick Posnansky, "Bigo bya Mugenyi," *Uganda Journal*, XXXIII (1969), 100–125; Posnansky, "Introduction," in Ruth H. Fisher, *Twilight Tales of the Black Baganda*; (London, 1969, 2nd. ed.).

17. E.C. Lanning, "Excavations at Mubende Hill," *Uganda Journal*, XXX (1966), 160.

18. E.C. Lanning, "The Earthworks at Kibengo, Mubende District," *Uganda Journal*, XXIV (1960), 189.

in general, trade penetration was slight before the late eighteenth century.

Ethnobotanical Evidence

The evidence for crop introductions has recently been studied in detail by McMaster for the banana and by Langlands for maize, the banana, and cassava.[19] The question of the origins of the banana is tied in with Indonesian contacts, which are discussed below. The evidence collected for the main American staples, cassava, corn (maize), sweet potatoes, etc., would suggest that they were just coming into cultivation by the early nineteenth century, though Murdock has suggested that the sweet potato might have spread earlier into East Africa with "Indonesian" crops like bananas, cocoyams, and yams along the yam belt to West Africa, ultimately to have been diffused back to Uganda along the same yam belt.[20] If any of this latter contention can be proved, it would appear that the Azande, who were expanding from west to east in the nineteenth century, had an important role in crop diffusion. Many varieties of yam were indigenous to Africa and their inclusion with the Indonesian list may be misleading.[21] Some of the cocoyams may also have had an indigenous provenance.

Though cassava and maize were both present in Uganda by 1862, they were probably new arrivals, possibly brought in as ancillaries to the coastal trade, though an origin from the west has been suggested for cassava and from the Ethiopian area for maize.[22] This again poses the question of western routes to Uganda along which the early beads might also have come. Crops

19. D.N. McMaster, "Speculations on the Coming of the Banana to Uganda," *Uganda Journal*, XXVII (1963), 163–175; B.W. Langlands, "Maize in Uganda," *Uganda Journal*, XXIX (1965), 215–121; "The Banana in Uganda 1860–1920," *Uganda Journal*, XXX (1966), 39–62; "Cassava in Uganda," *Uganda Journal*, XXX (1966), 211–218; M.D. Gwynne, "The Origin and Spread of Some Domestic Food Plants of Eastern Africa," below, 253, 261–270.
20. George Peter Murdock, *Africa: Its Peoples and their Culture History* (New York, 1959), 227–228.
21. D.G. Cowsey, *Yams* (London, 1967), 5–27.
22. W.N. Jones, *Manioc in Africa* (Stanford, 1959), 80; A.C.A. Wright, "Maize Names as Indicators of Economic Contacts," *Uganda Journal*, XIII (1949), 61.

which almost certainly came up from the east coast include the mango and citrus fruits. Little work has been done on either, but the widespread appearance of the mango and the number of varieties present, particularly in Buganda, is suggestive of a long cultivation, though the date for its introduction is impossible to ascertain. Thomas suggests that the introduction of the mango may have only been shortly before 1900,[23] although if the uncited evidence of Singh that the mango was present in Somaliland in the fourteenth century can be accepted, the diffusion inland could have taken place before the nineteenth century and explain the relatively established place of the mango in Buganda by 1900.[24]

Ethnographical Evidence

The question of Indonesian influence in the interlacustrine area has figured centrally in the arguments of Jones, his predecessors, such as Hornbostel as early as 1911, and their opponents.[25] Arguments have centered on both the musical instruments of the area, in particular the xylophone, and the ubiquitous banana. At present, beyond indicating that the banana has a respectable antiquity in Buganda, as evidenced by the proliferation of names of varieties, tools for preparing them, customs pertaining to them, and the number of varieties which have evolved, there can only be speculation as to its origin.

In discussing the origin of bananas, arguments have been advanced both for their arrival via the Sabaean route, through India and South Arabia to Ethiopia,[26] and for a great lakes route from Ethiopia to Uganda, but the evidence for neither is conclusive. No definite Indonesian cultural transplants have been found, and the musical theories, although possibly having a basis, indicate neither the scale of influence, the date, nor the route of diffusion. Wachsmann has indicated that the *entenga* drum chimes of

23. A.S. Thomas in J.D. Tothill, *Agriculture in Uganda* (Oxford, 1940), 486.
24. Lal Behari Singh, *The Mango* (London, 1960), 8.
25. A.M. Jones, *Africa and Indonesia*, (Leiden, 1963); Erich M. von Hornbostel, "Ueber ein akustische Kriterium für Kulturzusammenhange," *Zeitschrift für Ethnologie*, XLIII, (1911), 601–615.
26. Merrick Posnansky, "Bantu Genesis," *Uganda Journal*, XXV (1961), 86–93.

Buganda, which are tuned and played like the xylophone, have some affinities with drum ensembles from Ethiopia and possibly India.[27] For sewn boats the evidence is again inconclusive, as there is nothing indicating that they arrived on Lake Victoria earlier than the eighteenth century, by which time coastal contact was already well established.

In conclusion, the coastal impact on the interlacustrine kingdoms was late, certainly not prior to the seventeenth century, excepting the Indonesian crops (the number of which is being decreased through expanding palaeobotanical research) which may have come via various routes; the evidence that exists suggests that trade was of a slight nature before the nineteenth century, that even in the nineteenth century much of the trade was in the hands of Nyamwezi and other African middlemen, and that the "Arab" impact was confined to the period from 1844. For the earliest trade the evidence available is inconclusive as to routes, and many exotic items could have come just as easily from the west coast (the Congo basin) as from the east coast. Sufficient sites have been excavated or inspected within the region to state that coastal contact was slight and even the remarkably imperishable glass bead is such a rarity in any contexts prior to the nineteenth century that it is unlikely that further excavations will add very much new substantive information.

27. K.P. Wachsmann, "Some Speculations Concerning a Drum Chime in Buganda," *Man*, LXV (1965), 1–8.

SOME CONCLUSIONS FROM ARCHAEOLOGICAL
EXCAVATIONS ON THE COAST OF KENYA, 1948-1966

James Kirkman

Archaeological excavations on the coast of East Africa began in
1948 when the ruined town of Gedi in Kenya was proclaimed a
national park. During the next ten years I excavated at Gedi and
at Kilepwa near Gedi; at Mnarani, the old Kilifi, half way between
Mombasa and Malindi; at Ungwana at the mouth of the Tana
River; at Takwa on the island of Manda; and at Ras Mkumbuu
on the island of Pemba. From 1958 to 1970 I worked at Fort
Jesus, Mombasa, which was built by the Portuguese in 1593.

These excavations have disclosed a uniform, predominantly
Arab, urban culture, marked by houses, mosques, and tombs built
of rubble masonry, and by the use of imported porcelain and
glazed earthenware. This culture has been dated by its ceramics
to the fourteenth and fifteenth centuries. Evidence of an earlier
period was sparse, and in the pre-building levels. Clearly, before
the fourteenth century the standard of living on the mainland was
unpretentious. However, after that time a standard of comfort
and well-being was enjoyed which, without being artistic or
luxurious, would have been comparable with many towns in
Arabia. In the early seventeenth century this civilization came to
an end as a result of the southern migration from Somalia of the
Galla, whose limit of permanent occupation, or chronic aggression,
was probably a few miles north of Mombasa.

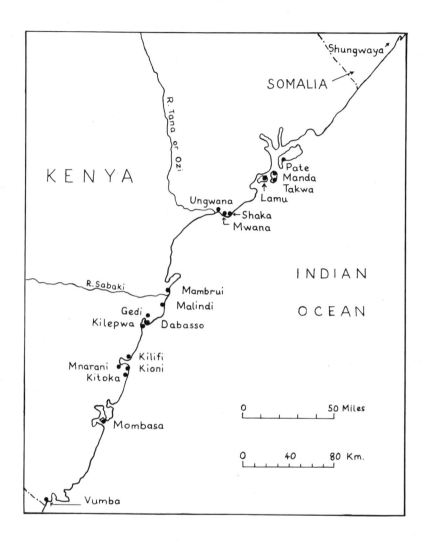

Archaeological and Other Sites of the Northern Kenya Coast

The history of the Bajun Islands, Lamu, Manda, and Pate, was different. Chittick's excavations have revealed a settlement at Manda going back to the ninth century and possibly earlier. Then came the Arab culture which continued on the islands, unaffected by the Galla occupation of the mainland.

Our knowledge of the pre-Portuguese culture of the coast of Kenya is derived from the study of the buildings and the objects found in them. Although Swahili must have existed as a spoken language, it was not a literary language, and no texts have survived; nor have graffiti yet been recorded earlier than the eighteenth century. Nothing in Arabic like the sixteenth-century history of Kilwa in Tanzania, recorded by the Portuguese, has survived.

The Buildings[1]

The houses at Gedi were characterized by a triple series of rooms and a sunken court in front, where guests would be received and where most of the life of the house would go on. The court was surrounded by a wall inside of which was a stone bench about eighteen inches high. The house proper had a platform in front approached by steps from the floor of the court. The normal façade consisted of two large doors, sometimes with a square window high up in the wall between them. In the older houses there were two long rooms, with a lavatory at the end of the outer room, and two small rooms, with a store or strong room without a door, at the back. Later a wall was built across the middle of the inner long room and the house was converted into a long room and two suites of two rooms each; sometimes at one side there was a pair of rooms leading into a small domestic court. In the walls were square niches for cupboards or shelves. In the lavatory was a washing bench at two levels, the lower level divided for use as a *bidet*. The roofs were of lime concrete carried on squared timbers, and the width of the rooms never exceeded eight feet, which was about the maximum length of beam which could be found to support such a weight of concrete. At the end of the sixteenth century, the courtyards tended to become wide

1. James Kirkman, "Historical Archaeology in Kenya 1948–1956," *The Antiquaries Journal*, XXXVII (1957), 16–28.

instead of narrow, indicating the possibility of a commercial or industrial use. The lavatory then stuck out into the court and was approached from the platform in front of the house, rather than from the house itself. The houses at Ungwana and Kilepwa have not been studied to the same extent as those at Gedi, and there may be local differences. The attention at Gedi given to the court-yard is perhaps exceptional.

The mosques were plain rectangles with aisles divided by rows of square pillars, with anterooms on one or both sides and a covered verandah generally on the east.[2] The roof was of lime concrete carried on beams set closely together; although the greatest span was eight feet, a span of seven or six was preferred. The *mihrab* was an alcove in the middle of the north wall, and the *minbar* of the *Jami'* (the Friday mosque) consisted of three steps. The doors were generally placed in the side walls. A curious feature of the mosques in Kenya is the preference for a single or triple row of pillars, which meant the whole effect was spoiled by the central row. Decoration was sparse and usually confined to the *mihrab*. It consisted of coral bosses carved with geometrical ornament, or porcelain and glazed earthenware bowls set in the pilasters or spandrels of the frame, or in the wall of the alcove itself. Outside was a well with a conduit, a cistern, and a lavatory.

The most interesting monuments and the sole architectural invention of the coastal culture of East Africa are the pillar tombs. These are tall, solid masonry pillars, from fifteen to twenty feet high, set in the middle of the east façade of a paneled tomb. The pillars take a variety of forms: rounded, octagonal, hexagonal, square, and fluted. The top is rounded or capped by a diminutive octagon or hexagon or, rarely, by a Chinese jar. Some Europeans say these pillars represent the male organ, but I am not satisfied that this is the true explanation. The oldest which have been investigated are the pillars of Kilepwa and Ras Mkumbuu (Pemba), which I consider to be of the thirteenth century. The Malindi pillar, one of the finest and the nearest in shape to a phallus, probably dates from the early fifteenth century. The relation of

2. Plans in P.S. Garlake, *Early Islamic Architecture of the East African Coast* (Oxford, 1966).

these pillars to the naturalistic phallic pillars of Kafa (Ethiopia) and Herimat (Somalia), and the acknowledged phallic monoliths of Madagascar, has still to be proved. The pillars had no standard shape, so the form they took was immaterial to their propriety or significance. If the original conception were phallic, it is clear that the builders had forgotten what they were trying to do by the time that the squares and octagons were being erected.[3]

The Objects Found in the Buildings

The period covered by the buildings and the pillars has been dated from the fourteenth to the sixteenth centuries by the finds of Yüan and Ming porcelain. The best collection of comparable pieces is at Ardebil in Iran.[4] Under these buildings were the relics of an earlier period, marked by the glazed earthenware known as *sgraffiato*. This earthenware was all of an eastern type, which I consider to be twelfth and thirteenth century. On the sites that I have dug in Kenya and on the coastal islands, it was not at all as plentiful as it has been on sites in Tanzania. No earlier material was found, such as Chittick has excavated on Tanzanian sites and now at Manda in Kenya. The civilization evinced by these sites in Kenya came to an end in the early seventeenth century. The last sherds of porcelain were Ming blue-and-white of Wan Li type. The post-Wan Li types, notably the dishes with elaborate paneled borders found in pre-1634 levels in Fort Jesus, were absent.

Fort Jesus was built by the Portuguese in 1593 and was taken by the Muscat Arabs in 1698. The finds included Portuguese and Indian, in addition to the Chinese and Islamic wares which continued to be imported into East Africa after 1700, as they had been in the past. From the fourteenth century to the middle of the nineteenth, the quantity of Chinese porcelain imported either equaled or, more often, exceeded all other foreign ceramics. It is clear that even though it was a more desirable commodity, it

3. James Kirkman, "The Great Pillars of Malindi and Mambrui," *Oriental Art*, IV, 2 (1958), 55–67.
4. John Alexander Pope, *Chinese Porcelains from the Ardebil Shrine* (Washington, 1956).

could not have been much more expensive. As a result of my recent excavations there is a ceramic succession valid for the coast of Kenya from the thirteenth century to the present day, which, as a result of Chittick's excavations at Manda, can be extended back to the ninth century.[5] The Chinese imports would have come via India. The principal ports concerned would have been Cambay, Cochin, Calicut, and, later, Surat and Bombay, though merchants from Malindi are mentioned at Malacca at the beginning of the sixteenth century.[6] There is no evidence of direct trade with China.

The principal external interest of these excavations is the comparison of ceramic patterns which have emerged with those from other sites on the Indian Ocean.[7] A similarity is already apparent in the ceramics and utensils, and is evidence of an Indian Ocean cultural unity which covered large distances and varying, often antipathetic, cultures. I think that it may also be traceable eventually in the humbler buildings and mosques, but Indian Ocean cultural unity is a subject which has never been studied.

The local earthenware consisted of cooking pots, lamps, jars, and eating bowls, which were competently made without the potter's wheel but had no pretense of being other than kitchen wares. The fact of their existence, however, is evidence that the settlements were established communities and that they did not depend exclusively on imported goods. The commonest forms were carinated cooking pots and open boat-shaped lamps; in the fifteenth century relish bowls with flat bases and straight sides appeared. The coastal ceramic was strongly influenced by the Semitic ceramic traditions which existed in the Near East long before the time of Islam, and in this respect differed considerably from the ceramic traditions of most other parts of Africa. The forms of the carinated bowls and lamps had an extraordinary affinity to those of the Middle Bronze Age of Palestine. Of course, by the time that these pots were made at Gedi and Ungwana they

5. Neville Chittick, "Discoveries in the Lamu Archipelago," *Azania*, II (1967), 40–55.
6. Tomé Pires, *Suma Oriental* (c. 1512–1515), in G.S.P. Freeman-Grenville, *The East African Coast* (Oxford, 1962), 125–126.
7. James Kirkman, "Les importations de céramique sur la côte du Kenya," *Revue de Madagascar*, 35 (1966), 35–44.

had become a naturalized coastal African ceramic form; the links in transmission have yet to be traced.

Finds other than ceramic were few. The most numerous were the medium-sized drawn (or cane) glass beads, red, blue, yellow, green, and black. Less common were the better quality wound and pressed beads in the same colors. In the fifteenth century a cheap variety of these beads was found that might be described as "looped," in which a number of strands were looped round a core, making a shape like a chrysalis. Less common were cornelians and crystals in the shape of hexagons and spheres. The cornelians came from the Cambay area, and the glass beads, I believe, were also made in India. Glass industries are attested by the Portuguese on the Malabar coast at Negapatam in 1597.[8] They also existed in Bengal.

There were also individual beads of great interest. A fine blue-and-white inlaid bead came from the palace at Gedi, and a mauve triangular bead was found at Ungwana, both in late sixteenth-century levels. One *millefiore* or "Rosetta" bead was found in a sixteenth-century level at Gedi. Locally-made beads consisted of the thin disks cut from ostrich egg, small scallops, and achatina snail shell, but the commonest were cylinders manufactured from clams and spider shell. They were numerous in all levels at Gedi but were less common in Fort Jesus.

Glass was also found. The most numerous fragments were from brown or green rosewater sprinklers, often with strands of glass wound round the neck. In the fifteenth and later centuries the lip, instead of being folded and tucked in, was cut off with a knife—a labor-saving device which simplified production but did not improve appearance. This form of vessel is, or was, made until recently in many parts of the Arab world. In addition there were bowls of clear glass and small flasks with molded or cut ornament in blue or clear glass. These were found in the thirteenth- and fourteenth-century levels.

Other small finds consisted of spindle whorls made from pieces

8. Joao Baptista Lavanha, *Naufragio da nao S. Alberto* (Lisbon, 1597), trans. in Charles R. Boxer, *The Tragic History of the Sea*, 1589–1622 (Cambridge, 1959), 133. For the dating of beads, see Chittick, *Kilwa*, II, ch. 29.

of pot, net sinkers, pipe bowls, small bronze chains, and eye pencils.

Literary evidence in the form of inscriptions was scanty; only at Mnarani was there a large number of funerary inscriptions from tombs of the fifteenth century. They are written in a form of floreate Neskhi script which is extremely difficult to read.

Linguistic and Ethnographical Evidence

Paleo-linguistic and ethnographical evidence has produced little. There has been no intensive study of the coastal dialects, other than the comparison between the old Swahili of Lamu and the standard Swahili of Zanzibar. It is possible that conclusions which will be of more than linguistic interest may be drawn from material which has been collected at Lamu. The place names of the coast are predominately Swahili, and the derivation of many of them, including Mombasa,[9] is unknown; some may be obsolete words, recognizable in other Bantu languages. Around Gedi there is a cluster of Galla place names—Gedi, Mida, and Dabasso— which indicate Galla settlements in the area.

The longest settled people on the coast of Kenya is a small tribe of hunters in the Witu area, who call themselves Da'alo and who speak a click language. They are the remnants of the pre-Bantu inhabitants and perhaps still reside in their ancestral home. The next are probably the Bajun, a group who live on the mainland and on the offshore islands between Kisimayu in Somalia and Lamu in Kenya. They are clearly of Arabo-African stock but distinct from the other Arabo-Africans or Swahili. They speak a dialect of Swahili close to Giriama, one of the northeast Bantu languages, which would be weakened by the removal of the many Arab loan words but which would nevertheless exist. I believe that the Bajun are the descendants of the lost Almozaid mentioned by Barros:

> The town of Magadoxo gained such power and state that it became the sovereign and head of all the Moors of the coast; but as the first tribe who came, called Emozaydy, held different opinions from the

9. The assumption that Mombasa is an Arabic word has still to be proved. I know of no Arabic word or root which can be fitted into Mombasa.

Arabs with regard to their creed, they would not submit to them and retreated to the interior, where they joined the kaffirs, intermarrying with them and adopting their customs, so that in every way they became *mestizes*. These are the people whom the Moors of the sea coast call Baduys, a common name as in this country we call the country people Alarves.[10]

Nevertheless, all of the clans except one have Somali eponyms,[11] and most of them appear to be more Arabo-Hamitic than Arabo-Bantu. To introduce Kushites, megalithic or otherwise, would be convenient, but, in default of any proof of their existence, premature.

As a result of Chittick's excavations some of the Arab settlements may be assumed to have been founded in the ninth century, thus confirming the accounts in Barros and in the nineteenth-century local histories. The earliest stream of immigrants, which on the evidence of the *Periplus* and Barros[12] I would designate as "the traders," came from the Yemen and came as individuals, but of these no evidence has yet been found. At a later stage, I believe as a consequence of the subjection of the Near East to the Ummayad Caliphate (*c*. A.D. 700), groups of fugitives arrived in East Africa mainly from the Persian Gulf.[13] These were the people of Manda and comprised the earliest wave of settlers, as opposed to the traders of the past. They, or rather the women among them, could not have been very numerous, as otherwise their wives would have ensured that Arabic was maintained as their language.

I distinguish four areas of settlement in Kenya. These are the islands of the Bajun, which we have already mentioned; the Lamu archipelago; the "Kingdom of Melinde"; and Mombasa and the

10. João de Barros, *Da Asia* (1552) in Freeman-Grenville, *The East African Coast*, 84.
11. Vinigi L. Grottanelli, *Pescatori dell'Oceano Indiano* (Roma, 1955), 204–205.
12. Hjalmar Frisk, *Le Périple de la Mer Erythrée* (Göteberg, 1927), 5–6, in Freeman-Grenville, *The East African Coast*, 1–2. See also Gervase Mathew, "The Dating and Significance of the *Periplus of Erythrean Sea*," above, 158–159, João de Barros, *Deçadas da India* (1777), II, 1, ii, 19–30, trans. in James Kirkman, *Ungwana on the Tana* (The Hague, 1966), 8–9.
13. Shaibu Faraji bin Hammed al Bakariya al Lamu (trans. William Hichens), "Khabar al Lamu—A Chronicle of Lamu," *Bantu Studies*, XII (1938), 1–33. See also Neville Chittick, "The Peopling of the East African Coast," above, 16.

south. The settlers in the Lamu archipelago came from the Yemen and from al-Sham. (Al-Sham normally means Syria, but it is also applied to the northern part of the Hijaz.[14]) Much later arrived the Nabhani, the ruling family of Pate, who claim to have been rulers of Oman.[15] The Kingdom of Melinde included the estuaries of the Tana and Sabaki Rivers, and its citizens are supposed to have come from Kufa.[16] The Kufans, according to the Lamu chronicle, were "notoriously seditious and notoriously cowardly," so there is every reason to suppose that after the invariably unsuccessful internal revolts there would be considerable migrations. Mombasa, probably its ally Kilifi, and Vumba, the state south of Mombasa, were the creations of the Shirazi. The Shirazi were more prominent in Tanganyika and Zanzibar than in Kenya. They claim to have come from Shiraz, but it is now being suggested that in fact they came from the Benadir coast of Somalia.[17] The date of their arrival is also a subject of controversy. I prefer the later date—the twelfth century—to the tenth century, which has been accepted hitherto; but I am loath, without stronger evidence than has been produced so far, to agree with the view that the Shirazi did not come directly from Persia. If the Shirazi occupation were an "expansion" rather than a "migration," it is extraordinary that there should be no record or oral tradition referring to it. In favor of the new hypotheses that the Shirazi came from the north are the Portuguese references to people "creeping like a slow plague down the coast."[18] But these refer to the primary period of settlement, so they support the earlier date

14. Private communication from the Rev. James Ritchie. I think this interpretation is a more plausible explanation than that "settlers from al-Sham" merely means subjects of the Caliphate, which at that time was based at Damascus. It is most unlikely that any body of settlers should have come from Syria directly without there being some mention of it in Arabic literature.

15. C.H. Stigand, *The Land of Zinj* (London, 1913), in Freeman-Grenville, *The East African Coast*, 241.

16. Enrico Cerulli, *Somalia* (Roma, 1957), I 3, 260.

17. J. Spencer Trimingham, *Islam in East Africa* (Oxford, 1964), 1–18; Neville Chittick, "The 'Shirazi' Colonization of East Africa," *The Journal of African History*, VI (1965), 275–294; Chittick, above, 41; Vinigi L. Grotanelli, "The Peopling of the Horn of Africa," above, 57; Trimingham, "The Arab Geographers and the East African Coast," above, 128–129.

18. João de Barros, *Da Asia*, in Freeman-Grenville, *The East African Coast*, 83.

which is unacceptable if we assign, as I think we should do, the coins of 'Ali bin Hasan to the founder of Kilwa. The answer may come when a history of Maqdishu is found.

The present coastal Africans belong to the group of northeastern Bantu known as the Nyika, or the Nine Tribes. According to their traditions, which were first collected by Guillain in 1846,[19] they were settled around Shungwaya in southern Somalia until they were driven south by the Galla at the end of the sixteenth and at the beginning of the seventeenth century. They fell back first to the Tana River, where they left behind the Pokomo tribe, and then into the hills behind the coastal plain. The only people mentioned in the oral tradition as being in possession of these hills were the semi-pigmy Berikomo. The existence of this people may be substantiated by the strong streak of steatopygy among the Giriama, one of the Nyika tribes, which does not exist among the others. On the coast, however, there must have been a normal type of Bantu-speaker to account for the mixed Swahili population of the towns. I believe that these Bantu-speakers were a branch of the northeastern Bantu related to the Shungwaya people and later absorbed by them. Two names have been recorded by the Portuguese. One is Mosungalos, the people who lived behind Mombasa, whose name has survived in a small tribe near Gelib in Somalia. The other is Segeju, the people who lived behind Malindi and who were a mixed Bantu-Galla or Bantu-Somali people. They also were fugitives from Shungwaya and have survived as Islamized Bantu in the neighborhood of Vumba in southern Kenya and Tanga in northern Tanganyika.[20] In the nineteenth century the Galla in the Shungwaya area were attacked by the Masai and the Somali and, with their cattle dying of east coast fever, were in decline. They were given their death blow in the 1860's by the "love feast" in which their leaders were massacred and the tribe sold as slaves by the Somali to the people whom they had oppressed for centuries.[21] By the end of the century the

19. Charles Guillain, *Documents sur l'histoire, la géographie et le commerce de l'Afrique orientale* (Paris, 1856), III, 242. See also above, 61.
20. João dos Santos, *Ethiopia Oriental* (Evora, 1609), in Freeman-Grenville, *East African Coast*, 150.
21. Cerulli, *Somalia*, I, 286–288.

Giriama had reoccupied all of the territory up to the Sabaki River. North of the Sabaki were Pokomo on the Tana River, Bajun and Swahili on the coast, and Boni and Sanya, subject castes of the Galla who may have arrived with them, in the immediate hinterland.

EXCAVATED SITES

Gedi[22]

The principal site of my excavations was the town of Gedi, ten miles from Malindi, which was investigated in order to be maintained as an historical monument. It is situated four miles from the sea and two miles from a navigable estuary, Mida Creek. The only attraction of the site, apart from its obscurity, was the presence of water which is nowhere abundant between Malindi and Mombasa. Today the wells of Gedi are dry, but there is good water only half a mile away. It was probably founded as the result of some dispute in Malindi, and seems never to have achieved a distinct position of its own. The name Gedi is a Galla word meaning "precious." In an unpublished history of the Pokomo it is mentioned as "Gedi Kilimani," meaning Gedi "on the hill," a common place name. Confirmation of the name Kilimani is found in the Berthelot map of Africa (1635) in the British Museum, in which a place between Kilifi and Malindi is marked as Quelman.[23]

The excavations at the Great Mosque, the Palace, and the Dated Tomb showed that the buildings were mostly fifteenth century, although there had been a considerable settlement in the fourteenth century. The characteristic foreign imports were Lung-ch'uan celadon, Ch'ing-pai, white, and blue-and-white porcelain, and polychrome and monochrome glazed earthenware. *Sgraffiato* was uncommon, both the incised and *champlevé* variety. In almost every level where it was found it occurred with Lung-ch'uan celadon, which I think indicates that Gedi was not founded until the thirteenth century.

22. James Kirkman, *The Arab City of Gedi: The Great Mosque* (Oxford, 1954); *idem, The Tomb of the Dated Inscription at Gedi* (London, 1960); *idem, Gedi: The Palace* (The Hague, 1963).
23. Eric Axelson, *Portuguese in South-East Africa*, 1600–1700 (Johannesburg, 1960), map facing 97.

The fourteenth-century levels were marked by the presence of celadon bowls and plates, particularly the bowls with carved long lotus leaf petals on the outside, and the coarse yellow glazed earthenware with geometrical pattern in black. These types were found below the floor of the Dated Tomb, i.e., in a level not later than 1399. Among them were a few sherds of a golden luster jug and a blue luster plate, which were certainly family heirlooms.

The fifteenth century was the golden age of Gedi. The town was rebuilt and there was a great increase in the quantity and variety of imports. Celadon continued to be imported, but blue-and-white bowls began to be preferred toward the end of the century. Most of the blue-and-white sherds were the post-Hsuan Te types. Among them were bowls made in Annam, in blue or sepia on cream with a varnished base. Other types included white, ch'ing-pai, and tz'u chou bowls, and brown, medium sized storage jars.

The yellow-and-black glazed wares were replaced about the middle of the century by the glossy lead glazed monochromes; blue, green, and turquoise were the favorite colors, but yellow, black, mauve, and purple were also found. Less common were the blue-and-white bowls with a tin glaze on a white body, or plain white bowls with an Arabic text carved in relief under the glaze. Both these types had occured in fourteenth-century levels but were more common in the fifteenth century. They seem to be the same types as were found at Wasit in Iraq.[24]

Early in the sixteenth century there was a break in occupation at Gedi. This, I believe, was the result of a punitive expedition sent by Mombasa against Malindi in 1529. The people of Malindi had joined with the Portuguese in the second sack of Mombasa, and when the Portuguese fleet continued on its way to India, a small garrison was left behind at Malindi. The attack against Malindi never took place, but it is possible that the expedition destroyed Gedi. This could be the reason why it was never mentioned by the Portuguese, although for eighty years they lived peacefully at Malindi, only ten miles away.

In the late sixteenth century Gedi was reoccupied by refugees

24. Fuad Safar, *Wasit: The Sixth Season's Excavations* (Cairo, 1945).

from the mainland cities farther north which were abandoned as a result of the southern advance of the Galla from Somalia. Some of the ruined houses were restored, making use of the old floors but at times altering the position of the entrance—an indication of the taking possession of an abandoned town, with attendant spiritual dangers. A new town wall was made, enclosing a much smaller area of eighteen instead of forty-five acres. This re-occupation was of short duration, possibly less than a generation. The Palace was divided into apartments, but the work was never finished. In one of the courts a pile of lime, which was being used for plastering a blocked door, was found lying where it had been dumped. The new inhabitants probably heard that the Galla had reached the Sabaki River, about fifteen miles away, and fled.

In the last levels the characteristic ceramic was Wan Li blue-and-white porcelain and a rather coarsely-painted glazed earthenware on a hard-baked red body. The decoration consisted of floral and geometrical designs in manganese black, green, and blue on a yellow, white, or gray ground. This ware is known from Baroda.[25] A simpler form of the same ware was merely decorated with chevrons on a flat rim and a star or spray in the bottom. In these levels also appeared a number of bowls and lamps in a sandy-buff colored earthenware, which had been made on a wheel with a professional touch that was absent from the rest of the unglazed earthenware. In view of the difference in the clay, I think they may have been imported, perhaps from Aden.

Kilepwa[26]

Kilepwa was a small settlement on an island in Mida Creek, about two miles from Gedi. It consisted of a small mosque, two pillar tombs, and a group of houses. It was clearly a family unit, corresponding perhaps to the European manor. The site had been occupied as early as the beginning of the thirteenth century, and abandoned at the end of the sixteenth although, from the scarcity of late Ming sherds, it must have had very little life during the

25. Bendapudi Subbarao, *Baroda through the Ages* (Baroda, 1953), Plate xiii, 1.
26. James Kirkman, "Excavations at Kilepwa," *The Antiquaries Journal* XXXII (1952), 168–184.

sixteenth century. Sherds of *sgraffiato* were found all over the site, so it may have had a large population in the pre-building period.

The most interesting feature was a tomb with an octagonal pillar. In the debris around it, among late sixteenth-century material, was found an early fourteenth-century blue-and-white dragon vase which had probably decorated the tomb.

In the lowest levels below the mosque were *sgraffiato* with the hatched background reminiscent of Sassanian silverwork and a gray-tinted tin glazed earthenware. Above these, under the first floor, were found Persian blue-and-white with a paste body and blue-gray and greenish white porcelain. Between the first and second floors of the mosque were found blue and green mono-chromes, blue and white bichromes on a red body, *champlevé sgraffiato*, and buff and olive brown celadon—the whole collection composing a characteristic fifteenth-century ceramic pattern.

Mnarani[27]

Mnarani, the old Kilifi, was built on a bluff on the south side of Kilifi Creek. The ruins consist of a large mosque with a fine group of ornamented tombs at the north end behind the *mihrab*, with more than a hundred feet of broken inscriptions, and a smaller mosque with an open arcade on the west of the *musalla*, apparently with no wall between arcade and *musalla*.

No *sgraffiato* was found, and the earliest levels contain yellow-and-black glazed earthenware and a little celadon. In the surface levels Islamic monochromes and fifteenth-century Chinese blue-and-white porcelain predominated. However, as at Kilepwa, a few sherds of late Ming porcelain showed that the site was still occupied in the sixteenth century.

Kilifi was a small state always at odds with Malindi and in alliance with Mombasa. About 1590 the shaykh of Kilifi was killed in a battle with the Segeju, the African tribe allied with Malindi, and Kilifi was absorbed into the Sultanate of Malindi-Mombasa. It was destroyed by the Galla some time after 1618, which is the last mention of it in Portuguese sources. The area of Kilifi state included two other sites, known as Kioni and Kitoka.

27. James Kirkman, "Mnarani of Kilifi," *Ars Orientalis*, III (1959), 95–112.

At Kioni the capital of a *mihrab* was found with an inscription in interlacing Kufic, which may be older than the fourteenth century.

Ungwana[28]

Another large site was Ungwana, near Kipini, almost certainly the town called Hoja by the Portuguese (from Ozi, an old name for the Tana River). Today it is about a quarter of a mile from the seashore, but at one time it may have been on it. Along the coast, within six miles, are two more towns called Shaka and Mwana. This area has no obvious attraction and the reason for the existence of these settlements is unknown.

The excavations at Ungwana were concentrated on the area of the two Jami' and on another elaborately decorated mosque which may have been a *chapelle royale*. There were six periods distinguishable: Periods I and II preceded the construction of the Jami'; Periods III and IV covered the life of the old Jami' and the building of the new; Periods V and VI, the rebuilding of the new Jami' and the last hundred years of the life of the town.

In the lowest levels (Periods I and II, dated 1200–1350) were found *sgraffiato* of the two types, incised and *champlevé*, and a tin glazed ware which was not found at Gedi. The *sgraffiato* was decorated with curling lines in the Samarran manner, but also with floral motifs and Arabic letters on a hatched ground. The tin glazed ware may be the type found by Chittick with Sassanian/Islamic jars in the upper levels of his deep fill deposit at Manda. However, all of these wares had a long life and the presence of *champlevé* types, I think, is a caution against too early dating. Similarily, the *sgraffiato* with hatched background was found in the later levels at Bhambor in Sindh, Pakistan, which are thirteenth century. The curling lines suggest an earlier type of *sgraffiato*, but I have not found it unaccompanied by sherds with the hatched background.

The next period (Period III, dated 1350–1450) was a great building period and was marked by celadon and Islamic yellow-and-black and green *sgraffiato* of Mamluk type. This last ware

28. Kirkman, *Ungwana*.

was found at Gedi below the court of the Great Mosque but not in such quantity as at Ungwana. Chinese blue-and-white was absent.

In Period IV early blue-and-white appeared. The earliest sherds, clearly post-Hsuan Te types, were accompanied by the yellow-and-black and the glossy monochromes. The anteroom of the old Jamiᶜ was decorated with a series of fine celadon bowls in the intrados of the cupolas of the roof. Another celadon bowl had been set above the *mihrab* of the new Jamiᶜ and was found in the humus in front of it. This period was brought to an end in 1505, when Hoja was sacked by Tristan da Cunha.

The last two periods (Periods V and VI) were marked by Chinese blue-and-white of Chia Ching and Wan Li types, the glossy Islamic monochromes, and the polychromes which were found in the last levels at Gedi. A new type, which was not found at Gedi but has occured at Fort Jesus, consisted of small bowls with a watery green glaze and *sgraffiato* decoration on the outside and a yellow glaze on the inside. They appear to be similar to an Egyptian ware made at Alexandria at this time.[29] The prominence of green *sgraffiato* at Ungwana confirms the connection which appears to have existed between Hoja and Egypt, as testified in the words of the shaykh of Hoja to Tristan da Cunha that "he was the subject of the Soldan [Sultan] of Cairo."[30]

Near the Jamiᶜ was the cemetery in which were two large tombs, one richly decorated with porcelain bowls and carved coral ornament in the form of bosses linked with cable molding, the other with panels with a cross *fitché* diaper. These panels are similar to those at the entrance of the Great Mosque of Veramin near Tehran, built in 1325. The bowls (except for a large plate of "Istanbul" type) which are believed to have decorated them, belong to the second half of the fifteenth century.

Hoja is mentioned by the Portuguese as late as the end of the seventeenth century but, apart from the watery green *sgraffiato*

29. M.A. Marzouk, "Three Signed Specimens of Mamluk Pottery from Alexandria," *Ars Orientalis*, II (1957), 497–501.

30. The Sultan of Cairo in 1505 was al-Ashraf Kansuh El Ghuri (1500–1516), who corresponded with the Venetians over the iniquities of the Portuguese and was defeated and killed by the Ottoman Turks at the Battle of Marg Dabik near Aleppo in 1516.

and a few stray pieces such as a Maria Theresa dollar and a blue monochrome bowl from the cemetery, nothing was found which could be later than the Wan Li period. The absence of K'ang Hsi porcelain and associated Islamic and local wares of the late seventeenth century indicates that the town had come to an end as an urban center.

Takwa[31]

Another small site which was examined was Takwa on the island of Manda, at the end of a creek leading off the entrance to Lamu harbor. Here was a large mosque which was built in the sixteenth century and abandoned in the seventeenth. On the shore was an unusual type of pillar tomb with a cylindrical pillar and an inscription with a date 1094 A.H. (A.D. 1682). In the cistern of the mosque was a blue-and-white plate of Portuguese majolica, with the cross of the Order of Christ. Takwa was never mentioned by the Portuguese. It was probably the retreat of a holy man who lived there for a time with his disciples. The tomb is still a place of annual pilgrimage, though the site is uninhabited owing to the absence of water.

Fort Jesus, Mombasa

The excavations at Fort Jesus produced material for the seventeenth, eighteenth, and nineteenth centuries. In spite of the fact that it was a fortress, not a town, there was no great difference in the finds from the excavations. There were four main strata: early Portuguese, 1593– c.1634; late Portuguese, c.1634–1698; early Omani and Mazrui, 1698–1837; and Zanzibari, 1837–1895.

The first period was defined by the raising of the bastions after the Arab revolt of 1631. In these levels the porcelain consisted of late Ming and transitional types, including dishes with the heavily decorated, paneled rims which have not been found on the earlier sites. The polychrome glazed earthenware was identical with wares which had been found in the surface levels at Gedi and Ungwana.

In the same levels had been found a coarse green or brown

31. James Kirkman, "Takwa: The Mosque of the Pillar," *Ars Orientalis,* II (1957), 175–182.

glazed stoneware on a gray or gray-buff body, consisting of straight-sided bowls and dishes with flat lips. At the end of the seventeenth century the import of this ware increased, and the forms included a small handled jar with a turned out lip. In the eighteenth century the body was frequently a soft buff instead of hard baked gray. The form of the base was more Chinese than Islamic, and I believe that this ware was made somewhere in Indonesia or Indochina. However, I cannot find any reference to it in the Dutch trading registers. It continued to be imported throughout the first half of the nineteenth century.

In addition there was the thin, red, polished ware of the Alemtejo, the blue-and-white majolica of Lisbon and Coimbra, and the salt glazed basins and demijohns which could have been made almost anywhere in Europe. Less common was a thin, black, polished ware, probably from India, and a pink, mica-dusted ware, which had also been found at Ungwana and Gedi and which would have been made in some part of the Arab world.

The second period is defined by the clearing up of the fort by the Arabs after the great siege (1696–1698) and particularly by the construction of the gunplatform over the filled-in captain's house. This must have been carried out soon after the capture of the fort because of the need to put it in a state of defense. In these levels Portuguese blue-and-white was found, but Ming had been replaced by K'ang Hsi. Unfortunately, there are no dated structures in the fort, other than a cavalier built in 1648, so the excavations have not helped in the dating of the various K'ang Hsi types. In these late seventeenth-century levels, *famille verte*, a great variety of blue-and-white, chocolate, *café-au-lait*, overglaze blue, *blanc de chine*, and the later celadon were found, but no rose pink. There was an increase in the importation of Persian blue-and-white, usually with Chinese designs. Other Islamic wares were scarce.

The unglazed earthenware of the first period had continued the ceramic tradition of the sixteenth century, with the addition of a new kind of appliqué ornament consisting of thin strips of clay making curvilinear or toothed motifs above the carination. These became more elaborate at the end of the century. The forms of the vessels were the same as the undecorated or incised specimens, so there can be no question of a difference of origin. Another variety, which appeared at the end of the seventeenth century, had a smoothed black surface with a bead rim and a sliced diamond-shaped ornament on the carination.

Besides the cooking pots and jars of local origin, there was a class of jars and carinated bowls in both red and black earthenware made on the wheel and with molded lips, which I believe came from Diu. They were in the same ceramic tradition as the pots from the excavations at Baroda,[32] and they ceased to be imported after the fall of the fort. In these levels also appeared the first sherds of the typical Indian chatty with round red body and black rings. This continued to be imported in increasing quantities throughout the eighteenth and nineteenth centuries. It was being made at Muscat in the nineteenth century.[33]

The early eighteenth century seems to have been a period of poverty in Mombasa. Most of the sherds of the rose pink porcelain belong to types of the second half of the century, with small sprays of blossoms and heavy borders of pink or mauve. The blue-and-white was limited to a monotonous choice between the "comb" pattern, the chrysanthemum, the rosette border, and later the trellis and spray and the *shou* character motifs. This period I believe continued well into the nineteenth century, and it was only after the expulsion of the Mazrui governors and the absorption of Mombasa by Zanzibar in 1837, that the import of European china began. The earliest specimens were the creamwares of Doulton type, mostly large dishes, small coffee cups, and plates and bowls of English print ware. In the second half of the century the Saar potteries, Utzschneider and Company at Saarguemines and Villeroy and Boch at Wallerfangen, were sending large quantities of flowered cups and bowls to East Africa. Chinese porcelain continued to be imported, and it was not until the middle of the century that it was ousted by European china. Persian blue-and-white had ceased to be imported after the first quarter of the eighteenth century. The commonest Islamic wares, probably also Persian, were small platters with a yellow glaze on a buff body.

32. Subbarao, *Baroda*, Figs., 20, 21, 23.
33. Guillain, *Documents*, III, 347.

Other wares consisted of jugs with four vertical handles in a blue or yellow glaze.

The local earthenware underwent a change of feeling after a long static period, as is shown in the carinated pots. The profile of the neck above the carination had been convex in the seventeenth century, but in the eighteenth it was made straight and square. At the end of the eighteenth century there was another change. The austere straight line was replaced by an exaggerated concave profile and projecting lip. In the middle of the nineteenth century the lip was chamfered to a flat vertical line. The changes in jars and relish bowls were not so marked. However, the relish bowls of the eighteenth century were generally stouter and tended to have straighter sides than their predecessors of the seventeenth century, and the burnishing was perfunctory or entirely omitted. In the small water jars a crimson painted neck became universal at the end of the seventeenth century and is characteristic of eighteenth-century levels. In the nineteenth the painting was sometimes omitted and this type of vessel became less common.

The importation of European beads is mentioned by the Portuguese, principally red coral and jet, but very few have been found in the excavations. At the end of the seventeenth century a number of new types appeared in the cane beads: a light opaque blue, an opaque and a transparent white, a transparent blue, and a red on green. In the nineteenth century, rings, spheres, and a candy-pink bead were imported in addition to the other types in use.

European glass had appeared in the late seventeenth century in the form of case bottles with pewter neck and screw cap. In the eighteenth these bottles continued to be imported but with a molded lip, and with them the conventional wine bottles with an uneven strand below the mouth for tying on the cork. They were probably made in England or France and would have been brought from India or Mauritius.

Some Suggestions for Further Research

The evidence of the excavations already carried out in Kenya has suggested that it was only in the fourteenth and fifteenth centuries that the Arab, or mixed Arabo-African, settlements attained more than a pioneer standard of living. This can, of course, be the accident of excavation, which may be disproved by excavations on the islands of Lamu, Pate, Mombasa, and Wasin, or on mainland sites like Ngomeni and Malindi. The excavations at Manda have shown that early Arab remains do exist, and further investigation at this site is most desirable.

The reason for the expansion of the fourteenth and fifteenth centuries may be connected with the increase in luxury goods and their adoption by a larger middle class than had before existed. This development has been seen in Europe, but its application to the southern hemisphere awaits a social and economic history of the Indian Ocean. The discovery of pre-Islamic sites is linked with that of the early Islamic sites, since the same factors would have been required: a good harbor, water, and some element of security.

Another field of research would be the investigation of the contribution made by indigenous people to the urban culture of the coast. There are two lines of research which might be followed with this end in view. One is the investigation of the significance and derivation of the pillar tomb, the most striking architectural feature on the coast of East Africa. The other is the study of the local earthenware, its northern associations, and to what extent it is a product of the urban communities and distinct from the pottery of the countryside. In this way it should be possible to confirm or modify the apparent absence of cultural interchange between the urban and tribal communities on the coast of East Africa.

THE ORIGIN AND SPREAD OF SOME DOMESTIC FOOD PLANTS OF EASTERN AFRICA

M.D. Gwynne

General Considerations

One of the initial centers of plant domestication was the Middle East. We assume that domestication probably first took place in this area during the eighth millennium B.C., and spread over a period of at least one hundred human generations.[1] Although the first plants concerned were what subsequently became wheat and barley, the process by which they became domesticated is most likely the same as the one through which other crop plants have passed. It is, therefore, worth briefly considering the general features of this process before proceeding further and discussing the origins of East African food plants.

The domestication of all food plants has involved unconscious and conscious selection for characteristics which permit easier harvest and give better yields. Thus, for example, in the early grain crops there was a movement away from ears that shattered, away from hulled grain, and, above all, away from crossbreeding and the continuance of great variability which resulted in the

I would like to thank Hugh Doggett and Jan B. Gillett for their many helpful comments and discussions.
1. Cyril D. Darlington, *The Genetics of Society*, reprinted from A.J. Gregor (ed.), *A Symposium on Race: an Interdisciplinary Approach* (Honolulu, 1963), 6.

uneven spread of flowering and germination throughout the season. The movement was toward a new and previously unknown habit which today is recognized as that of the cultivated plant. As a result grain crops tended to come into flower at the same time, and they began to be self-fertilizing instead of cross-fertilizing. The ears became tough and the grain could be thrashed out. Similarly the seed ripened together and, when planted, germinated at the same time.[2] These characteristics came from unintended selection due to regular sowing, regular tillage, and regular harvesting, all of which favored hereditary mutations leading to better yields.

When cultivators migrated to new areas, they took with them their skills, and, in some regions as they harvested their crops, they also took in the seeds of the local weeds. Selection, therefore worked on these weeds as well, with the result that a new crop sometimes arose; thus cultivated sorghum is thought to have originated from a weed of the wheat fields. Conscious and unconscious selection working together have built the world's crops and are processes which have continued almost without interruption to the present day.

Apart from twentieth-century introductions, the cultivated food plants of eastern Africa fall into four major groups:

1) The early arrivals from southwestern Asia (the Middle East) which came with the introduction of agriculture to the region.
2) Indigenous plants which were domesticated as a result of the introduction and spread of agriculture within Africa.
3) Later introductions from India and Southeast Asia.
4) Recent introductions from the Western Hemisphere.

It has been maintained that agriculture was first introduced into eastern Africa through Ethiopia and the eastern Sudan sometime during the third millennium B.C., and that it came initially from southwestern Asia. Soon, however, cultivators were growing indigenous plants as crops. Early crops thought to have originated in this manner are sorghum (*Sorghum bicolor*), finger millet (*Eleusine coracana*), and teff (*Eragrostis abyssinica*). Other vegetables

---

2. N.I. Vavilov, "Studies on the Origin of Cultivated Plants," *The Bulletin of Applied Botany*, XVI (1926), 139–248.

such as cowpea (*Vigna sinensis*) and earthpea (*Voandzeia sub-terranea*) probably developed in the same way at a later date. These new crops radiated out to the south and the east. Several, however, probably spread rapidly to the west, where they were further developed in a secondary center of plant domestication which arose in West Africa sometime about 1000 B.C. This subsequently led to the domestication of some West African plants, such as the oil palm (*Elaeis guineensis*), geocarpa groundnut (*Kerstingiella geocarpa*), and the Guinea yams (*Dioscorea cayennensis* and *D. rotundata*), some of which later moved into the eastern part of the continent.

Rice (*Oryza sativa*) is a difficult plant to consider as the cytological relationships among the varieties have not yet been fully worked out. Evidence suggests that it originated in Southeast Asia, spreading into Indonesia and through India and Persia into Egypt and Europe. Rice probably entered East Africa either directly from Indonesia or indirectly by way of India, and is therefore Group 3 in origin.[3] The problem is, however, more complicated for there is considerable cytological evidence that the West African cultivated rice (*O. glaberrima*) developed from its wild relative, *O. breviligulata* (which is endemic to West Africa), quite independently of the origin of *O. sativa* from the Asian *O. perennis*, and is therefore Group 2 by origin.[4] Thus it is possible that some of the West African Group 2 rice forms could have diffused eastwards across the continent and are now present in parts of eastern Africa. It will need further careful investigation to determine whether Group 2 as well as Group 3 rices occur in East Africa today.

The question of how Group 3 plants arrived in eastern Africa is a difficult one. On the botanical evidence several could have reached Africa either directly, by being transported across the Indian Ocean, or indirectly, by the coastal route through India and southern Arabia; at various times both routes were probably used. There is no botanical reason, however, for such plants not

3. D.H. Grist, *Rice* (London, 1953), 4.
4. Hiroko Morishima, Kokichi Hinatà, and Hiko-Ichi Oka, "Comparison of Modes of Evolution of Cultivated Forms From Two Wild Rice Species, *Oryza breviligulata* and *Oryza perennis*," *Evolution* XVII (1963), 170–181.

to have come along the coastal route via Iraq and Syria. It is easy to transport plants reproduced by seed, and those whose main method of propagation is vegetative could survive the coastal journey if the propagation parts were well packed, particularly if suitable intermediate cultivation points were available, such as Dhufar in South Arabia. Careful study of the cultivated plants of South Arabia, and of islands such as Socotra, would prove worthwhile, for it is possible that these plants might show considerable Southeast Asian affinities. (In addition such a study could shed light on the origin of the South Arabian Veddoid people and their connection with Southeast Asia.[5])

A further possibility is that the Southeast Asian crop elements were introduced into Africa by way of southern India without intermediate stops in South Arabia. The direct ocean voyage from southern India to the East African coast or Madagascar would, at the right time of year, present no great problems, and the time needed would still be within the life span of any properly prepared vegetative propagules. Only a surprisingly few people are needed successfully to introduce new plant and animal life; it would thus not have needed many voyages to establish new crops in Africa.

Two main imports via these routes were banana and sugar cane, both of which will be considered below, but in addition to them some twenty to thirty other important domestic plants reached eastern Africa in the same way, e.g., mango (*Mangifera indica*), taro (*Colocasia antiquorum*), and the pomegranate (*Punica granatum*), the last probably coming from Persia or Afghanistan.[6] Too little work has been done on these crops to say accurately when they reached the eastern coast. The mango, for example, is said by some[7] to have been introduced at the end of the nineteenth century, yet others report it as being in Somaliland in the fourteenth century.[8] The very large number of mango varieties seen in East Africa would suggest that it has long been cultivated in the area. However, this could equally well reflect the introduction of

5. Hugh Scott, *In the High Yemen* (London, 1942), 202.
6. Peter J. Greenway, "Origins of Some East African Food Plants," *The East African Agriculture Journal*, X (1944), 118.
7. A.S. Thomas, "Fruits and Vegetables" in J.D. Tothill (ed.), *Agriculture in Uganda* (Oxford, 1940), 488.
8. Lal Behari Singh, *The Mango* (London, 1960), 8. See also Posnansky, above, 224.

many varieties from India. Until the East African varieties have been botanically compared with those of Asia generally, it will be impossible to give a definite opinion.

Some plants in this same group are of uncertain origin, and it cannot be said how they first came to East Africa. One is the coconut (*Cocos nucifera*) because it is possible, although improbable, that the coconut reached the shores of tropical eastern Africa by natural means. Experiments carried out in Hawaii have shown that the coconut fruit can float in salt water for periods of up to 110 days and still remain viable;[9] with a favorable current this would provide enough time to transport it about three thousand miles. In 1928 and 1930 eruptions from a submerged crater threw up several new islands in the vicinity of Krakatoa, Indonesia. One of these, Anak Krakatoa IV, remained and, eighteen months later, was visited by biologists who found forty-one germinating coconuts on the shore. The distribution of the coconuts was quite random, and the active nature of the crater precluded introduction by human agency.[10] The area was destroyed by a further eruption in 1932, so that it is not known whether the coconuts became properly established. I have found germinating coconuts among beach debris on the Indian Ocean atolls of Farquar, Cosmoledo, and Astove.[11] There were no signs, however, of any older stages of establishment, and it is likely that such germinating plants are quickly destroyed by the abundant shore crabs. It is worth noting that there were no shore crabs present where the coconuts were germinating on Anak Krakatoa IV.[12] Apart from areas on the island of Trinidad, there is no other documented example of mature coconuts having become established as a result of natural dispersal.[13] It is most likely that they were introduced to eastern Africa by human agency.

Group 4 plants consist entirely of those types originally domesticated in the Western Hemisphere and introduced into

9. Reginald Child, *Coconuts* (London, 1964), 9.
10. A.W. Hill and W.D. Van Leeuwan, "Germinating Coconuts on a New Volcanic Island, Krakatoa," *Nature*, CXXXII (1933), 674–675.
11. During the course of the East African Marine Fisheries Research Organisation Indian Ocean Islands Expedition, 1967.
12. Hill and Van Leeuwan, "Krakatoa," 675.
13. Child, *Coconuts*, 10–11.

Africa after the first Portuguese visits to the Americas in the fifteenth century. It includes such plants as maize (*Zea mays*), groundnut (*Arachis hypogaea*), sweet potato (*Ipomoea batatas*), and cassava (*Manihot utilissima*), all of which have become well established in Africa. Although these plants were introduced to Africa comparatively recently, very little is known about the paths of their dispersion. It would seem, however, that these routes may have varied with the type of crop and its habitat requirements. Cassava, for example, is thought to have first reached the lakes area of East Africa from the west[14] while, on nonbotanical evidence, a possible route for maize found in the same area went from the east through Ethiopia.[15]

Having considered the origins of East African food crops in general terms, it is necessary to examine particular plants in each group to see what formed the basis for proposing the division into these groups. Wherever possible this entails the use of botanical evidence such as the distribution and relationships of present-day crop types, the latter determined mainly by cytological studies, and the evidence of ancient preserved plant remains from sites of archaeological significance. An assessment of this sort, however, has so far proved possible for very few African crops, and the movements of the majority of crops must still be inferred from the suggested migration of these few examples. Thus there is a very great need for more evolutionary studies by geneticists on cultivated plants and for greater attention to the collection and preservation of plant material during excavations by archaeologists.

Group 1 Plants—Wheat

From archaeological evidence it seems most likely that the first cultivated plants to be introduced into Africa (Group 1) were wheat and barley. Wheat is a grass belonging to the genus *Triticum* and consists of a polyploid series of species in which there are diploid, tetraploid, and hexaploid representatives with chromosome numbers of fourteen, twenty-eight, and forty-two respectively; the

14. B.W. Langlands, "Cassava in Uganda 1860–1920," *The Uganda Journal*, XXX (1966), 212.
15. A.C.A. Wright, "Maize Names as Indicators of Economic Contacts," *The Uganda Journal*, XIII (1949), 80.

basic chromosome number of the genus and the number of chromosomes in each genome is, therefore, seven. For convenience the haploid set of seven chromosomes of the diploid is termed the A genome. It can be shown that the tetraploid contains the A genome plus another B genome. Similarly the hexaploid contains both A and B genomes plus a third which is unfortunately termed the D genome.[16] Thus the relationships within the genus can be summarized:

$$
\begin{aligned}
\textit{Triticum diploid} &= 14 = \text{AA} \\
\textit{Triticum tetraploid} &= 28 = \text{AABB} \\
\textit{Triticum hexaploid} &= 42 = \text{AABBDD}
\end{aligned}
$$

This would imply that the tetraploids arose from hybridization between diploid wheat and a B genome species (shown experimentally to be the wild grass *Aegilops speltoides*). This hybridization was followed or accompanied by a doubling of the chromosome number. Later hybridization again took place, this time between the new tetraploid wheat and a third diploid species, the D genome donor (shown to be the wild grass *Aegilops squarrosa*), thus giving rise to the hexaploid wheats.

The wild diploid wheat species was probably growing on the hills of the Middle East before agriculture began. According to Helbaek it was shifted down to a lower level from its original hilly habitat (3,000–4,000 ft.) by the first cultivators and the change caused the development of a number of mutations out of which came the first cultivated wheat species, *Triticum monococcum*

16. *Chromosomes* are the paired structures which appear in the nucleus of a living cell when that cell starts to divide. They are normally present in each cell of an organism in a constant number, and they carry the genes or hereditary control factors. The *genome* is the basic chromosome set of a group of very closely related organisms in which all cell chromosome complements are multiples of this basic number. *Polyploid* is a cell chromosome set having more than the normal or *diploid* two members of each chromosome pair, e.g. *triploid* with three members, *tetraploid* with four members, *pentaploid* with five members, and *hexaploid* with six members, are all polyploids. Individual organisms with the chromosomes of their cells arranged as triploid and pentaploid are usually sexually sterile. *Haploid* is a chromosome set containing one member only of each type of chromosome as in the reproductive cells of a normal diploid. *Clone* is a group of individuals derived from asexually produced ancestor with the result that all have the same genetic composition.

or Einkorn.[17] The tetraploid, *T. dicoccoides* also probably arose before agriculture in the same area and was brought under cultivation at about the same time (7000 B.C.). The cultivated Emmer wheat of today (*T. dicoccum*) arose by selection from the varieties and mutations produced by the cultivation of *T. dicoccoides*.

During the sixth and fifth millennia B.C. wheat cultivation spread into the alluvial plains of Iraq and Egypt. Emmer wheat thrived under the new conditions, but the Einkorn did not and so gave way to the Emmer.

Hexaploid wheats probably originated somewhere in Asia Minor and were carried to new localities in Europe as weeds or "off-types" of the Einkorn and Emmer. In Europe they were found to be hardy enough to flourish in the rigorous mountain environment of the new lands. They also had the advantage that their grains were naked and the stalk (or rachis) on which the grains were carried was tough and nonshattering. The grains, therefore, could be thrashed out easily to give a grain supply more or less free from husk remains.

During the first millennium B.C., somewhere in or near Egypt, another new tetraploid wheat arose from the Emmer by mutation. This had a soft, loose husk and a tough rachis so that it also could be thrashed easily to give a clean grain supply. The new tetraploids, therefore, were an improvement on Emmer and replaced it wherever contact allowed until, today, Emmer does not occur in the Middle East.

Emmer probably reached the interior of Persia and the Indus Valley in the early third millennium, but its spread to the east is not well documented. By the end of the third millennium, however, hexaploid wheats were being grown in the Indus Valley, and later they became the major type cultivated.

Emmer reached Ethiopia by way of the Nile Valley with the introduction of agriculture sometime during Egyptian dynastic times, while it was still the major wheat crop in Egypt. It is not possible to date its arrival precisely, but Helbaek, when discussing

17. Hans Helbaek, "Domestication of Food Plants in the Old World," *Science*, CXXX (1959), 366.

a wheat spike obtained from a site at El Omari, Egypt, dated as late or middle and late Neolithic, mentions that the husk apices correspond to those of Emmer and that the husks of five of the eight preserved spikelets resemble the present-day Ethiopian type because of their narrowly converging vein tips.[18] This finding would suggest that Emmer wheats reached Ethiopia at an early date, possibly during the third millennium. (A good annotated list of Emmer wheat discoveries in the Nile Valley is given by Täckholm and Drar.[19])

The new tetraploids also reached the Ethiopian area although they never replaced the Emmer, which continues to be cultivated today under the name of Adjaz. The great range of habitats within the Ethiopian mountain region led to further variations arising and surviving so that several of the wheats formed distinct subspecies, but full differentiation into "acceptable" species did not occur. Thus Ethiopia became a secondary center of wheat diversification.

From Ethiopia the new types spread to the East through the Yemen and southern Arabia into India where, for example, *T. dicoccum* subsp. *abyssinicum* is still cultivated in small quantities amidst the basic wheats of the Indian area, the hexaploids *T. aestivum* and *T. sphaerococcum*.

Although many suitable habitats exist, there seems to be no record of wheat being grown to the south of the Ethiopian region until recent times, when, according to local tradition, Arab slavers introduced it from southern Arabia to Tabora and Karagwe (Tanzania) in the first half of the nineteenth century.[20]

18. Hans Helbaek, "Ancient Egyptian Wheats," *Proceedings of the Prehistory Society*, XXI (1955), 94.
19. Vivi and Gunnar Täckholm, in collaboration with Mohammed Drar, *Flora of Egypt* (Cairo, 1941), I, 242–246.
20. Greenway, *Origins*, 252. Date palms also occur at Tabora, which is well outside their normal range, and the same origin is attributed to them. Harry H. Johnston, *British Central Africa* (London, 1897), 426, also states that wheat was introduced into the Zambezi Valley by the Portuguese and into Nyasaland (now Malawi) by the early European missionaries. David Livingstone, *Missionary Travels and Researches in South Africa* (London, 1857), 639, records wheat being grown at Tete and Zumbo in the Zambezi Valley in 1856 but makes no comment on its introduction. He states (379), however, that it was introduced into Angola by Jesuits.

Group 2 Plants—Sorghum, Millet, and Ensete

Sorghum and *Eleusine* millet were probably the first of the indigenous African plants to be domesticated. The cultivated sorghums (*Sorghum bicolor*) are grasses belonging to the tribe Andropogonae. The genus *Sorghum* has a basic chromosome number of five and can be divided into six subgenera with varying chromosome numbers up to a haploid of twenty in *Heterosorghum*. According to Doggett, on whose work this account is based, the available evidence would suggest that the subgenus *Eusorghum* is sharply defined and genetically separated from the other subgenera in the group even though their distributions overlap. *Eusorghums* are found throughout Africa, the Mediterranean, India, and Southeast Asia and have both diploid (twenty chromosome) and tetraploid (forty chromosome) forms. It is very likely that the diploid *Eusorghums* are themselves ancient tetraploids. The *Eusorghums* can be further divided into the forms *Halepensia*, which are mostly tetraploid, and *Arundinacea*, which are diploid. The cultivated sorghums all belong to the *Arundinacea* form. The wild *Arundinacea Eusorghums* are generally grasses of river and swamp margins or weeds of cultivated and abandoned land, although some are grasses of arid areas, and they seem to be restricted to Africa, where they are continental in distribution.[21]

The wild *Arundinacea Eusorghums* have been split into a number of what have come to be termed species and varieties.[22] Whatever the exact status of these divisions, they serve to illustrate the degree of variability within the group. Of the seventeen species listed, fourteen are found in northeastern Africa (north of 10°S. and east of 25°E.), and of the twenty-one named varieties, nineteen occur in the same area. In West Africa only five of the species and five of the varieties occur, while for southern Africa the figures are six and eight respectively. These data would suggest that the center of greatest variability for the wild *Arundinacea Eusorghum* is northeastern Africa.

21. Hugh Doggett, "The Development of the Cultivated Sorghums," in Joseph Hutchinson (ed.), *Essays on Crop Plant Evolution* (Cambridge, 1965), 54–55.
22. J.D. Snowden, "The Wild Fodder Sorghums of the Section Eu-Sorghum," *The Journal of the Linnean Society of London—Botany*, LV (1955), 214–260.

The collection of cultivated *Eusorghum* forms is far from complete so that comments upon their distribution cannot be accurate. It would appear, however, that twenty-eight of the listed thirty-one cultivated species are found in Africa and of these, twenty occur in the northeast. In West Africa only eleven species have been found and in southern Africa only twelve. Of the twenty species in the northeast, eleven are not found in West Africa, whereas of the eleven West African forms, only four do not occur in the northeast also.

When considering the varieties the same sort of pattern emerges. So far eighty-seven varieties have been collected in the northeast and twenty-seven in the West. Of these twenty-seven, eight also occur in the northeast. In southern Africa forty varieties occur, of which twenty-one are also found in the northeast. Only one variety is found in all three zones.

Given that northeastern Africa is the center of variation of both the wild and the cultivated sorghums, it seems certain that the latter must have originated there. It is likely that the first cultivators to reach the Sudan and the Ethiopian region in the third millennium B.C. brought with them Emmer wheat. It is possible, therefore, that being accustomed to cereals these early cultivators developed some of the local plants such as *Eleusine* millet and sorghum for use in areas not well suited to wheat cultivation— particularly those at the lower altitudes. The wild *Eusorghums* would have been the most likely grasses to be improved and, indeed, their initial development may have been due to un- conscious selection of *Eusorghum* weeds in the wheat fields.

Very likely the early sorghums were carried south into East Africa by the agriculturalists of the Ethiopian region, and possibly it was for use with sorghum that the stone pestles, bowls, and grinding stones of Njoro River Cave, Kenya, were intended. The suggestion has been made that the original cultivators of the Ethiopian region did not develop sorghum but merely improved it on receiving it from West Africa.[23] The present distribution of both the wild and cultivated sorghums, however, makes it much more likely that the crop was developed in northeastern Africa,

23. George Peter Murdock, *Africa: Its People and Their Culture History* (New York, 1959), 68, 123.

probably in that area which forms the modern Republic of the Sudan. Agriculture must have reached West Africa at an early date, and a certain amount of secondary sorghum crop evolution took place there.

Doggett is of the opinion that Bantu-speaking peoples found sorghum and *Eleusine* millet grown by Kushites in East Africa.[24] He considers that they then adopted Kushite agricultural practices and that it was the cultivation of sorghum and millet that enabled them to spread into the savannah areas of subtropical eastern and southern Africa, mainly during the last thousand years. He points out that present-day practices for harvesting, seed selection, and threshing in the sorghum-growing areas of the central highlands of Ethiopia are almost identical to those of the Sukuma of Tanzania, and that these practices are very different from those of the peoples who occupy the intervening region today.

On linguistic grounds it is thought that cultivated sorghum reached India after the arrival of Sanskrit-speaking peoples, as there is no specific Sanskrit name for the crop. This would mean that it probably reached India sometime about 1500 B.C., most likely by way of the Arabian coast. Sorghum had reached the Middle East by 700 B.C., for there is a carving in the palace of Sennacharib at Timgad which clearly shows it. Archaeological evidence suggests that sorghum was not grown in Egypt before the Roman Byzantine period so that it cannot have entered the Middle East by way of the Nile Valley and Egypt. It must, therefore, have come by way of India, which the Persian name of *juar-i-hindi* would suggest. From the Middle East it must have spread into Europe and North Africa, for Pliny records the movement of sorghum from India to Italy during the first century A.D.[25]

From India, sorghum also spread eastwards through Burma and into mainland China. That this happened can be deduced from the similarities between modern Indian and Chinese cultivated sorghums, but the date of its entry into China is problematical, although some authorities consider it to have occured during the period 500 A.D. to 1000 A.D.

24. Doggett, *Sorghums*, 59–60.
25. Täckholm and Drar, *Flora*, 537–538.

The Chinese amber canes (*S. dochna*) are a group of sorghums found in India, Burma, Malaya, and Korea, but only in areas within easy access of the coast. They differ in character from the sorghums of the interior of China, and from their distribution it is likely that they were moved by coastal vessels. In southeastern Africa there is a sorghum variety (Collier) which can be placed with the amber canes, and it is probable that this represents an ancestral type for the amber canes which were probably developed in Southeast Asia from the introduction of an earlier "Collier" type from Africa, followed by introgression with a local sorghum such as *S. proposigum*.[26] The ambers are probably not a very ancient introduction to China; it is likely that the first arrival came by sea from Africa not more than a thousand years ago.

In view of the later discussion, under Group 3 plants, of the introduction of the banana to Africa, it is worth considering here the banana's close relative, *Ensete* (*E. ventricosum*). At present it is mainly grown by the Sidamo people of southern Ethiopia who, from the pith of the stem, manufacture a starchy foodstuff which forms the basis of their diet. *Ensete* reproduces sexually, forming viable seeds, but the Sidamo propagate it vegetatively by stimulating the production of suckers by hollowing out the stem and packing it with earth and livestock manure.[27] Simmonds considers that this system of intensive *Ensete* agriculture is a relic of a more widespread culture which was replaced in northern Ethiopia on the arrival of plough-and-seed farming invaders.[28] It has been pointed out that the famous "Plant of Naqada" design found on prehistoric pottery from Naqada near Qus in the Nile Valley and dating from middle predynastic times may actually represent *Ensete*.[29] If this is the case it would suggest that *Ensete* was, in Neolithic times, an important food plant in Upper Egypt when environmental conditions were wetter and more suitable for its growth, and that the present Ethiopian sites are relics of a wide-

26. Hugh Doggett, *in litt.*, 14 March 1967.
27. N.W. Simmonds, "Ensete Cultivation in the Southern Highlands of Ethiopia: a Review," *Tropical Agriculture*, XXXV (1958), 303.
28. N.W. Simmonds, *Bananas* (London, 1966), 268.
29. Vivi Laurent-Täckholm, "The Plant of Naqada," *Annales du service des antiquités de l'Egypte*, LI (1951), 302–304.

spread form of *Ensete* culture which was displaced by the arrival of grain cultivators and the onset of dry conditions. This could in turn imply that agriculture in the form of *Ensete* culture could have developed independently in this region. At the same time it would be difficult for an intensive form of *Ensete* agriculture, such as that practiced today, to exist without the livestock on which it depends for manure and for sucker production. An acceptable alternative would be to suggest that *Ensete* was an important food plant during the gathering phase of culture, when it was harvested as a wild plant. Later, with the introduction of grain agriculture from the north, *Ensete* was grown from seed. The fact that there are said to be some forty distinct kinds of *Ensete* cultivated in Ethiopia at present would imply extensive seed propagation in the past and support this view.[30] Later, with the arrival of livestock, the more complex method of asexual sucker propagation was developed. This would seem a logical and acceptable sequence and place *Ensete* among the Group 2 plants.

Group 3 Plants—the Banana and Sugar Cane

Of Group 3 plants, probably no single type has aroused more controversy over its point of origin and its subsequent spread than has the banana. In order to appreciate the problems associated with cultivated banana distribution, it is necessary to know something of the biology of the plant. Bananas are not woody plants, but herbs with a small compact stem at, or just below, ground level. What is normally termed the stem is actually a pseudo-stem made up of the bases of the leaves. The true stem produces the new leaves which grow up through the pseudo-stem to emerge in the leaf crown. Later, when the plant is mature, the true stem stops producing leaves, elongates, and itself grows up through the pseudo-stem and out at the top. Flowers are produced on the stem and fruit develops, after which the whole plant dies.

In cultivated bananas, fruit can develop without the normal stimulus of pollination, and therefore they need not contain seeds. This is unlike the situation in wild bananas where fruit development is entirely dependent upon fertilization and seed formation.

30. Simmonds, "Ensete," 305.

In the cultivated banana, therefore, sexually sterile plants can bear fruit. The majority of modern banana fruits are sterile due to a complex of causes among which are specific female sterility genes, triploidy, and chromosome structural change.

Sterile fruit on a plant with the life cycle of the banana would be a severe evolutionary and distributional shortcoming were it not that the banana produces vegetative shoots very efficiently by means of suckers from its underground stem. These suckers reproduce the genetic identity of the parent and mean, in effect, that the individual is immortal and, provided that the suckers are transported, it can be represented in widely differing localities. It is the suckers, therefore, that are used by man as the primary means of banana propagation, and it is the length of life of the uprooted suckers that governs the routes followed in banana dispersal. This does not mean that sexual reproduction does not occur, but only that it is very rare and it may be, for example, that no new banana variety has ever arisen in Africa by hybridization. Nor does it mean that new banana varieties never occur for they can, and do, by nonsexual structural changes in the chromosomes. It does mean, however, that the basic affinities of the new varieties are obvious and that their genomic composition can be worked out.[31]

Wild bananas are plants of disturbed habitats and quickly spring up from seeds in abandoned clearings. They cannot, however, stand root competition, particularly from grasses, so that they are rapidly eliminated from any habitat where grasses come to predominate. Similarly, they are intolerant of shade and soon die when the vegetation canopy closes over them. Under these conditions vegetative reproduction is of no great value as the suckers are soon killed off by competition so that reproduction must be entirely by seed, which is most usually dispersed by animals. Bananas could, therefore, be described as weeds of the forest which need high temperatures, humidities, and light intensities, and which spring up in transient, often man-made habitats; without human disturbance they would probably be rare plants.[32]

31. N.W. Simmonds, *The Evolution of the Bananas* (London, 1962), 76–126.
32. *Ibid.*, 34.

It is from such habitats that early man selected the first banana types and later, using suckers, was able to cultivate the non-seed bearing fruit forms which, under natural conditions, probably arose occasionally but which were unable to survive for more than the life of the individual plant. What might have been a disadvantage, therefore, has turned out to be beneficial, for in the frost-free tropics a banana with good seed-free fruits which can easily be propagated vegetatively is of much more value to man than one whose fruits are full of hard seeds.

Cultivated bananas belong to the family Musaceae which contains two genera, *Ensete*, which has already been considered, and *Musa*. The latter can be further divided into four sections, two of which, *Australimusa* and *Eumusa*, contain the edible bananas. Within the *Eumusa*, to which belong all the African cultivated bananas, six groups can be recognized on the basis of ploidy and the contributions made to the origin of the constituent cultivars by two wild species, *Musa acuminata* and *Musa balbisiana*. The genomes of these two species are customarily designated A and B respectively.[33]

The original domesticated bananas were probably diploid *acuminata* type (AA), but selection would soon favor any triploids (AAA) which arose because of their increased vigor, yield, and fewer seeds in the fruits. The present center of diversity of *acuminata* AA and AAA types is Malaysia, and there is little doubt that they originated there.

Transport by human agency of AA types into areas only marginally favorable to *acuminata* forms, but which were already occupied by wild *M. balbisiana*, probably gave rise to AB hybrids between the two. At present these hybrids are centered in India, but the type probably arose several times, for the cross is not difficult to make. Later, triploids of both AAB and ABB composition developed. These were successful, and therefore selected, because they were of hybrid composition with the *balbisiana* genome contributing an adaptation to those local climatic conditions which were not ideal for pure *acuminata* types, particularly with regard to severe seasonal water stress. At a later date these hybrid

33. Simmonds, *Bananas*, 52.

triploids returned to Malaysia to supplement the *acuminata* triploids.

The great inland cultivations of banana in Uganda and western Kenya, with their many somatic mutants, (i.e., varieties which have arisen by nonsexual means) are all primarily of triploid AAA clones and thus show strong affinities with Malaysia. Indeed, although they need not have come immediately from Malaysia (there could have been one or more intermediate cultivation sites, e.g., the Arabian coast and Madagascar), they must have been derived from ancestral material originating there. It is probable, however, that being AAA, they represent an early introduction made at a time before the AAB and ABB cultivars were widespread.

Banana suckers trimmed of leaves and packed for transport will survive for periods of up to one hundred days. Thus the estimated forty days needed for the direct sea voyage from Malaysia to Madagascar or the East African coast is well within the sucker lifespan.[34] So too would be the time needed to accomplish the various individual intermediate coastal stages if the plants were spread by ship along the Indian and Arabian coasts.

Bananas could have reached the lake area of East Africa from almost any point along the East African coast but particularly from the area between the Juba and Zambezi Rivers. New suckers from the original imports which were grown at the coast could be moved inland and planted at any suitable site along the route, with new material being moved forward again later. One obvious route would have been through the Usambara, Kilimanjaro, and Kenya highlands.

It must be remembered that the early introductions were of AAA plants. They are sensitive to severe water stress and to cold which would make it unlikely that any introductions reached the lake area from the north. Bugandan tradition, however, says that bananas were brought from the north by their legendary ancestor, Kintu, and it is quite possible that later, more resistant, triploid hybrids did come from the northeast.[35]

34. Simmonds, *Evolution*, 145.
35. G.A. Wainwright, "The Coming of the Banana to Uganda," *The Uganda Journal*, XVI (1952), 147. A full discussion of the arguments for and against the Kintu tradition is given in Merrick Posnansky, "Bantu Genesis," *The Uganda Journal*, XXV (1961), 89; D.M. McMaster,

The second great group of East African banana cultivations are the coastal types which extend inland as far as Moshi. These are mainly of triploid hybrids with some edible diploids, and they probably represent several subsequent introductions from the Indian and Malaysian areas. Some of these types did reach Uganda at an early stage, but they never supplanted the AAA types. Others spread into Zaire where recent research suggests that in the plantain group (AAB) the fifty-six recognized varieties are really homogenous in that they are derived from a single clonal source.[36] If this is so, it is an indication that they have been in cultivation in the area in large numbers for a long time and subject to considerable human selection.

The possibility of using the somatic mutation rate as a guide to the date of the first introduction of bananas to East Africa has been suggested. It is, however, very difficult to employ because of the many variables involved. Work carried out in Queensland has shown that the rate of change from Dwarf Cavendish to Giant Cavendish was approximately two mutants per million. Assuming, therefore, a lower mutation rate of one mutant per million, it can be seen that a cultivation which has produced a hundred million plants will have produced at least one hundred new mutants. A conservative estimate would be that the great banana-growing areas of inland East Africa are likely to have produced a total of not less than a trillion plants. This would make it possible for the rarest mutants to have arisen several times. Survival of mutants, however, depends not on their occurence but on whether the mutant is selected for further propagation, ignored, or deliberately destroyed.[37] Thus the degree of mutant variation observed in a given banana cultivation is not a direct result of the mutation rate, but rather a result of the degree of attention given to selecting the mutant types by the cultivator. It is, therefore, very difficult to use the mutation rate to calculate the age of any banana cultivation area other than to say that in those areas which contain

---

"Speculations on the Coming of the Banana to Uganda," *ibid.*, XXVII (1963), 168.

36. Simmonds, *Bananas*, 439.
37. Simmonds, *Evolution*, 147–148.

a large number of clonal mutants intensive banana culture must have been carried out for a long time.

From East Africa the banana is thought to have spread to the west coast of the continent where it was well established by the time that the first European travelers arrived. According to Simmond's hypothesis, there should be AAA forms present in West Africa which show East African affinities.[38] So far little is known about the clonal composition of the West African bananas, but some recent work on the bananas of Sierra Leone by Bakshi suggests that of the five common bananas now regarded as native to the area, all were of the AAB group while no AAA forms were found.[39] It must be emphasized, however, that these findings were based purely on vegetative characters and not on chromosome studies so that they cannot be regarded as conclusive. If true, they would suggest that the East African inland AAA cultivations are perhaps the remnants of a very early introduction from Malaysia, followed by a later but still early introduction of more environmentally tolerant AAB forms which circumstances allowed to spread inland through Zaire to West Africa. A still more recent series of introductions would result in other types, such as ABB, reaching coastal East Africa, but in their being still comparatively restricted in range. The dates of arrival of bananas in East Africa and their dispersal throughout the continent must therefore remain conjectural until extensive cytological studies have been carried out on the clones under cultivation in Madagascar, Central, and West Africa.

Another interesting Group 3 plant whose spread is closely tied to human population movements is the sugar cane, which is a grass belonging to the genus *Saccharum* of the Andropogonae. When it flowers it can reproduce freely by seed, but it is very sensitive to changes of day length so that sexual reproduction of some varieties in certain areas is irregular or never happens. A more usual method of propagating the numerous sugar varieties is by means of canes. The stems of the plant are divided into a

38. *Ibid.*, 144.
39. T.S. Bakshi, "Bananas of Southern Sierra Leone," *Economic Botany*, XVII (1963), 252–262.

number of sections or joints by cross partitions termed nodes. Lateral buds appear at the nodes, usually on alternate sides of the stem, and there also is a ring of root primordia at each node which, when suitably stimulated, gives rise to roots. The sugar cane is propagated asexually by taking stem cuttings having one or more buds. Properly wrapped these cuttings can remain viable for up to one hundred days. This is virtually the only method of dispersal open to domestic sugar cane. The fact, however, that many of the numerous varieties of the five major sugar cane species can and do interbreed on occasion (unlike banana) while all the varieties, including the sterile ones, can be propagated and spread asexually, makes the cytology very complex, with diploid chromosome numbers varying from forty-eight to one hundred ninety-four.[40]

The botanical field and laboratory work of Brandes has suggested that the history of domestic cane may be summarized as follows: The wild sugar cane species *Saccharum robustum*, which is localized in New Guinea, gave rise through polyploidy and human selection to a group of tropical cultivated canes which are generally termed *S. officinarum*. At a much later stage migrating forms of *S. officinarum* in Southeast Asia hybridized with forms of the widely distributed wild *S. spontaneum*, and gave rise to several groups of thin subtropical cultivated canes among which are the better known *S. sinense* and *S. barberi*.[41]

Brandes postulates three main movements away from New Guinea. The first of these took the sugar cane eastwards to the Solomon Islands, the New Hebrides, and New Caledonia. The second took a westerly direction to Indonesia, the Philippines, and, eventually, to northern India. South of the Tropic of Cancer, above which *S. officinarum* does not flower, the *sinense* and *barberi* thin canes developed by hybridization with *S. spontaneum*. In the selective processes of the early agriculturists, the hybrids were singled out as better suited to the more vigorous climatic conditions of the north, and so they became dominant there. The

40. A.C. Barnes, *The Sugar Cane* (London, 1964), 35–36.
41. E.W. Brandes, "Origin, Dispersal and Use in Breeding of the Melanesian Garden Sugar-Canes and Their Derivatives, *Saccharum officinarum* L.," *The Proceedings of the Ninth International Society of Sugar Cane Technologists*, I (1956), 727.

third main movement probably began somewhere about 500 A.D. to 1000 A.D. and took the cane eastward from the New Hebrides to Fiji, Tonga, and on to Hawaii and Easter Island.[42] From India the cane spread westward, reaching Europe during the fourth century B.C. There had, however, been earlier local introductions into Persia, Arabia, and Egypt.[43]

Sugar cane was well established on the East African coast when the Portuguese arrived in the fifteenth century. It is most likely that it reached East Africa by being transported in stages along the coast from India and Arabia during the previous thousand years, although it could equally well have come directly from Indonesia to East Africa, for the length of life of the stem cuttings is considerably longer than the time needed for the direct sea voyage.

There is no botanical evidence to support either hypothesis as little is known about the cytology and relationships of the sugar canes of eastern Africa. It should be mentioned, however, that the wild sugar cane, *S. spontaneum*, is present throughout East Africa as far south as Malawi.

Group 4 Plants—the Cassava

Although Group 4 plants are recent introductions to Africa, their spread is not well understood, particularly in eastern Africa, for historical data relating to them are few, and they have not been on the continent long enough for genetic variation to become obvious and of use in considering movement pathways. Typical of Group 4 plants is cassava (*Manihot utilissima*)[44] which is eaten as a staple or a supplementary food in almost every part of tropical Africa south of the Sahara and north of the Zambezi River. Although often thought to be indigenous to Africa, it is American in origin.

Cassava was first introduced into Africa by the Portuguese who brought it from Brazil to their various stations along the West African coast. The earliest successful introductions were made in

42. *Ibid.*, 735–739.
43. Barnes, *Sugar Cane*, 2.
44. Also known as manioc in South America and French-speaking Africa, and as tapioca in Malaya, Ceylon, and India.

the area around the mouth of the Congo River, and from there cassava spread all over central Africa. It was probably taken to upper Guinea at about the same time as it reached Zaire, but the local peoples were at first reluctant to incorporate it into their agriculture. It was almost certainly introduced to Portuguese stations in eastern Africa at a much later date than in the west.

So far it has not been possible to establish with any accuracy when cassava was first introduced into Zaire. There are reports of it occurring in 1593, and it was definitely being grown in Angola by the 1660s. Cassava had probably penetrated to the heart of the Congo basin within 150 years of the discovery of the New World. At first it was primarily used as a vegetable, being simply sliced and cooked, and only later were more complex processing methods developed. Cassava continued to spread eastward during the eighteenth and nineteenth centuries, passing through the territories of the Shongo, Luba, Lunda, Bemba, and Bisa who occupied the grasslands to the south of the rain forest.[45]

Cassava was also grown in the tropical forest, but its movements there are less well understood. Stanley found cassava all along the Congo River in 1876–1877, and he relied on it as food for his expedition of 1887–1889 when he moved along the Aruwimi and Ituri Rivers. He put the point at which it began to be of less importance as the Panga Falls on the Aruwimi, which are about seventy-five miles from the nearest grassland.[46]

It is not known when cassava was first introduced to the east coast of Africa but it is thought to have been sometime between 1700 and 1750, although some authorities think it was brought in during the Portuguese occupation of the Kenyan and Tanzanian coasts in the early sixteenth century.[47] It was not taken to India or the Indian Ocean islands until late in the eighteenth century.[48]

Cassava probably was not introduced into the hinterland of East Africa until after 1800, the main centers of dispersal being Zanzibar and Moçambique. Only around Lake Tanganyika does cassava introduced from the east meet cassava coming through

45. William O. Jones, *Manioc in Africa* (Stanford, 1959), 62–67.
46. Henry M. Stanley, *In Darkest Africa* (London, 1890), I, 186.
47. Reginald Coupland, *East Africa and Its Invaders* (Oxford, 1938), 70.
48. Jones, *Manioc*, 81.

Zaire from the west. From the accounts of the early nine-teenth-century European travelers, it would seem that cassava was unimportant in East Africa except along the coast and in the vicinity of Lake Tanganyika, to which it had probably come from the west. After 1850 cultivation rapidly increased, and in 1875 Stanley found cassava in Uganda, although Speke had not recorded it there only thirteen years before.[49]

Conclusion

These accounts of individual crops show how difficult it is to give dates for plant movement based only on botanical study, and they emphasize the need for archaeological support for any hypotheses put forward. Botanical evidence on its own will show only affinities and trends and suggest possible migration pathways. Probably no domestic plant can move without the aid of human cultivators, so that positive statements with regard to dispersal movements must await the accumulation of archaeological evidence. It would also probably be a mistake to consider the use of only one pathway in any given movement, for it is much more likely that more than a single route was used in nearly every case—some perhaps simultaneously. Furthermore, the spread of a crop need not necessarily be related to the spread of a people; it could take place independently of population movements through contact between peoples with illustrations of the benefits of a new crop, or the diffusion could even be caused by acts of nature. In Africa, for example, a large number of seed-eating birds and one in particular, the red-billed finch or *Quelea*, can occur in flocks containing astronomical numbers.[50] It is not generally realized that these birds prefer to eat sweet seed grains, so that when both sweet and bitter grains occur together, the bitter ones are always left. This is particularly true for sorghum which, with its open unprotected seed head, is ideally suited to bird predation. The earlier unorganized nature of the East African countryside, with large areas of bushland between farming sites, encouraged the

49. Langlands, "Cassava," 211.
50. There were an estimated million *Quelea* in East Africa in 1960.

development of large flocks of seed-eating birds. The result was that throughout their range the birds effectively restricted the culture of sweet-grained types of sorghum. This had a secondary effect in that flour from the bitter grains has a tendency to become very acid and is also prone to weevil attack. Thus the sorghum flour ration for each family had to be prepared every day. The advantages of maize, with its sweet grains which were protected from bird attack by the cob husk and with its flour which could be stored, were quickly realized by the African cultivators; the new crop therefore prospered at the expense of the old.

Cassava can be propagated not only from seeds but also by stem cuttings and most clones are multiplied in this way. The easy vegetative cultivation of cassava would, therefore, be quickly taken up by a people used to growing bananas. In many other areas, however, cassava was adopted as a staple because it was seen still to yield food in quantity when most other crops had been devoured by locusts. Thus, like maize, cassava's resistance to one of Africa's natural biological hazards aided its rapid spread through the continent.

In spite of the obvious difficulties in dating the actual introduction of various food crops it has been possible to distinguish a main sequence—Groups 1, 2, 3, and 4. This should provide a foundation and a framework on which to build as further botanical research sheds light on the evolutionary pathways followed, and as new archaeological evidence becomes available.

APPENDIX 1

NOTES ON ARABIC SOURCES OF INFORMATION
ON EAST AFRICA

J. Spencer Trimingham

To help readers unacquainted with the Muslim geographers to
understand the background, I shall try to show, within the context
of the historical development of Muslim geography, the different
approaches of the writers and the diversity of their material.

The material relating to East Africa which is provided by the
Muslim writers is very piecemeal. In spite of the fact that it formed
part of the vast Indian Ocean trading complex, to them East Africa
was of peripheral interest.

The works of the astronomers, geographers, and travelers,
which are described subsequently, supply the main body of information, but a variety of other writings provide supplementary
material. Information is found in such histories as al-Ya'qūbī's
Ta'rīkh,[1] composed in A.D. 875–880, which contains an account
of the Beja. Odd references will be found in bestiaries, works
on mineralogy, and the like. For example, al-Bīrūnī's book on

1. Al-Ya'qūbī (ed. Theodore Houtsma) *Historiae* (Leiden, 1883), i, 217-219.

the *Science of Drugs*,[2] written *c.* 1050, describes how the Zanj col-
lect and treat cowries; and his famous *Book on India*, A.H. 432
(A.D. 1041) provides evidence on the existence of maritime relations between Sōmanāth and the Sofāla of the Zanj: "The reason why
in particular Somanāth has become so famous is that it was a
harbor for seafaring people and a station for those who went to
and fro between Sufāla in the country of the Zanj and China."
(*Alberuni's India*, ii, 104). He also seemed to know of the connection
between the Indian and Atlantic Oceans: the Sea of the Berbers
"stretches from Aden to Sufalah of the Zanj, beyond which no
ship ventures because of the great risks involved. Beyond this point
it joins the Western Ocean [the Atlantic]."[3] In Maqrīzī's description
of Cairo (III, ii, 302) we find references to such things as sewn
boats which supplements or is derived from al-Mas'ūdī's remarks.

Adab Literature and Travelers' Narratives

These accounts are most valuable for the Indian Ocean since most
of the writers and travelers had little interest in East Africa and at
the same time little access to information. However, for the early
period these books, written primarily for entertainment, are our
only sources of information.

An early example (*akhbār*-type) is the account of the Indian
Ocean travels of "Sulaimān the Merchant" and others written by
an anonymous author in 237 (851), and supplemented by Abu Zaid
es-Hasan as-Sīrāfī in 304 (916).[4] Throughout these tales information is given on winds and weather, navigational hazards, stages,
ports of call, and the like; in addition to information on the Indian
Ocean and the Far East, they contain references to the Zanj.

Far more important is the book of sailor's tales, collected between A.D. 930 and 947 by Captain Buzurg ibn Shahriyār, called
'*Ajā'ib al-Hind* (*Marvels of India*), which is useful for Qanbalū, and
which also contains other important material on Bilād az-Zanj and
the Indian Ocean.

2. Aṣ-Ṣaidana, Arabic text included with (ed. A. Zeki Validi Togan) Bīrūnī's
    Picture of the World (Delhi, 1937), 77.
3. For quotes by Yāqūt, see W. Jwaideh, *The Introductory Chapters of Yāqūt's
    Mu'jam al-Buldān*,(Leiden, 1959), 31.
4. Gabriel Ferrand, *Voyage du marchand arabe Sulaiman en Inde et en Chine
    redigé en* 851 (237 *A.H.*), *suivi de remarques par Abu Zaid Hasan* (*vers* 916)
    (Paris, 1920); Jean Sauvaget, *Relation de la Chine et de l'Inde* (Paris, 1948).

The famous *adab* writer al-Jāḥiẓ (d. 255 [869]) included the occasional reference to Zanj in his book of anecdotal rhetoric called *Kitāb al-bayān wa 't-tabyīn* (see, for example, Cairo edition, ii, 26–27) and "The Book of Animals," an anthology of passages concerned with animals.

Al-Mas'ūdī (d. 346 [957]) is our best source of information for this early period. Although we place him among *adab* writers, and not the geographers, we mean no disparagement thereby, since without his work we should know little about East Africa in the tenth century. He made use of existing material and supplemented it by firsthand information gathered during his extensive travels which included, as has been seen, a visit to the East African island of Qanbalū. His most famous book, written on almost encyclopaedic, though unsystematic, lines is the *Murūj adh-dhahab* ("Golden Pastures"), written about 332–336 (943–948) and subsequently revised. His *Kitāb at-tanbīh wa'l-ishrāf*, written in A.D. 955, is a useful supplementary work. Mas'ūdī's exact geographical knowledge was limited, but because he was not tied to any official geographical dogma and could make use of firsthand information, he was frequently closer to the true situation (as regards the Indian Ocean, for example) than the geographers,. On the other hand, he was capable of saying that on one clime-band all important towns must be on the same latitude. This is similar to Idrīsī's later misinterpretation of the first clime, which included the East African coast and Indonesia.

Ibn Baṭṭūṭa (d. 779 [1377]), the greatest of the travelers, was not mentioned in the essay but cannot be ignored in this account of writers in Arabic who provide information about East Africa. After his last journey (across the Sahara to the state of Māli in West Africa in 753–754 [1352–1353]) he settled in his native Morocco and dictated an account of his wanderings.[5] Though there are indications that he kept some record, for he mentions notes being stolen, he made many errors in place names and became confused about dates. He traveled along the east coast of Africa (1329?), visiting Maqdishū, calling at Mombasa, and by

5. C. Defrémery and B. R. Sanguinetti (ed. and trans.), *Tuḥfat an-Nuẓẓār* (Paris, 1853–1859), 4v.; English translation, Hamilton A. R. Gibb, *The Travels of Ibn Battuta* (Cambridge, 1958, 1962, 1971), 3v.

implication spending some time at Kilwa. Apart from Maqdishū his accounts are meager and present many problems of interpretation, so much so that I have questioned whether he actually went farther south than Maqdishū.

The Astronomers

Mūsā al-Khwārizmī (d. after 232 [847]) in his *Kitāb ṣūrat al-Arḍ* (Treatise concerning the Face of the Earth), redacted between 201 and 210 [817 and 826], utilized, rearranged, and developed Ptolemy's geographical tables and blended them with the Hindu and Persian material which divided the inhabited earth into climes. His work was continued by the mid-tenth century Suhrāb, who suggested ways to design a map of the world from the coordinates he provided, and proposed the provision of a text to illustrate the maps. This suggestion might have led to an understanding between the astronomers, with their concern for exact evidence and the provision of tables of latitudes and longitudes, and the geographers. But it was not followed up, and the geographers continued to hold to their fixed ideas, which led to the distortion of both their maps and their conceptions of the configuration of the Indian Ocean.

The only other work of this type referred to in the article is al-Bīrūnī's *Qānūn al-Masʿūdī*, composed in A.D. 1030, with which mathematical geography came into its own. Al-Bīrūnī was a genius of vast range, but his other works, chiefly relating to trade, provide only incidental material on our subject.

No doubt material relating to East Africa may be found in other astronomical and astrological works, such as the *Muntahā' al-idrāk* of al-Kharaqī (d. 527 [1132]). At least the astronomers knew that one could sail around South Africa and into the Atlantic Ocean.

Then there are the *zījs*, handbooks for the practicing astronomer, which also have not been referred to in this essay. They contain tables listing cities with their geographical coordinates and are more valuable for the better-known parts of the world. E. S. Kennedy and Fu'ad Haddad of the American University of Beirut have compiled a collection of place-names, obtained from these tables and other geographical writings, on 8000 punched cards, giving latitudes and longitudes, together with the variants, for some 2500 towns and other localities.

The Early Geographers — A.D. 800 to A.D. 900

Muslim geography arose from the need for itineraries and revenue-books in connection with the administration of the Islamic empire. One of the earliest and best developed itineraries was the *Kitāb al-Masālik wa'l-mamālik* (first draft 232 [846], second revised edition 272 [885]), of which only an abridgment has survived, by Ibn Khurdādhbih, at one period the director of posts in the province of 'Irāq-'Ajamī (al-Jabal).[6] Although well acquainted with Ptolemy's astronomical divisional method, he concerned himself principally with giving descriptions of the main trade-routes of the Muslim world, the towns on these routes, and the distances between them.

Such route-books developed into geographical treatises while still showing the nature of their origin. (Al-Mas'ūdī has some disparaging remarks about the dry, factual method of compiling these books [*Murūj*, Pellat edition, i, 240–241]). We have referred to three of these early books: al-Ya'qūbī's *Kitāb al-Buldān* (composed *c.* 278 [891–892]), Ibn al-Faqīh al-Hamadhānī's treatise (written *c.* 290 [903]) of a similar title, of which only a compendium has come down to us; and Aḥmad ibn Rustah's *Kitāb al-A'lāq an-Nafīsa* (BGA VII), written around 290 [902].

These early geographers have little information to offer about East Africa except in their general references to the Zanj or Bilād az-Zanj. Similarly, early books concerning the land-tax and postal services, such as Abu'l-Faraj al-Baghdādī's *Kitāb al-Kharāj*, contain no material on East Africa.

The Balkhī School of Geographers — A.D. 900 to 1000.

In the tenth century another distinctive geographical school was formed. A book called *Ṣuwar al-Aqālīm* (Representations of the Climes) by Abu Zaid al-Balkhī (d. 322 [933]) provides a new point of departure. Al-Balkhī divided the inhabited part of the earth into twenty regions, for which he used the term *iqlīm* (pl. *aqālīm*),

6. Ibn an-Nadīm (ed. Gustav Flügel), *The Fihrist [The Index] of A.D. 988* (1871–1872), 149.

"clime," providing a map for each *iqlīm* and a chapter intended to be descriptive of each map. Some of al-Balkhī's maps have survived, though not the text; he was succeeded by others who continued and developed his work. The first of these successors was al-Iṣṭakhrī, whose *Kitāb al-mamālik* was compiled between 318 and 321 (930 and 933), but was not published until 340 (951).

Ibn Ḥawqal continued al-Iṣṭakhrī's work in his *Ṣūrat al-Arḍ*, which was finished in A.D. 977. He provided valuable new material, especially for the Nilotic Sudan, and revised the maps—showing Qanbalū, which is missing in al-Iṣṭakhrī's work, in the correct position.

With this group we may include al-Maqdisī. The author says that he completed his *Aḥsan at-taqāsīm fī maʿrifat al-aqālīm* at Shiraz in 375 (985), but he subsequently incorporated later information. Thr "climes" (*aqālīm*) mentioned in the title of this book, as with others in the same group, refer to distinctive geographical divisions, not to latitudinal bands. The geographers had no use for mathematical geography. Al-Maqdisī discarded many of the old catalog-type listings; his work is especially valuable for the sociological and cultural information which it provides.

To this group also belongs the anonymous *Ḥudūd al-ʿĀlam* (Countries of the World), which was begun in Persian in 372 [982–983]. It is probably a commentary dealing with a map or maps which have not survived. It makes use of al-Iṣṭakhrī (> Balkhī), but the author did not know the works of Ibn Ḥawqal or al-Maqdisī. He devoted more attention to the non-Muslim world than did the other members of this school and included interesting material on Nubia, Ḥabash, the Western Sudan, and Zangistān, such as the following on "The Country of Zangistān and its Towns":

It is the largest (*mihtarīn*) country in the south. Some of its eastern regions adjoin Zābaj; its north adjoins the Great Sea; some of its western parts adjoin Abyssinia; on its south are mountains. Their soil is (full of) gold-mines. The country is situated opposite Pārs, Kirmān, and Sindh. The people are full-faced (*tamām-ṣūrat*), with large bones, and curly hair (*jaʿd-mū*). Their nature is that of wild animals (*dadhagān va bahāʾim*). They are extremely black. Enmity reigns between them and the Abyssinians and Zābaj.

1. M.LJĀN (M.ljmān?), a town of the Zang on the sea-coast (*bar karāna-yi daryā*). It is the haunt of the merchants visiting these parts.
2. SUFĀLA, the seat of the Zang king.
3. HWFL (حو فل), the town which in this country is by far the richest in goods (*bisyār-khwāstatarīn*). (trans. V. Minorsky, 1937, 163)

No problem in understanding the directions will be experienced if one looks at an Arab map of the Indian Ocean such as on p. 283, simplified delineation, based on a map of al-Iṣṭakhrī.

The order of countries south of the equator, from east to west, in the *Ḥudūd* (83) is: Zāba (Zābaj), Zangistān, Ḥabasha, Baja, and Nūba. Zangistān is placed opposite Fārs and Kirmān.

It is surprising that Qanbalū is not mentioned. It was known through Mas'ūdī and Buzurg, though the first geographer to cite it (text and maps) was Ibn Ḥawqal. It seems rather far-fetched to read حو فل (Ḥawfal) as قنـبلو (Qanbalū) or (Qanbalā). Yet it may be the name of the island rather than of the town. Sufāla, as with al-Bīrūnī a little later, is the seat of the Zanj kings.

The first syllable in MLJĀN/MLJMĀN may be *mul* (but I gather that the manuscript at this point is bad). *Mul* was the navigators' term for the coastline or mainland used in the route-books (e.g. Ibn Mājid) and even in the History of Kilwa: "This island is under the control of the *mul* pagans," i.e. the coastal tribes.[7] Also Ibn Baṭṭūṭa has a Mul-Jāwa on the shores of the Gulf of Siam (Cairo edition, 1928, ii, 155). Mul-Jān or Mul-Jumān would then be Jān or Jumān of the Main.

The Balkhī school's particular value was the fact that it related maps and descriptive material. Unfortunately, with respect to East Africa, these writers restricted themselves largely to the territories of Islam. Al-Maqdisī stated (BGA, 1906, 9) that he was concerned only with Muslim states and not those of the *kuffār*, "both on account of the fact that we have never entered them, and also that there seems no profit in mentioning them." Ibn Ḥawqal, though not interested in the Western Sudan, had a most important account of Nilotic Sudan, its Niles, and their inhabitants, both Christian

7. S.A. Strong (ed.), *Journal of the Royal Asiatic Society* (1895), 413 and cf. 417.

and pagan. But in their comprehensive descriptions of the world, its seas, islands, etc., these geographers included the East African coast and islands, mentioning Bilād az-Zanj, in their descriptions of the Indian Ocean (Baḥr Fāris), but placing the Zanj country opposite Sindh. With them, Bilād al-Wāq-Wāq, and also the Island of Wāq-Wāq (= Sumatra), whose inhabitants were also called Wāq-wāqian Zangīs, referred to Malaysia = Indonesia.

The Idrīsī Tradition—A.D. 1000 to 1300

Al-Idrīsī (493–562 [1099–1166]), is the Muslim geographer best-known to the Western world because he worked under the patronage of King Roger of Sicily and made Palermo the center of his studies. No complete edition of his *Nuzhat al-Mushtāq* (finished in 549 [1154]) has yet been published, and the sectional studies that have been made do not include East Africa. He also wrote a route-book, important for East Africa, called *Uns al-muhaj wa rawḍ al-furaj* (edited 588 [1192]), which is often confused with *Rawḍ al-uns wa nuzhat an-nafs*. Both works are still in manuscript, but the relationship between his various works need not concern us here.

Idrīsī carried on the astronomers' custom of dividing the inhabited world into seven clime-bands, but, in addition, he divided each clime into ten sections and provided maps for each section, making seventy maps in all,. In spite of his distortion of the Indian Ocean through adherence to traditional theories, he collected valuable material—even though much of this is difficult to interpret—concerning the countries bordering that ocean and its islands.

Tuulio has suggested that the sectional maps which illustrate our Idrīsī manuscripts were constructed on the basis of the text, and not the text after the maps, as with the Balkhī school.[8] This suggestion facilitates our interpretation of the maps, but means that one needs the text before it is possible to make full use of the maps. The Mediterranean coast, being based upon observation, is fairly accurate, whereas the East African coast is extended to the far east, parallel to the equator, in what is practically a straight line.

8. O. J. Tuulio, "Du nouveau sur Idrisi," *Studia Orientalia*, VI (1936), 44–62.

Ibn Sa'īd al-Maghribī (611–674 [1214–1275]) was a most valuable successor to Idrīsī. Although he followed the same lines, his work frequently corrected the old and provided new material. Of his *Kitāb Jughrafiyā fī 'l-Aqālīm as-sab'* only a summary survives, and the published *Kitāb Basṭ al-arḍ fī ṭūlihā wa 'l-arḍ*, quoted in the essay, is another even shorter summary. He provided coordinates of the most important places from which a map could be drawn, distorted it is true for the Indian Ocean but still valuable for place relationships. His new material on Africa was taken from "The Book of Ibn Fāṭima" (written about A.D. 1250) which is lost. We have also quoted from the regional study by Ibn al-Mujāwir (d. 690 [1291]), entitled *Kitāb al-Mustabṣir* and written about 630 [1232], which has important topographical descriptions of South Arabia.

Cosmoramic Geographers—A.D. 1300 to 1450

After Ibn Sa'īd we have a succession of geographical compilers. They provide little original material, but we must call attention to them since they are frequently quoted in references to East Africa and given an authority which they do not deserve.

The *Taqwīm al-Buldān* of the Syrian prince Abu'l-Fidā (final redaction in 721 [1321]), however, is more than a mere compilation, both in its systematic rearrangement of material from the geographers and astronomers and by its incorporation of new material, especially concerning non-Muslim regions. It utilizes the coordinates from al-Bīrūnī's *Qānūn*, Ibn Sa'īd's *Basṭ al-arḍ*, and the tenth-century tables, *Kitāb al-aṭwāl*.

Al-Qazwīnī (A.D. 1203–1283) was a compiler of an entirely different type, but his works contain some African material derived from a lost work of Abu'r-Rabī' Sulaimān al-Multānī.[9] Superior to al-Qazwīnī's works but less appealing to the general public is *Nukhabat ad-dahr* by ad-Dimishqī (d. 728 [1327]), which provides a few references to East Africa not found elsewhere, but which are difficult to control.

9. Al-Qaswīnī (ed. F. Wüstenfeld), *Āthār al-Bilād* (Göttingen, 1848). The popularity of his *'Ajā' ib al-buldān*, a later arrangement of the *Athār*, led to the production of a number of eastern editions, the last in Beirut in 1950.

The *Kharīdat al-'Ajā'ib* by Sirāj ad-dīn ibn al-Wardī (d. c. 850 [1446]) is sometimes also quoted as an authoritative work in reference to East Africa, but it seems to be almost entirely copied from other works. For example, it contains an account of the Zanji riding and fighting on cattle without mentioning that the information came from al-Mas'ūdī and was therefore hundreds of years old by the time al-Wardī used it. The first chapter is almost entirely based upon the first chapter of Yāqūt's *Mu'jam*.

An original work of the period, *Masālik al-abṣār fī mamālik al-amṣār* by Ibn Faḍl Allāh al-'Umarī (1301–1349), valuable for West Africa, has been only partially edited or studied, and I do not know if it contains anything concerning East Africa.

Other Sources
Geographical Dictionaries
The only one utilized is the *Mu'jam al-Buldān* of Yāqūt. Yāqūt, of Greek origin, was captured and sold as a slave, then manumitted in A.D. 1199. He worked on his dictionary between A.D.1212 and his death in 1229. His work is a geographical encyclopaedia and includes a gazetteer, with topographical, historical, biographical, and even literary information, as well as geographical information from works which have been lost.

Nautical Instructions, Guides, and Route-Books.
These come later than the period under discussion but they often provide valuable supplementary or confirmatory evidence. Their information on the East African routes and coastal distinguishing marks and landing-places is of great value, but has hardly been used by students.

Al-Maqdisī showed that such practical works were compiled at an early date, but none of these has survived.[10] There are other indications that the Arabs inherited nautical instructions from the Persians of the Sassanian period (nautical Arabic is well-stocked with Middle-Persian words), and that Sīrāf became the coordinating navigational center until its destruction by an earthquake. Both al-Maqdisī (10–11) and al-Mas'ūdī (Pellat edition, 1962, i,

10. *Aḥsan at-taqāsim* [*Descriptio Imperii Moslemici*] (BGA, Leiden, 1906), 10–11.

115) showed that the reason why these practical books did not influence geography was because their observations did not square with the geographers' inherited dogma. The earliest extant guide dates from the late fifteenth century and is by Shihāb ad-dīn Aḥmad ibn Mājid, famous as the pilot of Vasco da Gama from Malindi to India in 1498. The most important of his many nautical guides (compiled between 867 [1462] and 896 [1490]) is called *Kitāb al-Fawā'id*. Successors whose works have survived include Sulaimān al-Mahrī and the Muḥiṭ, or "Ocean," of Sīdī 'Alī Re'īs ('Alī ibn al-Ḥusain) compiled in 1554 in Turkish from Arabic and Persian guides.

The assessment of the value of the heterogeneous material extracted from the geographical and other writings is not easy. The usual methods of literary and historical criticism, if combined with a skeptical, practical, and sensible outlook (not always evident with regard to discussions of early East African sources), can be used fairly satisfactorily. We have to relate the information to the dates, more generally the period, from which it derives, and determine whether it comes from firsthand observation or hearsay, from an older or more recent writer, and whether it was intended to entertain, inform, or record. All of the material has to be seen within the context of the Indian Ocean, rather than that of Africa. We have shown that the dichotomy between astronomical and geographical knowledge and the distorted outlook inherited from non-Muslim geography have been particularly unfortunate in formulating conceptions of the Indian Ocean. The Balkhī school found the method of dividing the world into clime-bands unsatisfactory and initiated a regional approach, though they used the same word "clime." This school was sound, and its work illuminating, but these writers were not much interested in non-Muslim regions. Then Idrīsī approved the clime-band method with unfortunate consequences.

The geographers utilized and improved the work of their predecessors on sound lines, but the later cosmoramic type of writers have produced difficulties since their aim was unscientific and their criteria for the inclusion of information in their books were the bizarre and the marvellous. Abu'l-Fidā' cannot be classed with these writers since he worked on scientific lines and carefully cited his sources, ad-Dimishqī much less so. Yāqūt sometimes mentions his sources, sometimes forgets to do so, and frequently we cannot be sure to what date his information relates. Without this basic information it is almost impossible accurately to date and control references.

NOTES ON CHINESE TEXTS CONTAINING
REFERENCES TO EAST AFRICA

Paul Wheatley

I. The two earliest accounts of East Africa in Chinese records, relating to *Muâ-liĕn* (Meroe) and *Puât-b'uat-liək* (*Barbarā*), both date from the seventh decade of the ninth century:

A. *Ching-hsing Chi* 經 行 記 (*Record of Travels*) by Tu Huan 杜 環, in which *Muâ-liĕn* was first mentioned, was an account of the author's decennial captivity among the Arabs, by whom he had been taken prisoner at the battle of the Talas river in 751. Although the work itself has been lost, fragments have been preserved in several subsequent histories and encyclopedias:

(i) *T'ung Tien* 通 典 ("Comprehensive Institutes"), in 200 chüan, was completed by Tu Yu 杜 佑 in about 812 after some thirty-six years of study, collection, and organization. It is divided into eight sections on, respectively, political economy, literary graduation, government offices, rites, music, military discipline, geography, and national defense, each arranged in chronological order and incorporating materials from the earliest times to the end of the T'ang T'ien-pao period (755). This work is regarded as one of the more reliable of Chinese encyclopedias and was accorded high praise by the editors of the catalog of the Ch'ing imperial library, *Ch'in-ting Ssŭ-k'u Ch'üan-shu Tsung-mu* 欽 定 四 庫 全 書 總 目. Information relating to *Muâ-liĕn* is to be found in chüan 193.

(ii) *T'ung Chih* 通 志 ("Historical Collections"), in 200 chüan, is a massive history of China from the legendary times of Fu Hsi 伏 羲 to the end of the T'ang dynasty (A.D. 906). It was completed by Cheng Ch'iao 鄭 樵 in about 1150, and is arranged in five sections entitled respectively *Imperial Records, Biographies of Empresses, Register, Compendia* (in which the notice of *Muâ-liĕn* occurs) and *Biographies*. *Muâ-lien* is described in Chüan 196.

(iii) *Wen-hsien T'ung-k'ao* 文 獻 通 考, compiled in 348 chüan by Ma Tuan-lin 馬 端 臨, was designed as a comprehensive history of Chinese civilization. It was based fundamentally on the *T'ung Tien*, but a great deal of later material was added by the compiler himself, including much that was omitted from the Sung dynastic history. To Tu Yu's eight sections (which he expanded into nineteen topics) Ma Tuan-lin added five more dealing with *Bibliography, The Imperial Lineage, Appointments, Uranography,* and *Phenomena*. The work was begun in about 1254 but, although it was completed in about 1280, was not published until 1319. *Muâ-liĕn* is the subject of a notice in Chüan 339.

(iv) *T'ai-p'ing Huan Yü Chi* 太 平 寰 宇 記 ("General Description of the World Compiled in the T'ai-p'ing Reign-Period"), by Yüeh Shih 樂 史, is a general statistical and descriptive topography of the Empire in 193 chüan, together with some data relating to neighboring countries. It was compiled between 976 and 983. *Muâ-liĕn* is among the countries listed in Chüan 177.

(v) *Hsin T'ang-Shu* 新 唐 書 ("New T'ang Annals") is one of the twenty-five officially approved standard histories which have justly been called "the world's greatest repository of historical information." All are arranged on a fairly uniform pattern, beginning with information on *Imperial Records* and proceeding through *Memoirs, Miscellanea,* and *Biographies*, the last of which includes materials relating to foreign countries, incorporated with the lives of eminent statesmen and envoys. The official history of T'ang was first compiled in 945 but was alleged by the literary cognoscenti of the time to exhibit unwarranted prolixity, excessive generalization, want of discrimination, and frequent omissions so that a second version was commissioned under the editorship of Ou-yang Hsiu 歐 陽 修 and Sung Ch'i 宋 祁. These two versions are known as *Chiu T'ang-Shu*

("Old T'ang Annals") and *Hsin T'ang-Shu* respectively. Although the latter was not completed until 1061, its information relates, of course, to the period of the T'ang dynasty, that is from 618 to 906. It incorporates a great deal of additional matter omitted from the "Old T'ang Annals," including the notice of *Muâ-liĕn*, though that particular passage is abbreviated to such a degree that the meaning is distorted. The paragraph in question is to be found in Chüan 221 B.

B. The earliest mention of *Puât-b'uât-liǝk* occurs in the *Yu-yang Tsa-tsu* 酉 陽 雜 俎 ("Assorted dishes from Yu-yang"), written by Tuan Ch'eng-shih soon after the middle of the ninth century. In this work Tuan collected together a great deal of unusual information elicited from a wide range of informants. Here we find the earliest notice of *Barbarā*, which occurs in chüan 4, folio 3 verso.

The *Yu-yang Tsa-tsu* was published in the *Chin-tai Pi-shu* 津 逮 秘 書 by Mao Chin 毛 晉, who lived from 1598 to 1657. This edition comprises a nominal twenty chapters with a ten-chapter supplement. An edition of 1608 by Li Yün-hao 李 雲 鵠 was reprinted in the collectanea *Hu-pei Hsien Cheng I-shu* 湖 北 先 正 遺 書 and *Ssŭ-pu Ts'ung-k'an* 四 部 叢 刊. A fragmentary version in only two chapters is reproduced in the *I-yüan Chün-hua* 藝 苑 捃 華, the *Lung-wei Pi-shu* 龍 威 秘 書, the *Shuo K'u* 說 庫, and the *T'ang-tai Tsung-shu* 唐 代 叢 書, and an abridged edition is included in the *Shuo-fu* 說 郛. Friedrich Hirth also mentions a fairly reliable edition in Chang Hai-p'eng's 張 海 鵬 collectaneum entitled *Hsüeh-chin T'ao-yüan* 學 津 討 原 of 1805 (*Journal of the American Oriental Society*, XXX [1909–1910], 17–18).

The notice of *Puât-b'uât-liǝk* which appeared originally in the *Yu-yang Tsa-tsu* was subsequently incorporated in the *Hsin T'ang-Shu*, but once again in such abbreviated form that the implications of at least one passage were grossly distorted.

II. The chief Chinese source of information about Africa in Sung times, indeed a prime source for maritime trade throughout the seas and islands bordering southern and eastern Asia, is the *Chu-fan-chih* 諸 蕃 志 ("Gazetteer of Foreigners") published by Chao Ju-kua

趙 汝 适 in about 1225. A brief notice in a descriptive library catalogue, the *Chih-chai shu-lu chieh-t'i* 直 齊 書 錄 解 題, compiled by Ch'en Chen-sun 陳 振 孫 in the middle of the thirteenth century, refers to Chao Ju-kua as Superintendent of Maritime Trade (*Shihpo-shih* 市 舶 使) in Fu-chien. He would, therefore, have been stationed at Ch'üan-chou 泉 州, a post which would have afforded him exceptional opportunities of obtaining information about foreign countries from the merchants and sailors who frequented that port.

Chao's book is divided into two sections, the first of which comprises descriptions of countries in South and East Asia and as far west as the African coast and the Mediterranean littoral, that is, of those lands which bordered the Arab sea route to the West. The second section is devoted to systematic descriptions of the principal foreign products entering into maritime trade. Much of the information in both these sections occurs neither in any previous Chinese work nor in any other Sung topography, so it must be assumed that Chao Ju-kua acquired it through his personal association with overseas traders. Such, for example, is the matter relating to *Tiung-lji* (possibly Shungwaya) and *Tsəng-b'uat* (*Zangibār*). In other instances, however, Chao combined his own information with that already available in an earlier work. This was the *Ling-wai Tai-ta* 嶺 外 代 答 ("Information from Beyond the Mountains"), which had been compiled by Chou Ch'ü-fei 周 去 非, one-time Assistant Sub-Prefect at Kuei-lin 桂 林, in 1178. This work, in ten chüan, professed to be supplementary to the *Kuei-hai yü-heng chih* 桂 海 虞 衡 志, a topography of the southern provinces of the Empire by Fan Ch'eng-ta 范 成 大, and to that earlier account added summary outlines of a number of foreign countries. Chao's paragraph on *Kuən-luən Tsəng-kji* is taken, with only minor changes in wording, from this work of Chou Ch'ü-fei, while the notice of *Puât-b'uât-liək* is a compound of materials from both sources. There is a somewhat expanded discussion of this last country in the Sung encyclopedia *Shih-lin Kuang-chi* 事 林 廣 記, which was compiled by Ch'en Yüanching 陳 元 靚 at some time between 1100 and 1250, but which was not printed until 1325.

Information about the *Zanj* coast has also been included in the official Sung history (*Sung Shih* 宋 史, chüan 490), dealing with the period from 960 to 1279 and compiled by T'o-T'o (Toktaga) 脫 脫 and Ou-yang Hsüan 歐 陽 玄 in about 1345. In the past, the *Sung Shih* has not enjoyed a reputation for reliability, but the notice of *Tsəng-d'ân*, as far as can be ascertained at present, would seem to bear the stamp of authenticity. Whereas the previously mentioned works, apart from *ad hoc* renderings of paragraphs here and there, remain untranslated into European languages, there is an English version of *Chu-fan-chih* by Friedrich Hirth and W.W. Rockhill, *Chau Ju-kua: His Work on the Chinese and Arab Trade in the Twelfth and Thirteenth Centuries, Entitled Chu-fan-chi* (St. Petersburg, 1911).

The *Tao-i Chih-lüeh* 島 夷 誌 略 ("Description of the Island Barbarians") is a description in 100 sections of ninety-nine countries, ports, and noteworthy localities ranging from the Moluccas to Arabia and the African coast. It was compiled in 1349 by Wang Ta-yüan 汪 大 淵 (cognomen Huan Chang 煥 章), who had himself traded in foreign parts in the 1330's. The influence of Chao Ju-kua is apparent in the arrangement of the text but there are only five direct quotations, and localities mentioned in *Chu-fan-chih* often appear in Wang's work under different orthographies. The *Zanj* coast, for example, appears in the hitherto unrecorded form *Tsəng-b'uât-lâ*. In addition to the localities mentioned in this paper there are several others, so far unidentified, which may eventually prove to have been situated on the East African coast. The *Tao-i Chih-lüeh* has been the subject of an exegetical study by Fujita Toyohachi 藤 田 豐 八, *Tao-i Chih-lüeh Chiao-chu* 島 夷 誌 略 校 注, published in *Hsüeh-t'ang Tsung-k'e* 雪 堂 叢 刻, and a partial English translation is incorporated in W.W. Rockhill's "Notes on the relations and trade of China with the Eastern Archipelago and the coast of the Indian Ocean during the fourteenth century," *T'oung Pao*, XIV (1913) 473–476, XV (1914), 419–447; XVI (1915), 61–159, 236–271, 374–392, 435–467, 604–626.

III. Information on East Africa deriving from the great Ming naval expeditions into the Indian Ocean has been preserved in three works:

A. *Wu-pei-chih* 武 備 志 ("Notes on Military Preparedness") by Mao Yüan-i 茅 元 儀, which incorporates a set of combined nautical charts and sailing directions for voyages in the Indian Ocean and China Seas, the African material occurring in chüan 240, folios 19 recto – 20 verso. The preface is dated 1621 but the work was not presented to the throne until 1628, so we know that it was printed subsequent to the latter date. However, there is reason to think that the nautical information contained in chüan 240 may be some two centuries older. Mao Yüan-i was a grandson of a certain Mao K'un 茅 坤, who lived from 1511 to 1601 and collaborated with Hu Tsung-hsien 胡 宗 憲, an expert on coastal defense. Internal and external considerations both imply that the *Wu-pei-chih* charts are based on the collated logs of the several voyages undertaken by the Ming fleets between 1405 and 1433. Possibly the original collation had taken the form of a compass directory or *chen-wei* [-*pien*] 鍼 位 [編] of the type mentioned by Huang Sheng-ts'eng 黃 省 曾 in the sixteenth century (preface to *Hsi-yang Chao-kung Tien-lu* 西 洋 朝 貢 典 錄 ("A Record of the Tributary Nations of the West," A.D. 1520) and which is probably represented by the still unpublished manuscript sailing directory preserved in the Bodleian Library under the rubric *Laud Or. 145.*

The *Wu-pei-chih* charts were subsequently reproduced in a compilation entitled *Wu-pei Pi-shu* 武 備 秘 書, and tracings from that source were published by George Phillips, "The Seaports of India and Ceylon," *Journal of the China Branch of the Royal Asiatic Society*, XX (1885), 209–226; XXI (1886), 30–42. The African section of Phillips's tracing has been reprinted by J.J.L. Duyvendak in Youssouf Kamal, *Monumenta cartographica Africae et Ægypti*, III, v (Cairo, 1935); his *China's Discovery of Africa* (London, 1949), plate V; in Teobaldo Filesi, *Le relazioni della Cina con l'Africa nel Medio-evo* (Milano, 1962), 103; and folios 19 recto – 20 verso of chüan 240 of the *Wu-pei-chih* itself by Paul Wheatley, "The Land of Zanj: Exegetical Notes on Chinese Knowledge of East Africa Prior to A.D. 1500," in *Geographers and the Tropics: Liverpool Essays* (Liverpool, 1964), 166–167. The whole of chüan 240 has recently been reprinted with annotations under the title *Cheng-Ho hang-hai t'u* 鄭 和 航 海 圖 (Pei-ching, 1961).

B. *Hsing-ch'a Sheng-lan* 星 槎 勝 覽 ("Triumphant Vision of the Starry Raft" [i.e. a ship carrying an imperial envoy]), written in

1436 by Fei Hsin 費 信, a man belonging to the scholar class who had sailed as a junior officer on some of the Ming naval expeditions into the Indian Ocean. The text usually quoted consists of four chüan in *Ku-chin Shuo-hai* 古 今 說 海 (1544), of one chüan in *Chi-lu Hui-pien* 紀 錄 彙 編 (1617), and again of four chüan in both the *Hsüeh-hai Lei-pien* 學 海 類 編 and the *Che-ku Ts'ung-ch'ao* 澤 古 叢 鈔. This recension does not differentiate between the countries visited by Fei Hsin himself and those on which he reported by hearsay, but another, of only two chüan, in the *T'ien-i-ko* 天 一 閣 does make this distinction. Paul Pelliot established the interrelation ships of these recensions in "Les grands voyages maritimes chinoi-au début du XVe siècle," *T'oung Pao*, XXX (1933), 246–339. The African countries reported on by Fei Hsin were Maqdishū, Brava, Juba, and Malindi.

C. *Ming Shih* 明 史 ("History of the Ming Dynasty"). Descriptions of these same four countries have also been included in chüan 326 of the official history of the Ming dynasty (1368–1643), which was begun as early as 1646, completed in 1736 under the direction of Chang T'ing-yü 張 廷 玉, and first printed in 1739.

BIBLIOGRAPHY

Abdallah, Yohanna B. (trans. Meredith Sanderson), *The Yaos* (Zomba, 1919).

Allen, T. W., "A Group of Ninth Century Manuscripts," *Journal of Philology*, XXI (1893), 48–53.

Alpers, Edward A., "The Mutapa and Malawi Political Systems to the Time of the Ngoni Invasions," in Terence O. Ranger (ed.), *Aspects of Central African History* (London, 1967), 1–28.

Andrade, A. A. de, *Relações de Moçambique Setecentista* (Lisbon, 1955).

Anon., *Cheng-ho hang-hai t'u* (Pei-ching, 1961).

Anon, *Archaeology in New China* (Peking, 1961).

Anon., *La Poterie malgache, catalogue de l'exposition poterie malgache* (Tananarive, 1964).

Antiquities Department of Tanganyika, *Annual Report* [by H.N. Chittick] (Dar es Salaam, 1958).

Arkell, A. J., "The Iron Age in the Sudan," *Current Anthropology*, VII (1966), 451–452

Aroutiounov, S. A., "Problèmes des liens historico-culturelles du bassin pacifique," *Sovietskaia Ethnografica*, IV (1964), 68–75.

Axelson, Eric, *South-East Africa*, 1488–1530 (Johannesburg, 1940).

————, *Portuguese in South-East Africa*, 1600–1700 (Johannesburg, 1960).

Balfour, I. B., *The Botany of Sokotra* (Edinburgh, 1888).

Balog, Paul, *The Coinage of the Mamluk Sultans of Egypt and Syria* (New York, 1964).

Barros, João de, *Deçadas da Asia* (Lisbon and Madrid, 1552–1615), 4v.

Béart, Charles, *Jeux et jouets de l'ouest africain* (Dakar, 1955).

Bent, Theodore, *Southern Arabia* (London, 1900).

Bokshchanin, A. A., "Poseshchenie stran Afriki morskimi ekspeditsiyami Chzhen Khe v nachale XV veka" ["Visitation of African Countries by naval expeditions of Chzhen Khe in the beginning of the XV century"], *Istorii mirovoi kul'tury* [History of World Culture], VI (1959).

—————————, "K istorii plavanii Chzhen Khe" ["Towards a history of the voyages of Chzhen Khe"], *Kratkie soobshch., Instituta narodov*

Azii [Short Communications of the Institute of the peoples of Asia], (1962).

Boone, Olive, *Les Xylophones du Congo belge* (Tervuren, 1936).

Bosch, F. D. K., *Selected Studies in Indonesian Archaeology* (The Hague, 1961).

Bowen, Richard LeBaron, "Egypt's Earliest Sailing Ships," *Antiquity*, XXXIV (1960), 117–131.

Boxer, Charles R., *Fidalgoes in the Far East* (The Hague, 1948).

——, and Carlos de Azevedo, *Fort Jesus and the Portuguese in Mombasa*, 1593–1729 (London, 1960).

Bretschneider, Emilii, *On the Knowledge of the Arabs Possessed by the Chinese* (London, 1871).

Breuil, Henri, *The White Lady of the Brandberg* (London, 1955).

Buck, Peter H., *The Ethnology of Mangereva* (Honolulu, 1938).

Buhler, Alfred, "Plangi," *International Archives of Ethnography*, XLVI (1952), 4–35.

Burton, Richard F., *Zanzibar; City, Island, Coast* (London, 1872) 2v.

Callenfels, P. V. van Stein, "Prehistoric Sites on the Karama River (West Toraja-land, Central Celebes)," *Journal of East Asiatic Studies*, I (1968), 82–97.

Cashmore, T. H. R., "A Note on the Chronology of the Wanyika," *Tanganyika Notes and Records*, 57 (1961), 153–172.

Caton-Thompson, Gertrude, *Zimbabwe Culture* (Oxford, 1931).

——, "Zimbabwe; All Things Considered," *Antiquity*, XXXVIII (1964), 99–102.

Cerulli, Enrico, "Gruppi etnici nelle Somalia," *Archivo per l'Antropologia e la Etnologia*, *LXIV* (1934), 127–148.

——, *Somalia: scritti vari editi ed inediti* (Rome, 1957), 3v.

Champion, A., *The Agiryama of Kenya* (London, 1967).

Chang Hsing-lang, "The Importation of Negro Slaves to China Under the T'ang Dynasty," *Bulletin of the Catholic University of Peking*, VII (1930), 37–59.

——, *Chung-Hsi chiao-t'ung shih-liao hui-p'ien* (Pei-p'ing, 1930).

Charlesworth, M. P. "Some Notes on the Periplus Maris Erythraei," *Classical Quarterly*, XXII (1928), 92–100.

Cheng Hao-sheng, *Cheng Ho* (Ch'ung-ch'ing, 1945).

Chin Yün-ming, "Cheng-Ho ch'i-tz'u-hsia Hsi-yang nien-yüeh k'ao-cheng," *Fu-chien Wen-hua*, XXVI (1937), 1–48.

Chittick, H. Neville, "A Note on Stone-Built Enclosures in South Nyanza, Kenya," *Man*, LXV (1965), 147.

——, "Ibn Baṭṭuṭa and East Africa," *Journal de la Société des Africanistes*, XXXVIII (1968), 239–241.

——, *Kisimani Mafia: Excavations at an Islamic Settlement on the East African Coast* (Dar es Salaam, 1961).

————, "Kilwa: A Preliminary Report," *Azania*, I (1966), 1–36.

————, "Discoveries in the Lamu Archipelago," *Azania*, II (1967), 37–67.

————, "An Archaeological Reconnaissance of the Southern Somali Coast," *ibid.*, IV (1969), 115–130.

————, "The 'Shirazi' Colonization of East Africa," *Journal of African History*, VI (1965), 275–294.

————, *Kilwa: An Islamic Trading City on the East African Coast* (Nairobi, 1974), 2v.

Christensen, Arthur, *L'Iran sous les Sassanides* (Copenhagen, 1936).

Christie, Anthony H., "An Obscure Passage from the Periplus," *Bulletin of the School of Oriental and African Studies*, XIX (1957), 345–353.

Claessen, H. J. M., "A Comparison Between the Theories of Sharp and Suggs about Polynesian Long-Distance Voyaging," *Bijdragen tot de Taal, Land- en Volkenkunde*, CXX (1964), 140–162.

Clark, J. Desmond, "Notes on Archaeological Work Carried Out During 1966 in Northern Malawi," *The Society of Malawi Journal*, XX (1967), 12–16.

Cole, Sonia, *The Prehistory of East Africa* (New York, 1965).

Condominas, G., "Le Lithophone préhistorique de Ndut Lieng Krak," *Bulletin de l'Ecole Française d'Extrême Orient*, XLV (1952), 359–392.

Creswell, K. A. C., *Early Muslim Architecture* (London, 1909), 2v.

Dahl, Otto C., *Malgache et Maanjan* (Oslo, 1951).

————, *Les Débuts de l'orthographe malgache* (Oslo, 1966).

Dammann, Ernst, "Erzählungen eines Digo zur Geschichte seines Stammes," *Zeitschrift für Eingeborene Sprachen*, XXIX (1938–1939), 292–311.

————, "Zur Geschichte der Digo," *Zeitschrift für Eingeborene Sprachen*, XXXIV (1944), 53–69.

————, "Ein Nachtrag zur Geschichte der Digo," *Afrika und Uebersee*, XLIV (1960), 37–40.

————, "Zur Ueberlieferung der Segedju," in *Beiträge zur Völkerforschung: Jahrbuch des Museums für Völkerkunde zu Leipzig* (Berlin, 1961), 981–998.

Darroch, R. G., "Some notes on the early History of the Tribes Living on the Lower Tana," *Journal of East African and Uganda National History Society*, XVII (1943), 244–254, 370–394.

Datoo, B. A., "Rhapta: the Location and Importance of East Africa's first Port," *Azania*, V (1970), 65–75.

Davidson, Janet M., "Archaeology in Samoa and Tonga," *Newsletter, New Zealand Archaeological Association*, VIII (1965), 59–71.

Deschamps, Hubert, *Histoire de Madagascar* (Paris, 1960).

Diller, Aubrey, *The Tradition of the Minor Greek Geographers* (Lancaster, 1952).

Dodd, Edward, *Polynesian Seafaring* (Lymington, 1972).

Donque, Gérald, "Le contexte des anciennes migrations: vents et cou-rants dans l'Océan Indien," *Annales de l'Université de Madagascar,* III (1965), 43-59.

Drake-Brockman, R. E., *British Somaliland* (London, 1912).

Drake, F. S. (ed.), *Symposium on Historical, Archaeological, and Linguistic Studies in South-East Asia* (Hong Kong, 1967).

Dubins, Barbara, "The Comoro Islands: A Bibliographical Essay," *African Studies Bulletin,* XII (1969), 131-137.

Duriyanga, Phra Chen, *Thai Music* (Bangkok, 1956).

Duyvendak, J. J. L., "Ma Huan Re-examined," *Verhandelingen der Koninklijke Akademie van Wetenschappen te Amsterdam,* XXXII (1933), 1-74.

————, "The True Dates of the Chinese Maritime Expeditions in the Early Fifteenth Century," *T'oung Pao,* XXXIV (1938), 341-412.

————, *China's Discovery of Africa,* (London, 1949).

Dyen, Isidore, *A Lexicostatistical Classification of the Austronesian Languages,* (Baltimore, 1965).

Elkiss, Terry H., "Kilwa Kisiwani: The Rise of an East African City State," *African Studies Review,* XVI (1973), 119-130.

Elliot, J. A. G., "A. Visit to the Bajun Islands," *Journal of African Studies,* XXVI (1925-1926), 147-245, 338, 351.

Emory, Kenneth P., and Yosihiko Sinoto, "Les Conséquences des récentes découvertes archéologiques en Polynésie Oriental," *Bulletin de la Société des Etudes Océaniennes,* XII (1964), 406-414.

Fabricius, B., *Arriani Alexandrine Periplus Maris Erythraei* (Dresden, 1848).

Fadiman, Jeffrey A., "Early History of the Meru of Mt. Kenya," *Journal of African History,* XIV (1973), 9-27.

Fagan, Brian, "Early Iron Age Pottery in Eastern and Southern Africa," *Azania,* I (1966), 101-109.

————, *Southern Africa* (London, 1966).

————, "The Iron Age of Zambia," *Current Anthropology,* VII (1966), 453-462.

————, *Iron Age Cultures in Zambia* (London, 1967-1968), 2v.

Fan Wen-t'ao, *Cheng-Ho hang-hai-t'u k'ao* (Ch'ung-ch'ing, 1943).

Faublée, Jacques (ed.), *L'Ethnographie de Madagascar* (Paris, 1946).

Ferrand, Gabriel, "Les Voyages des Javanais à Madagascar," *Journa Asiatique,* XV (1910), 881-330.

————, "Le K'ouen-louen et les anciennes navigations interocéaniques dans les mers du sud," *T'oung Pao,* XIII (1919), 239-333, 431-492; (1920), 201-241.

————, "Les Sultans de Kilwa," *Mémorial Henri Basset, Publications de l'Institute des Hautes Etudes Marocaines,* XVII (1928), 239-260.

Filesi, Teobaldo, *I viaggi dei Cinesi in Africa nel Medioevo* (Rome, 1961).

————, *Le relazioni della Cine con l'Africa nel Medioevo* (Milan, 1962).

Forke, Alfred, "Mu Wang und die Königin von Saba," *Mitteilungen des Seminars für Orientalische Sprachen,* VII (1904), 117–172.

Fosbrooke, Henry A., "Early Iron Age Sites in Tanganyika Relative to Traditional History," in J. Desmond Clark (ed.), *Proceedings of the Third Pan-African Congress on Prehistory,* 1955 (London, 1957), 318–325.

Fox, Robert B., "The Calatagan Excavations," *Philippine Studies,* VII (1959), 325–390.

Franke, Otto, *Geschichte des Chinesischen Reiches* (Berlin, 1930–1953), 5v.

Freeman-Grenville, G. S. P., "A New Hoard and Some Unpublished Variants of the Coins of the Sultans of Kilwa," *Numismatic Chronicle,* XIV (1954), 220–224.

————————, "Coinage in East Africa before Portuguese Times," *Numismatic Chronicle,* XVII (1957), 151–175.

————————, "East African Coin Finds and their Historical Significance," *Journal of African History,* I (1960), 31–42.

————————, *The Medieval History of the Coast of Tanganyika* (London, 1962).

————————, "Coins from Mogadishu, c. 1300 to c. 1700," *Numismatic Chronicle,* III (1963), 179–200.

————————, "Coin Finds and their Significance for East African Chronology," *ibid.,* XI (1971), 283–301.

Fripp, C. E., "A Note on Mediaeval Chinese-African Trade," *Nada,* XVII (1940), 88–96.

————, "Chinese Mediaeval Trade with Africa," *ibid.,* XVIII (1941), 18.

Frisk, Hjalmar (ed.), *Le Périple de la Mer Erythrée* (Göteborg, 1927).

Fuchs, Walter, *The Mongol Atlas of China by Chu Ssu-pen and the Kuang-Yü-T'u* (Pei-p'ing, 1946).

————, "Was South Africa Already Known in the 13th Century?" *Imago Mundi,* IX (1953), 50–51.

Gardin, J. C., "Poteries de Bamiyan," *Ars Orientalis,* II (1957), 242–243.

————, *Lashkari Bazar: une résidence royale ghaznéuide, Mémoires de la Delegation Archéologique Française en Afghanistan,* XVIII (Paris, 1963).

Garlake, P. S., *Early Islamic Architecture of the East African Coast* (Oxford, 1966).

————, *Great Zimbabwe* (London, 1973).

Ghosh, A., *The City in Early Historical India* (Simla, 1973).

Girace, A., "Le Coste della Somalia e i Cinesi," *Corriere della Somalia,* CCVII (1954).

Godlewski, Aleksander, "La Recherche océanienne dans la Pologne d'aujourd'hui," *Journal de la Société des Océanistes,* XX (1964), 79–84.

Gonda, Jan, *Sanskrit in Indonesia* (Nagpur, 1952).

Grace, George W., "The Linguistic Evidence," *Current Anthropology,* V (1964), 361–368.

Gray, John M., "Portuguese Records Relating to the Segeju," *Tanganyika Notes and Records,* 29 (1950), 85–98.

———, "A History of Kilwa," *Tanganyika Notes and Records*, 31 (1951), 1–2 ; 32 (1952), 11–37.

———, *History of Zanzibar* (London, 1961).

Green, R. C., "Archaeology in Western Samoa," *Newsletter, New Zealand Archaeological Association*, VII (1964), 45–50.

Grottanelli, Vinigi L., "I Bantu del Giuba nelle tradizioni dei Wazegua," *Geographica Helvetica*, VIII (1953), 249–260.

———, "Asiatic Influences in Somali Culture," *Ethnos*, 12 (1947), 153–181.

———, *Pescatori dell'Oceano Indiano* (Rome, 1955).

———, "A Lost African Metropolis," in J. Lukas (ed.), *Afrikanistiche Studien Dietrich Westermann zum 80. Geburtstag* (Berlin, 1955), 231–242.

———, "The Peopling of the Horn of Africa," *Africa* (Roma), XXVII (1972), 363–394.

Guignes, Joseph de, *Mémoire dans lequel on prouve que les Chinois sont une colonie égyptienne* (Paris, 1760).

Guillain, Charles (ed.), *Documents sur l'histoire, la géographie et le commerce de l'Afrique Orientale* (Paris, 1856–1857), 4v.

Gutman, B., *Das Recht der Chagga* (Munich, 1926).

Haddon, A. C., and James Hornell, *Canoes of Oceania* (Honolulu, 1938).

Harries, Lyndon (ed.), "The Founding of Rabai: A Swahili Chronicle," *Swahili*, 31 (1960), 140–149.

Harris, Alfred and Grace, "Property and the Cycle of Domestic Groups in Taita," in Robert F. Gray and Philip H. Gulliver (eds.), *The Family Estate in Africa* (Boston, 1964), 117–154.

Harris, Grace, "Taita Bride-Wealth and Affinal Relationships," in Meyer Fortes (ed.), *Marriage in Tribal Societies* (Cambridge, 1962), 55–81.

Hadi Hasan, *A History of Persian Navigation* (London, 1928).

Haudricourt, André G., "Nature et culture dans la civilization de l'Igname: l'origine des clones et des clans," *L'Homme*, IV (1964), 93–104.

Heekeren, H. R. van, *The Bronze-Iron Age of Indonesia* (The Hague, 1958).

Heine–Geldern, Robert von, "Prehistoric Research in the Netherlands Indies," in Pieter Honig (ed.), *Science and Scientist in the Netherlands Indies* (New York, 1945), 129–167.

Heyerdahl, Thor, "Plant Evidence for Contacts with America before Columbus," *Antiquity*, XXXVIII (1964), 120–132.

Hichens, Walter (ed.), "Khabar Lamu," *Bantu Studies*, XII (1938), 1–33.

Hiernaux, Jean, "Human Biological Diversity of Central Africa," *Man*, I (1966), 287–306.

Hirth, Friedrich, *China and the Roman Orient* (Shanghai, 1885).

———, "The Mystery of Fu-lin," *Journal of the American Oriental Society*, XXX (1909), 1–31.

———, "Early Chinese Notices of East African Territories," *Journal of the American Oriental Society*, XXX (1909), 46–57.

———, and W. W. Rockhill, *Chau Ju-kua: His Work on the Chinese and Arab Trade in the Twelfth and Thirteenth Centuries, Entitled Chu-fan-chi* (St. Petersburg, 1911).

Hornbostel, Erich M. von, "Ueber ein akustische Kriterium für Kulturzusammenhänge," *Zeitschrift für Ethnologie*, XLIII (1911), 601–615.

Hornell, James, "Indonesian Influence on East African Culture," *Journal of the Royal Anthropological Institute*, LXIV (1934), 305–332.

———, *Water Transport* (Cambridge, 1946).

Hourani, George F., *Arab Seafaring in the Indian Ocean in Ancient and Early Medieval Times* (Princeton, 1951).

Hrbek, Ivan, "The Chronology of Ibn Baṭṭūta's Travels, "*Archiv Orientalni*, XXX (1962), 409–486.

Hsia Nai, "China and Africa – Historical Friendship," *China Reconstructs*, XI (1962), 27–29.

Huffman, T. N., "The Rise and Fall of Zimbabwe," *Journal of African History*, XIII (1972), 353–366.

Huntingford, G. W. B., "The Azanian Civilization of Kenya," *Antiquity*, VII (1933), 153–165.

Hunwick, J. O., "Some Notes on the Term *Zanj* and Its Derivatives in a West African Chronicle," *Research Bulletin* (Ibadan), IV (December, 1968), 41–51.

Hutton, J. H., "West Africa and Indonesia: A Problem in Distribution" *Journal of the Royal Anthropological Institute*, LXXVI (1946), 5–12.

Janse, Olov R. T., "Some Notes on the Sa-huynh Complex," *Asian Perspectives*, III (1959), 109–11.

Jones, A. M., "Indonesia and Africa: The Xylophone as a Culture Indicator," *Journal of the Royal Anthropological Institute*, LXXXIX (1959) 155–168.

———, *Africa and Indonesia* (Leiden, 1964).

———, "The Influence of Indonesia: The Musicological Evidence Reconsidered," *Azania*, IV (1969), 131–145.

Kamal, Youssouf (ed.), *Monumenta cartographica Africae et Ægypti* (Cairo, 1935–1939), 14v.

Kaudern, Walter, *Musical Instruments in Celebes* (The Hague, 1929).

Kayamba, H. M. T., "Notes on the Wadigo," *Tanganyika Notes and Records*, 23 (1947), 80–96.

Kent, Raymond K., "Madagascar and Africa: I. The Problem of the Bara," *Journal of African History*, IX (1968), 387–408.

———, *Early Kingdoms in Madagascar, 1500–1700* (New York, 1970).

Kirby, Percival R., "The Indonesian Origin of Certain African Musical Instruments," *African Studies*, XXV (1966), 3–21.

———, "Thoughts on The Origins of South African Society," *South African Journal of Science*, LXIII (1967), 137–139.

Kircher, Athanasius, *Œdipus Ægyptiacus* (Rome, 1652–1655).

———, *China monumentis qua profanis illustrata* (Amsterdam, 1667).

298   BIBLIOGRAPHY

Kirkman, James S., *The Arab City of Gedi. Excavations at the Great Mosque* (Oxford, 1954).

———, *The Tomb of the Dated Inscription at Gedi* (London, 1960).

———, *Gedi: The Palace* (The Hague, 1963).

———, *Men and Monuments of the East African Coast* (London, 1964).

———, *Ugwana on the Tana* (The Hague, 1966).

———, *Fort Jesus: a Portuguese Fortress on the East African Coast* (Oxford, 1974).

———, "The Kenya Littoral," *Current Anthropology*, VII (1966), 347–348.

Koechlin, Raymond, "Les Céramiques musulmanes de Suse au Musée du Louvre," *Mémoires de la Mission Archéologique de Perse*, XIX (1928), 1–109.

Kunst, Jaap, "A Musicological Argument for Relationship Between Indonesia—Probably Java—and Central Africa," *Proceedings of the Musical Association*, LXII (1935–1936), 57–69.

———, *Music in Java* (The Hague, 1949).

———, "The Origin of the Kemanak," *Bijdragen*, LXVI (1960), 263–269.

Lambert, H. E., *The Use of Indigenous Authorities in Tribal Administration: Studies of the Meru in Kenya Colony* (Capetown, 1947).

———, "Land Tenure among the Kamba," *African Studies*, VI (1947), 157–175.

Leakey, Mary D., W. E. Owen, and Louis S. B. Leakey, "Dimple-based Pottery from Central Kavirondo, Kenya," *Occasional Papers of the Cornydon Memorial Museum* (Nairobi, 1948), II.

Leur, J. C. van, *Indonesian Trade and Society: Essays in Asian Social and Economic History* (The Hague, 1955).

Lewis, David, "Polynesian Navigational Methods," *The Journal of the Polynesian Society*, LXXIII (1964), 364–373.

Lewis, Herbert S., "Historical Problems in Ethiopia and the Horn of Africa," *Annals of the New York Academy of Sciences*, XCVI (1962), 504–511.

———, "The Origins of African Kingdoms," *Cahiers d'Etudes Africaines*, VI (1966), 402–407.

———, "The Origins of the Galla and Somali," *Journal of African History*, VII (1966), 27–46.

Lewis, I. M., "The Galla in Northern Somaliland," *Rassegna di Studi Etiopici*, XV (1959–1960), 21–38.

———, "The Somali Conquest of the Horn of Africa," *Journal of African History*, I (1960), 213–230.

Liesegang, Gerhard, "Archaeological Sites on the Bay of Sofala," *Azania*, VII (1972), 147–159.

Lindblom, Gerhard, "Anteckningar öfver Taveta-folkets etnologi," *Ymer*, XIII (1913), 158–185.

———, *The Akamba in British East Africa* (Uppsala, 1916).

————, *Kamba Riddles, Proverbs and Songs* (Uppsala, 1934).

————, *Kamba Tales of Supernatural Beings and Adventures* (Uppsala 1935).

————, *Carved Initiation Sticks and Bows from Taveta, Kenya Colony* (Stockholm, 1950).

Lobato, Alexandre, *A Expansão Portuguesa em Moçambique de 1498 a 1530* (Lisbon, 1954–1960), 3v.

Lormian, Henri, *L'Art malgache* (Paris, 1929).

Lupi, E. do C., *Angoche – Breve memoria sobre uma das capitanias-morls do Districto de Moçambique* (Lisboa, 1907).

McCall, Daniel F., "Swahili Loanwords: Whence and When," in Daniel F. McCall, Norman R. Bennett, and Jeffrey Butler (eds.), *Eastern African History* (New York, 1969), 28–73.

MacDowall, David W., "The Early Western Satraps and the Date of the Periplus," *Numismatic Chronicle*, IV (1964), 271–280.

Maclaren, P. I. R., *The Fishing Devices of Central and Southern Africa* (Livingstone, 1958).

Marwick, Max G., "History and Tradition in East Central Africa Through the Eyes of the Northern Rhodesian Cewa," *The Journal of African History*, IV (1963), 375–390.

Matheson, Sylvia A., *Persia: An Archaeological Guide* (London, 1972).

Mathew, Gervase, "Chinese Porcelain in East Africa and on the Coast of S. Arabia," *Oriental Art*, II (1956), 50–55.

————, "Some Reflections on African Trade Routes," *Research Review* (Legon), III (1967), 63–71.

Mauny, Raymond, *Les Navigations médiévales sur les côtes sahariennes antérieures à la découverte portugaise* (Lisbon, 1960).

————, "Le Périple de la mer Erythrée et le problème du commerce romain en Afrique au sud du Limes," *Journal de la Société des Africanistes*, XXXVIII (1968), 19–34.

Mayers, W. F., "Chinese Explorations of the Indian Ocean During the Fifteenth Century," *The China Review*, III (1874–1875), 219–225, 321–331; IV (1875–1876), 61–67, 173–190.

Middleton, John, and Greet Kershaw, *The Kikuyu and Kamba of Kenya* (London, 1965).

Miller, J. Innes, *The Spice Trade of the Roman Empire* (Oxford, 1969).

Mills, J. V., "Notes on Early Chinese Voyages," *Journal of the Royal Asiatic Society* (1951), 3–27.

————, "Chinese Coastal Maps," *Imago Mundi*, XI (1954), 151–168.

Molet, Louis, *Le Bain royal à Madagascar* (Tananarive, 1956).

Mollat, M. (ed.), *Sociétés et Compagnies de l'Océan Indien* (Paris, 1972).

Mookerji, Radha K., *Indian Shipping: A History of the Sea-Borne Trade and Maritime Activity of the Indians from the Earliest Times* (Bombay, 1957).

Morton, R. F., "The Shungwaya Myth of Miji Kenda Origins: A Problem of Nineteenth-Century Kenya Coastal History," *International Journal of African Historical Studies*, V (1972), 397–423.

Mulder, W. Z., "The 'Wu Pei Chih' Charts, " *T'oung Pao*, XXXVII (1944), 1–14.

Murdock, George Peter, *Africa: Its People and Their Culture History* (New York, 1959).

————, "Genetic Classification of the Austronesian Languages: A Key to Oceanic Culture History," *Ethnology*, III (1964), 116–126.

Needham, John Turberville, *De inscriptione quadam Ægyptiaca Taurini inventa et Characteribus Ægyptiis olim et Sinis communibus exarata, idolo cuidam antiquo in regia universitate servato...* (Rome, 1761).

Needham, Joseph, *Science and Civilisation in China* (Cambridge, 1954–1962), 4v.

Nenquin, Jacques, *Contributions to the Study of the Prehistoric Cultures of Rwanda and Burundi* (Tervuren, 1967).

Ngala, R. G., *Nchi na Desturi za Wagiryama* (Nairobi, 1949).

Nilakanta Sastri, K. A., *History of Sri Vijaya* (Madras, 1949).

Nooteboom, C., *Die Boomstamkano in Indonesie* (Leiden, 1932).

Ogot, Bethwell A., and John A. Kieran (eds), *Zamani: A Survey of East African History* (Nairobi, 1968).

Palm, C. H. M., "Polynesians in the Pacific," *Bijdragen tot de Taal-, Land- en Volkenkunde*, CXX (1964), 69–108.

Pauw, C. de, "Recherches philosophiques sur les Egyptiens et les Chinois," *Œuvres Philosophiques* (Paris, 1774–1795), IV, V.

Paravey, Charles de, "Archéologie primitive. Traditions primitives conservées dans les hiéroglyphs des anciens peuples..." *Annales de Philosophie Chrétienne* (Paris, 1853), 192–207.

Paribeni, Roberto, "Ricerche sul luogo dell'antica Adulis (Colonia Eritrea), "*Monumenti Antichi pubblicati per cura della Reale Accademia dei Lincei*, XVIII (1908), 439–572.

Peacock, B. A. V., "A Short Description of Malayan Prehistoric Pottery," *Asian Perspectives*, III (1961), 121–156.

Pelliot, Paul, "Les Anciens Rapports entre l'Egypte et l'Extrême-Orient," *Comptes Rendus du Congrès International de Géographie*, V (1926), · 21–22.

————, "Les Grands Voyages maritimes chinois au début du XVe siècle," *T'oung Pao*, XXX (1933), 237–455.

————, *Notes on Marco Polo* (Paris, 1959, 1963), 2v.

Perera, B. J., "The Foreign Trade and Commerce of Ancient Ceylon,", *The Ceylon Historical Journal*, I (1951), 109–119; II (1952), 192–204, 301–320.

Pigraud, T. O. Th., *Java in the Fourteenth Century: A Study in Cultural History* (The Hague, 1960).

Pirenne, Jacqueline, "La Date du Périple de la Mer Erythrée," *Journal Asiatique*, CCXLIX (1961), 441–459.

————, *Le Royaume sud-arabe de Qataban et sa datation* (Louvain, 1961).

Porée–Maspero, Eveline, *Etude sur les rites agraires des Cambodgiens* (Paris, 1962–1969), 3v.

Posnansky, Merrick, "Bantu Genesis," *Uganda Journal*, XXV (1961), 86–93.

————, "CA* Comment," *Current Anthropology*, VII (1966), 473.

————, "Kingship, Archaeology and Historic Myth," *Uganda Journal*, XXX (1966), 1–12.

————, (ed.), *Prelude to East African History* (London, 1966).

————, "The Iron Age in East Africa," in W. W. Bishop and J. D. Clark (eds.), *Background to Evolution in Africa* (Chicago, 1967).

Prins, A. H. J., *Coastal Tribes of the North-East Bantu* (London, 1952).

————, "Shungwaya, die Urheimat der Nordost-Bantu," *Anthropos*, L (1955), 273–282.

————, "The Shungwaya Problem: Traditional History and Cultural Likeness in Bantu Northeast Africa," *Anthropos*, LXVII (1972), 9–35.

————, "The Geographical Distribution of the North-East Bantu Populations," *Tijdschrift Koninklijk Nederlandskundig Genootschap*, III (1955) 232–240.

————, "On Swahili Historiography," *Journal of the East African Swahili Committee*, 28 (1958), 26–40.

————, "De zeekant van Lamu," *Mens en Maatschappij*, XXXIV (1959) 209–221.

————, *Swahili-speaking Peoples of Zanzibar and the East African Coast* (London, 1961).

————, *Sailing from Lamu* (Assen, 1965).

Quaritch Wales, H. G., *The Indianisation of China and of South-East Asia* (London, 1968).

Reitlinger, Gerald, "The Interim Period in Persian Pottery; An Essay in Chronological Revision," *Ars Islamica*, V (1938), 155–178.

Rich, E. E., and C. H. Wilson (eds.), *The Cambridge Economic History of Europe* (Cambridge, 1967), IV.

Richards, D. S. (ed.), *Islam and the Trade of Asia* (Oxford, 1970).

Riley, Carroll L., *et al.* (eds.), *Man Across the Sea: Problems of Pre-Columbian Contacts* (Austin, 1971).

Roberts, Andrew (ed.), *Tanzania Before* 1900 (Nairobi, 1968).

Robinson, K. R., "A Preliminary Report on the Recent Archaeology of Ngonde, Northern Malawi," *Journal of African History*, VII (1966), 169–188.

————, "The Leopard's Kopje Culture: Its Position in the Iron Age of Southern Rhodesia," *South African Archaeological Bulletin*, XXI (1966), 5–51.

Rockhill, W. W., "Notes on the Relations and Trade of China with the Eastern Archipelago and the Coast of the Indian Ocean During the Fourteenth Century," *T'oung Pao*, XIV (1913), 473–476, XV (1914),

419–447, XVI (1915), 61–159, 236–271, 374–392, 435–467, 604–626.

Rouffaer, Gerrit P., "Waar kwamen de Muti Salah van Timor vandaan," *Bijdragen voor Land-, Taal-, en Volkenkunde*, VI (1899), 409–675.

Rouget, G., "La Musique à Madagascar," in Jacques Faublée (ed.) *L'Ethnographie de Madagascar* (Paris, 1946).

Sachs, Curt, *Les Instruments de musique de Madagascar* (Paris, 1938).

Santos, Joao dos, *Ethiopia Oriental* (Evora, 1609).

Sarre, Friedrich, "Die Kleinfunde von Samarra und ihre Ergebnisse für das islamische Kunstgewerbe," *Der Islam*, V (1914), 180–195.

Sassoon, Hamo, "Engaruka, Excavations During 1964," *Azania*, I (1966), 79–99.

————, "New Views on Engaruka, Northern Tanzania: Excavations Carried Out for the Tanzania Government in 1964 and 1966," *Journal of African History*, VIII (1967), 201–217.

Sauer, Jonathan D., *Plants and Man on the Seychelles Coast: A Study in Historical Biogeography* (Madison, 1967).

Sauvaget, Jean, (trans.) '*Akhbar aṣ-Ṣin wa'l-Hind: Relation de la Chine et l'Inde, rédigée en* 851 (Paris, 1948).

————, "Sur d'anciennes instructions nautiques arabes pour les mers de l'Inde," *Journal Asiatique*, CCXXXVI (1948), 11–20.

Schafer, Edward H., "Notes on Tuan Ch'eng-shih and his Writings," *Etudes Asiatiques*, XVI (1963), 14–33.

————, *The Golden Peaches of Samarkand* (Berkeley, 1963).

Schoff, Wilfrid H. (trans.), *The Periplus of the Erythrean Sea* (New York, 1912).

Schnitger, F. M. *The Archaeology of Hindoo Sumatra* (Leiden, 1937).

————, *Forgotten Kingdoms in Sumatra* (Leiden, 1939).

Schwarz, E. H. L., "The Chinese Connection with Africa," *Journal of the Royal Asiatic Society of Bengal*, IV (1938), 175–193.

Seddon, David, "The Origins and Development of Agriculture in East and Southern Africa," *Current Anthropology*, IX (1968), 489–494.

Sharp, Andrew, *Ancient Voyagers in Polynesia* (Sydney, 1963).

————, "Those Polynesian Voyages," *American Anthropologist*, LXVII (1965), 102–103.

Shinnie, Peter L., "Socotra," *Antiquity*, XXXIV (1960), 100–110.

———— (ed.), *The African Iron Age* (Oxford, 1971).

Sicard, Harald von, "The Ancient Sabi–Zimbabwe Trade Route," *Nada* XL (1963), 6–16.

Smith, S. P., *Hawaiki* (London, 1921).

Smolla, G., "Prähistorische Keramik aus Ostafrika," *Tribus*, VI (1965), 35–64.

Soedjatmoko, *et al.* (eds.), *An Introduction to Indonesian Historiography* (Ithaca, 1965).

Soejono, R. P., "Indonesia," *Asian Perspectives*, VI (1963), 34–43.

Soekmono, R., "Early Civilisations of Southeast Asia," *Journal of the Siam Society*, XLVI (1958), 17-20.

Soerensen, Per, "The 'Shaman Grave,' " *Felicitation Volumes of Southeast-Asian Studies*, II (1965), 303--318.

Solheim, Wilhelm G., "Two Major Problems in Bornean (and Asian) Ethnology and Archaeology," *Sarawak Museum Journal*, 13-14 (1960), 1-5.

——, "Sa-huynh Pottery Relationships in Southeast Asia," *Asian Perspectives*, III (1961), 97-188.

——, "Further Notes on the Kalanay Pottery Complex in the Philippines," *Asian Perspectives*, III (1961), 157-166.

——, "Pottery and the Malayo-Polynesians," *Current Anthropology*, V (1964), 360, 376-384, 400-403.

——, *The Archaeology of Central Philippines: A Study Chiefly of the Iron Age and Its Relationships* (Manila, 1964).

——, "Indonesian Culture and Malagasy Origins," *Taloha*, I (1965), 33-42.

——, "A Preliminary Report on a New Pottery Complex in Northeastern Thailand," *Felicitation Volumes of Southeast-Asian Studies*, II (Bangkok, 1965), 249-254.

——, ' Further Relationships of the Sa-huynh-Kalanay Pottery Tradition," *Asian Perspectives*, VIII (1966), 196-210.

——, Barbara Harrisson, and Lindsey Wall, "Niah 'Three Colour Ware' and Related Prehistoric Pottery from Borneo," *Asian Perspectives*, III (1966), 463-469.

Soper, Robert C., "Kwale: An Early Iron Age Site in South-eastern Kenya," *Azania*, II (1967), 1-17.

——, "Iron Age Sites in North-eastern Tanzania," *Azania*, II (1967), 19-36.

Sopher, David E., *The Sea Nomads. A Study Based on the Literature of The Maritime Boat of Southeast Asia* (Singapore, 1965).

Sousa, João de, *Documentos Arabicos para a historia Portuguesa copiados dos originaes da Torre do Tombo* (Lisbon, 1790).

Southall, Aidan W. (ed.), *Social Change in Modern Africa* (London, 1961).

Stein, Mark Aurel, "Archaeological Reconnaissance in Southern Persia," *The Geographical Journal*, LXXXIII (1934), 119-134.

Stigand, Chauncey Hugh, *The Land of Zinj* (London, 1913).

Strandes, Justus, *Die Portugiesenzeit von Deutsch und Englisch Ost Afrika* (Berlin, 1899).

Strong, Sandford Arthur, "The History of Kilwa," *Journal of the Royal Asiatic Society*, XX (1895), 385-430.

Stuhlmann, Franz, *Beiträge zur Kulturgeschichte von Ostafrika* (Berlin, 1909).

Stumpf, C., "Tonsystem und Musik der Siamesen," *Beiträge zur Akustik und Musikwissenschaft*, III (1901), 127–140.

Summers, Roger, *Inyanga* (Cambridge, 1958).

————, "The Iron Age of Southern Rhodesia," *Current Anthropology*, VII (1966), 463–469.

————, *Zimbabwe: A Rhodesian Mystery* (Cape Town, 1964).

Sutton, John E. G., "The Archaeology and Early Peoples of the Highlands of Kenya and Northern Tanzania," *Azania*, I (1966), 37–57.

————, " 'Ancient Civilizations' and Modern Agricultural Systems in the Southern Highlands of Tanzania," *ibid.*, IV (1969), 1–14.

————, *The East African Coast: An Historical and Archaeological Review* (Nairobi, 1966).

Thomassen à Thuessink van der Hoop, Abraham Nicholas Jan, *Megalithic Remains in South Sumatra* (Zutphen, 1933).

Tibbetts, G. R., "Pre-Islamic Arabia and South-East Asia," *Journal of the Malayan Branch of the Royal Asiatic Society*, XXIX (1956), 182–208.

————, *Arab Navigation in the Indian Ocean before the Coming of the Portuguese* (London, 1971).

Toussaint, Auguste (ed.), *Early American Trade with Mauritius* (Port Louis, 1954).

————, *Bibliography of Mauritius* (1502–1954) (Port Louis, 1956).

————, *Répertoire des archives de l'Ile de France pendant la régie de la Compagnie des Indes*, 1715–1768 (Nerac, 1956).

————, *L'Administration française de l'Ile Maurice et ses archives*, 1721–1810 (Port Louis, 1965).

Tracey, Hugh T., *Chopi Musicians* (London, 1948).

Trowell, Margaret, and K. P. Wachsmann, *Tribal Crafts of Uganda* (Oxford, 1953).

Tuulio, O. J., "Du Nouveau sur Idrisi," *Studia Orientalia*, VI (1936), 1–242.

Upton, J. M., "The Persian Expedition, 1934–1935, " *Bulletin of the Metropolitan Museum of Art*, XXXI (1936), 176–180.

Urbain–Faublée, Marcel, *L'Art malgache* (Paris, 1963).

Valette, Jean, "De l'Origine des Malgaches", *Annales de l'Université de Madagascar*, III (1965), 15–320.

van der Sleen, Wicher, "Ancient Glass Beads of East and Central Africa and the Indian Ocean," *Journal of the Royal Anthropological Institute*, LXXXVIII (1958), 203–216.

————, *Handbook on Beads* (Liège, 1967).

Velgus V., "Strany Mo-lin' i Bo-sa-lo (Lao-bo-sa) v srednevekovykh Kitaiskikh izvestiyakh ob Afrike" [The countries of Mo-lin and Bo-sa-lo (Lao-bo-sa) in Medieval Chinese information about Africa], *Africana*, XC (1966), 104–121.

————, "O srednevekovykh kitaiskikh izvestiyakh ob Afrike i yazyki narodov Afriki" [On medieval Chinese information about Africa and certain problems of its study], *Africana*, XC (1966), 84–103.

Vérin, Pierre, "Retrospective et Problèmes de l'archéologie à Madagascar," *Asian Perspectives*, VI (1962), 198–218.

——, "L'Ancienne civilisation de l'Isandra," *Taloha*, I (1965), 249–285.

——, "Aperçu sur l'histoire ancienne de Madagascar," *Rythmes du Monde*, XL (1966), 3–6.

—— "L'Archéologie à Madagascar," *Azania*, I (1966), 119–137.

——, (ed.), "Archéologie et Anthropologie des Hautes Terres et de l'Afrique orientale," *Taloha*, III (1970), entire issue [16 articles].

——, "Histoire ancienne du nord-ouest de Madagascar," *ibid.*, V (1972), entire issue.

Wachsman, Klaus P. (ed.), *Essays on Music and History in Africa* (Evanston, 1971).

AUTHORS

H. NEVILLE CHITTICK, F. S. A., is a graduate of the University of Cambridge and received a postgraduate diploma in archaeology from the same institution. He assisted on various excavations in the Middle East in 1950–1952, and from 1952 to 1956 was curator of museums in the Republic of Sudan. From 1957 to 1961 he was Director of the Antiquities Department of Tanganyika, and since 1961 has been Director of the British Institute in Eastern Africa. He is the author of *Kilwa: An Islamic Trading City on the East African Coast* (London, 1974), 2v.; *Kisimani Mafia* (Dar es Salaam, 1961); with Peter Shinnie, *Ghazali: A Monastery in the Northern Sudan* (Khartoum, 1961); and numerous articles on the history and archaeology of Eastern Africa. He edits *Azania*.

ROBERT I. ROTBERG is professor of history and political science, The Massachusetts Institute of Technology, and a research fellow of the Center for International Affairs, Harvard University. A graduate of Oberlin College, Princeton University, and the University of Oxford, he previously taught at Harvard University. He is the author or editor of a dozen books, including *Joseph Thomson and the Exploration of Africa* (London, 1971); *Haiti: The Politics of Squalor* (Boston, 1971); *Protest and Power in Black Africa* (New York, 1970); *Africa and its Explorers* (Cambridge, Mass., 1970); *A Political History of Tropical Africa* (New York, 1965); *The Rise of Nationalism in Central Africa* (Cambridge, Mass., 1965); and *The Family in History* (New York, 1973). He edits *The Journal of Interdisciplinary History*.

COUNT VINIGI L. GROTTANELLI was professor of ethnology and director of the Istituto di Etnologia at the University of Rome. He has carried out research in Somalia (1932–1933 and 1951–1952), in Ethiopia (1937 and 1939), in Madagascar (1960), and in Ghana (1954, 1961, 1963, 1969–1971). He is an editor of *The Encyclopaedia of World Art*. From 1947 to 1960 he was a member of the executive council of the International African Institute, London. He is a vice-president of the International Union of the Anthropological and Ethnological Sciences

(1964–1973). The author of some ninety books and articles, mainly on African ethnology, his principal work is *Ethnologica* (Milan, 1965–1966, second edition 1976), 3v. He is a counsellor, Societa Italiana di Anthropologia e Etnologia, Florence, an honorary member, Royal Anthropological Institute of Great Britain and Ireland, foreign fellow, American Anthropological Association, and a member of the Deutsche Gesellschaft für Volkerkunde and the Société des Africanistes. He has been a visiting professor at the University of Pittsburgh.

MICHAEL DOUGLAS GWYNNE is Senior Research Fellow in Tropical Ecology at Balliol College, Oxford. Formerly Head of the Plant Physiology and Ecology Division of the East African Agriculture and Forestry Research Organization in Kenya, he is now working on animal habitat utilization with the UNDP/FAO Kenya Range Management Project. He is the author of numerous scientific publications in the fields of tropical ecology, rangeland utilization, tropical agriculture, and natural history.

JAMES SPEDDING KIRKMAN, O.B.E., Ph.D. (Cantab), F.S.A., after an early career in the Far East and the Middle East became warden. Coast Historical Sites of Kenya (1948–59) and Curator, Fort Jesus Museum (1960–72). He is the author of *The Arab City of Gedi: The Great Mosque* (Oxford, 1954); *Gedi: The Palace* (The Hague, 1963); *Men and Monuments on the East African Coast* (London, 1964); *Ungwana on the Tana* (The Hague, 1966); *Fort Jesus, a Portuguese Fortress on the East African Coast* (Oxford, 1973); and numerous articles.

THE REV. ANTHONY GERVASE MATHEW, O.P., F.S.A., of Balliol College, Oxford, is university lecturer in Byzantine studies, member of the Faculty of History and the Sub-Faculty of Anthropology in the University of Oxford and lecturer on African history and archaeology. He undertook archaeological surveys for the Tanganyika Government in 1950, for the British Somaliland Protectorate in 1951, for the Government of Uganda in 1953, and in South Arabia in 1961. He also was responsible for an archaeological report on the High Commission Territories in 1962. He has been visiting professor of African history at the University of Ghana, 1963, and at the University of California, Los Angeles, 1965. He is the author of: *Byzantine Painting* (London, 1951), *Byzantine Aesthetics* (London, 1963), *The Court of Richard II* (London, 1967), numerous articles, and edited (with Roland Oliver) *History of East Africa I* (Oxford, 1963).

MERRICK POSNANSKY was educated at the Universities of Nottingham and Cambridge. From 1956 to 1958 he was warden of the Prehistoric Sites of the Royal National Parks of Kenya. In 1958, he went to Uganda where he served as curator of the Uganda Museum (1958–1962), assistant director of the British Institute of History and Archaeology in East Africa (1962–1964), and director of African Studies at Makerere University College (1965–1967). Editor of the *Uganda Journal* from 1962 to 1966, he was founder-president of the Museums Association of Middle Africa and served as a visiting professor in African history at the University of California, Los Angeles, in 1966. He is presently professor of archaeology at the University of Ghana in Legon. He edited *Prelude to East African History* (Nairobi, 1966) and has written numerous articles on excavations of all ages in East Africa.

AIDAN SOUTHALL, professor of anthropology, University of Wisconsin, was formerly professor of sociology and social anthropology, dean of the Faculty of Social Sciences, and chairman of the East African Institute for Social Research at Makerere University College. He received his B.A. (Cantab.) in 1942 and Ph.D. (University of London) in 1952. He is the author of *Alur Society* (Cambridge, 1956), and the editor of *Social Change in Modern Africa* (London, 1961).

THE REV. DR. JOHN SPENCER TRIMINGHAM was educated at the Universities of Birmingham (Social Studies) and Oxford (Arabic and Persian), and a theological college. He became administrative secretary of the Church Missionary Society's mission in the (then) Anglo-Egyptian Sudan, at the same time travelling extensively in Africa pursuing studies of Islam in that continent. Subsequently, he went to the University of Glasgow as lecturer in Islamic Studies, then became Reader in Arabic and head of the Department of Arabic and Islamic Studies. From 1964 to 1971 he was a visiting professor in the department of history at the American University of Beirut. He now teaches Islamic Studies at the Near East School of Theology in Beirut. He is the author of *Sudan Colloquial Arabic* (Oxford 1946); *Islam in the Sudan* (London, 1949); *Islam in Ethiopia* (London, 1952); *Islam in West Africa* (Oxford, 1959); *A History of Islam in West Africa* (London, 1962); *Islam in West Africa* (Oxford, 1964); *The Influence of Islam upon Africa* (London, 1968); *The Sufi Orders in Islam* (Oxford, 1971).

PIERRE VERIN received a first degree from l'Ecole Nationale de la France d'Outre-Mer (Madagascar section), a Licence en Droit, Diplômes de l'Ecole des Langues Orientales Vivantes (Malagasy and Oceaniac languages), an M.A. in Anthropology from Yale University, and is both a Docteur en Préhistoire and a Docteur d'Etat en Histoire from the Université de Paris. He studied a Carib village of St. Lucia (West Indies), did archaeological fieldwork in the Society and Austral

Islands (French Polynesia), and in Madagascar, and became maître de conférence and director of the Center for Archaeology at the Université de Madagascar. In 1973 he became head of the history department of the University Center of Guadeloupe. He is the author of *L'Ancienne Civilisation de Rurutu* (Paris, 1968) and numerous articles on Madagascar and the Pacific. He is a regional editor of *Asian Perspectives*.

PAUL WHEATLEY received academic degrees from the Universities of Liverpool and London, and has taught in the Universities of Malaya, California, and London. He now holds a dual appointment as professor of Geography and of Social Thought at the University of Chicago. His publications include *The Golden Khersonese* (Kuala Lumpur, 1961), *Sung Maritime Trade* (Singapore, 1961), *The Malay Peninsula in Ancient Times* (Singapore, 1964), and *The Pivot of the Four Quarters* (Edinburgh, 1971). He is a member of the editorial boards of *The Journal of Interdisciplinary History*, *The Journal of Urban History*, and *The Journal of Southeast Asian Studies*.

INDEX

NOTE: Proper names and indentifications in non-Roman script are not included.

318   INDEX

Granite, 92
Graphite pottery, *see* Pottery and ceramics
Graves, 52; at Bur Gao, 28. *See also* Tombs
Gray, John Milner, British jurist and author, 216
Graziosi, Paolo, Italian archaeologist, 45
Greeks, 20, 52, 60, 75, 147–148, 150, 152, 154, 158–159, 161, 162, 281. *See also* Graeco-Roman
Grohmann, A., German classicist, 70
Grottanelli, Count Vinigi L., Italian ethnologist, 6, 27
Groundnuts, 250, 253
Guardafui, Cape, 3, 9, 11, 12, 30, 44, 69, 71, 116, 125, 161
Guillain, Captain Charles, French sailor and author, 68, 236
Guinea, 269
Gujerat, India, 12, 109
Gum copal, 14
Gurra, people, Somalia, 57
Guthrie, Malcolm, British linguist, 17
Gwynne, Michael, British scientist, 4–5, 15

Ḥabash, Ḥabasha, Bilād al-Ḥabasha, Zunūj al-Ḥabasha, Nīl al-Ḥabasha, *see* Ethiopia
Haberland, Eike, German anthropologist, 53–56
Habesho, ethnic designation, 63
Hackin, Joseph, French orientalist, 159
Hadaftimo, mountains, Arabia, 101
Hadimu, people, Kenya, 72
Hadramaut, Arabia, 39–43, 106–107, 109; Wadi Hadramaut, 160
Hadrami sgraffiato pottery, *see* pottery and ceramics
Hadza-Tindiga, people, Tanzania, 47
Hafun, Ḥafūnī, *see* Ras Hāfūn
Hairstyles, 98
al-Hamadhānī, Ibn al-Faqīh, Arab geographer, 276
Hamarani, people, Somalia, 68
al-Hamdānī, al-Hasan ibn-Ahmad, Arab author, 92, 134
Hamitic, 46–47, 59, 84, 120–121; 'proto-Hamite', 49; Hamito-Semitic, 49; "Hamitization", 56, 61; pre-Hamitic Bushmanoid hunters, 109; Nilo-Hamitic language, 193
Harar, *see* Falhūn
Hargeisa, Somalia, 45
Hatshepsut, Egyptian queen, 69
Haudricourt, André, French botanist, 177
Hawaii, 212, 252, 268
Ḥawfal, Qanbalu?, 278
Hawiyya (Hāwiya), people, Somalia, 57, 63, 74, 125, 142; Hāwiya nomads, 122
Haywood, Captain C.W., British naval officer, 162
Hébert, Jean Claude, French author, 168, 170, 175, 177, 195, 200–202, 209
Helay, *see* Elay
Helbaek, Hans, botanist, 254–256
Hellenistic, *see* Greeks
Hemp (bhang, marijuana), 222
Henning, W.B., British orientalist, 20–21
Herimat, pillars of, Somalia, 230
Hero of Alexandria, 152
Herzfeld, Ernst, German orientalist, 20
Hijaz, Arabia, 12, 50, 64, 235

Prehistoric cultures, 45–46, 49–
50, 59
Pre-Islamic, see Islam
Products, indigenous, 8, 10, 14,
70, 75, 104–109, 120–121, 124,
131, 133, 161. See also Timber;
Ebony; Ivory; Tortoise shell;
Animal skins; Gold; etc.
Protein, 2, 21, 54–55, 60, 101
See also Animals, domestic-
ated; Food; Grains; Meat;
Milk
Proto-Indonesian, see Indones-
ians
Ptolemaeus, Claudius, of Alex-
andria (Ptolemy) geographer
and astronomer, 8, 20, 84, 110,
116, 118, 134, 151, 155, 162,
275–276; Geography, 20, 119,
149, 151–152, 154–155, 157–
158,   161–162,   275–276;
Accanae Emporion,   139;
Cube Emporion, 139; Cape
of Perfumes,   84;   Barbaric
Gulf, 84
Ptolemy   III   and   Ptolemaic
Egypt, 11, 27, 161–162
Puât-b'uât-liǝk (Barbarā?) 284,
286, 287
Punt, land of, 68–69
Puraloi islands, in the Periplus,
163
Pygmies, 193, 236

Qahtani, people, Arabia, 36, 74
Qā'idat al-Barābar, 142
Qaljūr, in Idrisi, 139, 142
Qaljūriyya swords, 142
Qamar, in Idrisi, 131, 142–144
Qana, inscription of, 159
Qanbalu, Pemba?, 11, 23, 31,
42, 116, 121–122, 124, 126, 129
–137, 143, 146, 273–274, 277–
278; Jazīrat Qanbalū, 146.

See also Verdure, Isle of
Qānūn al-Mas'udi, by al-Bīrūnī,
275, 280
Qarfūna (Qarfūa, Qarfawa, Qar-
qūna, Qurūnū), in Idrisi, 125,
139
Qarmatians and Qarāmita,
Arabia, 36, 123
Qarnūa (Qarnawa), in Idrisi, 127,
140
Qarqūna (Farfūna), in Idrisi, 142
al-Qazwīnī, Arab compiler, 100,
280
Quartz, 220–221
Qubbat Arīn (Qubbat Uzain), in
Idrisi, 143
Queensland, Australia, 265
Quelman (Kilimani), see Gedi
Qulzum, Ethiopia?, 135
Qumr (Madagascar), 87, 119,
124–125, 127, 144–145; Qumr
Zangi, 86–88, 94, 109. See also
Madagascar
Qumriyya, old capital of Qumr,
145
Qur'anic texts, 13, 103
Qus, Egypt, 260

Racial types, 5, 14, 17–23, 25–
28, 32, 39, 42–43, 46, 48–50,
54, 58–63, 68–69, 71, 75, 86–
88, 95, 109, 123, 127, 171, 175,
201, 206–211, 213, 227, 236.
See also Physical character-
istics; Genetic composition
Radiocarbon dating, 18
Rāfāta, in Ptolemy, 119
Rāfatī and Rāqatā (Bāqatī), in
Idrisi, 139
Rafts, see Boats
Ragusa, Cardinal John of, 150
Rahanwen, people, Somalia, 46,
62
Rains, 44, 99